ENGLAND, WALES & CHANNEL ISLANDS

Turn to the page shown for the start of each county

CONTENTS

SCOTLAND

Moray p372

Highland p358

Aberdeenshire p340

Perth and Kinross p373

Argyll & Bute p341

Fife p356

Stirling p384

City of Glasgow p357

City of Edinburgh p349

Midlothian p371

Borders (Scottish) p378

South Ayrshire p383

Dumfries and Galloway p345

ENGLAND

WALES

INTRODUCTION

Andrew Warren, Managing Director, Condé Nast Johansens Ltd.

The rapid growth of exciting new hotel spas throughout Great Britain & Ireland is now reflected in the title of this Guide.

You can easily identify those hotels offering spa facilities by referring to the symbols at the foot of each page entry.

You also have the opportunity to purchase 'Gift Vouchers' for the first time. Gift Vouchers make a superb present for anniversaries, weddings, special occasions or as a corporate incentive. Full details can be found on our website, www.johansens.com.

Once again, our team of dedicated Regional Inspectors have been busy visiting existing and new recommendations and we all very much hope that you will enjoy the results!

You can pass your opinions and observations back to us via the 'Guest Survey Forms' printed in this Guide and you can also take advantage of our 'Special Offers' at www.johansens.com

Above all, please remember to mention 'Johansens' when you make an enquiry or reservation and again when you arrive.

THE CONDÉ NAST JOHANSENS PROMISE

Condé Nast Johansens is the most comprehensive illustrated reference to annually inspected, independently owned accommodation and meetings venues throughout Great Britain, Europe and North America.

It is our objective to maintain the trust of guide users by recommending by annual inspection a careful choice of accommodation offering quality, excellent service and value for money.

Our team of over 50 dedicated Regional Inspectors visit thousands of hotels, country houses, inns and resorts throughout the world to select only the very best for recommendation in the 2005 editions of our Guides.

No hotel can appear unless it meets our exacting standards.

1

CONDÉ NAST JOHANSENS GUIDES

Recommending only the finest hotels in the world

As well as this Guide, Condé Nast Johansens also publishes the following titles:

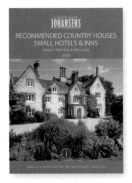

RECOMMENDED COUNTRY HOUSES, SMALL HOTELS & INNS, GREAT BRITAIN & IRELAND

Smaller, more rural properties, ideal for short breaks or more intimate stays

RECOMMENDED HOTELS & SPAS, EUROPE & THE MEDITERRANEAN

A wonderful choice of properties including châteaux, resorts, charming countryside hotels and stylish city hotels.

RECOMMENDED HOTELS, INNS & RESORTS, NORTH AMERICA, BERMUDA, CARIBBEAN, MEXICO, PACIFIC

A diverse collection of properties across the region, including exotic ocean front resorts, historic plantation houses and traditional inns.

RECOMMENDED VENUES, GREAT BRITAIN & EUROPE

Venues that cater specifically for business meetings, conferences, product launches, events and celebrations.

When you purchase two Guides or more we will be pleased to offer you a reduction in the cost.

The complete set of five Condé Nast Johansens Guides may be purchased as 'The International Collection'.

To order any Guides please complete the order form on page 460
or call FREEPHONE 0800 269 397

HOW TO USE THIS GUIDE

To find a hotel by location:

- Use the county maps at the front to identify the area of the country you wish to search.

- Turn to the relevant county section where hotels are featured alphabetically by location.

- Alternatively use the maps on pages 447–458 at the rear of the Guide. These maps cover all regions of Great Britain & Ireland and each hotel is marked.

There are over 50 properties which did not feature in our last (2004) edition and these are identified with a "NEW" symbol at the top of the page.

To find a hotel by its name or the name of its nearest town look in the indexes on pages 436–442.

The indexes also list recommended hotels by their amenities such as spa, swimming pool, golf, etc.

If you cannot find a suitable hotel where you wish to stay, you may decide to choose one of Condé Nast Johansens Recommended Country Houses, Small Hotels or Inns as an alternative. These more intimate establishments are listed by place names on pages 407–411.

Once you have made your choice please contact the hotel directly. Rates are per room, including VAT and breakfast (unless stated otherwise) and are correct at the time of going to press but should always be checked with the hotel before you make your reservation. **When making a booking please mention that Condé Nast Johansens was your source of reference.**

We occasionally receive letters from guests who have been charged for accommodation booked in advance but later cancelled. Readers should be aware that by making a reservation with a hotel, either by telephone, e-mail or in writing, they are entering into a legal contract. A hotelier under certain circumstances is entitled to make a charge for accommodation when guests fail to arrive, even if notice of the cancellation is given.

All guides are obtainable from bookshops, by calling Freephone 0800 269397, by using the order coupons on pages 459–464 or at www.johansens.com/bookshop

CONDÉ NAST JOHANSENS

Condé Nast Johansens Ltd., 6-8 Old Bond Street, London W1S 4PH
Tel: +44 (0)20 7499 9080 Fax: +44 (0)20 7152 3565
Find Condé Nast Johansens on the Internet at: www.johansens.com
E-Mail: info@johansens.com

Publishing Director:	Stuart Johnson
P.A. to Publishing Director:	Amelia Dempster
Hotel Inspectors:	Jean Branham
	Geraldine Bromley
	Robert Bromley
	Pat Gillson
	Marie Iversen
	Pauline Mason
	John O'Neill
	Mary O'Neill
	Fiona Patrick
	Liza Reeves
	John Sloggie
	Nevill Swanson
	David Wilkinson
	Helen Wynn
Production Manager:	Kevin Bradbrook
Production Controller:	Laura Kerry
Senior Designer:	Michael Tompsett
Copywriters:	Clare Barker
	Sasha Creed
	Norman Flack
	Debra Giles
	Rozanne Paragon
	Leonora Sandwell
Marketing Coordinator:	Siobhan Smith
Client Services Director:	Fiona Patrick
PA to Managing Director:	Siobhan Smith
Managing Director:	Andrew Warren

Copyright © 2004 Condé Nast Johansens Ltd.

Condé Nast Johansens Ltd. is part of The Condé Nast Publications Ltd.
ISBN 1 903665 18 3
Printed in England by St Ives plc
Colour origination by Graphic Facilities
Distributed in the UK and Europe by Portfolio, Greenford (bookstores).
In North America by Casemate Publishing, Havertown (bookstores).

www.hildon.com

2004 AWARDS FOR EXCELLENCE

The winners of the Condé Nast Johansens 2004 Awards for Excellence

The Condé Nast Johansens 2004 Awards for Excellence were presented at the Awards Dinner held at The Dorchester hotel, London, on November 10th, 2003. Awards were offered to those properties worldwide that represented the finest standards and best value for money in luxury independent travel. An important source of information for these awards was the feedback provided by guests who completed Johansens Guest Survey reports. Guest Survey forms can be found on page 460.

Most Excellent London Hotel Award

NUMBER SIXTEEN – London, England, p191

"Freshly refurbished behind an immaculate pillared façade, the hotel is a haven of calm and tranquillity with a conservatory opening onto an award winning garden."

Most Excellent City Hotel Award

GREEN BOUGH HOTEL – Cheshire, England, p45

"Chester's premier small luxury hotel - within walking distance of the city, bedrooms feature original cast iron beds, plasma screen TV's and Jacuzzi baths."

Most Excellent Service Award

RIVERSIDE HOUSE – Derbyshire, England, p82

"Care and enthusiasm are given to generate a relaxed and pampered stay."

Most Excellent Restaurant Award

THE FRENCH HORN – Berkshire, England, p28

"Beautiful floodlit views over the Thames at night. The restaurant spit roasts local duck on an open fire, using the freshest ingredients and combining French and British cuisine."

Most Excellent Spa Award

CHEWTON GLEN – Hampshire, England p147

"The remodelled spa opened in spring 2002 with the addition of dedicated heat treatment areas, Hydrotherapy pool, Canadian hot tub and expanded treatment list – a haven of tranquillity and comfort."

The International Mark of Excellence

For further information, current news,
e-club membership, hotel search, Preferred Partners,
online bookshop and special offers visit:

www.johansens.com

Annually Inspected for the Independent Traveller

THE BATH PRIORY HOTEL AND RESTAURANT

WESTON ROAD, BATH, SOMERSET BA1 2XT

Directions: 1 mile west of the centre of Bath. Please contact the hotel for precise directions.

Web: www.johansens.com/bathpriory
E-mail: mail@thebathpriory.co.uk
Tel: 0870 381 8345
International: +44 (0)1225 331922
Fax: 01225 448276

Price Guide: (incl. full English breakfast)
double/twin from £245

Standing in 4 acres of gardens, The Bath Priory Hotel is close to some of England's most famous and finest architecture. Within walking distance of Bath city centre, this Georgian, mellow stone building dates from 1835, when it formed part of a row of fashionable residences on the west side of the city. Visitors will sense the luxury as they enter the hotel; antique furniture, many superb oil paintings and objets d'art add interest to the 2 spacious reception rooms and the elegant drawing room. Well-defined colour schemes lend an uplifting brightness throughout, particularly in the tastefully appointed bedrooms. The classical style of Michelin-starred head chef, Robert Clayton, is the primary inspiration for the cuisine, served in 3 interconnecting dining rooms which overlook the gardens. An especially good selection of wines can be recommended to accompany meals. Private functions can be accommodated both in the terrace, pavilion and the Orangery. The Roman Baths, Theatre Royal, Museum of Costume and a host of bijou shops offer plenty for visitors to see. The Garden Spa consists of a fitness suite, swimming pool, sauna, steam room and health and beauty spa.

Our inspector loved: *The Magnolia Room with bay windows overlooking the beautiful gardens.*

THE BATH SPA HOTEL

SYDNEY ROAD, BATH, SOMERSET BA2 6JF

Nestling in 7 acres of mature grounds dotted with ancient cedars, formal gardens, ponds and fountains, The Bath Spa Hotel's elegant Georgian façade can only hint at the warmth, style, comfort and attentive personal service. It is a handsome building in a handsome setting with antique furniture, richly coloured carpeting and well defined colour schemes lending an uplifting brightness throughout. The bedrooms are elegantly decorated; the bathrooms are luxuriously appointed in mahogany and marble. The Bath Spa Hotel offers all amenities that guests would expect of a 5-star hotel, for example WiFi provided by Kooku, whilst retaining the character of a homely country house. Chef Andrew Hamer's imaginative, contemporary style is the primary inspiration for the award-winning cuisine served in the 2 restaurants. For relaxation there is a fully equipped health and leisure spa which includes an indoor swimming pool, gymnasium, sauna, Jacuzzi, 3 treatment rooms, hair salon, tennis court and croquet lawn. Apart from the delights of Bath, there is motor racing at Castle Combe and hot air ballooning nearby.

Our inspector loved: This elegant, luxurious and comfortable hotel.

Directions: Exit M4 at jct18 onto the A46, follow signs to Bath for 8 miles until the major roundabout. Turn right onto A4 follow City Centre signs for a mile, at the 1st major set of traffic lights turn left toward the A36. At mini roundabout turn right then next left after Holburne Museum into Sydney Place. The hotel is 200 yards up the hill on the right.

Web: www.johansens.com/bathspa
E-mail: sales@bathspahotel.com
Tel: 0870 381 8346
International: +44 (0)1225 444424
Fax: 01225 444006

Price Guide:
double/twin £230–£260
4-poster £350–£380

COMBE GROVE MANOR HOTEL & COUNTRY CLUB

BRASSKNOCKER HILL, MONKTON COMBE, BATH, SOMERSET BA2 7HS

This exclusive 18th-century Country House Hotel is conveniently located just 2 miles from the beautiful city of Bath. Built on the hillside site of an ancient Roman settlement, Combe Grove Manor is set in 69 acres of beautiful private gardens and woodlands, with awe-inspiring panoramic views over the magnificent Limpley Stoke Valley and surrounding areas. The Manor House features luxurious four-poster rooms and suites with Jacuzzi baths, whilst the rooms in the Garden Lodge have spectacular views, some with private balconies. All 40 bedrooms are lavishly appointed and individual in design with superb en-suite facilities. Within the hotel's grounds are some of the finest leisure facilities in the south west, including indoor and outdoor heated pools, hydrospa beds and steam room, 4 all-weather tennis courts, a 5-hole par 3 golf course and a 16-bay driving range. Guests may use the fully-equipped gym, aerobics studio, sauna and solaria or simply indulge in the full range of treatments offered by professionally trained staff in the Clarins beauty rooms. There is also a choice of 2 superb restaurants; the elegant main restaurant features delicious traditional style cuisine and fine wines, whereas the informal Eden Bistro offers an exciting contemporary international menu.

Directions: Set south-east of Bath, off the A36 near the University. A map can be supplied on request.

Web: www.johansens.com/combegrovemanor
E-mail: info@combegrovemanor.com
Tel: 0870 381 8438
International: +44 (0)1225 834644
Fax: 01225 834961

Price Guide:
single from £130
double/twin from £130
suite from £300

Our inspector loved: The wonderful view of the Limpley Stoke Valley.

THE FRANCIS HOTEL

QUEEN SQUARE, BATH, SOMERSET BA1 2HH

This classic Regency town house lies in the very centre of this striking and exciting city, and minutes away from the many attractions that it has to offer. The stunning Abbey, historical Roman Baths, Pump Room and Thermae Bath Spa are all within a stone's throw, making The Francis the ideal base from which to explore, not just the historical tourist trail, but also the many fine shops, cafés and restaurants. The hotel itself has some 95 air conditioned en-suite bedrooms, each of which is decorated with careful flair – Regency stripes pay homage to the building's Georgian origins, but are brought up to date with exciting chenilles, damasks, stripes and checks. This modern approach is echoed by the style of food, sample dishes such as fresh aparagus, parma ham, poached egg, hollandaise sauce or grilled yellow fin tuna, slow roasted tomatoes grilled aubergine and mozzarella, are served in The Square Restaurant, whilst more informal suppers are available in the Caffébar. There are 2 well-equipped meeting rooms available for conferences, product launches and meetings; and with London Paddington being less than 2 hours away, The Francis is a great location for the business traveller as well as weekenders. Weddings can also be organised and catered for.

Our inspector loved: The newly refurbished bedrooms – smart, crisp and comfortable.

Directions: The Francis is located on Queen Square, a short distance from The Circus. Simply follow the A4 through route, which forms the north side of Queen Square.

Web: www.johansens.com/francis
E-mail: sales.francis@macdonald-hotels.co.uk
Tel: 0870 381 8728
International: +44 (0)1225 424105
Fax: 01225 319715

Price Guide:
double £112-£130
suite £172-£200

THE ROYAL CRESCENT HOTEL

16 ROYAL CRESCENT, BATH, SOMERSET BA1 2LS

The Royal Crescent Hotel is a Grade I listed building of the greatest historical and architectural importance and occupies the central 2 houses of one of Europe's finest masterpieces. The Royal Crescent is a sweep of 30 houses with identical façades stretching in a 500ft curve. Built by 1775, the hotel was completely refurbished in 1998 and the work undertaken has restored many of the classical Georgian features with all the additional modern comforts. Each of the 45 bedrooms is equipped with air conditioning, the Cliveden bed, video/compact disc player and personal facsimile machine. Pimpernel's restaurant offers a relaxed and informal dining atmosphere, presenting a contemporary menu. Comprehensively equipped, the secure private boardroom provides self-contained business meeting facilities. Exclusive use of the hotel can be arranged for a special occasion or corporate event. Magnificent views of Bath and the surrounding countryside may be enjoyed from the hotel's vintage river launch and hot air balloon. The Bath House is a unique spa, in which to enjoy both complementary therapies and holistic massage. Adjacent to this tranquil setting is the gym with cardio-vascular and resistance equipment.

Directions: Detailed directions are available from the hotel on booking.

Web: www.johansens.com/royalcrescent
E-mail: info@royalcrescent.co.uk
Tel: 0870 381 8874
International: +44 (0)1225 823333
Fax: 01225 339401

Price Guide: (room only)
double/twin from £280
suite from £450

Our inspector loved: The spacious elegant suites and prime location in Bath.

THE WINDSOR HOTEL

69 GREAT PULTENEY STREET, BATH BA2 4DL

Elegant wrought-iron railings front this attractive town house situated in the heart of the best preserved Georgian city in Britain. Grade I listed and refurbished to the highest standards, The Windsor Hotel stands on one of the finest boulevards in Europe just a short stroll from the Royal Crescent, Circus, Assembly Rooms and Roman Baths. The hotel's tall front windows look across Georgian façades inspired by Palladio, whilst rooms at the back have views of the rolling hills beyond. Enchanting interior décor complements the strong and pleasing architectural style and fine furniture and fabrics abound. Each individually designed en suite bedroom and suite is the essence of high quality and comfort. Afternoon tea or after-dinner drinks can be enjoyed in an exquisite drawing room while memorable menus are served in a small Japanese restaurant which overlooks its own special garden. Great Pulteney Street leads onto Pulteney Bridge and the city's tempting boutiques, antique shops and highly acclaimed restaurants. Within easy reach are Longleat Estate, Ilford Manor, the American Museum and Limpley Stoke Valley. Parking is available.

Our inspector loved: *The homely relaxed atmosphere.*

Directions: From junction18 off the M4, enter Bath along the A4 London Road. Turn left into Bathwick Street, then right into Sydney Place and right again into Great Pulteney Street.

Bath

Taunton   Yeovil

Web: www.johansens.com/windsorhotel
E-mail: sales@bathwindsorhotel.com
Tel: 0870 381 9003
International: +44 (0)1225 422100
Fax: 01225 422550

Price Guide:
single £85-£115
double/twin £135-£195
suite £275

HOMEWOOD PARK

HINTON CHARTERHOUSE, BATH, SOMERSET BA2 7TB

Directions: On the A36 6 miles from Bath towards Warminster.

Web: www.johansens.com/homewoodpark
E-mail: res@homewoodpark.com
Tel: 0870 381 8605
International: +44 (0)1225 723731
Fax: 01225 723820

Price Guide:
single from £120
double/twin from £150
suites from £270

Standing amid 10 acres of beautiful grounds and woodland on the edge of Limpley Stoke Valley, designated area of outstanding natural beauty is Homewood Park, one of Britain's finest privately-owned smaller country house hotels. This lovely 19th-century building has an elegant interior, adorned with beautiful fabrics, antiques, oriental rugs and original oil paintings. Lavishly furnished bedrooms offer the best in comfort, style and privacy. Each of them has a charm and character of its own and most have good views over the Victorian garden. The outstanding cuisine overseen by chef Jean de La Rouziere has won the hotel an excellent reputation. The à la carte menu uses wherever possible produce from local suppliers. A range of carefully selected wines, stored in the hotel's original medieval cellars, lies patiently waiting to augment lunch and dinner. Before or after a meal guests can enjoy a drink in the comfortable bar or drawing rooms, both of which have a log fire during the cooler months. The hotel is well placed for guests to enjoy the varied attractions of the wonderful city of Bath with its unique hot springs, Roman remains, superb Georgian architecture and American Museum. Further afield but within reach are Stonehenge and Cheddar caves.

Our inspector loved: Calm, cosy and relaxing - always a warm welcome.

HUNSTRETE HOUSE

HUNSTRETE, NR BATH, SOMERSET BS39 4NS

In a classical English landscape on the edge of the Mendip Hills stands Hunstrete House. This unique hotel, surrounded by lovely gardens, is largely 18th century, although the history of the estate goes back to 963AD. Each of the bedrooms is individually decorated and furnished to a high standard, combining the benefits of a hotel room with the atmosphere of a charming private country house. Many offer uninterrupted views over undulating fields and woodlands. The reception areas exhibit warmth and elegance and are liberally furnished with beautiful antiques. Log fires burn in the hall, library and drawing room through the winter and on cooler summer evenings. The Terrace dining room looks out on to an Italianate, flower-filled courtyard. A highly skilled head chef offers light, elegant dishes using produce from the extensive garden, including organic meat and vegetables. The menu changes regularly and the hotel has an excellent reputation for the quality and interest of its wine list. In a sheltered corner of the walled garden there is a heated swimming pool for guests to enjoy. For the energetic, the all-weather tennis court provides another diversion. The hotel is also available for exclusive use wedding and corporate events with a marquee to seat up to 120 people.

Our inspector loved: The pretty courtyard - an ideal spot for a light lunch or pre-dinner drinks.

Directions: From Bath take the A4 towards Bristol and then the A368 to Wells.

Web: www.johansens.com/hunstretehouse
E-mail: reservations@hunstretehouse.co.uk
Tel: 0870 381 8630
International: +44 (0)1761 490490
Fax: 01761 490732

Price Guide:
single from £145
double/twin from £170
suite from £265

MOORE PLACE HOTEL

THE SQUARE, ASPLEY GUISE, MILTON KEYNES, BEDFORDSHIRE MK17 8DW

Directions: Only a 2-minute drive from the M1/junction 13.

Web: www.johansens.com/mooreplace
E-mail: manager@mooreplace.com
Tel: 0870 381 8745
International: +44 (0)1908 282000
Fax: 01908 281888

Price Guide:
single £55–£105
double/twin £75–£145
suite £150–£210

Built in 1786, Moore Place Hotel is a delightful country house hotel set in the centre of the peaceful village of Aspley Guise, and only 1.5 miles from the M1. Sympathetically extended to create extra accommodation, the new wing frames the attractive patio courtyard, rock garden, lily pool and waterfall. In May 2003, an additional 10 guest rooms were opened in the converted, listed cottage; each maintaining a very special character of its own. All 64 bedrooms are well-appointed and offer little extras such as trouser press, hairdryer, welcome drinks and large towelling bathrobes to make each visit special, for both business and leisure travellers alike. The attractive Victorian-style conservatory houses the highly acclaimed Greenhouse Restaurant, which is open to residents as well as non-residents, and serves cuisine rated amongst the best in the area. The menu is traditional English with European influences and is enhanced by a selection of fine wines; private dinners, conferences and special celebrations can be accommodated in 5 private function rooms. Moore Place Hotel is ideally situated for exploring the surrounding countryside and places of interest such as Bletchley Park, Waddesdon Manor, Woburn Abbey and Whipsnade Zoo to name but a few.

Our inspector loved: The newly available spacious and attractive rooms in the cottage.

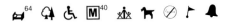

MONKEY ISLAND HOTEL

OLD MILL LANE, BRAY-ON-THAMES, MAIDENHEAD, BERKSHIRE SL6 2EE

The name Monkey Island derives from the medieval Monk's Eyot. Circa 1723, the island was purchased by Charles Spencer, the third Duke of Marlborough, who built the fishing lodge now known as the Pavilion and the fishing temple, both of which are Grade I listed. The Pavilion's Candles Lounge overlooks acres of riverside lawn and is an ideal spot for a relaxing cocktail. The award-winning Pavilion Restaurant perched on the island's narrowest tip, boasts fine English cuisine and friendly service. The River Room is suitable for weddings or other large functions, whilst the Regency-style boardroom is perfect for small parties. The whole hotel and island is available for exclusive use to create a truly memorable occasion. There are 26 comfortable bedrooms and suites in the Temple House. The Wedgwood Room, with its splendid ceiling in high-relief plaster, and the octagonal Temple Room, provide further examples of the conference facilities. Monkey Island is 1 mile downstream from Maidenhead, within easy reach of Royal Windsor, Eton, Henley and London. The hotel offers weekend breaks from £90 per person and in the summer, boat hire and picnic days.

Our inspector loved: The hotel's island setting in the midst of the River Thames.

Directions: Jct 8/9 M4 - Take A308 from Maidenhead towards Windsor; turn left following signposts to Bray. Entering Bray, go right along Old Mill Lane, which goes over M4; the entrance to the hotel is on the left after approx ¼ mile.

Web: www.johansens.com/monkeyisland
E-mail: reception@monkeyisland.co.uk
Tel: 0870 381 8742
International: +44 (0)1628 623400
Fax: 01628 784732

Price Guide:
single from £110
double/twin £140–£190
suite £295

FREDRICK'S – HOTEL RESTAURANT SPA

SHOPPENHANGERS ROAD, MAIDENHEAD, BERKSHIRE SL6 2PZ

Directions: Leave M4 at junction 8/9, take A404(M) and leave at first exit 9A signed Cox Green/White Waltham. Turn left into Shoppenhangers Road towards Maidenhead. Fredrick's is on the right.

Web: www.johansens.com/fredricks
E-mail: reservations@fredricks–hotel.co.uk
Tel: 0870 381 8531
International: +44 (0)1628 581000
Fax: 01628 771054

Price Guide:
single from £195
double/twin from £260
suite from £390

'Putting people first' is the guiding philosophy behind this sumptuously equipped deluxe hotel. Guests can expect to receive uncompromising service from this second generation family-run establishment. Extensive landscaped gardens furnished with an array of contemporary artwork overlook the fairways and greens of Maidenhead Golf Club. The spectacular addition of Fredrick's exclusive Spa offers the ultimate in relaxation and is the first in the UK equipped with its own private flotation suite. Guests can indulge in restorative treatments such as Rasul or LaStone therapies. In the hotel, minute attention to detail is evident in the luxurious bedrooms, all immaculate with gleaming, marble bathrooms, whilst some of the suites have their own patio or balcony. A quiet drink can be enjoyed in the light airy wintergarden lounge, and in warmer weather on the patio, before entering the 3 AA Rosette air-conditioned restaurant. Gourmet cuisine, which has received recognition from leading guides for many years, is served in elegant surroundings enhanced by a collection of fine art and sculpture. As well as being suitable for relaxation, leisurely spa breaks and fine dining, Fredrick's is perfectly located for conferences and corporate hospitality. Fredrick's, easily accessible from Windsor, Henley, Ascot and London is also ideal for those needing an overnight stay close to Heathrow Airport.

Our inspector loved: The new spa with so many tempting relaxation treats.

CLIVEDEN

TAPLOW, BERKSHIRE SL6 0JF

Cliveden, winner of the 2004 Tea Council and AA award for "Best Country House Hotel for Afternoon Tea", is Britain's only 5 Red AA Star hotel that is also a stately home. Set in 376 acres of gardens and parkland overlooking the Thames, this former home of Frederick, Prince of Wales, 3 Dukes and the Astor family has been at the centre of Britain's social and political life for over 300 years. It is exquisitely furnished in a classical English style; oil paintings, antiques and objets d'art abound. The guest rooms and suites are spacious and luxurious and the choice of dining rooms and the scope of the menus are superb. Spring Cottage, secluded in its own gardens on the edge of the River Thames, provides unrivalled peace and privacy. Guests can enjoy a range of treatments in the Cliveden Spa, roam the magnificent gardens or enjoy a river cruise. A choice of sports, including indoor and outdoor swimming, tennis, squash, gymnasium, golf, clay pigeon shooting, horse riding and polo lessons are also available. Well-equipped, the 2 secure private boardrooms provide self-contained business meeting facilities. Exclusive use of the house can be arranged. Cliveden is part of the von Essen hotel collection.

Our inspector loved: *Its' splendour and elegance combined with comfort and relaxation.*

Directions: From M4 junction 7. A4 towards Maidenhead. After a few miles, turn right into Berry Hill and follow the road for ¾ miles. Cliveden is on your left hand side via a grand entrance.

Web: www.johansens.com/cliveden
E-mail: Reservations@clivedenhouse.co.uk
Tel: 0870 381 8432
International: +44 (0)1628 668561
Fax: 01628 661837

Price Guide:
(full English breakfast incl. VAT)
double/twin from £295
suites from £480

DONNINGTON VALLEY HOTEL & GOLF CLUB

OLD OXFORD ROAD, DONNINGTON, NEWBURY, BERKSHIRE RG14 3AG

Directions: Leave the M4 at junction 13, go south towards Newbury on A34, then follow signs for Donnington Castle. The hotel is on the right before reaching the castle.

Web: www.johansens.com/donningtonvalley
E-mail: general@donningtonvalley.co.uk
Tel: 0870 381 8484
International: +44 (0)1635 551199
Fax: 01635 551123

Price Guide:
single from £165
double/twin £165–£190
suite from £230

Uncompromising quality is the hallmark of this award winning hotel built in contrasting styles in 1991 with its own golf course. The grandeur of the Edwardian era has been captured by the interior of the hotel's reception area with its splendid wood-panelled ceilings and impressive overhanging gallery. Each individually designed bedroom has been thoughtfully equipped to guarantee comfort and peace of mind. In addition to the standard guest rooms Donnington Valley offers a number of non-smoking rooms, family rooms, superior executive rooms and luxury suites. With its open log fire and elegant surroundings, the Piano Bar is an ideal place to meet friends or enjoy the relaxed ambience. Guests lunch and dine in the 2 AA rosettes Winepress Restaurant, which offers fine British cuisine which is complemented by an extensive choice of wines and liqueurs – Donnington Valley Hotel was the 2004 winner of the Taittinger/Condé Nast Johansens wine List of the Year. 18-hole par 71 golf course is a stern test for golfers of all abilities, through a magnificent parkland setting. Special corporate golfing packages are offered and tournaments can be arranged.

Our inspector loved: *This very comfortable hotel with its exceptional staff, glorious flowers and grounds.*

NEWBURY MANOR HOTEL

LONDON ROAD, NEWBURY, BERKSHIRE RG14 2BY

Surrounded by 9 acres of lush meadows and mature woodlands on the edge of Newbury, this hidden gem of serenity epitomises the elegant English manor of old where superior standards of hospitality, service and comfort still exist. This attractive Grade II listed building, with an imposing white pillared entranceway, is exquisitely furnished and decorated to offer every luxury and facility and many rooms boast views over the river and countryside. Deep chairs and sofas, fine fabrics, antiques, floral decorations and rich carpeting contribute to the elegant ambience. The 33 spacious bedrooms and suites, many with balconies or patios, open onto manicured grounds through which runs a tranquil river, are beautifully appointed and feature facilities that discerning guests have come to expect in a luxury hotel. From four-poster and queen-size beds to a Jacuzzi in the impressive art deco style bathrooms. Award-winning head chef, Simon Mckensie, creates innovative and tempting modern European cuisine to match the imaginative décor of a restaurant listed high in The Good Food Guide. Lunch and more informal evening dining can be enjoyed in the nearby RiverBar, a refurbished Grade II listed watermill overlooking rushing weir waters where the rivers Kennet and Lambourn meet.

Our inspector loved: *Everything about this perfect hotel! Especially the informal RiverBar.*

Directions: Take the M4/junction 13 to Newbury then follow signs to the A4 Reading. Pass the BP garage on the left and continue over the small roundabout. The hotel is 300 yards on the right.

Web: www.johansens.com/newburymanor
E-mail: enquiries@newbury-manor-hotel.co.uk
Tel: 0870 381 9275
International: +44 (0)1635 528838
Fax: 01635 523406

Price Guide:
double/twin £145
suites £165–£295

THE VINEYARD AT STOCKCROSS

NEWBURY, BERKSHIRE RG20 8JU

Directions: From M4, exit Jct13, A34 towards Newbury, then Hungerford exit. 1st roundabout Hungerford exit, 2nd roundabout Stockcross exit. Hotel on right.

Web: www.johansens.com/vineyardstockcross
E-mail: general@the-vineyard.co.uk
Tel: 0870 381 8965
International: +44 (0)1635 528770
Fax: 01635 528398

Price Guide: (excluding VAT)
single/double/twin £169–£240
suite £310–£630

The Vineyard at Stockcross, Sir Peter Michael's "restaurant-with-suites" is a European showcase for the finest Californian wines including those from the Peter Michael Winery. Head Sommelier, Edoardo Amadi, has selected the best from the most highly-prized, family-owned Californian wineries, creating one of the widest, most innovative, international wine lists. Awarded 5 Red Stars and 4 Rosettes by the AA, the modern British cuisine matches the calibre of the wines. Pure flavours, fresh ingredients and subtle design blend harmoniously with the fine wines. A stimulating collection of paintings and sculpture includes the keynote piece,"Fire and Water" by William Pye FRBS and "Deconstructing the Grape", a sculpture commissioned for The Vineyard Spa. A vine-inspired steel balustrade elegantly dominates the restaurant and the luxurious interior is complemented by subtle attention to detail throughout with stunning china and glass designs. The 49 well-appointed bedrooms include 31 suites offering stylish comfort with distinctive character. The Vineyard Spa features an indoor pool, spa bath, sauna, steam room, gym and treatment rooms.

Our inspector loved: *The space, the light, the sophistication and more than a "touch of the sublime."*

THE REGENCY PARK HOTEL

BOWLING GREEN ROAD, THATCHAM, BERKSHIRE RG18 3RP

Ideally situated for access to both London and the South West, the Regency Park is a modern hotel that takes great pride in providing not only the most sophisticated facilities but combining them with the most attentive service and care. The style is neat and crisp with an understated elegance throughout, from the airy and spacious bedrooms to the array of meeting venues housed in the Business Centre. The Parkland Suite is a beautiful setting for any occasion, and with its own entrance and facilities for up to 200 guests it is the ideal place for wedding receptions and parties, as well as conferences and launches. "Escape" is the name of the leisure complex, and true to its name it really is a place where state-of-the-art technology and sheer luxury meet to form a special feature. The serenity of the 17m swimming pool and the large health and beauty salon create an instantly relaxing atmosphere where fully qualified staff offer holistic health and beauty treatments. The Watermark Restaurant again has a contemporary elegance and attractive views over the Waterfall gardens, reflected in its excellent menu of modern flavours and fusions. There is even a children's menu to ensure all guests are catered for. Weekend breaks available.

Our inspector loved: The spacious and open feel of this contemporary hotel.

Directions: Between Newbury and Reading. Leave M4 at Jct12 or 13; the hotel is signposted on A4, on the western outskirts of Thatcham.

Web: www.johansens.com/regencypark
E-mail: info@regencyparkhotel.co.uk
Tel: 0870 381 8852
International: +44 (0)1635 871555
Fax: 01635 871571

Price Guide:
single £95–£229
double/twin £110–£229
suite £233–£385

THE FRENCH HORN

SONNING-ON-THAMES, BERKSHIRE RG4 6TN

Directions: Leave the M4 at J8/9. Follow A404/M then at Thickets Roundabout turn left on A4 towards Reading for 8 miles. Turn right for Sonning. Cross Thames on B478. Hotel is on right.

Web: www.johansens.com/frenchhorn
E-mail: info@thefrenchhorn.co.uk
Tel: 0870 381 8532
International: +44 (0)1189 692204
Fax: 01189 442210

Price Guide:
single £110–£165
double/twin £140–£205

For over 150 years The French Horn, nestling beside the Thames near the historic village of Sonning with its pretty riverside walks,has provided a charming riverside retreat from the busy outside world. Today, although busier on this stretch of the river, it continues that fine tradition of comfortable accommodation and outstanding cuisine in a beautiful setting. It is as ideal for a midweek or weekend break as it is for an executive meeting or private dinner. The bedrooms and suites are comfortable and homely and many have river views. The old panelled bar provides an intimate scene for pre-dinner drinks and the Condé Nast Johansens award winning restaurant with its' speciality of locally reared duck, spit roasted here over an open fire. By day the restaurant is a lovely setting for lunch, while by night diners can enjoy the floodlit view of the graceful weeping willows which fringe the river. Dinner is served by candlelight and the cuisine is a mixture of French and English cooking using the freshest ingredients, complemented by The French Horn's fine and extensive wine. Places of interest in the area include Henley, Windsor Stratfield Saye, and Mapledurham. There are numerous golf courses, equestrian centres and fishing. Shooting can be arranged at Bisley, there are leisure facilities at the local nearby spa as well as local theatre to enjoy.

Our inspector loved: *It's traditional charm and pretty riverside location.*

THE SWAN AT STREATLEY

STREATLEY-ON-THAMES, BERKSHIRE RG8 9HR

In a beautiful setting on the banks of the River Thames, this hotel offers visitors comfortable accommodation. All of the 46 bedrooms, many of which have balconies overlooking the river, are appointed with individual décor and furnishings. The hotel's innovative cuisine ensures it maintains its 2 AA Rosettes. Guests can dine in the Cygnetures restaurant, which, with the Cygnet Bar and outdoor terrace, offers superb riverside views. Business guests are well catered for with 6 conference suites – all with natural daylight. Moored alongside the hotel is the Magdalen College Barge – a unique venue for small meetings and cocktail parties. Reflexions leisure club is equipped with a heated 'fitness' pool, sauna, sunbeds, spa bath, steam room and a wide range of exercise equipment. Cruising on the river may be arranged by the hotel and golf, horse riding, and clay pigeon shooting are available locally. Events in the locality include Henley Regatta and Newbury Races, while Windsor Castle, Blenheim Palace, Oxford and London's airports are easily accessible. Special breaks such as "family weekends," "winter warmers," "summer sizzler," racing and romance are available.

Our inspector loved: Its riverside location and attractive terrace.

Directions: M4 junction 12. A340 to Pangbourne. A329 to Streatley. Turn right at Streatley traffic lights. The hotel is on the left before the bridge. Only 20 minutes from the M4

Web: www.johansens.com/swanatstreatley
E-mail: sales@swan-at-streatley.co.uk
Tel: 0870 381 8928
International: +44 (0)1491 878800
Fax: 01491 872554

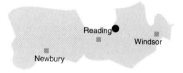

Price Guide:
single from £110
double/twin from £138
suites from £175

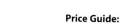

29

Sir Christopher Wren's House Hotel & Spa

THAMES STREET, WINDSOR, BERKSHIRE SL4 1PX

A friendly and welcoming atmosphere makes Sir Christopher Wren's House a perfect location for guests wanting to combine shopping and sightseeing with leisure. Built by the famous architect in 1676, it nestles beneath the ramparts and towers of Windsor Castle, beside the River Thames and Eton Bridge. With a quiet charm and dignity of its own, the hotel combines fine furnishings from the past with contemporary modern design. Additions to the original house, include a beautiful pavillion overlooking the Thames and Riverside terrace. There are 90 bedrooms available for guests, all richly furnished to the highest standards and, while some feature a balcony and river views, others overlook the famous castle. All offer a full range of amenities, including state-of-the-art technology. For longer stays guests may wish to use the hotels' apartments. Stroks Riverside Restaurant and attractive open terrace offers a good selection of beautifully cooked and well-presented meals. The hotel also has a top class gym with outdoor spa pool and beauty treatments. The Windsor area has a great deal to offer, for those with time to explore. Among the many attractions within easy reach are Windsor Castle, Eton College, river excursions Royal Ascot, Thorpe Park, Henley, Savill Gardens and Legoland.

Directions: Windsor is just 2 miles from Jct 6 of the M4. Follow one-way system with River Thames on your left towards Datchet. Turn left into Thames Street. The hotel's car park (by arrangement) is on the left. (Thames Street is pedestrianised).

Web: www.johansens.com/sirchristopher
E-mail: reservations@wrensgroup.com
Tel: 0870 381 8896
International: +44 (0)1753 861354
Fax: 01753 860172

Price Guide:
single from £70–£155
double/twin from £80–£232
suite from £200–£283

Reading
Windsor
Newbury

Our inspector loved: *The glorious river views from Stroks Restaurant and terrace - plus the well equipped spa.*

STIRRUPS

MAIDENS GREEN, BRACKNELL, BERKSHIRE RG42 6LD

Set back from the road, this family-owned and run hotel sits amidst 10 acres of pretty grounds, which extend to the rear and sides. Its comfortable walk through bar is popular with guests and locals alike, and serves excellent bar meals and real ales in an informal atmosphere. Alternatively the award-winning restaurant offers an á la carte menu and an extensive wine list. Most of the well-sized freshly updated bedrooms, each with its distinctive style and charm, have views over the gardens, and provide all the facilities one would expect; they range from standard rooms to junior suites, several of which are suitable for families. The hotel is as ideal a location for a relaxed weekend break as it is for business and corporate events and meetings. There are 3 bright and pleasant conference rooms and 2 syndicate rooms, catering for 2 to 100 delegates. Stirrups is also a popular choice for weddings, and has been granted a licence to conduct civil ceremonies. Its convenient location means it is within easy reach of Windsor, Legoland, Royal Ascot and London. Weekend breaks and Legoland packages are available

Our inspector loved: *This friendly country hotel with its pretty gardens and bedrooms.*

Directions: From the M4 take J8/9, and join the A330 towards Ascot. Turn right onto the B3022 and the hotel is 200 yards on the left. From the M3 take J3 onto the A332.

Web: www.johansens.com/stirrups
E-mail: reception@stirrupshotel.co.uk
Tel: 0870 381 9238
International: +44 (0)1344 882284
Fax: 01344 882300

Price Guide:
single from £105
double/twin from £110
suite from £140

HOTEL DU VIN & BISTRO

CHURCH STREET, BIRMINGHAM B3 2NR

Directions: From the M6, jct 6 take the A38 to the city centre. Take the flyover and exit at St Chad's Circus signposted "Jewellery Quarter". Take the second left into Great Charles Street, then the first left into Livery Street. Take the third turning right into Barwick Street then right into Church Street.

Web: www.johansens.com/hoteduvinbirmingham
E-mail: info@birmingham.hotelduvin.com
Tel: 0870 381 8618
International: +44 (0)121 200 0600
Fax: 0121 236 0889

Price Guide:
double/twin from £125
studios from £195

Hotel du Vin & Bistro, originally the Birmingham Eye Hospital, is a unique venue in the heart of cosmopolitan Birmingham. Its stunning early Victorian architecture enhances the luxury of the tasteful, modern interior design. 66 tranquil bedrooms emphasize simplicity and quality with superb beds, luxurious Egyptian linens and attention to detail. The hotel has 2 bars: The Bubble Lounge is based on a Venetian café and serves over 50 different types of champagne; The Cellar Bar features an eye-catching oil painting of a lobster, the colourful backdrop for its vast selection of wines; big, comfortable sofas, low-lighting and relaxation are essential to the Cigar Divan. The hotel's excellent chef chooses only the freshest of local ingredients to create a sumptuous feast, which is served in the elegant surrounds of the Bistro. Guests may unwind and pamper themselves in the hotel's private health and beauty spa, which features state-of-the-art equipment, sauna, steam room, massage, aromatherapy and a range of wonderful beauty treatments using natural ingredients. Only minutes away from Birmingham's old city centre, there is fantastic shopping, waterways, art galleries, theatres and the Symphony Hall nearby.

Our inspector loved: *The ambience and décor in the bistro - and the food and wine!.*

      SPA

NEW HALL

WALMLEY ROAD, ROYAL SUTTON COLDFIELD, WEST MIDLANDS B76 1QX

Cocooned by a lily filled moat and surrounded by 26 acres of beautiful gardens and parkland, New Hall dates from the 12th century and is reputedly the oldest fully moated manor house in England. This prestigious hotel is full of warmth and luxury and exudes a friendly, welcoming atmosphere. New Hall proudly holds the coveted RAC Gold Ribbon Award, and AA Inspectors' Hotel of the Year for England 1994. The cocktail bar and adjoining drawing room overlook the terrace from which a bridge leads to the yew topiary, orchards and sunlit glades. The superbly appointed bedrooms and individually designed suites offer every modern comfort and amenity and have glorious views over the gardens and moat. A 9-hole par 3 golf course and floodlit tennis court are available for guests' use, as are a heated indoor pool, Jacuzzi, sauna, steam room and gymnasium. For those wishing to revitalise mind, body and soul, New Hall offers a superb range of beauty treatments. Surrounded by a rich cultural heritage, New Hall is convenient for Lichfield Cathedral, Warwick Castle, Stratford-upon-Avon, the NEC and the ICC in Birmingham. The Belfry Golf Centre is also nearby.

Our inspector loved: The grounds, the topiary and the moat with its abundant lilies.

Directions: From exit 9 of the M42, follow A4097 (ignoring signs to A38 Sutton Coldfield). At B4148 turn right at the traffic lights. New Hall is 1 mile on the left.

Web: www.johansens.com/newhall
E-mail: newhall@thistle.co.uk
Tel: 0870 381 8756
International: +44 (0)121 378 2442
Fax: 0121 378 4637

Price Guide:
single from £166
double/twin from £200
suite from £230

HOTEL DU VIN & BISTRO

THE SUGAR HOUSE, NARROW LEWINS MEAD, BRISTOL BS1 2NU

Set around a courtyard dating from the 1700s, this hotel comprises 6 listed warehouses that have been used for a number of industrial purposes over the centuries. The imposing 100-foot chimney is a lasting testimony to the buildings' impressive past and other distinctive vestiges relating to this period feature inside. The individually named bedrooms are decorated with fine fabrics such as Egyptian linen and offer a good range of facilities including oversized baths and power showers. Guests may relax in the convivial cocktail bar with its walk-in cigar humidor or enjoy a glass of wine from the well-stocked cellar before dining in the Bistro. The traditional menu has been created using the freshest local ingredients and is complemented by an excellent wine list. Throughout the property the cool, understated elegance is evident as is the owners' attention to even the smallest detail. The hotel has a selection of specially designed rooms for private meetings or dinner parties. Do not expect stuffy formality at the Hotel du Vin!

Our inspector loved: *Relaxed, informal and comfortable with a great atmosphere in the buzzy bistro.*

Directions: Follow the M32 and then follow signs for the city centre. Go past Broadmead Shopping Centre on your left, and approx 500 yards further on the War Memorial in the centre. Turn right and get onto the opposite side of the carriageway. The hotel is located about 400 yards further down on the left, offset from the main road.

Web: www.johansens.com/hotelduvinbristol
E-mail: info@bristol.hotelduvin.com
Tel: 0870 381 8616
International: +44 (0)117 925 5577
Fax: 0117 925 1199

Price Guide:
double/twin from £130
studio suite from £180

Chipping Sodbury

Bristol

Bristol Airport

Bath

HARTWELL HOUSE HOTEL, RESTAURANT & SPA

OXFORD ROAD, NEAR AYLESBURY, BUCKINGHAMSHIRE HP17 8NL

Standing in 90 acres of gardens and parkland landscaped by a contemporary of Capability Brown, Hartwell House has both Jacobean and Georgian facades. This beautiful country house is a Grade 1 listed building, and was the residence in exile of King Louis XVIII of France from 1809 to 1814. The large ground floor reception rooms, with oak panelling and decorated ceilings, have antique furniture and fine paintings that evoke the elegance of the 18th century. There are 46 individually designed bedrooms and suites some in the house and some in Hartwell Court, the restored 18th century stables. The dining room is the setting for excellent food awarded 3 AA Rosettes (gentlemen are requested to wear a jacket at dinner), and there are also 2 private dining rooms. The Old Rectory, Hartwell with its 2 acres of gardens, tennis court and swimming pool, provides superb accommodation and offers great comfort and privacy. The Hartwell Spa adjacent to the hotel includes an indoor heated pool, whirlpool spa bath, steam room, saunas, gymnasium and 4 beauty salons. Situated in the Vale of Aylesbury, the hotel is only 45 minutes from London Heathrow, 1 hour from London and 20 miles from Oxford. Blenheim Palace, Waddesdon Manor and Woburn Abbey are just some of the nearby attractions. Dogs are permitted only in Hartwell Court bedrooms. Owned and restored by Historic House Hotels Limited.

Directions: Off the A418 between Oxford and Aylesbury. 2 miles from Aylesbury

Web: www.johansens.com/hartwellhouse

E-mail: info@hartwell–house.com

Tel: 0870 381 8585

International: +44 (0)1296 747444

Fax: 01296 747450

Price Guide: (inc continental breakfast)
single from £155
double/twin from £260
suites from £360

Our inspector loved: The grandeur of this lovely English country house.

STOKE PARK CLUB

PARK ROAD, STOKE POGES, BUCKINGHAMSHIRE SL2 4PG

Amidst 350 acres of sweeping parkland and gardens, Stoke Park Club is the epitome of elegance and style. For more than 900 years the estate has been at the heart of English heritage, playing host to lords, noblemen, kings and queens. History has left an indelible mark of prestige on the hotel and today it effortlessly combines peerless service with luxury. The magnificence of the Palladian mansion is echoed by the lavishly decorated interior where intricate attention to detail has been paid to the décor with antiques, exquisite fabrics and original paintings and prints ensuring that each room is a masterpiece of indulgence. All 21 individually furnished bedrooms and suites are complemented by marble en-suite bathrooms and some open onto terraces where an early evening drink can be enjoyed as the sun descends over the lakes and gardens. 8 beautiful function rooms, perfect for private dining and entertaining, also continue the theme of tasteful elegance. Since 1908 the hotel has been home to one of the finest 27-hole championship parkland golf courses in the world, Stoke Poges, and the addition of an all indulging spa, health and racquet pavilion re-affirms the hotel's position as one of the country's leading sporting venues. Luxury facilities include 11 beauty treatment rooms, indoor swimming pool, state-of-the-art gymnasium and studio and 13 tennis courts.

Directions: From the M4 take junction 6 or from the M40 take junction 2 then the A344. At the double roundabout at Farnham Royal take the B416. The entrance is just over 1 mile on the right.

Web: www.johansens.com/stokepark
E-mail: info@stokeparkclub.com
Tel: 0870 381 8915
International: +44 (0)1753 717171
Fax: 01753 717181

Price Guide:
single £275
suite £395

Milton Keynes

Aylesbury

High Wycombe

Our inspector loved: The wonderful views and the temptation of the spa.

      SPA

TAPLOW HOUSE HOTEL

BERRY HILL, TAPLOW, NR MAIDENHEAD, BUCKINGHAMSHIRE SL6 0DA

Elegance, comfort, efficient service and a warm welcome are the hallmarks of this stunning Georgian hotel. Situated on the border between Berkshire and Buckinghamshire, it is a peaceful haven near Windsor and close to London Heathrow Airport, Henley-on-Thames, Ascot and Cliveden. The city of London is also within easy reach. As you sweep up the driveway, you are greeted by a fine Country House, which was originally a gift from James I to Hampson, Governor of Virginia. Set in 6 acres of beautiful gardens and boasting Europe's largest tulip tress, Taplow House Hotel is the perfect setting for a meeting, private event, wedding or relaxing overnight stay. The hotel offers a pleasing combination of period charm and state of the art business amenities. All 32 bedrooms, most with fine views over the grounds, have spacious en suite bathrooms. The restaurant lends itself to a fine dining experience, whilst the Garden Terrace on a balmy summer day is ideal for afternoon tea or cocktails. Weekend breaks and special packages are available.

Our inspector loved: The comfortable bar and glorious gardens.

Directions: From M4 junction 7. A4 towards Maidenhead after approximately 2 miles and once under a railway bridge, turn right into Berry Hill. The hotel is on the right after 150 yards.

Web: www.johansens.com/taplowhouse
E-mail: reception@taplow.wrensgroup.com
Tel: 0870 381 8939
International: +44 (0)1628 670056
Fax: 01628 773625

Price Guide: (room only)
single £95–£130
double/twin £120–£200
suite £170–£260

DANESFIELD HOUSE HOTEL AND SPA

HENLEY ROAD, MARLOW-ON-THAMES, BUCKINGHAMSHIRE SL7 2EY

Directions: Danesfield is situated between Henley-on-Thames and Marlow and is easily accessed by the M4 junction 8/9 and the M40.

Web: www.johansens.com/danesfieldhouse
E-mail: sales@danesfieldhouse.co.uk
Tel: 0870 381 8474
International: +44 (0)1628 891010
Fax: 01628 890408

Price Guide:
single £190
double/twin £230
suites £285

Danesfield House is set within 65 acres of gardens and parkland overlooking the River Thames and offering panoramic views across the Chiltern Hills. It is the third house since 1664 to occupy this lovely setting and it was designed and built in sumptuous style at the end of the 19th century. After years of neglect the house has been fully restored, combining its Victorian splendour with the very best modern hotel facilities. Among the many attractions of its luxury bedrooms, all beautifully decorated and furnished, are the extensive facilities they offer. These include 2 telephone lines (one may be used for personal fax), satellite TV, in-room movies, mini bar, trouser press, hair dryers, bath robes and toiletries. Guests can relax in the magnificent drawing room with its galleried library or in the sun-lit atrium. There is a choice of 2 restaurants, the Oak Room and Orangery Brasserie, both of which offer a choice of international cuisine. The hotel also has 6 private banqueting and conference rooms. Leisure facilities include the award-winning luxurious spa with 20-metre pool, sauna, steam room, gymnasium and superb treatment rooms. Windsor Castle, Marlow, Henley and Oxford are nearby.

Our inspector loved: *Its position overlooking the river and Chiltern Hills beyond.*

HOTEL FELIX

WHITEHOUSE LANE, HUNTINGDON ROAD, CAMBRIDGE CB3 0LX

Hotel Felix combines Victorian and modern architecture and sits in 4 acres of landscaped gardens offering peaceful surroundings, yet is within minutes' reach of Cambridge with its famous contrast of high-tech science parks and beautiful medieval university buildings. The furniture in the hotel's public areas is handmade and the décor softly neutral with splashes of colour and carefully selected sculptures and artwork. All of the 52 en-suite bedrooms comprise king-sized beds and state-of-the-art communication facilities. Rooms have elegant proportions and are light and airy with high ceilings and views over the gardens. A restaurant and adjacent Café Bar act as a focal point and guests experience modern cuisine with a strong Mediterranean influence or continental coffees and pastries, fine teas, wine and champagne by the glass. Hotel Felix specialises in private corporate and celebration dining and its 4 meeting rooms with natural daylight and ISDN connections will accommodate 34 boardroom and 60 theatre style. Other activities to be enjoyed in Cambridge are visits to Kings College, the Botanical Gardens, Fitzwilliam Museum and punting on the River Cam. Nearby places of interest include Ely, Bury St Edmunds and the races at Newmarket.

Our inspector loved: The romantic bedroom hidden away in the top of the house.

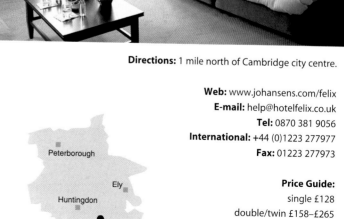

Directions: 1 mile north of Cambridge city centre.

Web: www.johansens.com/felix
E-mail: help@hotelfelix.co.uk
Tel: 0870 381 9056
International: +44 (0)1223 277977
Fax: 01223 277973

Price Guide:
single £128
double/twin £158–£265

THE CAMBRIDGE BELFRY

CAMBOURNE, CAMBRIDGE CB3 6BW

Directions: Exit the M11 at junction 13 and join the A428 west. Cambourne is on the left after approximately 6 miles.

Web: www.johansens.com/cambridgebelfry
E-mail: cambridge@marstonhotels.com
Tel: 0870 381 9312
International: +44 (0)1954 714600
Fax: 01954 714610

Price Guide:
single from £112
double/twin from £134
suite from £137

Modern, light and airy, this 4-star hotel stands at the gateway of Cambourne Village, conveniently close to the M11 and within a 15-minute drive of historic Cambridge with its contrasting hi-tech science parks, botanical gardens, river punting and beautiful medieval university buildings. The Belfry's doors open out onto either a lovely lakeside setting or a spacious and restful courtyard garden where guests can enjoy cool drinks and social chats during long summer days. Furniture in the hotel's public rooms is sleek and comfortable and combines excellently with the softly coloured décor highlighted with commissioned paintings and artwork depicting the city and its colleges. Well proportioned and beautifully appointed en-suite bedrooms offer every facility. Guests also have a choice of 19 executive rooms and 2 suites on the first and second floors with 6 exclusive, individually styled penthouse suites on the third floor. 2 bars provide comfortable relaxation prior to dining in the stylish Bridge restaurant where the varied menu is complemented by an extensive wine list. Lighter meals and snacks are available at Brooks Brasserie. Leisure facilities include, swimming pool, a spa bath, steam and sauna rooms, exercise studio and spa therapy. Flexible conference and function facilities are available.

Our inspector loved: *The extensive range of original artwork by Jane Ford - especially the life drawings of puntsmen.*

THE HAYCOCK

WANSFORD, PETERBOROUGH, CAMBRIDGESHIRE PE8 6JA

The Haycock is a handsome old coaching inn of great charm, character and historic interest. It was host to Mary Queen of Scots in 1586 and Princess Alexandra Victoria, later Queen Victoria in 1835. Overlooking the historic bridge that spans the River Nene, the Hotel is set in a delightful village of unspoilt cottages. Recently restored to private ownership, The Haycock is enjoying a renewed attention to detail – the fragrance of fresh flowers, upgrading and refurbishment. All bedrooms are individually designed and equipped to the highest standards with beautiful soft furnishings. The restaurant is renowned for the high quality of its classic cuisine complemented by a selection of interesting and outstanding wines with dishes utilising the freshest local ingredients. A purpose-built ballroom, with lovely oak beams and its own private garden, is a popular venue for a wide range of events, including balls, wedding receptions and Christmas parties. The Business Centre has also made its mark; it is well-equipped with every facility required and offers flexibility to cater for meetings, product launches, seminars and conferences. Places of interest nearby include Stamford, Burghley House, Nene Valley Railway, Elton Hall, Rutland Water and Peterborough Cathedral.

Our inspector loved: The welcoming atmosphere characterised by the friendly staff, hand painted mural and luxurious bathrooms.

Directions: Clearly signposted on the A1, a few miles south of Stamford, on the A1/A47 intersection west of Peterborough.

Web: www.johansens.com/haycock
E-mail: sales@thehaycock.co.uk
Tel: 0870 381 8587
International: +44 (0)1780 782223
Fax: 01780 783031

Price Guide:
single from £80
double/twin room from £115
four posters from £165
junior suite from £185

THE ALDERLEY EDGE HOTEL

MACCLESFIELD ROAD, ALDERLEY EDGE, CHESHIRE SK9 7BJ

This privately owned award-winning hotel has 52 bedrooms including the Presidential and Bridal Suites, which are beautifully decorated to a high standard. Located in the sumptuous conservatory, the restaurant offers exceptional views and the highest standards of cooking; fresh produce, including fish delivered daily, is provided by local suppliers. Specialities include hot and cold seafood dishes, puddings served piping hot from the oven and a daily selection of unusual and delicious breads, baked each morning in the hotel bakery. The food is complemented by an extensive wine list, featuring a wide range of champagnes and wines. Special wine and champagne dinners are held quarterly. In addition to the main conference room there is a suite of meeting and private dining rooms. The famous Edge walks are nearby, as are Tatton and Lyme Parks, Quarry Bank Mill and Dunham Massey. Manchester's thriving city centre is 15 miles away and the airport is a 20-minute drive.

Directions: Follow M6 to M56 Stockport. Exit Jct 6, take A538 to Wilmslow. Follow signs 1½ miles to Alderley Edge. Turn left at end of the main shopping area on to Macclesfield Rd (B5087). The hotel is 200 yards on the right. From M6 take Jct 18 and follow signs for Holmes Chapel and Alderley Edge.

Web: www.johansens.com/alderleyedge
E-mail: sales@alderleyedgehotel.com
Tel: 0870 381 8307
International: +44 (0)1625 583033
Fax: 01625 586343

Price Guide:
single £55–£174
double £99–£240
suite from £250

Our inspector loved: The dining experience in the Alderley Restaurant with its extensive list of champagnes and wines.

THE CHESTER CRABWALL MANOR

PARKGATE ROAD, MOLLINGTON, CHESTER, CHESHIRE CH1 6NE

Crabwall Manor can be traced back to Saxon England, prior to the Norman Conquest. Set in 11 acres of mature woodland on the outskirts of Chester, this Grade II listed manor house has a relaxed ambience, which is enhanced by staff who combine attentive service with friendliness and care. The interior boasts elegant drapes complemented by pastel shades which lend a freshness to the décor of the spacious lounge and reception areas, whilst the log fires in the inglenook fireplaces add warmth. The hotel has won several awards for their renowned cuisine, complemented by an excellent selection of fine wines and outstanding levels of accommodation. 7 meeting suites and a further 10 syndicate rooms are available. The Reflections leisure club features a 17-metre pool, gymnasium, dance studio, sauna, spa pool and juice bar. Those wishing to be pampered will enjoy the 3 beauty treatment rooms. 100 yards from the hotel guests have reduced green fees at Mollington Grange 18 hole championship golf course. The ancient city of Chester with its many attractions is only 1½ miles away. Weekend breaks available.

Our inspector loved: *The excellent exclusive leisure club with its large swimming pool and beauty retreat.*

Directions: Go to end of the M56, ignoring signs to Chester. Follow signs to Queensferry and North Wales, taking the A5117 to next roundabout. Turn left onto the A540, towards Chester for 2 miles. The hotel is on the right.

Web: www.johansens.com/crabwallmanor
E-mail: crabwallmanor@marstonhotels.com
Tel: 0870 381 8423
International: +44 (0)1244 851666
Fax: 01244 851400

Price Guide:
single from £151
double/twin from £181–£198
suite from £225–£350

NEW

THE CHESTER GROSVENOR AND GROSVENOR SPA

EASTGATE, CHESTER, CHESHIRE CH1 1LT

Directions: In the centre of Chester on Eastgate. 24-hour NCP car parking available – follow signs to Grosvenor Precinct Car Park

Web: www.johansens.com/chestergrosvenor
E-mail: chesgrov@chestergrosvenor.co.uk
Tel: 0870 381 9264
International: +44 (0)1244 324024
Fax: 01244 313246

Price Guide:
single £190-£235
double/twin £215-£350
suite £335-£700

Located in the centre of Chester this Grade II listed building invites guests to take a step back in time and enjoy the opulence and refinement of a bygone era. Awarded Five Red Stars from the AA and Five Stars from the RAC, this highly acclaimed hotel is just a short walk from the "Rows", medieval galleried streets, Roman walls, Chester cathedral and one of the oldest racecourses in England. Each of the air-conditioned 80 guest rooms and suites is individually decorated and features a queen or king-size bed. Morning coffee, lunch and afternoon tea are all served in the relaxing and comfortable Library and Archive room whilst Michelin-starred cuisine is savoured in The Arkle, where modern, imaginative dishes are complemented by a very impressive list of fine wines and liqueurs. The less formal, Parisian-style La Brasserie provides an alternative dining option. The Grosvenor Spa comprises five treatment rooms, where both Western and Eastern techniques are practised. Facilities include: thermal suite, salt grotto, crystal steam room, ice fountain and herb-sauna. For the more athletic, the hotel's fitness centre is adjacent to the spa. Conference facilities for up to 250 delegates can be accommodated.

Our inspector loved: *The new innovative spa, which is an excellent addition to Chester's finest hotel.*

GREEN BOUGH HOTEL

60 HOOLE ROAD, CHESTER, CHESHIRE CH2 3NL

Proprietors Janice and Philip Martin have worked ceaselessly to create this friendly, relaxing haven, which is now Chester's premier small luxury hotel. The 15 sumptuous bedrooms and suites have been completely refurbished using Italian wall coverings and fabrics in keeping with the Roman theme which is evident throughout the hotel. Original oil paintings depicting scenes from a bygone era in Pompeii add to the exclusive ambience. Bedrooms feature original antique cast-iron beds and some have four-posters, plasma televisions, CD players and Jacuzzi baths. There are 7 deluxe bedrooms and 1 master suite in the Lodge. This totally non-smoking hotel enjoys an outstanding reputation reflected in the prestigious awards it has accumulated: Regional Small Hotel of the Year 2002, RAC Blue Ribbon, ETC Gold Award, Excellence in England Finalist 2003. The Olive Tree restaurant offers a fine dining experience bringing together an eclectic mix of aromas and flavours to produce imaginative and innovative dishes for the à la carte and table d'hôte menus, which are complemented by wines from the extensive cellar. The hotel is located within walking distance of the ancient and historic city of Chester and centrally placed for easy access to Snowdonia, Cumbria, Manchester and Liverpool. There is ample off-road parking.

Our inspector loved: The Roman theme prevalent throughout the hotel.

Directions: Leave M53 at Jct12. Take A56 into Chester for 1 mile. The Green Bough Hotel is on the right.

Web: www.johansens.com/greenbough
E-mail: luxury@greenbough.co.uk
Tel: 0870 381 8571
International: +44 (0)1244 326241
Fax: 01244 326265

Price Guide:
single from £90/€115
double/twin from £125/€175
suites from £195/€250

NUNSMERE HALL

TARPORLEY ROAD, OAKMERE, NORTHWICH, CHESHIRE CW8 2ES

Directions: Leave M6 at junction 19, take A556 to Chester (approximately 12 miles). Turn left onto A49. Hotel is 1 mile on left.

Web: www.johansens.com/nunsmerehall
E-mail: reservations@nunsmere.co.uk
Tel: 0870 381 8772
International: +44 (0)1606 889100
Fax: 01606 889055

Price Guide:
single £140–£165
double/twin £195–£230
junior suites £260–£350

Set in peaceful Cheshire countryside and surrounded on three sides by a lake, Nunsmere Hall epitomises the elegant country manor where superior standards of hospitality still exist. Wood panelling, antique furniture, exclusive fabrics, Chinese lamps and magnificent chandeliers evoke an air of luxury. The 29 bedrooms and 7 junior suites, most with spectacular views of the lake and gardens, are beautifully appointed with king-size beds, comfortable breakfast seating and marbled bathrooms containing soft bathrobes and toiletries. The Brocklebank, Delamere and Oakmere business suites are air-conditioned, soundproofed and offer excellent facilities for boardroom meetings, private dining and seminars. The restaurant has a reputation for fine food and uses only fresh seasonal produce. Twice County Restaurant of the Year in the Good Food Guide. A snooker room is available and there are several championship golf courses nearby. Oulton Park racing circuit and the Cheshire Polo Club are next door. Golf pitch and putt is available in the grounds. Archery and air rifle shooting by arrangement. Although secluded, Nunsmere is convenient for major towns and routes. AA 3 Red Star and 2 Rosettes.

Our inspector loved: This elegant country house surrounded by its own lake.

ROWTON HALL HOTEL

WHITCHURCH ROAD, ROWTON, CHESTER, CHESHIRE CH3 6AD

Set in over 8 acres of award-winning gardens, Rowton Hall is located at the end of a leafy lane, only 3 miles from Chester city centre. Built as a private residence in 1779, it retains many of its original features, including extensive oak panelling, a self-supporting hand-carved staircase, an original Inglenook fireplace and an elegant Robert Adam fireplace. Each luxury bedroom is individually and tastefully decorated with attention to detail, and is equipped with every modern amenity, including private bathroom, satellite television, direct dial telephone with modem points, personal safe, luxury bathrobes, trouser press and hostess tray. Dining in the oak-panelled Langdale Restaurant is a delight; every dish is carefully created by head chef, Matt Hulme, who uses the finest ingredients from local markets and the Hall's gardens to produce exquisite cuisine. Guests can enjoy the indoor Health Club and relax in the Jacuzzi, steam room or sauna. For the more energetic, a workout in the well-equipped gymnasium and dance studio is available and 2 floodlit all-weather tennis courts are within the grounds. Four main conference and banqueting suites make the Hall an ideal venue for meetings, weddings, private dining or conferences and corporate events for up to 200 guests. Marquee events can be arranged in the gardens.

Our inspector loved: The lovingly tended gardens.

Directions: From the centre of Chester, take A41 towards Whitchurch. After 3 miles, turn right to Rowton village. The hotel is in the centre of the village.

Web: www.johansens.com/rowtonhall
E-mail: rowtonhall@rowtonhall.co.uk
Tel: 0870 381 8871
International: +44 (0)1244 335262
Fax: 01244 335464

Price Guide:
single £137–£170
double/twin £149–£185
suites £375

CREWE HALL

WESTON ROAD, CREWE, CHESHIRE CW1 6UZ

Directions: From the M6, exit at junction 16 and follow the A500 towards Crewe. At the first roundabout take the last exit. At the next roundabout take the first exit. After ¼ mile turn right into the drive.

Web: www.johansens.com/crewehall
E-mail: crewehall@marstonhotels.com
Tel: 0870 381 8458
International: +44 (0)1270 253333
Fax: 01270 253322

Price Guide:
single £177–£417
double/twin £219–£459
suite £274–£459

Set in vast, impressive grounds, the magnificent Crewe Hall is the jewel of Cheshire. Once the seat of the Earls of Crewe and owned by the Queen as part of the estate of the Duchy of Lancaster, this stately home transports guests back to an age of splendour and luxury where quality and service were imperative. An exquisite Jacobean carving, which adorns the lavish main entrance, is reflected over the whole exterior from the balustraded terraces to the tip of the tall West Wing Tower. Crewe Hall's beautiful interior boats a confident juxtaposition between the traditional and modern. The newly refurbished and air-conditioned west wing, with its stylish, contemporary décor, is contrasted with the traditional home rooms, which have magnificent panelling and marble, huge stone fireplaces, intricate carvings, stained glass and antique furniture. Regarded as one of the finest specimens of Elizabethan architecture, the staircase in the East Hall climbs majestically upwards. Guests can dine in the quiet, elegant dining room or the informal Brasserie, which has a unique revolving bar (whose smooth motion means you will not notice you are moving until the view has suddenly changed) and offers imaginative, delicious meals complemented by international beers and wines.

Our inspector loved: *The eclectic mix of the traditional and modern.*

HILLBARK HOTEL

ROYDEN PARK, FRANKBY, WIRRAL CH48 1NP

Surrounded by 240 acres of parkland, Hillbark hotel is a magnificent Elizabethan style mansion with a fascinating history and views over the Dee estuary and hills of North Wales. It was originally built in Birkenhead for the soap manufacturer, Robert William Hudson. Germany's Crown Prince Wilhelm was so impressed by it that he built a replica of it for himself in Potsdam, Germany. It is there that the famous Potsdam Agreement was signed at the end of World War II. In 1931, the mansion was moved brick by brick to its present location in Frankby on the Wirral Peninsula. There are many extraordinary features in the hotel - a Jacobean fireplace dates from 1527 and was taken from Sir Walter Raleigh's home and there are beautiful stained glass windows by William Morris. The library was originally in a stately home in Gloucestershire whilst the dining room doors are from an old tea clipper. Delicious and imaginative haute cuisine is served in the 2 stylish restaurants together with an excellent choice of fine wines from the cellar. Hillbark is ideal for that special celebration where up to 500 guests can be catered for. For that extra touch Rolls Royce and Bentley motor cars are available to collect from airports and rail stations. Leisure activities include world-class golf and windsurfing.

Our inspector loved: The oak panelling in this magnificent Elizabethan style black and white timber house.

Directions: M53 Jct 3 A552. Then A551 towards Upton. After the hospital turn left onto Arrowe Brook Road, then left onto Arrowe Brook Lane, then over roundabout. Hillbark is on the left

Web: www.johansens.com/hillbark
E-mail: enquiries@hillbarkhotel.co.uk
Tel: 0870 381 9128
International: +44 (0)151 625 2400
Fax: 0151 625 4040

Price Guide:
single £140
double/twin £160–£195
suite £195–£345

MERE COURT HOTEL

WARRINGTON ROAD, MERE, KNUTSFORD, CHESHIRE WA16 0RW

Directions: From M6, exit at junction 19. Take A556 towards Manchester. After 1 mile turn left at traffic lights onto A50 towards Warrington. Mere Court is on the right.

Web: www.johansens.com/merecourt
E-mail: sales@merecourt.co.uk
Tel: 0870 381 8727
International: +44 (0)1565 831000
Fax: 01565 831001

Price Guide:
single £95–£125
double/twin £115–£140

This attractive Edwardian house stands in 7 acres of mature gardens and parkland in one of the loveliest parts of Cheshire. Maintained as a family home since being built in 1903, Mere Court has been skilfully restored into a fine country house hotel offering visitors a peaceful ambience in luxury surroundings. Comforts and conveniences of the present mix excellently with the ambience and many original features of the past. The bedrooms have views over the grounds or ornamental lake. All are individually designed and a number of them have a Jacuzzi spa bath and mini bar. Facilities include safes, personalised voice mail telephones and modem points. Heavy ceiling beams, polished oak panelling and restful waterside views are features of the elegant Aboreum Restaurant, which serves the best of traditional English and Mediterranean cuisines. Lighter meals can be enjoyed in the Lounge Bar. The original coach house has been converted into a designated conference centre with state-of-the-art conference suites and syndicate rooms accommodating up to 120 delegates. Warrington, Chester, Manchester Airport and many National Trust properties are within easy reach.

Our inspector loved: *The oak-panelled restaurant overlooking the ornamental lake.*

THE STANNEYLANDS HOTEL

STANNEYLANDS ROAD, WILMSLOW, CHESHIRE SK9 4EY

Stanneylands is a handsome country house set in several acres of impressive, tranquil gardens with a collection of unusual trees and shrubs. Guests experience a truly warm welcome in a unique and special atmosphere, where luxurious comfort provides the perfect setting for business or pleasure. The bedrooms have recently been refurbished to a high standard. A sense of quiet luxury prevails in the reception rooms, where classical décor and comfortable furnishings create a relaxing ambience. In the award-winning restaurant guests can choose from an enticing blend of innovative and traditional English and international cuisine. Stanneylands is an excellent venue for both private and business events. The Oak Room accommodates up to 60 people, whilst the Stanley Suite is available for conferences and larger celebrations. The hotel is conveniently located for Manchester and its airport, as well as the bustling market towns and industrial heritage of the area. Special corporate and weekend rates are available.

Our inspector loved: The newly refurbished front lounge and bedrooms.

Directions: 3 miles from Manchester International Airport. Come off at Junction 5 on the M56 (airport turn off). Follow signs to Cheadle/Wilmslow, turn left into station road, bear right onto Stanneylands Road.

Web: www.johansens.com/stanneylands
E-mail: sales@stanneylandshotel.co.uk
Tel: 0870 381 8909
International: +44 (0)1625 525225
Fax: 01625 537282

Price Guide:
single £70–£135
double/twin £102–£150
suite £150

THE NARE HOTEL

CARNE BEACH, VERYAN-IN-ROSELAND, TRURO, CORNWALL TR2 5PF

Directions: Follow the road to St Mawes. 2 miles after Tregony Bridge turn left for Veryan. The hotel is 1 mile beyond Veryan.

Web: www.johansens.com/nare
E-mail: office@narehotel.co.uk
Tel: 0870 381 8755
International: +44 (0)1872 501111
Fax: 01872 501856

Price Guide:
single £96-£183
double/twin £182-£336
suite £324-£530

Peace, tranquillity and stunning sea views make The Nare a real find. Superbly positioned, the hotel overlooks the fine sandy beach of Gerrans Bay, facing south and sheltered by The Nare and St Mawes headlands. In recent years extensive refurbishments have ensured comfort and elegance without detracting from the country house charm of this friendly family-run hotel. All bedrooms are close to the sea, many with patios and balconies taking advantage of the spectacular outlook. In the main dining room guests can enjoy the sea views from 3 sides of the room where local seafood, such as lobster and delicious homemade puddings, are served with Cornish cream, complemented by an interesting range of wines. The Quarterdeck Restaurant is open all day serving morning coffee, light luncheons, cream teas and offers relaxed dining in the evening. The Nare remains the highest rated AA 4 star hotel in the south west with 2 Rosettes for its food. Surrounded by subtropical gardens and National Trust land the hotel's seclusion is ideal for exploring the coastline and villages of the glorious Roseland Peninsula. It is also central for many of Cornwall's beautiful houses and gardens including the famous Heligan. Guests arriving by train or air are met, without charge, by prior arrangement, at Truro Station or Newquay Airport. The hotel is open throughout the year, including Christmas and New Year.

Our inspector loved: *The magnificent location and beautiful presentation .*

THE GREENBANK HOTEL

HARBOURSIDE, FALMOUTH, CORNWALL TR11 2SR

Surrounded by the vibrant atmosphere of Falmouth, the Greenbank is the only hotel on the banks of one of the world's largest and deepest natural harbours. Because of its position as a ferry point to Flushing, its history stretches back to the 17th century, and visitors have included Florence Nightingale and Kenneth Grahame, whose letters from the hotel to his son formed the basis for his book "The Wind in the Willows". Seaward views from the hotel are stunning, and reaching out from each side are lovely clifftop paths leading to secluded coves where walkers can relax while enjoying a paddle in clear blue waters and breathing in fresh, clean sea air. Most of the charming, delightfully furnished and well equipped en-suite bedrooms enjoy panoramic views across the harbour to Flushing and St Mawes. Keen appetites will be well satisfied by the variety of dishes offered in the Harbourside Restaurant with seafood and local lamb specialities on the menu. There are opportunities locally for golf, sailing, riding and fishing. Interesting places nearby include Cornwall's National Maritime Museum, several heritage sites and many National Trust properties and gardens.

Our inspector loved: The magnificent location and breathtaking views across Falmouth harbour's ever changing scenery.

Directions: Take the A39 from Truro and on approaching Falmouth join the Old Road going through Penryn. Turn left at the second roundabout where the hotel is signposted.

Web: www.johansens.com/greenbank
E-mail: sales@greenbank-hotel.com
Tel: 0870 381 8573
International: +44 (0)1326 312440
Fax: 01326 211362

Price Guide:
single £70–£90
double/twin £115–£175
suite £190–£235

53

BUDOCK VEAN - THE HOTEL ON THE RIVER

NEAR HELFORD PASSAGE, MAWNAN SMITH, FALMOUTH, CORNWALL TR11 5LG

Directions: From the A39, Truro to Falmouth road, follow the brown tourist signs for Trebah Garden. Budock Vean appears ½ mile after passing Trebah on the left-hand side.

Web: www.johansens.com/budockvean
E-mail: relax@budockvean.co.uk
Tel: 0870 381 8392
International: reservations+44 (0)1326 252100
Fax: 01326 250892

Price Guide: (including dinner)
single £68–£111
double/twin £136–£222
suites £232–£292

This family-run, 4-star Cornwall Tourist Board Hotel of the Year 2002 & 2003, is nestled in 65 acres of award-winning gardens and parkland with a private foreshore on the tranquil Helford River. Set in a designated area of breathtaking natural beauty, the hotel is a destination in itself with outstanding leisure facilities and space to relax and be pampered. The AA Rosette restaurant offers excellent cuisine using the finest local produce to create exciting and imaginative 5-course dinners, with fresh seafood being a speciality. On site are a golf course, large indoor swimming pool, tennis courts, a billiard room, boating, fishing, and the Natural Health Spa. Awarded the South West Tourism Large Hotel of the Year 2003. The local ferry will take guests from the hotel's jetty to waterside pubs, to Frenchman's Creek or to hire a boat. The hotel also takes out guests on its own 32-foot "Sunseeker". A myriad of magnificent country and coastal walks from the wild grandeur of Kynance and the Lizard to the peace and tranquillity of the Helford itself, as well as several of the Great Gardens of Cornwall, are in the close vicinity.

Our inspector loved: *This beautiful, peaceful, tranquil away from it all escape.*

Newquay   Bodmin

Penzance   ● Falmouth

Isles of Scilly

MEUDON HOTEL

MAWNAN SMITH, NR FALMOUTH, CORNWALL TR11 5HT

Set against a delightfully romantic backdrop of densely wooded countryside between the Fal and Helford Rivers, Meudon Hotel is a unique, family-run, superior retreat with sub-tropical gardens leading to its own private sea beach. The French name originates from a nearby farmhouse built by Napoleonic prisoners of war and called after their eponymous home village in the environs of Paris. 9 acres of sub-tropical gardens are coaxed into early bloom by the Gulf Stream and mild Cornish climate; Meudon is safely surrounded by 200 acres of beautiful National Trust land and the sea. All bedrooms are in a modern wing, have en-suite bathrooms and each enjoys spectacular garden views. Many a guest is enticed by the cuisine to return; in the restaurant fresh seafood, caught by local fishermen, is served with wines from a judiciously compiled list. Rich in natural beauty with a myriad of watersports and country pursuits to indulge in, you can play golf free at nearby Falmouth Golf Club and 5 others in Cornwall, sail aboard the hotel's skipperd 34-foot yacht or just laze on the beach.

Our inspector loved: The warm relaxing atmosphere throughout.

Directions: From Truro A39 torwards Falmouth at Hillhead roundabout take 2nd exit. The hotel is 4 miles on the left.

Web: www.johansens.com/meudon
E-mail: wecare@meudon.co.uk
Tel: 0870 381 8730
International: +44 (0)1326 250541
Fax: 01326 250543

Price Guide: (including dinner)
single £120
double/twin £240
suite £330

Fowey Hall Hotel & Restaurant

HANSON DRIVE, FOWEY, CORNWALL PL23 1ET

Situated in five acres of beautiful grounds overlooking the Estuary, Fowey Hall Hotel is a magnificent Victorian mansion renowned for its excellent service and comfortable accommodation. The fine panelling and superb plasterwork ceilings add character to the spacious public rooms. Located in either the main house or the Court, the 24 bedrooms include 12 suites and interconnecting rooms. All are well-proportioned with a full range of modern comforts. The panelled dining rooms provide an intimate atmosphere where guests may savour the local delicacies. Using the best of regional produce, the menu comprises tempting seafood and fish specialities. The hotel offers a full complimentary crèche service. Guests may swim in the indoor swimming pool or play croquet in the gardens. Older children have not been forgotten and "The Garage" in the courtyard is well-equipped with table tennis, table football and many other games. Outdoor pursuits include sea fishing, boat trips and a variety of water sports such as sailing, scuba-diving and windsurfing. There are several coastal walks for those who wish to explore Cornwall and its beautiful landscape.

Directions: On reaching Fowey, go straight over 3 mini roundabouts and follow the road all the way eventually taking a sharp right bend, take the next left turn and Fowey Hall drive is on the right.

Web: www.johansens.com/foweyhall
E-mail: info@foweyhall.com
Tel: 0870 381 8529
International: +44 (0)1726 833866
Fax: 01726 834100

Price Guide: (min 2 nights incl dinner)
double/twin from £160
superior double from £185
suite from £210

Newquay   Bodmin

Penzance   Falmouth

Isles of Scilly

Our inspector loved: *The beautiful proportioned rooms, the grandeur yet wonderful warm welcome for families.*

TRENYTHON MANOR HOTEL & SPA

TYWARDREATH, NEAR FOWEY, CORNWALL PL24 2TS

Built between 1854 and 1872 by an Italian architect, Trenython Manor stands amidst 25 acres of wooded parkland. The manor boasts an interesting and varied history; originally home to Colonel Peard, a former Bishop's palace, a Great Western Railway Convalescent Home and host to the Daphne Du Maurier Festival of Arts. The Italian influence is evident throughout the hotel with its grand staircase and colonnades together with attractive oak panelling, Italian fabrics and fine marble. The 24 bedrooms and suites are beautifully decorated with no expense spared to ensure pure luxury! The panelled dining room, featuring carved wood obtained from Worcester Cathedral, York Minster and many churches, provides a magnificent setting for meals prepared from only the freshest of ingredients. More informal meals can be taken in the lounge bar. The manor's recently opened Health & Beauty Salon offers a great variety of treatments to guests wishing to relax and be pampered by the professional staff. Trenython is only 3 miles away from glorious Cornish beaches and in an ideal position to explore Bodmin Moor, the rugged north coast of Cornwall and the Eden Project. Many water sports as well as shark fishing trips can be arranged.

Our inspector loved: Location, comfort and tranquillity – so peaceful.

Directions: From Exeter join the A30 towards Cornwall then the B3269 signposted Lostwithiel. Take the A390 St Austell/Fowey B3269, follow Fowey signs for approximately 4 miles. The hotel is then signposted.

Newquay   Bodmin

Penzance   Falmouth

Isles of Scilly

Web: www.johansens.com/trenython
E-mail: hotel@trenython.co.uk
Tel: 0870 381 9139
International: +44 (0)1726 814797
Fax: 01726 817030

Price Guide:
single from £105
double £125-£225

HELL BAY

BRYHER, ISLES OF SCILLY, CORNWALL TR23 0PR

Bryher is the smallest community of the Isles of Scilly, 28 miles west of Land's End, and Hell Bay its only hotel. It stands in a spectacular and dramatic setting in extensive lawned grounds on the rugged West Coast overlooking the unbroken Atlantic Ocean. Described as a "spectacularly located getaway-from-it-all destination that is a paradise for adults and children alike" .. and it is. Outdoor heated swimming pool, gym, sauna, spa bath, children's playground, games room and par 3 golf course ensure there is never a dull moment. Daily boat trips available so that you can discover the islands, the world famous tropical Abbey Garden is on the neighbouring island of Tresco. White sanded beaches abound with an array of water sports available. Dining is an integral part of staying at Hell Bay and the food will not disappoint; as you would expect, seafood is a speciality. Closed December to March

Directions: The Isles of Scilly are reached by helicopter or boat from Penzance or fixed-wing aircraft from Southampton, Bristol, Exeter, Newquay and Lands End. The hotel can make all necessary travel arrangements and will co-ordinate all transfers to Bryher on arrival.

Web: www.johansens.com/hellbay
E-mail: contactus@hellbay.co.uk
Tel: 0870 381 8591
International: +44 (0)1720 422947
Fax: 01720 423004

Price Guide: (including dinner)
suites £220–£450

Our inspector loved: From stepping off the boat on arrival - the perfect haven

Newquay   Bodmin

Penzance   Falmouth

Isles of Scilly

TREGLOS HOTEL

CONSTANTINE BAY, NEAR PADSTOW, CORNWALL PL28 8JH

"Betjeman country," with its dramatic headlands and sweeping Atlantic views, is the lovely setting for this recently awarded 4-star hotel. The magnificent refurbishment of the entrance lounge welcomes guests to its warm, friendly and relaxing atmosphere where every modern comfort is available. The hotel has remained in the ownership of the same family for over 30 years and has maintained the highest standards, providing first-class service surrounded by tasteful décor. Each of the bedrooms and suites is a no-smoking area and overlook the stunning Constantine Bay but the best place to relax during the day are the elegant and comfortable lounges and new conservatory that leads onto a large decking area. The Cornish sea air is guaranteed to sharpen any appetite and the hotel's restaurant offers tempting menus for all tastes, including fresh local seafood and fine traditional cuisine, complemented by superb wines. Manager Wally Vellacott is among the best sommeliers in the country; a runner-up in the Premier Crew Awards! For sheer relaxation, there is a heated indoor pool and Jacuzzi, snooker and pool tables and the Treglos spa offering a varierty of beauty and massage treatments. The hotel's landscaped gardens offer a quiet retreat, while further afield there are numerous country and cliff top walks. 5 self-catering apartments are available in the hotel grounds.

Our inspector loved: This well presented friendly country house.

Directions: From St Merryn take the B3276 for ¼mile. Constantine Bay and Treglos are well signposted. Newquay Airport is 8 miles away.

Web: www.johansens.com/treglos
E-mail: stay@tregloshotel.com
Tel: 0870 381 8951
International: +44 (0)1841 520727
Fax: 01841 521163

Price Guide: (including dinner)
single £69–£92.50
double/twin £138–£185

59

TALLAND BAY HOTEL

PORTHALLOW, CORNWALL PL13 2JB

Directions: The hotel is signposted from the A387 Looe–Polperro road.

Web: www.johansens.com/tallandbay
E-mail: info@tallandbayhotel.co.uk
Tel: 0870 381 8937
International: +44 (0)1503 272667
Fax: 01503 272940

Price Guide:
single £90–£145
double/twin £130–£195

Newquay   Bodmin

Penzance   Falmouth

Isles of Scilly

Surrounded by 2 acres of beautiful sub-tropical gardens and with dramatic views over Talland Bay, this lovely old Cornish manor house is a real gem. Each of the 23 bedrooms has its own individual character and is traditionally furnished. Many offer stunning views of the sea and the garden's magnificent Monterey pines. In the bathrooms, fluffy bathrobes and Molton Brown toiletries are just some of the extra touches that are the hotel's hallmark. The award-winning, 2 AA Rosetted restaurant is under the guidance of chef, Shay Cooper, who moved to Talland Bay directly from a restaurant with 4 AA Rosettes and a Michelin star. The menu is essentially modern British and incorporates high quality, fresh local produce complemented by fine wines specially selected by the owners. The hotel organises a number of exclusive weekends combining gourmet food with superb entertainment – such as an evening of jazz or classical music or a wine masterclass with one of the world's leading experts. Talland Bay is also noted for its splendid Christmas and New Year "house party" breaks. There are fabulous coastal walks all year round while, in summer, putting and croquet can be played on the beautiful lawns and the heated outdoor swimming pool, with its south-facing terrace, is a constant temptation. In the winter, there is a chance to read that favourite book by a roaring log fire.

Our inspector loved: *The location, and charming, friendly atmosphere.*

THE ROSEVINE HOTEL

PORTHCURNICK BEACH, PORTSCATHO, ST MAWES, TRURO, CORNWALL TR2 5EW

At the heart of Cornwall's breathtaking Roseland Peninsula, the Rosevine is an elegant and gracious late Georgian hotel that offers visitors complete comfort and peace. The Rosevine stands in its own landscaped grounds overlooking Portscatho Harbour, a traditional Cornish fishing village. The superbly equipped bedrooms are delightfully designed, with some benefiting from direct access into the gardens and from their own private patio. This is the only hotel in Cornwall to hold the awards of 3 AA Red Stars and the RAC Blue Ribbon and Triple Dining Rosettes. The restaurant serves exceptional food, using the freshest seafood and locally grown produce. After dining, guests can relax in any of the 3 tastefully and comfortably presented lounges, bathe in the spacious indoor heated pool, or read in the hotel's well stocked library. Visitors to the region do not forget the walks to the charming villages dotted along the Roseland Peninsula, and the golden sand of the National Trust maintained beach, which immediately faces the hotel. Children and family holdays are especially catered for. Visitors can also take river trips on small ferries, once the only means of travel around the peninsula. The hotel is ideally placed for the Eden Project, Heligan, National Trust gardens and the beautiful Cathedral city of Truro.

Our inspector loved: *The magnificent coastal views, the peace and comfort.*

Directions: From Exeter take A30 towards Truro. Take the St Mawes turn and the hotel is signed to the left.

Web: www.johansens.com/rosevinehotel
E-mail: info@rosevine.co.uk
Tel: 0870 381 8867
International: +44 (0)1872 580206
Fax: 01872 580230

Price Guide:
single £85–£185
double/twin £170–£245
suite £250–£350

THE LUGGER HOTEL

PORTLOE, NR TRURO, CORNWALL TR2 5RD

Directions: Turn off A390 St Austell to Truro onto B3287 Tregony. Then take A3048 signed St Mawes, after 2 miles take left fork following signs for Portloe.

Web: www.johansens.com/lugger
E-mail: office@luggerhotel.com
Tel: 0870 381 8708
International: +44 (0)1872 501322
Fax: 01872 501691

Price Guide: (including dinner)
double/twin £200–£310

Set on the water's edge and sheltered on three sides by green rolling hills tumbling into the sea, this lovely little former inn is as picturesque as any you will come across. Reputedly the haunt of 17th-century smugglers The Lugger Hotel overlooks a tiny working harbour in the scenic village of Portloe on the unspoilt Roseland Peninsula. It is a conservation area of outstanding beauty and an idyllic location in which to escape the stresses of today's hectic world. Seaward views from the hotel are stunning and reaching out from each side are lovely coastal paths leading to secluded coves. Welcoming owners Sheryl and Richard Young have created an atmosphere of total comfort and relaxation whilst retaining an historic ambience. The 21 bedrooms have every amenity; each is en suite, tastefully decorated and furnished, whilst some are situated across an attractive courtyard. A great variety of dishes and innovative dinner menus are offered in the restaurant overlooking the harbour. Local seafood is a specialty with crab and lobster being particular favourites. For beach lovers, the sandy stretches of Pendower and Carne are within easy reach, as are many National Trust properties and gardens, including the Lost Gardens of Heligan and the Eden project.

Our inspector loved: *This little gem so idyllically tucked away.*

THE GARRACK HOTEL & RESTAURANT

BURTHALLAN LANE, ST IVES, CORNWALL TR26 3AA

This family-run hotel, secluded and full of character, ideal for a family holiday, is set in 2 acres of gardens with fabulous sea views over Porthmeor Beach, the St Ives Tate Gallery and the old town of St Ives. The bedrooms in the original house are in keeping with the style of the building. The additional rooms are modern in design. All rooms have private bathrooms. Superior rooms have either four-poster beds or whirlpool baths. A ground-floor room has been fitted for guests with disabilities. Visitors return year after year to enjoy informal yet professional service, good food and hospitality. The restaurant specialises in seafood especially fresh lobsters. The wine list includes over 70 labels from ten regions. The lounges have books, magazines and board games for all and open fires. The small attractive leisure centre contains a small swimming pool with integral spa, sauna, solarium and fitness area. The hotel has its own car park. Porthmeor Beach, just below the hotel, is renowned for surfing. Riding, golf, bowls, sea-fishing and other activities can be enjoyed locally. St Ives, with its harbour, is famous for artists and for the new St Ives Tate Gallery. Gateway to coastal footpaths.

Our inspector loved: This family-run relaxed informal hotel overlooking Porthmeor Beach.

Directions: A30–A3074–B3311–B3306. Go ½ mile, turn left at mini-roundabout, hotel signs are on the left as the road starts down hill.

Web: www.johansens.com/garrack
E-mail: enquiry@garrack.com
Tel: 0870 381 8536
International: +44 (0)1736 796199
Fax: 01736 798955

Price Guide:
single £68–£72
double/twin £117–£175

THE WELL HOUSE

ST KEYNE, LISKEARD, CORNWALL PL14 4RN

Directions: Leave the A38 at Liskeard and take the A390 to town centre. Then take the B3254 south to St Keyne Well and hotel.

Web: www.johansens.com/wellhouse
E-mail: enquiries@wellhouse.co.uk
Tel: 0870 381 8975
International: +44 (0)1579 342001
Fax: 01579 343891

Price Guide:
single from £75
double/twin £115–£170
family suite from £180

The West Country is one corner of England where hospitality and friendliness are at their most spontaneous and nowhere more so than at The Well House, just beyond the River Tamar. New arrivals are entranced by their first view of this lovely Victorian country manor. Its façade wrapped in rambling wisteria and jasmine trailers is just one of a continuous series of delights including top-quality service, modern luxury and impeccable standards of comfort and cooking. The hotel is professionally managed by proprietor Nick Wainford and manager Mark Watts, whose attention to every smallest detail has earned their hotel numerous awards, among them AA 2 Red Stars and the restaurant 3 Rosettes. From the tastefully appointed bedrooms there are fine rural views and each private bathroom offers luxurious bath linen, soaps and gels. Continental breakfast can be served in bed – or a traditional English breakfast may be taken in the dining room. Chef Glenn Gatland selects fresh, seasonal produce to create his balanced and superbly presented cuisine. Tennis and swimming are on site and the Cornish coastline offers matchless scenery for walks. The Eden Project and the Lost Gardens of Heligan are a short drive away.

Our inspector loved: *The beautiful newly presented bar and restaurant complementing the fine cuisine.*

ALVERTON MANOR

TREGOLLS ROAD, TRURO, CORNWALL TR1 1ZQ

Standing in the heart of the cathedral city of Truro and rising majestically over immaculate surrounds, Alverton Manor, awarded 2 AA Rosettes, is the epitome of a mid-19th-century family home. With its handsome sandstone walls, mullioned windows and superb Cornish Delabole slate roof, this elegant and gracious hotel is reminiscent of the splendour of a bygone era and proudly defends its claim to a Grade II* listing. Built for the Tweedy family over 150 years ago, it was acquired by the Bishop of Truro in the 1880s and later occupied by the Sister of the Epiphany before being taken over and restored to its former glory. Owner Michael Sagin and his talented and dedicated staff take pride in not only providing a high standard of service and modern English cuisine but also in enthusiastically maintaining a welcoming and relaxing ambience that attracts guests time and again. A superb entrance hall with a huge, decorative York stone archway leads to rooms that are comfortable in a quiet, elegant way. Lounges are restful, finely furnished, tastefully decorated and warmed by open fires in winter. The dining room is exquisite, and each of the 33 bedrooms has been individually designed to provide a special character, from the intimate to the grand. Golf, sailing and fishing nearby. Special golf and garden breaks available.

Our inspector loved: The peace and tranquillity throughout this former beautiful nunnery.

Directions: Exit the M5, junction 30 and join the A30 through Devon into Cornwall at Fraddon and join the A39 to Truro.

Web: www.johansens.com/alverton
E-mail: reception@alvertonmanor.co.uk
Tel: 0870 381 9152
International: +44 (0)1872 276633
Fax: 01872 222989

Price Guide:
single £80
double £130-£150
suite £170

LOVELADY SHIELD COUNTRY HOUSE HOTEL

NENTHEAD ROAD, ALSTON, CUMBRIA CA9 3LF

Directions: The hotel's driveway is by the junction of the B6294 and the A689, 2¼ miles east of Alston.

Web: www.johansens.com/loveladyshield
E-mail: enquiries@lovelady.co.uk
Tel: 0870 381 8705
International: +44 (0)1434 381203
Fax: 01434 381515

Price Guide:
single £70–£120
double/twin £140–£240

Reached by the A646, one of the worlds 10 best drives and 2½ miles from Alston, England's highest market town, Lovelady Shield, nestles in 3 acres of secluded riverside gardens. Bright log fires in the library and drawing room enhance the hotel's welcoming atmosphere. Owners Peter and Marie Haynes take great care to create a peaceful and tranquil haven where guests can relax and unwind. The 5-course dinners prepared by master chef Barrie Garton, rounded off by homemade puddings and a selection of English farmhouse cheeses, have consistently been awarded AA Rosettes for the past 10 years for food. Many guests first discover Lovelady Shield en route to Scotland. They then return to explore this beautiful and unspoilt part of England and experience the comforts of the hotel. Golf, fishing, shooting, pony-trekking and riding can be arranged locally. The Pennine Way, Hadrian's Wall and the Lake District are within easy reach. Facilities for small conferences and boardroom meetings are available. Open all year, Special Christmas, New Year, and short breaks are offered with special rates for 2 and 3-day stays.

Our inspector loved: This informal relaxing hotel set in a picturesque valley.

HOLBECK GHYLL COUNTRY HOUSE HOTEL

HOLBECK LANE, WINDERMERE, CUMBRIA LA23 1LU

The saying goes that all the best sites for building a house in England were taken long before the days of the motor car. Holbeck Ghyll has one such prime position. It was built in the early days of the 19th century and is superbly located overlooking Lake Windermere and the Langdale Fells. Today this luxury hotel has an outstanding reputation and is managed personally and expertly by its proprietors, David and Patricia Nicholson. As well as being awarded the RAC Gold Ribbon and 3 AA Red Stars they are among an élite who have won an AA Courtesy and Care Award, Holbeck Ghyll was 2002 Country Life Hotel of the Year. The majority of bedrooms are large and have spectacular and breathtaking lake views. All are recently refurbished to a very high standard and include decanters of sherry, fresh flowers, fluffy bathrobes and much more. There are 6 suites in the lodge. The oak-panelled restaurant, awarded a coveted Michelin star and 3 AA Rosettes, is a delightful setting for memorable dining and the meals are classically prepared, with the focus on flavours and presentation, while an extensive wine list reflects quality and variety. The hotel has an all-weather tennis court and a health spa with gym, sauna and treatment facilities.

Our inspector loved: The delicious dinner in the oak-panelled restaurant with extensive views over Lake Windermere.

Directions: From Windermere, pass Brockhole Visitors Centre, then after ½ mile turn right into Holbeck Lane. Hotel is ½ mile on left.

Carlisle

Penrith

Windermere

Kendal

Web: www.johansens.com/holbeckghyll
E-mail: stay@holbeckghyll.com
Tel: 0870 381 8601
International: +44 (0)15394 32375
Fax: 015394 34743

Price Guide: (including 4 course dinner)
single from £125
double/twin £190–£360
suite £220–£360

ROTHAY MANOR

ROTHAY BRIDGE, AMBLESIDE, CUMBRIA LA22 0EH

Directions: ¼ mile from Ambleside on the A593 to Coniston. Closed 3rd-28th January.

Web: www.johansens.com/rothaymanor
E-mail: hotel@rothaymanor.co.uk
Tel: 0870 381 8869
International: +44 (0)15394 33605
Fax: 015394 33607

Price Guide:
single £78–£115
double/twin £135–£165
suite £180–£200

A short walk from the centre of Ambleside and ¼ mile from Lake Windermere, this Regency country house hotel, set within landscaped gardens, has been personally managed by the Nixon family for over 35 years. Renowned for its relaxed, comfortable and friendly atmosphere, each of the 16 bedrooms in the hotel is individually designed, some with balconies overlooking the garden, and there are 3 spacious, private suites, 2 of which are situated within the grounds. Family rooms and suites are also available, and a ground-floor bedroom and one suite designed with particular attention to the comfort of those with disabilities. A varied menu is prepared with flair and imagination using local produce whenever possible, complemented by a personally compiled wine list. Guests are entitled to free use of nearby Low Wood Leisure Club with swimming pool, sauna, steam room, gym, Jacuzzi, squash courts, sunbeds and a health and beauty salon. Local activities such as walking, sightseeing, cycling, sailing, horse riding, golf and fishing (permits available) can be arranged. Alternatively, spend the day cruising on Lake Windermere. Special interest holidays from October-May include: gardening, antiques, walking, photography, bridge, music, painting and Lake District heritage. Small functions and conferences can be catered for and short breaks are available all year.

Our inspector loved: *The delicious home-made cakes and biscuits.*

TUFTON ARMS HOTEL

MARKET SQUARE, APPLEBY-IN-WESTMORLAND, CUMBRIA CA16 6XA

This distinguished Victorian coaching inn, owned and run by the Milsom family, has been refurbished to provide a high standard of comfort. The bedrooms evoke the style of the 19th century, when the Tufton Arms became one of the premier hotels in Victorian England. The kitchen is run under the auspices of David Milsom and Shaun Atkinson, who spoil guests for choice with a gourmet dinner menu as well as a grill menu, the restaurant being renowned for its fish dishes. Complementing the cuisine is an extensive wine list. There are conference and meeting rooms including the air-conditioned Hothfield Suite which can accommodate up to 100 people. Appleby, the historic county town of Westmorland, stands in splendid countryside and is ideal for touring the Lakes, Yorkshire Dales and Pennines. It is also a convenient stop-over en route to Scotland. Members of the Milsom family also run The Royal Hotel in Comrie. Superb fishing for wild brown trout on a 24-mile stretch of the main River Eden, salmon fishing can be arranged on the lower reaches of the river. Shooting parties for grouse, duck and pheasant are a speciality. Appleby has an 18-hole moorland golf course.

Our inspector loved: *Being taken fishing by Nigel Milsom on the River Eden.*

Directions: In centre of Appleby (bypassed by the A66), 38 miles west of Scotch Corner, 13 miles east of Penrith (M6 junction 40), 12 miles from M6 junction 38.

Web: www.johansens.com/tuftonarms
E-mail: info@tuftonarmshotel.co.uk
Tel: 0870 381 8956
International: +44 (0)17683 51593
Fax: 017683 52761

Price Guide:
single £69.50–£107.50
double/twin £95–£140
suite £155

69

NETHERWOOD HOTEL

LINDALE ROAD, GRANGE-OVER-SANDS, CUMBRIA LA11 6ET

Directions: Take the M6, exit 36 then the A590 towards Barrow-in-Burness. Then the B5277 into Grange-Over-Sands. The hotel is on the right before the town.

Web: www.johansens.com/netherwood
E-mail: enquiries@netherwood-hotel.co.uk
Tel: 0870 381 8729
International: +44 (0)15395 32552
Fax: 015395 34121

Price Guide:
single £80–£110
double £120-£180

Carlisle

Penrith

Windermere

Kendal

This dramatic and stately residence was built as a family house in the 19th century, and still retains its family ambience in the careful hands of its long-standing owners, the Fallowfields. Impressive oak panelling is a key feature of the property and provides a marvellous backdrop to the public areas – the lounge, lounge bar and ballroom, where log fires roar in the winter months. All of the bedrooms have en-suite facilities, and many have been furnished to extremely high modern standards; all have picturesque views of the sea, woodland or gardens. The light and airy restaurant is housed in the conservatory area on the first floor of the property, maximising the dramatic views over Morecambe Bay. Here, a daily changing menu of freshly prepared specialities caters for a wide variety of tastes and is complemented by an extensive selection of fine wines. A stunning indoor swimming pool and fitness centre is a delightful haven and a keen favourite with families – the pool even has toys for younger guests - whilst an extensive range of beauty treatments, massage and complementary therapies is available at "Equilibrium", the hotel's health spa. Special breaks available.

Our inspector loved: The oak panelling in the hall and lounge and the stunning views over Morecambe Bay.

      SPA

ARMATHWAITE HALL HOTEL

BASSENTHWAITE LAKE, KESWICK, CUMBRIA CA12 4RE

With an awe-inspiring backdrop of Skiddaw Mountain and the surrounding Lakeland fells, on the shores of Bassenthwaite Lake, the romantic Armathwaite Hall is the perfect location for lovers of boating, walking and climbing. Amidst 400 acres of deer park and woodland, this 4-star country house is a tranquil hideaway for those wishing to relax and escape from modern day living, where comfort is intensified by an emphasis on quality and old-fashioned hospitality, as you would expect of a family-owned and run hotel. The timeless elegance of this stately home is complemented by original features such as wood panelling, magnificent stonework, artworks and antiques. Beautiful bedrooms are decorated in a warm, traditional style and guests can arrange to have champagne, chocolates and flowers on their arrival. The Rosette restaurant offers exceptional cuisine created by Masterchef Kevin Dowling, who uses the finest local seasonal produce. In the Spa there is a gym, indoor swimming pool and a holistic Beauty Salon. Clay pigeon shooting, quad bike safaris, falconry, mountain biking, tennis and croquet are all available, with sailing, fishing and golf nearby. Family friendly with a programme of activities for children and the attraction of Trotters World of Animals on the estate, home to many traditional favourites and endangered species.

Our inspector loved: The spectacular views over Bassenthwaite Lake.

Directions: Take the M6 to Penrith. At J40 take the A66 to Keswick roundabout then the A591 towards Carlisle. Go 8 miles to Castle Inn junction, turn left and Armathwaite Hall is 300 yards ahead.

Carlisle

Penrith

Windermere

Kendal

Web: www.johansens.com/armathwaite
E-mail: reservations@armathwaite-hall.com
Tel: 0870 381 8478
International: +44 (0)17687 76551
Fax: 017687 76220

Price Guide:
single £75–£160
double/twin£150–£310

NEW

THE LODORE FALLS HOTEL

BORROWDALE, KESWICK, CUMBRIA CA12 5UX

Directions: Take the M6 at junction 40. Take the A66 into Keswick then the B5289 to Borrowdale. After 3 minutes, the hotel is on the left-hand side. The nearest railway station is Penrith.

Web: www.johansens.com/lodorefalls
E-mail: info@lodorefallshotel.co.uk
Tel: 0870 381 9314
International: +44 (0)17687 77285
Fax: 017687 77343

Price Guide:
single from £72
double from £132
suite from £234

Carlisle

Penrith

Windermere

Kendal

Imagine a place with stunning lake and mountain views – the Lodore Falls Hotel is such a place. Situated in the picturesque Borrowdale Valley with 20 acres of lake frontage and landscaped gardens and with the famous Lodore waterfalls in the grounds, this hotel offers not only a magnificent setting in the heart of the Lake District, but also the very best in hospitality. The 71 en-suite Fell and Lake View Rooms, including family rooms and luxurious suites, some with balconies, have every modern amenity, such as Playstations and Internet access. Light meals and coffee can be enjoyed in the comfortable lounges, whilst the cocktail bar is the ideal venue for a pre-dinner drink. The superb Lake View restaurant serves the best in English and Continental cuisine accompanied by fine wines after a long day exploring the surroundings. Free midweek golf is available at nearby Keswick Golf Club, and the hotel's leisure facilities include an indoor and outdoor swimming pool, sauna, gymnasium, tennis and squash court and beauty salon. In addition to an outdoor children's playground an activity programme is also available for 2 hours daily during school holidays. The hotel's large function suites can accommodate up to 200 guests – ideal for weddings, conferences and meetings.

Our inspector loved: *Having a stroll up to the Lodore Falls before dinner.*

SHARROW BAY COUNTRY HOUSE HOTEL

HOWTOWN, LAKE ULLSWATER, PENRITH, CUMBRIA CA10 2LZ

Now in its 57th year, Sharrow Bay is known to discerning travellers the world over, who return again and again to this magnificent lakeside hotel. It wasn't always so. The late Francis Coulson arrived in 1948, he was joined by the late Brian Sack in 1952 and the partnership flourished, to make Sharrow Bay what it is today. All the bedrooms are elegantly furnished and guests are guaranteed the utmost comfort. In addition to the main hotel, there are 2 cottages nearby, the Gate House Lodge and Bank House which offer similarly luxurious accommodation. All the reception rooms are delightfully decorated. Sharrow Bay is universally renowned for its wonderful cuisine. The team of chefs, led by Johnnie Martin and Colin Akrigg, ensure that each meal is a special occasion, a mouth-watering adventure! With its private jetty and 12-acres of lakeside gardens Sharrow Bay offers guests boating, swimming and fishing. Fell-walking is a challenge for the upwardly mobile. Sharrow Bay is the oldest British member of Relais et Châteaux.

Our inspector loved: The newly refurbished bedrooms up at Bank House with their stunning views across Lake Ullswater.

Directions: Take the M6, junction 40, A592 to Lake Ullswater, into Pooley Bridge, then take Howtown road for 2 miles.

Web: www.johansens.com/sharrowbaycountryhouse
E-mail: info@sharrowbay.co.uk
Tel: 0870 381 8891
International: +44 (0)17684 86301/86483
Fax: 017684 86349

Price Guide: (including 6-course dinner and full English breakfast)
single £150–£250
double/twin £320–£440
suites from £450

THE INN ON THE LAKE

LAKE ULLSWATER, GLENRIDDING, CUMBRIA CA11 0PE

Directions: Leave the M6 at junction 40, then take the A66 west. At the first roundabout, by Rheged Discovery Centre, head towards Pooley Bridge then follow the shoreline of Lake Ullswater to Glenridding.

Web: www.johansens.com/innonthelake
E-mail: info@innonthelakeullswater.co.uk
Tel: 0870 381 8640
International: +44 (0)17684 82444
Fax: 017684 82303

Price Guide:
single £72
double from £132
four poster £184

Carlisle

Penrith

Windermere

Kendal

With its 15 acres of grounds and lawns sweeping down to the shore of Lake Ullswater, The Inn on the Lake truly boasts one of the most spectacular settings in the Lake District. Recently bought and refurbished by the Graves family, it now offers a wide range of excellent facilities as well as stunning views of the surrounding scenery. Downstairs, comfortable lounges provide a calm environment in which to relax with a drink, whilst dinner can be enjoyed in the Lake View restaurant. Most of the 46 en-suite bedrooms look across to the Lake or the fells and 4 lake view four-poster rooms add an extra touch of luxury. The hotel welcomes wedding ceremonies and receptions and is happy to provide a full private function service as well as conference facilities for up to 120 business delegates. The list of nearby leisure activities for children and adults alike is endless; rock climbing, pony trekking, canoeing, windsurfing, sailing and fishing are all available. Trips around the Lake can be taken aboard the Ullswater steamers and many of the most stunning Lake District walks begin in this area.

Our inspector loved: Strolling across the lawned garden down to Lake Ullswater.

RAMPSBECK COUNTRY HOUSE HOTEL

WATERMILLOCK, LAKE ULLSWATER, NR PENRITH, CUMBRIA CA11 0LP

A beautifully situated hotel, Rampsbeck Country House stands in 18 acres of landscaped gardens and meadows leading to the shores of Lake Ullswater. Built in 1714, it first became a hotel in 1947, before the present owners acquired it in 1983. Thomas and Marion Gibb, with the help of Marion's mother, Marguerite MacDowall, completely refurbished Rampsbeck with the aim of maintaining its character and adding only to its comfort. Most of the well-appointed bedrooms have lake and garden views. Three have a private balcony and the suite overlooks the lake. In the elegant drawing room, a log fire burns and French windows lead to the garden. Guests and non-residents are welcome to dine in the intimate candle-lit restaurant. Imaginative menus offer a choice of delicious dishes, carefully prepared by Master Chef Andrew McGeorge and his team. A good bar lunch menu offers light snacks as well as hot food. Guests can stroll through the gardens, play croquet or fish from the lake shore, around which there are designated walks. Lake steamer trips, riding, golf, sailing, wind-surfing and fell-walking are available nearby. Closed January to mid-February. Dogs by arrangement only.

Our inspector loved: The wonderful views of Lake Ullswater and the beautiful landscaped gardens.

Directions: Leave M6 at junction 40, take A592 to Ullswater. At T-junction at lake turn right; hotel is 1½ miles on left.

Web: www.johansens.com/rampsbeckcountryhouse
E-mail: enquiries@rampsbeck.fsnet.co.uk
Tel: 0870 381 8848
International: +44 (0)17684 86442
Fax: 017684 86688

Carlisle
Penrith
Windermere
Kendal

Price Guide:
single £65–£140
double/twin £120–£240
suite £240

GILPIN LODGE

CROOK ROAD, WINDERMERE, CUMBRIA LA23 3NE

Directions: M6 exit 36. A591 Kendal bypass then B5284 to Crook.

Web: www.johansens.com/gilpinlodge
E-mail: hotel@gilpinlodge.com
Tel: 0870 381 8546
International: +44 (0)15394 88818
Fax: 015394 88058

Price Guide: (including 5 course dinner)
single £160
double/twin £220–£290

This elegant, luxurious family-run country house hotel is set in 20 acres of woodland, moors and country gardens, 2 miles from Lake Windermere and 12 miles from the M6. The original building, tastefully extended and modernised, dates from 1901 and the long-standing staff, as much a feature of the house as the Cunliffe family, ensure a relaxed ambience alongside friendly, personal care and attention to detail. All the senses are delicately pampered; the profusion of fresh flower arrangements, picture-lined walls, antique furniture and log fires in winter, are all part of Gilpin hospitality. The sumptuous bedrooms have en-suite bathrooms and every comfort; some have patio doors, split levels and whirlpool baths. The exquisite food, created by a team of 8 chefs, has received 3 AA Rosettes and 4 RAC Dining Awards; the wine list contains 175 labels from 13 different countries. The beautiful gardens are the perfect place in which to muse whilst savouring the beautiful Lakeland scenery. This is Wordsworth and Beatrix Potter country and there are several stately homes, gardens and castles to visit nearby. Guests are entitled to free use of a nearby leisure club and Windermere golf course is ½ mile away. English Tourist Board Gold award, AA 3 Red Stars, RAC Gold Ribbon award, AA Ten Top Country Retreat, AA Ten Top Small Hotel. A Pride of Britain Hotel. (See website for guided tour.)

Our inspector loved: The superb service and new garden room.

STORRS HALL

LAKE WINDERMERE, CUMBRIA LA23 3LG

From this magnificent listed Georgian manor house not another building can be seen, just a spectacular, seemingly endless view over beautiful Lake Windermere. Built in the 18th century for a Lancashire shipping magnate, Storrs Hall stands majestically in an unrivalled peninsular position surrounded by 17 acres of landscaped, wooded grounds which slope down to half a mile of lakeside frontage. Apart from Wordsworth, who first recited "Daffodils" in the Drawing Room at Storrs, the hotel was frequented by all the great Lakeland poets and Beatrix Potter. Furnished with antiques and objets d'art including a private collection of ship models, it reflects the maritime fortunes which built it. Now part of the English Lakes Hotels group the Hall has 29 beautifully furnished bedrooms, each en suite, spacious and with every comfort. Most of the rooms have views over the lake, and equally splendid views are enjoyed from an exquisite lounge, study and cosy bar. The Terrace Restaurant is renowned for the superb cuisine prepared by head chef Craig Sherrington. Guests receive complimentary use of leisure club facilities at sister hotel, Low Wood, just 3 miles away. Special breaks available.

Our inspector loved: *Strolling in the gardens on the shore of Lake Windermere.*

Directions: Situated on the A592, 2 miles south of Bowness and 5 miles north of Newby Bridge.

Web: www.johansens.com/storrshall
E-mail: storrshall@elhmail.co.uk
Tel: 0870 381 8919
International: +44 (0)15394 47111
Fax: 015394 47555

Carlisle

Penrith

Windermere

Kendal

Price Guide:
single from £125
double/twin £150–£310
suite £310

LINTHWAITE HOUSE HOTEL

CROOK ROAD, BOWNESS-ON-WINDERMERE, CUMBRIA LA23 3JA

Situated in 14 acres of gardens and woods in the heart of the Lake District, Linthwaite House overlooks Lake Windermere and Belle Isle, with Claife Heights and Coniston Old Man beyond. Here, guests will find themselves amid spectacular scenery, yet only a short drive from the motorway network. The hotel combines stylish originality with the best of traditional English hospitality. Superbly decorated en-suite bedrooms, most of which have lake or garden views. The comfortable lounge is the perfect place to unwind and there is a fire on winter evenings. In the restaurant excellent cuisine features the best of fresh, local produce, accompanied by a fine selection of wines. Within the hotel grounds, there is a 9-hole putting green and a par-3 practice hole. Fly fishermen can fish for brown trout in the hotel tarn. Guests have complimentary use of a private swimming pool and leisure club nearby, while fell walks begin at the hotel's front door. The area around Linthwaite abounds with places of interest: this is Beatrix Potter and Wordsworth country, and there is much to interest the visitor.

Directions: From the M6, junction 36 follow Kendal by-pass for 8 miles. Take the B5284, Crook Road, for 6 miles. 1 mile beyond Windermere Golf Club, Linthwaite House is signposted on the left.

Web: www.johansens.com/linthwaitehouse
E-mail: admin@linthwaite.com
Tel: 0870 381 8694
International: +44 (0)15394 88600
Fax: 015394 88601

Price Guide:
single £125–£150
double/twin £125–£270
suite £250–£295

Our inspector loved: *Walking through the landscaped gardens up to the tarn with its spectacular views of Lake Windermere.*

LAKESIDE HOTEL ON LAKE WINDERMERE

LAKESIDE, NEWBY BRIDGE, CUMBRIA LA12 8AT

Lakeside Hotel offers you a unique location on the water's edge of Lake Windermere. It is a classic, traditional Lakeland hotel offering 4-star facilities and service. All the bedrooms are en suite and enjoy individually designed fabrics and colours, many of the rooms offer breathtaking views of the lake. Guests may dine in either the award-winning Lakeview Restaurant or Ruskin's Brasserie, where extensive menus offer a wide selection of dishes including Cumbrian specialities. The Lakeside Conservatory serves drinks and light meals throughout the day – once there you are sure to fall under the spell of this peaceful location. Berthed next to the hotel there are cruisers which will enable you to explore the lake from the water. To enhance your stay, there is a leisure club including a 17m indoor pool, gymnasium, sauna, steam room and health and beauty suites. The hotel offers a fully equipped conference centre and many syndicate suites allowing plenty of scope and flexibility. Most of all you are assured of a stay in an unrivalled setting of genuine character. The original panelling and beams of the old coaching inn create an excellent ambience, whilst you are certain to enjoy the quality and friendly service. Special breaks available.

Our inspector loved: Enjoying a delicious afternoon tea in the Lakeside conservatory watching the boats sail by.

Directions: From the M6, junction 36 join the A590 to Newby Bridge then turn right over bridge towards Hawkshead. The hotel is 1 mile on the right.

Web: www.johansens.com/lakeside
E-mail: sales@lakesidehotel.co.uk
Tel: 0870 381 8672
International: +44 (0)1539 530001
Fax: 015395 31699

Price Guide:
single from £130
double/twin £170–£250
suite from £270

CALLOW HALL

MAPPLETON ROAD, ASHBOURNE, DERBYSHIRE DE6 2AA

The approach to Callow Hall is up a tree-lined drive through the 44-acre grounds. On arrival visitors can take in the splendid views from the hotel's elevated position, overlooking the valleys of Bentley Brook and the River Dove. The majestic building and Victorian gardens have been restored by resident proprietors, David, Dorothy, son Anthony and daughter, Emma Spencer, who represent the fifth and sixth generations of hoteliers in the Spencer family. The famous local Ashbourne mineral water and homemade biscuits greet guests in the spacious period bedrooms. Fresh local produce is selected daily for use in the kitchen, where the term "homemade" comes into its own. Well hung and personally selected meat, home-cured bacon, sausages, fresh bread, traditional English puddings and melt-in-the-mouth pastries are among the items prepared on the premises, which can be enjoyed by non-residents. Visiting anglers can enjoy a rare opportunity to fish for trout and grayling along a mile-long private stretch of the Bentley Brook, which is mentioned in Izaak Walton's "The Compleat Angler". Callow Hall is ideally located for some of England's finest stately homes. Closed at Christmas. East Midlands Airport is 35 minutes away.

Directions: Take the A515 through Ashbourne towards Buxton. At the Bowling Green Inn on the brow of a steep hill, turn left, then take the first right, signposted Mappleton and the hotel is over the bridge on the right.

Web: www.johansens.com/callowhall
E-mail: stay@callowhall.co.uk
Tel: 0870 381 8400
International: +44 (0)1335 300900
Fax: 01335 300512

Price Guide:
single £85–£110
double/twin £130–£165
suite £190

Sheffield
Glossop
Chesterfield
Bakewell
Nottingham
Derby

Our inspector loved: *The two generations of Spencer family who bring such warmth to Callow Hall, a true delight.*

THE IZAAK WALTON HOTEL

DOVEDALE, NEAR ASHBOURNE, DERBYSHIRE DE6 2AY

This converted 17th-century farmhouse hotel, named after the renowned author of "The Compleat Angler", enjoys glorious views of the surrounding Derbyshire Peaks. The River Dove runs in the valley below. The Izaak Walton is ideal for guests wishing to indulge in a warm welcome and a relaxing ambience. The 36 en-suite bedrooms are diverse in their designs; some have 4-poster beds whilst others are located in the old farmhouse building and still retain their old oak beams and décor. The Haddon Restaurant, with an AA Rosette, has a diverse menu of creative yet traditional cuisine. Informal meals and light snacks can be enjoyed in the Dovedale Bar. The hotel is ideal for family parties, out of the way meetings and conferences. Leisure pursuits include rambling, fishing (the hotel has 4 rods on the River Dove and private tuition is available), mountain biking and hand-gliding. Places of interest nearby include the Peak District, Alton Towers, the Staffordshire Potteries and fine country properties such as Chatsworth House and Haddon Hall. The hotel as inclusive packages available to include Chatsworth House, Alton Towers and Uttoxeter racecourse.

Our inspector loved: *Going to the hotel and really switching off. An Amazing location.*

Directions: Dovedale is 2 miles north-west of Ashbourne between A515 and A52.

Web: www.johansens.com/izaakwalton
E-mail: reception@izaakwaltonhotel.com
Tel: 0870 381 8642
International: +44 (0)1335 350555
Fax: 01335 350539

Price Guide:
single £89-£110
double/twin £115–£176

RIVERSIDE HOUSE

ASHFORD-IN-THE-WATER, NR BAKEWELL, DERBYSHIRE DE45 1QF

This graceful Georgian mansion nestles peacefully on the banks of the river Wye in one of the Peak District's most picturesque villages. It is an intimate gem of a country hotel, a tranquil rural retreat in the finest traditions of classic hospitality and friendliness. Small and ivy-clad, Riverside House sits majestically in the heart of secluded grounds that feature exquisite landscaped gardens and lawns. Elegance, style, intimacy and informality abound within its interior. Individually designed en suite bedrooms have their own distinctive character and are comfortably and delightfully furnished with rich fabrics and antique pieces. An atmosphere of complete relaxation is the hallmark of the welcoming public rooms whose large windows offer superb views. Guests can enjoy a distinctive fusion of modern English, International and local cuisine in the excellent and charming 2 AA Rosette awarded restaurant where service is of the highest quality. As well as being conveniently situated to explore the glories of the Peak District, Chatsworth House and Haddon Hall, the hotel is also an ideal base for guests wishing to visit the Derbyshire Dales, Lathkill and Dovedale.

Directions: Exit M1 at junction 29. Take A617 to Chesterfield, then A619 to Bakewell, then take A6 to Ashford-in-the-Water. Riverside House is at the end of the villge main street next to the Sheepwash Bridge.

Web: www.johansens.com/riversidehouse
E-mail: riversidehouse@enta.net
Tel: 0870 381 8860
International: +44 (0)1629 814275
Fax: 01629 812873

Price Guide:
single £90–£120
double/twin £135–£160

Our inspector loved: The attention to detail everywhere.

HASSOP HALL

HASSOP, NEAR BAKEWELL, DERBYSHIRE DE45 1NS

The recorded history of Hassop Hall reaches back 900 years to the Domesday Book, to a time when the political scene in England was still dominated by the power struggle between the barons and the King, when the only sure access to that power was through possession of land. By 1643, when the Civil War was raging, the Hall was under the ownership of Rowland Eyre, who turned it into a Royalist garrison. It was the scene of several skirmishes before it was recaptured after the Parliamentary victory. Since purchasing Hassop Hall in 1975, Thomas Chapman has determinedly pursued the preservation of its outstanding heritage. Guests can enjoy the beautifully maintained gardens as well as the splendid countryside of the surrounding area. The bedrooms, some of which are particularly spacious, are well furnished and comfortable. A four-poster bedroom is available for romantic occasions. A comprehensive dinner menu offers a wide and varied selection of dishes, with catering for most tastes. As well as the glories of the Peak District, places to visit include Chatsworth House, Haddon Hall and Buxton Opera House. Christmas opening – details on application. Inclusive rates available on request.

Our inspector loved: Its very special attention to detail.

Directions: From the M1, exit 29 (Chesterfield), take the A619 to Baslow, then the A623 to Calver. Turn left at the lights to B6001. Hassop Hall is 2 miles on the right.

Web: www.johansens.com/hassophall
E-mail: info@hassophallhotel.co.uk
Tel: 0870 381 8586
International: +44 (0)1629 640488
Fax: 01629 640577

Price Guide: (excluding breakfast)
double/twin £79–£149

EAST LODGE COUNTRY HOUSE HOTEL

ROWSLEY, NR MATLOCK, DERBYSHIRE DE4 2EF

Directions: Set back from the A6 in Rowsley village, 3 miles from Bakewell. The hotel entrance is adjacent to the B6012 junction to Sheffield/Chatsworth.

Web: www.johansens.com/eastlodgecountryhouse
E-mail: info@eastlodge.com
Tel: 0870 381 8496
International: +44 (0)1629 734474
Fax: 01629 733949

Price Guide:
single £80
double/twin from £100

This graceful 17th-century lodge on the edge of the Peak District was originally built as the East Lodge to Haddon Hall, the Derbyshire seat of the Duke of Rutland. Converted to a hotel in the 1980s, East Lodge is now owned and run by Joan and David Hardman and their attentive staff. The lodge has won many accolades including a Gold award and AA 3 star 79%. The attractive conservatory, charming restaurant and spacious hall offers high levels of comfort combined with a warm and relaxed atmosphere. The 14 en-suite bedrooms are tastefully furnished, each having its own distinctive character. Imaginative lunches and dinners are served daily in the excellent AA Rosetted restaurant with lighter meals available in the conservatory. A wide selection of fine wines is on offer. Set in 10 acres of attractive gardens and surrounded by rolling Derbyshire countryside, East Lodge provides a tranquil setting for relaxing breaks, conferences and corporate activity/team building events. The nearby Peak District National Park, boasts some of the country's most spectacular walks. The famous stately homes, Chatsworth House and Haddon Hall, are within 2 miles. Bakewell, Buxton, Matlock and Crich are a short drive away.

Our inspector loved: *This quintessential English retreat, delightful.*

CAVENDISH HOTEL

BASLOW, DERBYSHIRE DE45 1SP

This enchanting hotel offers travellers an opportunity to stay on the famous Chatsworth Estate, close to one of England's greatest stately houses, the home of the Duke and Duchess of Devonshire. The hotel has a long history of its own – once known as the Peacock Inn on the turnpike road to Buxton Spa. When it became The Cavendish in 1975, the Duchess personally supervised the transformation, providing some of the furnishings from Chatsworth, and her design talents are evident throughout. Guests receive a warm welcome before they are led to the luxurious bedrooms, all of which overlook the Estate. Harmonious colours, gorgeous fabrics and immense comfort prevail. Every imaginable extra is provided, from library books to bathrobes. Breakfast is served until lunchtime – no rising at cockcrow – and informal meals are served from morning until bed-time in The Garden Room. Sit at the kitchen table and watch super food being prepared as you dine. At dusk you can sample cocktails and fine wines in the bar before dining in the handsome restaurant with its imaginative menu and extensive list of carefully selected wines. Climbing The Peak, exploring The Dales, fishing, golf and Sheffield's Crucible Theatre are among the many leisure pursuits nearby.

Our inspector loved: This timeless property and dining in the gallery restaurant enjoying excellent company.

Directions: Take the M1, junction 29, A617 to Chesterfield then A619 west to Baslow.

Web: www.johansens.com/cavendish
E-mail: info@cavendish–hotel.net
Tel: 0870 381 8412
International: +44 (0)1246 582311
Fax: 01246 582312

Price Guide: (excluding breakfast)
single from £100
double/twin from £130

85

FISCHER'S

BASLOW HALL, CALVER ROAD, BASLOW, DERBYSHIRE DE45 1RR

Directions: Baslow is within 12 miles of the M1 motorway, Chesterfield and Sheffield. Fischer's is on the A623 in Baslow.

Web: www.johansens.com/fischers
E-mail: m.s@fischers–baslowhall.co.uk
Tel: 0870 381 8523
International: +44 (0)1246 583259
Fax: 01246 583818

Price Guide:
single £100-£120
double/twin £120–£180
suite £150

Situated on the edge of the magnificent Chatsworth Estate, Baslow Hall enjoys an enviable location surrounded by some of the country's finest stately homes and within easy reach of the Peak District's many cultural and historical attractions. Standing at the end of a winding chestnut tree-lined driveway, this fine Derbyshire manor house was tastefully converted by Max and Susan Fischer into an award-winning country house hotel in 1989. Since opening, Fischer's has consistently maintained its position as one of the finest establishments in the Derbyshire/South Yorkshire regions earning the prestigious Johansens Most Excellent UK Restaurant award in 2001. Whether staying in the area for private or business reasons, it is a welcome change to find a place that feels less like a hotel and more like a home, combining comfort and character with an eating experience which is a delight to the palate. Max presides in the kitchen, which offers exciting Michelin-starred gourmet menus and is also a wonderful setting in which to enjoy superb value for money lunches and the less formal Max's table d'hôte menu. Baslow Hall has facilities to cater for small conferences or private functions. With prior notification in advance arrangements can be made to park a helicopter nearby.

Our inspector loved: *The experience of Fischer's. So welcoming too. It is truly special.*

THE LEE WOOD HOTEL & RESTAURANT

THE PARK, BUXTON, DERBYSHIRE SK17 6TQ

Situated in the heart of the Peak District, in the delightful market town of Buxton, The Lee Wood is an ideal base for both relaxing weekends, exploring the countryside or as a backdrop for weddings and conferences. The building was built in 1832, and has been sympathetically decorated in-keeping with its heritage, and stylish new conference facilities have been added this year. With 40 bedrooms, the hotel is an ideal size for annivarsary and reunion celebrations, and the personal and attentive service ensures an extremely comfortable stay. The large conservatory restaurant has sweeping views over the gardens and complements the hotel's fine cuisine. The restaurant, awarded 2 AA Red Rosettes, place an emphasis on a balance between traditional English favourites and lighter international recipes. The more informal Canyons Brasserie is delightful and frequently serves pre-dinner suppers to guests, particularly during the Buxton Opera Festival – the theatre is within walking distance of the hotel. There is a staggering collection of places to visit locally, including the majestic Chatsworth House, as well as Haddon Hall, Peveril Castle, Pooles Cavern and Country Park. The Lee Wood is also extremely popular with those wishing to explore the beautiful and unspoilt local scenery.

Our inspector loved: *The delightful lunch, following a walk through the garden to Buxton.*

Directions: From north: M1, jct 29 Chesterfield–Baslow–Buxton. M6, jct 19 then A537 Knutsford– Macclesfield–Buxton. M56/M60 and M62 Stockport then A6 to Buxton. From south: M1, jct 23A/24 take A50 for approx 19 miles then Ashbourne A515 to Buxton. M6, jct14 Stone A53 to Leek/Buxton.

Web: www.johansens.com/leewood
E-mail: leewoodhotel@btinternet.com
Tel: 0870 381 8687
International: +44 (0)1298 23002
Fax: 01298 23228

Price Guide: (room only)
single £85
double/twin £100

RINGWOOD HALL HOTEL

RINGWOOD ROAD, BRIMINGTON, CHESTERFIELD, DERBYSHIRE S43 1DQ

Since its purchase by Lyric Hotels in November 1999, a sensitive and tasteful refurbishment has created one of the finest country house hotels in north east Derbyshire. The charming Grade II exterior invites guests into the impressive reception area with intricate plaster frieze work, a galleried landing and glazed dome ceiling. 29 acres of gardens and parkland provide a magnificent backdrop and feature original Victorian gardens that provide vegetables and herbs for the kitchen. Finest local produce is used for the extensive menus in the Expressions Restaurant, and numerous conference packages are on offer. This is a wonderful setting for wedding receptions and civil ceremonies, and the unique Helidining experience, which includes helicopter pick up from Sheffield City Airport and romantic meal for 2, is a perfect way to celebrate a special occasion. Situated on the edge of the Peak District, there is plenty to explore in the surrounding area. Families can enjoy nearby theme parks such as Alton Towers, whilst those interested in history may visit Chesterfield Museum, Hardwick Hall and Bolsover Castle. Local events, such as the Chatsworth Country Fair, take place throughout the year. An exclusive health and fitness club opened in 2002.

Directions: From junction 30, M1 take the A619 towards Chesterfield, passing through Mastin Moor and Staveley. Continue on the A619 and rising out of the valley the hotel is set back on the left.

Web: www.johansens.com/ringwood
E-mail: ringwood-hall-reception@lyrichotels.co.uk
Tel: 0870 381 8857
International: +44 (0)1246 280077
Fax: 01246 472241

Price Guide:
single from £75
double/twin from £95
suite from £100

Sheffield
Glossop
Chesterfield
Bakewell
Nottingham
Derby

Our inspector loved: The grounds; a real surprise so close to Chesterfield.

RIBER HALL

MATLOCK, DERBYSHIRE DE4 5JU

There could be few more picturesque settings than this stately Elizabethan manor house standing in its own walled garden in the foothills of the Pennine range. Views over the Peak National Park are outstanding and the atmosphere is one of total tranquillity. Privately owned and managed by the same family for over 30 years the latest round of awards stands testament to their skill and high standards of service. The 14 spacious bedrooms are each furnished with period antiques and elegant beds, the majority of which are four-poster. The log fires and oak beams of the lounge convey an instant sense of intimacy and timelessness. The restaurant is renowned for its attentive service, game (when in season) and inspired French classical and modern English cuisine. The excellent wine list has also been rated AA Wine Award Finalist in the Top 25 in the UK for the third consecutive year. This is the perfect setting for both weddings and conferences and there is much to see in the surrounding area for conference delegate or wedding guest with time to spare. Chatsworth House, Haddon Hall and many world heritage sites are within easy reach. The beautiful Peak District scenery is breathtaking. East Midlands, Sheffield and Birmingham Airports are all nearby.

Our inspector loved: *This totally unspoilt wonderful historic manor house. Derbyshire history at its best, with food and wines to match.*

Directions: 20 minutes from junction 28 of the M1, off the A615 at Tansley; 1 mile further to Riber.

Web: www.johansens.com/riberhall
E-mail: info@riber-hall.co.uk
Tel: 0870 381 8854
International: +44 (0)1629 582795
Fax: 01629 580475

Price Guide:
single £95–£105
double/twin £123–£165

NORTHCOTE MANOR COUNTRY HOUSE HOTEL

BURRINGTON, UMBERLEIGH, DEVON EX37 9LZ

Directions: From Exeter stay on the A377 towards Barnstaple (do not enter Burrington village). The driveway to Northcote Manor is opposite the Portsmouth Arms pub on the A377.

Web: www.johansens.com/northcotemanor
E-mail: rest@northcotemanor.co.uk
Tel: 0870 381 8767
International: +44 (0)1769 560501
Fax: 01769 560770

Price Guide:
single from £99
double/twin from £140
suite from £240

This 18th-century manor with grounds high above the Taw River Valley offers an ambience of timeless tranquillity. Situated in 20 acres of peaceful Devonshire countryside, Northcote Manor provides complete relaxation and refreshment. Extensive refurbishment has created 11 luxury bedrooms and suites, resulting in a total redesign of the décor in the spacious sitting rooms, hall and restaurant. One of the south west's leading country houses, the Manor has received a series of accolades. In 2002: Condé Nast Johansens Country Hotel of the Year; and AA 3 Red Stars. In 2004: the RAC Gold Ribbon Award; The Which? Hotel Guide; Tourist Board Silver Award; Michelin 2 Red Turrets Award; RAC Cooking Award level 3; and AA 2 Rosettes. Exmoor and Dartmoor are within easy reach and guests may visit RHS Rosemoor and the many National Trust properties nearby. A challenging 18-hole golf course is next door whilst outstanding fishing from the Taw River, at the bottom of the drive, can be arranged with the Gillie. The area also hosts some of the best shoots in the country. A tennis court and croquet lawn are on site. Helicopters can land at Eaglescott Airfield, approximately 2 miles away. Special breaks are available.

Our inspector loved: *The peaceful, calm location and atmosphere of warmth and welcome.*

MILL END

DARTMOOR NATIONAL PARK, CHAGFORD, DEVON TQ13 8JN

Gleaming white under slate grey roof tiles and with windows and doors opening onto a beautiful English country garden, Mill End is an idyllic hideaway in Dartmoor's National Park. The lawned garden with its wide, deeply shrubbed and colourful borders runs down to the languid waters of the River Teign, a water wheel slowly turns in the courtyard to the enjoyment of guests and diners. Built in the mid 1700s the hotel was a former flour mill, and inside there are numerous little corner nooks, paintings and old photographs that imbue a feeling of seclusion, enhanced by the smell of wood smoke and polished wood. The delightful en-suite bedrooms have undergone major refurbishment incorporating excellent décor, lovely fabrics and attractive local hand-crafted furniture. Plus, of course, every facility one would expect. The elegance of the dining room is matched by the delicious award-winning cuisine of Master Chef of Great Britain– Wayne Pearson. His menus are full and varied; one shouldn't miss, for example, lobster ravioli with seared scallops and lemon grass broth followed by grilled turbot with aubergine caviar and a dark chocolate tort with burnt orange sauce and rosewater ice cream. An 18-hole golf course is nearby and pony trekking and shooting can be arranged.

Our inspector loved: The tastefully relaxing newly refurbished lounge and the stunning location.

Directions: From the M5 exit at junction 31 towards Okehampton. Take the A382 at Merrymount roundabout towards Moretonhampstead. Mill End is on the right.

Web: www.johansens.com/millend
E-mail: info@millendhotel.com
Tel: 0870 381 8734
International: +44 (0)1647 432282
Fax: 01647 433106

Price Guide:
single £70–£110
double/twin £110–£160
suite £170–£210

89

BOVEY CASTLE

NORTH BOVEY, DARTMOOR NATIONAL PARK, DEVON TQ13 8RE

Ideally situated within the 368 square miles of Dartmoor National Park and surrounded by moorland, woodlands and rivers, Bovey Castle offers guests the utmost in style, elegance and tranquillity. Built in 1906 for Viscount Hambledon, son of the business baron WH Smith, and transformed into a grand country estate by the 1920s it is now owned by Peter de Savary. Focus on returning this great house to its former glory was then undertaken and remaining true to the standards that the art deco period aspired to has created relaxed luxury and glamour. Sumptuous accommodation in 65 individually designed rooms range from Valley View rooms, with their outlook across Dartmoor, to the triple aspect Chairman's Suites, with views over the gardens, moors and the 1st and 18th holes of the estate's challenging golf course, designed in 1926 to rival Gleneagles and Turnberry. The castle interior is very special with grand oak panelled drawing rooms, ornate broad stairways, a magnificently restored Cathedral Room, with vaulted ceiling, and a superbly crafted Great Hall, which opens onto stone balustraded terraces. The main dining room, where exceptional cuisine is served, is equally impressive in the style of an original art deco Palm Court. Fully equipped spa, indoor swimming pool and many leisure pursuits from riding and shooting to falconry and exclusive fishing.

Directions: Take the M5 and exit at junction 30, join the A38 to Newton Abbot and pick up signs for Moretonhampstead. Follow signs for Princetown - Castle Drive and the hotel is 3 miles on the left-hand side.

Web: www.johansens.com/boveycastle
E-mail: enquiries@boveycastle.com
Tel: 0870 381 9286
International: +44 (0)1647 445016
Fax: 01647 445020

Price Guide: (room only, excluding VAT)
single from £135
double £180-£290
suite £350-£1,500

Our inspector loved: This majestic castle and magnificent location.

COMBE HOUSE HOTEL & RESTAURANT

GITTISHAM, HONITON, NEAR EXETER, DEVON EX14 3AD

Combe House is a wildly romantic Grade I Elizabethan manor hidden in 3,500 acres of Devon's finest estates where magnificent Arabian horses and pheasants roam freely. Total peace and tranquillity together with generous hospitality can be enjoyed here in this warm and welcoming atmosphere created by the comfy sofas, flamboyant flowers and roaring log-fires. 15 intimate bedrooms and suites, many with panoramic views, are decorated with style and individuality. The candle-lit restaurant serves innovative, contemporary British cuisine prepared by Master Chef of Great Britain, Philip Leach, perfectly complemented by a well-chosen wine list, including a specialist Chablis collection. The recently restored Georgian Kitchen is the ideal setting for a highly individual private lunch or dinner, dining by lamps and candlelight. Down Combe's mile-long drive is Gittisham, once described by H.R.H. Prince Charles as "the ideal English village," with its thatched cottages, Norman church and village green. The World Heritage Jurassic coast, from Lyme Regis to Sidmouth, Honiton antique shops, numerous historic houses and gardens, the cathedral of Exeter and the wide open spaces of Dartmoor can all be explored.

Our inspector loved: The warmth and welcome of this beautifully located Elizabethan manor.

Directions: From the M5 take exit 28 to Honiton and Sidmouth or exit 29 to Honiton. Follow signs to Fenny Bridges and Gittisham.

Web: www.johansens.com/combehousegittisham
E-mail: stay@thishotel.com
Tel: 0870 381 8440
International: +44 (0)1404 540400
Fax: 01404 46004

Price Guide:
single £125–£165
double/twin £140–£198
suite £275–£295

FAIRWATER HEAD COUNTRY HOUSE HOTEL

HAWKCHURCH, AXMINSTER, DEVON EX13 5TX

Directions: Exit M5 at junction 25 onto A358. Then left onto A35 towards Bridport; left onto B3165 to Lyme Regis, Crewkerne road. Follow signs for Hawkchurch and hotel on left.

Web: www.johansens.com/fairwaterhead
E-mail: info@fairwaterheadhotel.co.uk
Tel: 0870 381 8511
International: +44 (0)1297 678349
Fax: 01297 678459

Price Guide: (including dinner)
single £110–£120
double/twin £180–£200

In an idyllic setting on the Devon, Dorset and Somerset borders, Fairwater Head – also the name of the stream's source – not only has its own magnificent landscaped gardens but is situated at the highest point of the land and boasts the most spectacular views over the Axe valley. Built from local stone and with a rich local history, this is a perfect retreat for guests seeking peace and tranquillity from which to explore the Devon and Dorset environs. The bedrooms are charming, both in the main house and the "garden rooms", and most overlook the beautiful grounds and open countryside. The spacious dining room is light and airy, and again has wonderful views, and it is here that a superb menu of traditional and contemporary cuisine is served – awarded 1 AA Rosette. This is an area rich in countryside walks and historic houses and gardens, and there is also Forde Abbey, picturesque Lyme Regis, and a donkey sanctuary nearby. Escorted tours and special breaks are available.

Our inspector loved: *The delightful peaceful location and the first class menu's offered by the newly appointed chef.*

ILSINGTON COUNTRY HOUSE HOTEL

ILSINGTON VILLAGE, NEAR NEWTON ABBOT, DEVON TQ13 9RR

The Ilsington Country House Hotel stands in 10 acres of beautiful private grounds within the Dartmoor National Park. Run by friendly proprietors, Tim and Maura Hassell, the delightful furnishings and ambience offer a most comfortable environment in which to relax. Stylish bedrooms all boast outstanding views across the rolling pastoral countryside and every comfort and convenience to make guests feel at home. The distinctive candle-lit dining room is perfect for savouring the superb cuisine, awarded an AA Rosette, created by talented chefs from fresh local produce. The library is ideal for an intimate dining party or celebration whilst the conservatory or lounge is the place for morning coffee or a Devon cream tea. There is a fully-equipped, purpose-built gymnasium, heated indoor pool, sauna, steam room and spa. Some of England's most idyllic and unspoilt scenery surrounds Ilsington, with the picturesque villages of Lustleigh and Widecombe-in-the-Moor close by. Guests have easy access to the moors from the hotel. Riding, fishing and many other country pursuits can be arranged. Special breaks are available.

Our inspector loved: The outstanding and beautiful location, and warm atmosphere within.

Directions: From the M5 join the A38 at Exeter following Plymouth signs. After approximately 12 miles, exit for Moretonhampstead and Newton Abbot. At the roundabout follow signs for Ilsington.

Web: www.johansens.com/ilsington
E-mail: hotel@ilsington.co.uk
Tel: 0870 381 8635
International: +44 (0)1364 661452
Fax: 01364 661307

Price Guide:
single from £86
double/twin from £126

DEVON - LEWDOWN (NR OKEHAMPTON)

LEWTRENCHARD MANOR

LEWDOWN, NEAR OKEHAMPTON, DEVON EX20 4PN

Directions: Located off the A386, 6 miles south of the A30. 30 miles from junction 31 on the M5 at Exeter.

Web: www.johansens.com/lewtrenchard
E-mail: info@lewtrenchard.co.uk
Tel: 0870 381 9177
International: +44 (0)1566 783222
Fax: 01566 783332

Price Guide:
single £100–£130
double/twin £140–£210
suite £220–£250

This beautiful Jacobean manor is tucked away within its own estate on rolling Devon hills, and with just 9 exquisite bedrooms is a delightful retreat from city life. Built in 1600 by the Monk family it was later embellished by the Victorian hymn writer Rev Sabine Baring Gould, and today is a stunning example of ornate ceilings, elegant carved oak staircases and leaded light windows. Carefully incorporated family antique pieces and elegant soft furnishings to create a sense of luxury combined with a warmth that is truly welcoming. Each of the bedrooms looks out over the valley, and the oak-panelled dining room with its coffered ceiling provides a stunning backdrop for some excellent cooking and superb wines. The restaurant has won 2 Rosettes for its exquisitely prepared and artistically presented cuisine, which is based on the freshest of local ingredients. The estate offers clay pigeon shooting and rough shooting and fishing, making this an ideal place for weekend parties, as well as an idyllic setting for weddings and functions. Exeter is on the doorstep with its cathedral and sophisticated shops, whilst Devon's numerous tourist attractions are all within easy reach.

Our inspector loved: The warm informal atmosphere in this beautiful manor house.

    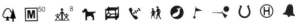

Barnstaple

Exeter
Sidmouth

Plymouth

THE ARUNDELL ARMS

LIFTON, DEVON PL16 0AA

In a lovely valley close to the uplands of Dartmoor, The Arundell Arms is a former coaching inn, which dates back to Saxon times. Its flagstone floors, cosy fires, paintings and antiques combine to create a haven of warmth and comfort in an atmosphere of Old World charm. One of England's best-known sporting hotels for more than half a century, it boasts 20 miles of exclusive salmon and trout fishing on the Tamar, and 5 of its tributaries, and a famous school of fly fishing. Guests also enjoy a host of other country activities, including hill walking, shooting, riding and golf. The hotel takes great pride in its elegant 3 AA Rosette restaurant, presided over by Master Chef's Philip Burgess and Nick Shopland. Their gourmet cuisine has won the restaurant an international reputation. A splendid base from which to enjoy the wonderful surfing beaches nearby, The Arundell Arms is also well placed for visits to Tintagel and the historic houses and gardens of Devon and Cornwall and the Eden Project. Only 45 minutes from Exeter and Plymouth, it is also ideal for the business executive, reached by major roads from all directions. A spacious conference suite is available.

Our inspector loved: *A haven for fishing, outdoor sports and the finest cuisine.*

Directions: Lifton is approximately ¼ mile off the A30, 2 miles east of Launceston and the Cornish Border.

Web: www.johansens.com/arundellarms
E-mail: reservations@arundellarms.com
Tel: 0870 381 8323
International: +44 (0)1566 784666
Fax: 01566 784494

Price Guide:
single £70–£90
double/twin from £146
suite £220

SOAR MILL COVE HOTEL

SOAR MILL COVE, SALCOMBE, SOUTH DEVON TQ7 3DS

Directions: A384 to Totnes, then A381 to Soar Mill Cove.

Web: www.johansens.com/soarmillcove
E-mail: info@soarmillcove.co.uk
Tel: 0870 381 8897
International: +44 (0)1548 561566
Fax: 01548 561223

Price Guide:
single £94–£160
double/twin £180–£220
suite from £216

Owned and loved by the Makepeace family who, for over 25 years, have provided a special blend of friendly yet professional service, this hotel is spectacularly set in a flower-filled combe, facing its own sheltered sandy bay and entirely surrounded by 2000 acres of dramatic National Trust coastline. While it is perhaps one of the last truly unspoiled corners of South Devon, Soar Mill Cove is only 15 miles from the motorway system (A38). "Serendipity", the fine dining restaurant holds 3 RAC Dining Awards and this luxury 4-star hotel is the AA's highest rated in Devon. All the bedrooms are at ground level, each with a private patio opening onto the gardens, which in spring or summer provides wonderful alfresco opportunities. In winter, the efficient double glazing keeps cooler weather at bay. A strict "no conference policy" guarantees that the peace of guests shall not be compromised. Both the indoor and outdoor pools are spring-water fed, the former being maintained all year at a constant 88°F. Here is Keith Stephen Makepeace's award-winning cuisine, imaginative and innovative, reflecting the very best of the West of England; fresh crabs and lobster caught in the bay are a speciality. Soar Mill Cove is situated midway between the old ports of Plymouth and Dartmouth.

Our inspector loved: The beautifully newly presented suites and as always the breathtaking location.

THE TIDES REACH HOTEL

SOUTH SANDS, SALCOMBE, DEVON TQ8 8LJ

This luxuriously appointed hotel is situated in an ideal position for those wishing to enjoy a relaxing or fun-filled break. Facing south in a tree-fringed sandy cove just inside the mouth of the Salcombe Estuary it has an extensive garden on one side, the sea and a safe bathing sandy beach a few steps opposite and, to the rear, a sheltering hill topped by the subtropical gardens of Overbecks. The Tides Reach has been under the supervision of owners, the Edwards family, for more than 35 years and they have built up a reputation for hospitality and courteous service. The atmosphere is warm and friendly, the décor and furnishings tasteful and comfortable. All 35 spacious bedrooms are en suite, well equipped and decorated with flair and originality. The lawned garden centres around an ornamental lake with waterfall and fountain which is surrounded by landscaped tiers of colourful plants, shrubs and palms. Overlooking it is the restaurant where chef Finn Ibsen's excellent gourmet cuisine has earned AA Rosettes. A superb indoor heated swimming pool is the nucleus of the hotel's leisure complex which includes a sauna, solarium, spa bath, gymnasium, squash court, snooker room and hair & beauty salon . The hotel has facilities for windsurfing, sailing and canoeing.

Our inspector loved: The warm welcome, superb location and relaxing ambience.

Directions: From the M5, exit at junction 30 and join the A38 towards Plymouth. Exit for Totnes and then take the A381.

Web: www.johansens.com/tidesreach
E-mail: enquires@tidesreach.com
Tel: 0870 381 8947
International: +44 (0)1548 843466
Fax: 01548 843954

Price Guide: (incl dinner)
single £75–£140
double/twin £132–£300

BUCKLAND-TOUT-SAINTS

GOVETON, KINGSBRIDGE, DEVON TQ7 2DS

Directions: Signed from A381 between Totnes and Kingsbridge.

Web: www.johansens.com/bucklandtoutsaints
E-mail: buckland@tout–saints.co.uk
Tel: 0870 381 8391
International: +44 (0)1548 853055
Fax: 01548 856261

Price Guide:
single from £80
double/twin from £150
suite from £300

One of the top 200 hotels in Britain and Ireland, Buckland-Tout-Saints is an impressive Grade II* listed manor house, built in 1690 during the reign of William and Mary. Recently refurbished to a superb standard, the wonderful hospitality and cuisine that guests enjoy at this hotel today would certainly have impressed its royal visitors of the past. Idyllic amongst its own woodlands and beautiful gardens, it is invitingly close to the spectacular beaches and dramatic cliffs of the Devonshire coastline. A warm and welcoming atmosphere prevails throughout, from the leather-clad couches of the convivial bar to the family of bears – Teddy Tout-Saints – whose individual members welcome guests to their de luxe rooms and suites. Many of these delightful period style rooms enjoy stunning views across the beautiful South Hams countryside with its moorland and river estuaries. Gastronomic delights using fresh local fish, meat and game accompanied by an equally tantalising selection of fine wines and vintage ports are served in the award-winning Queen Anne Resturant. Conferences, weddings and seminars are effortlessly accommodated in the Kestrel Rooms, where helpful staff and elegant surroundings ensure a successful occasion. Several well-known golf courses and sailing centres such as Salcome and Dartmouth are nearby. Details of golf breaks are available via the hotels website.

Our inspector loved: The location and feel of tranquillity.

HOTEL RIVIERA

THE ESPLANADE, SIDMOUTH, DEVON EX10 8AY

A warm welcome awaits guests arriving at this prestigious award-winning hotel. With accolades such as the AA Courtesy and Care Award and more recently, the Which? Hotel Guide's Hotel of the Year 1999, it comes as no surprise that Peter Wharton's Hotel Riviera is arguably one of the most comfortable and most hospitable in the region. The exterior, with its fine Regency façade and bow fronted windows complements the elegance of the interior comprising handsome public rooms and beautifully appointed bedrooms, many with sea views. Perfectly located at the centre of Sidmouth's historic Georgian esplanade and awarded 4 stars by both the AA and the RAC, the Riviera is committed to providing the very highest standard of excellence which makes each stay at the property a totally pleasurable experience. Guests may dine in the attractive salon, which affords glorious views across Lyme Bay, and indulge in the superb cuisine, prepared by Swiss and French trained chefs. The exceptional cellar will please the most discerning wine connoisseur. Activities include coastal walks, golf, bowling, croquet, putting, tennis, fishing, sailing, riding and exploring the breathtaking surroundings with its gardens, lush countryside and stunning coastline. Short breaks are available.

Our inspector loved: The superb newly presented bedrooms overlooking Lyme Bay.

Directions: The hotel is situated at the centre of the esplanade.

Web: www.johansens.com/riviera
E-mail: enquiries@hotelriviera.co.uk
Tel: 0870 381 8624
International: +44 (0)1395 515201
Fax: 01395 577775

Price Guide: (including 7 course dinner):
single £109–£143
double/twin £196–£264
suite £284–£304

THE PALACE HOTEL

BABBACOMBE ROAD, TORQUAY, DEVON TQ1 3TG

Directions: From seafront follow signs for Babbacombe. Hotel entrance is on the right.

Web: www.johansens.com/palacetorquay
E-mail: info@palacetorquay.co.uk
Tel: 0870 381 8798
International: +44 (0)1803 200200
Fax: 01803 299899

Price Guide:
single £75–£85
double/twin £150–£170
executive £199
suite £240–£280

Once the residence of the Bishop of Exeter, the privately owned Palace Hotel is a gracious Victorian building set in 25 acres of beautifully landscaped gardens and woodlands. The comfortable bedrooms are equipped with every modern amenity and there are also elegant, spacious suites available. Most rooms overlook the hotel's magnificent grounds. The main restaurant provides a high standard of traditional English cooking, making full use of fresh, local produce, as well as offering a good variety of international dishes. The cuisine is complemented by a wide selection of popular and fine wines. Light meals are also available from the lounge and during the summer months, a mediterranean-style menu is served on the terrace. A host of sporting facilities has made this hotel famous. These include a short par 3 9-hole championship golf course, indoor and outdoor swimming pools, 2 indoor and 4 outdoor tennis courts, 2 squash courts, saunas, snooker room and a well-equipped fitness suite. Places of interest nearby include Dartmoor, South Hams and Exeter. Paignton Zoo, Bygone's Museum and Kent's Cavern are among the local attractions.

Our inspector loved: This gracious hotel - beautiful grounds and the fact one can stay onsite and forget the car.

ORESTONE MANOR HOTEL & RESTAURANT

ROCKHOUSE LANE, MAIDENCOMBE, TORQUAY, DEVON TQ1 4SX

Stylishly refurbished as a colonial manor house, Orestone Manor is a luxury country house hotel and restaurant located on the rural fringe of Torquay, with stunning views across the Torbay coastline and Lyme Bay. The house was built in 1809 and was once the home of painter John Calcott Horsley RA, whose celebrated portrait of his brother-in-law, Isambard Kindom Brunel, hangs in the National Gallery. He is also renowned for having painted the very first Christmas card. Each room has its own décor and character with full amenities and luxury en-suite bathrooms; some have their own terrace or balcony. Excellent service and superb food and wine can be enjoyed in the 2 AA Rosette restaurant. Using only the best seasonal local produce – some from Orestone's own gardens – light lunches, snacks and afternoon teas are served in the conservatory or on the terrace, whilst a full set lunch and à la carte dinner menu are available in the restaurant. Numerous places of interest are close by, including Dartmoor, Exmoor and many National Trust properties and gardens, as well as a wide range of activities and picturesque coastal walks. Whether for a relaxing break, afternoon tea, lunch with friends or a special dinner, Orestone Manor provides the perfect setting, and adds style and elegance to any occasion.

Our inspector loved: The beautiful location and overall ambience, quite superb.

Directions: About 3 miles north of Torquay on the A379 (Formerly B3199). Take the coast road towards Teignmouth.

Web: www.johansens.com/orestonemanor
E-mail: enquiries@orestone.co.uk
Tel: 0870 381 8794
International: +44 (0)1803 328098
Fax: 01803 328336

Price Guide:
single £89–£139
double/twin £119–£199

THE OSBORNE HOTEL & LANGTRY'S RESTAURANT

MEADFOOT BEACH, TORQUAY, DEVON TQ1 2LL

Directions: The hotel is in Meadfoot, to the east of Torquay.

Web: www.johansens.com/osborne
E-mail: enq@osborne-torquay.co.uk
Tel: 0870 381 8795
International: +44 (0)1803 213311
Fax: 01803 296788

Price Guide:
single £55–£90
double/twin £95–£200
suite £120–£225

The combination of Mediterranean chic and the much-loved Devon landscape has a special appeal, which is reflected at The Osborne. The hotel is the centrepiece of an elegant recently refurbished Regency crescent in Meadfoot, a quiet location within easy reach of the centre of Torquay. Known as a "country house by the sea", the hotel offers the friendly ambience of a country home complemented by the superior standards of service and comfort expected of a hotel on the English Riviera. Most of the 29 bedrooms have magnificent views and are decorated in pastel shades. Overlooking the sea, Langtry's acclaimed award-winning restaurant provides fine English cooking and tempting regional specialities, whilst the Brasserie has a menu available throughout the day. Guests may relax in the attractive 6-acre gardens and make use of indoor and outdoor swimming pools, gymnasium, sauna, solarium, tennis court and putting green – all without leaving the grounds. Sailing, archery, clay pigeon shooting and golf can be arranged. Devon is a county of infinite variety, with its fine coastline, bustling harbours, tranquil lanes, sleepy villages and the wilds of Dartmoor. The Osborne is ideally placed to enjoy all these attractions.

Our inspector loved: The magnificent location and the ambience of a country house by the sea.

PERCY'S COUNTRY HOTEL & RESTAURANT

COOMBESHEAD ESTATE, VIRGINSTOW, DEVON EX21 5EA

A soft, tranquil ambience filters through every part of this stylish, charming Devon hideaway. Set amongst 130 acres of unspoilt countryside and with stunning wildlife that will enthrall and enchant, Percy's is ideal for those wishing to relax and unwind in a smoke and child-free environment. Against the backdrop of the breathtaking and striking wilds of Dartmoor and Bodmin Moor, Percy's combines modern architectural intelligence and traditional country house comfort with eye-catching results. The highly acclaimed and fully certified organic restaurant, winner of the 2003 Johansens Restaurant of the Year, only serves the freshest of ingredients. The fish bought at auction is only a few hours old, vegetables and a bespoke breed of lamb are nurtured on the estate and there is a choice of home produced eggs rich in natural flavour and colour. Guest rooms feature understated luxury with soothing colours, king-size beds, Jacuzzis, DVD players and freshly baked lavender and walnut shortbread to savour. Guests are welcome to explore the surrounding grounds with the company of any one of the 3 black resident Labradors.

Our inspector loved: The peaceful "away-from-it-all" location.

Directions: From Okehampton take the A3079 to Metherell Cross. After 8.3 miles turn left. The hotel is 6.5 miles on the left. See website for more comprehensive details.

Web: www.johansens.com/percys
E-mail: info@percys.co.uk
Tel: 0870 381 8817
International: +44 (0)1409 211236
Fax: 01409 211460

Price Guide:
single from £90
double from £150

LANGDON COURT HOTEL & RESTAURANT

DOWN THOMAS, PLYMOUTH, DEVON PL9 0DY

Originally built for Katherine Parr, the 6th wife of Henry VIII, this Grade II listed Tudor manor has even earlier origins, evidence of which can be found in its cellars. Rebuilt in 1648, the house is now surrounded by fields and woodland and has its own Jacobean walled gardens and well kept lawns. Behind its impressive grey façade lie tiled floors, warmly painted stone walls and classic, uncluttered furnishings. Some of the 17 bedrooms are simply stunning, and more than half are currently undergoing an upgrading programme to create the same, unparalleled standard. 3 function suites, Calmady, Cory and Courtney, are available for wedding receptions, shooting and house parties. An impressive menu is served in the modern brasserie, the bar or on the terrace, specialising in fish and seafood. Year round, the best produce and organically farmed meats are selected from local suppliers, and the cellar holds well-established favourites along with wines from the New World. The hotel has a direct path to the beach at Wembury, access to the coastal paths, and is ideally placed for exploring the South Hams countryside, numerous National Trust properties and the Eden project.

Directions: From Exeter join the A38 towards Plymouth then take the exit signed Plymouth, Yelverton Plymstock into Brixton. Follow Brixton Tor/Otter Nurseries and carry on the Leyford Lane. Turn left into the hotel's drive.

Web: www.johansens.com/langdon
E-mail: enquiries@langdoncourt.co.uk
Tel: 0870 381 9157
International: +44 (0)1752 862358
Fax: 01752 863428

Price Guide:
single from £65
double £95-£150

Our inspector loved: The new beautifully appointed bedrooms and ensuites and of course the cuisine.

WOOLACOMBE BAY HOTEL

SOUTH STREET, WOOLACOMBE, DEVON EX34 7BN

Woolacombe Bay Hotel stands in 6 acres of grounds, leading to 3 miles of golden sand. Built by the Victorians, the hotel has an air of luxury, style and comfort. All rooms are en suite with satellite TV, baby listening device, ironing centre, some with a balcony. Traditional English and French dishes are offered in the dining room. Superb recreational amenities on-site include unlimited free access to tennis, squash, indoor and outdoor pools, billiards, bowls, croquet, dancing and films, a health suite with steam room, sauna, spa bath with high impulse shower. Power-boating, fishing, shooting and riding can be arranged and preferential rates are offered for golf at the Saunton Golf Club. There is a "Hot House" aerobics studio, beauty salon, cardio vascular weights room, solariums, masseur and beautician. However, being energetic is not a requirement for enjoying the qualities of Woolacombe Bay. Many of its regulars choose simply to relax in the grand public rooms and in the grounds, which extend to the rolling surf of the magnificent bay. A drive along the coastal route in either direction will guarantee splendid views. Exmoor's beautiful Doone Valley is an hour away by car. Closed January.

Our inspector loved: The first-class facilities, the genuine welcome and total feel of relaxation.

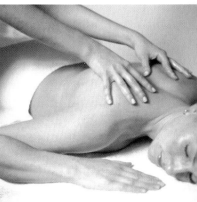

Directions: At the centre of the village, off main Barnstaple–Ilfracombe road.

Web: www.johansens.com/woolacombebay
E-mail: woolacombe.bayhotel@btinternet.com
Tel: 0870 381 9007
International: +44 (0)1271 870388
Fax: 01271 870613

Price Guide: (including dinner)
single £92–£152
double/twin £184–£304

Barnstaple
Exeter
Sidmouth
Plymouth

WATERSMEET HOTEL

MORTEHOE, WOOLACOMBE, DEVON EX34 7EB

Directions: From the M5, junction 27, follow the A361 towards Ilfracombe. Turn left at the roundabout and follow signs to Mortehoe.

Web: www.johansens.com/watersmeet
E-mail: info@watersmeethotel.co.uk
Tel: 0870 381 8972
International: +44 (0)1271 870333
Fax: 01271 870890

Price Guide: (including dinner)
single £98–£150
double/twin £140–£285

In a setting of incomparable beauty the Watersmeet is situated in one of the finest and most dramatic locations in the South West, it commands an elevated position at the waters edge above Combesgate Beach with steps leading directly to the sandy beach. The magnificent views of the rugged coastline to Lundy Island can be enjoyed from the large picture windows in the reception rooms ensuring that guests can admire the ever-changing coastline. Now under new ownership of Michael and Amanda James a tasteful refurbishment has transformed the bedrooms, consistent with the high standard of the hotel, to include all accruements for luxury living. All boast superb uninterrupted sea views and many have balconies. Award winning imaginative menus combine the use of the finest quality local ingredients with thoughtfully balanced dishes, taken in the pavilion AA Rosette restaurant while admiring the sunsets by candlelight. Lunch and tea may be taken alfresco on the terrace or in the picturesque tea garden. Recreational facilities include heated outdoor and indoor pool with newly installed hot spa and steam room. Scenic coastal walks along National Trust land and Saunton Sands Championship Golf Course are nearby. The excellent reputation of the hotel with the impeccable service, relaxation theme and home from home ambiance continues to attract guests year after year.

Our inspector loved: The new leisure facilities and refurbished bedrooms.

LANGTRY MANOR

DERBY ROAD, EAST CLIFF, BOURNEMOUTH, DORSET BH1 3QB

This fine house was built in 1877 by Edward VII (then Prince of Wales) as a home for his mistress Lillie Langtry. The concept of a themed luxury hotel was created by the present owners exactly a hundred years later. The Kings Suite is a fine spacious room, which features an original Jacobean four-poster bed and a huge oak inglenook fireplace with hand painted scenes of Shakespeare in gold leaf and blue/white enamel. Other rooms (including Lillies) have four-posters and corner spa baths and are all designed to engender a romantic ambience- a natural for honeymoons, anniversary's and birthdays. Saturday night guests are invited to take part in a delicious 6 course Edwardian Banquet displayed and served in the quite splendid Dining Hall with its minstrels gallery and stained glass windows. The banquet also features a short interlude of words and music based on the Life of the "Jersey Lillie". Some of the individually designed bedrooms offered are close by in The Lodge- where Lillie & Edward stayed as the guests of the owner Lord Derby during the building of the Manor. Guests can enjoy complimentary use of the state of the art leisure club just 2 minutes away. Sandy beaches, Hardy Country, the New Forest, art galleries, theatres and gardens are nearby.

Our inspector loved: *From the smiling welcome to the red rose on the pillow - everything delights.*

Directions: Take A338 Wessex Way to the station. First exit at roundabout, over next roundabout, first left into Knyveton Road, second right into Derby Road.

Web: www.johansens.com/langtrymanor
E-mail: lillie@langtrymanor.com
Tel: 0870 381 8681
International: +44 (0)1202 553887
Fax: 01202 290115

Price Guide:
single from £95
double/twin £139.50–£219.50

THE AVONMOUTH HOTEL AND RESTAURANT

95 MUDEFORD, CHRISTCHURCH, DORSET BH23 3NT

Built in the 1830s as a gentleman's residence, this charming, Grade II listed hotel stands in extensive grounds on a quiet area of the waterfront with magnificent views over Mudeford Quay, Hengistbury Head and Christchurch Estuary. Privately owned, it has recently undergone sympathetic refurbishment and offers the highest standards of accommodation, service and cuisine. Each en-suite bedroom is distinctively styled, tastefully furnished and has every home comfort. Guests have a choice of bedrooms in the Georgian main house or in the Orchard Wing, situated in the landscaped garden, which slopes gently down to the harbour edge. Dining in the delightful Quays Restaurant, with its panoramic window views and sunny terrace, is a real pleasure; classic dishes, with a touch of imagination, are prepared by talented executive chef Nigel Popperwell, formerly personal chef to fashion designers Tommy Hilfiger and Valentino and Ainsley Harriott's successor at London's Westbury Hotel. A heated outdoor swimming pool is popular with visitors from June to August and for the more energetic there are sailing and windsurfing in the estuary. Bournemouth and Christchurch's attractions are within easy reach while the lovely walks, rambling trails and villages of the New Forest are just 15 minutes away.

Directions: From the M25/M3/M27, take the A35 Lyndhurst to Christchurch. At Sainsbury roundabout follow signs to Mudeford. Continue on the main route through the village, past a parade of shops on the right and the hotel is on the left.

Web: www.johansens.com/avonmouth
E-mail: info@avonmouth-hotel.co.uk
Tel: 0870 381 9333
International: +44 (0)1202 483434
Fax: 01202 479004

Price Guide:
single from £80
double/twin from £100
double/twin with water view £130

Our inspector loved: *The amazing waterside location and the stunning views from the newly refurbished restaurant and lounge area.*

PLUMBER MANOR

STURMINSTER NEWTON, DORSET DT10 2AF

An imposing Jacobean building of local stone, occupying extensive gardens in the heart of Hardy's Dorset, Plumber Manor has been the home of the Prideaux-Brune family since the early 17th century. Leading off a charming gallery, hung with family portraits, are 6 very comfortable bedrooms. The conversion of a natural stone barn lying within the grounds, as well as the courtyard building, has added a further 10 spacious bedrooms, some of which have window seats overlooking the garden and the Develish stream. 3 interconnecting dining rooms comprise the restaurant, where a good choice of imaginative, well-prepared dishes is presented, supported by a wide-ranging wine list. Chef Brian Prideaux-Brune's culinary prowess has been recognised by all the major food guides. Open for dinner every evening and Sunday lunch. The Dorset landscape, with its picture-postcard villages such as Milton Abbas and Cerne Abbas, is close at hand, while Corfe Castle, Lulworth Cove, Kingston Lacy and Poole Harbour are not far away. Riding can be arranged locally; however, if guests wish to bring their own horse to hack or hunt with local packs, the hotel provides free stabling on a do-it-yourself basis. Closed during February.

Our inspector loved: The very essence of real country living - and desserts to die for!

Directions: Plumber Manor is 2 miles south-west of Sturminster Newton on the Hazelbury Bryan road, off the A357.

Web: www.johansens.com/plumbermanor
E-mail: book@plumbermanor.com
Tel: 0870 381 8829
International: +44 (0)1258 472507
Fax: 01258 473370

Price Guide:
single £90–£110
double/twin £100–£170

THE PRIORY HOTEL

CHURCH GREEN, WAREHAM, DORSET BH20 4ND

Directions: Wareham is on the A351 to the west of Bournemouth and Poole. The hotel is beside the River Frome at the southern end of the town near the parish church.

Web: www.johansens.com/priorywareham
E-mail: reservations@theprioryhotel.co.uk
Tel: 0870 381 8841
International: +44 (0)1929 551666
Fax: 01929 554519

Price Guide:
single from £110
double/twin from £140
suite from £295

Dating from the early 16th century, the one-time Lady St Mary Priory has, for hundreds of years, offered sanctuary to travellers. In Hardy's Dorset, "Far From the Madding Crowd", it placidly stands on the bank of the River Frome in 4 acres of immaculate gardens. Steeped in history, The Priory has undergone a sympathetic conversion to a hotel, which is charming yet unpretentious. Each bedroom is distinctively styled, with family antiques lending character and many rooms have views of the Purbeck Hills. A 16th-century clay barn has been transformed into the Boathouse, consisting of 4 spacious luxury suites at the river's edge. Tastefully furnished, the drawing room, residents' lounge and intimate bar together create a convivial atmosphere. The Garden Room Restaurant is open for breakfast and lunch, while splendid dinners are served in the vaulted stone cellars. There are moorings for guests arriving by boat. Dating back to the 9th century, the market town of Wareham has more than 200 listed buildings. Corfe Castle, Lulworth Cove, Poole and Swanage are all close by with superb walks and beaches.

Our inspector loved: *The tranquil calm of this truly delightful hotel.*

DORSET - WEYMOUTH (FLEET)

MOONFLEET MANOR

FLEET, WEYMOUTH, DORSET DT3 4ED

Overlooking Chesil Beach, a unique feature of the Dorset coast, Moonfleet Manor is both a luxury hotel and a family resort. The owners have applied the same flair for design evident in their other family friendly properties, Woolley Grange, The Ickworth Hotel and Fowey Hall in Cornwall. The use of a variety of unusual antiques and objects from around the world lends a refreshing and individual style to this comfortable and attractive hotel. Bedrooms are beautifully decorated and furnished and a range of amenities ensures that guests enjoy standards of maximum comfort and convenience. Enthusiastic and attentive staff work hard to ensure that guests feel at home, whatever their age. Moonfleet's dining room, whose décor and style would do credit to a fashionable London restaurant, offers an excellent and varied menu based on fresh local produce but bringing culinary styles from around the world. Facilities at the hotel include an indoor swimming pool with squash and tennis courts for the more energetic. Key places of interest nearby include Abbotsbury, Dorchester, Corfe Castle and Lulworth Cove, whilst in Weymouth itself the Sea Life Park, The Deep Sea Adventure and The Titanic Story are worth a visit.

Our inspector loved: *Its unique, stylish provision for families with children.*

Directions: Take the B3157 Weymouth to Bridport Road, then turn off towards the sea at the sign for Fleet.

Web: www.johansens.com/moonfleetmanor
E-mail: info@moonfleetmanor.com
Tel: 0870 381 8744
International: +44 (0)1305 786948
Fax: 01305 774395

Price Guide:
single from £95
double/twin £135–£285
suite £285–£385

HEADLAM HALL

HEADLAM, NR GAINFORD, DARLINGTON, COUNTY DURHAM DL2 3HA

Directions: Headlam is 2 miles north of Gainford off A67 Darlington–Barnard Castle road.

Web: www.johansens.com/headlamhall
E-mail: admin@headlamhall.co.uk
Tel: 0870 381 8590
International: +44 (0)1325 730238
Fax: 01325 730790

Price Guide:
single £75–£105
double/twin £90–£120
suite from £130

This magnificent 17th-century Jacobean mansion stands in 4 acres of formal walled gardens. The grand main lawn, ancient beach hedges and flowing waters evoke an air of tranquillity. Located in the picturesque hamlet of Headlam and surrounded by over 200 acres of its own rolling farmland, Headlam Hall offers guests a special ambience of seclusion and opulence. The traditional bedrooms are all en suite and furnished to a high standard, many with period furniture. The restaurant offers the very best of modern English and Continental cuisine with the kitchen team enjoying a fine reputation for their dishes. An extensive well-chosen wine list highlights the dining experience. Guests may dine in the tasteful surroundings of either the Panelled room, the Victorian room, the Patio room or Conservatory. The main hall features huge stone pillars and the superb original carved oak fireplace, which has dominated the room for over 300 years. The elegant Georgian drawing room opens on to a stepped terrace overlooking the main lawn. The hotel also offers extensive conference facilities and a fine ballroom, the Edwardian Suite with its oak floor and glass ceiling, suitable for up to 150 people. The vast range of leisure facilities include an indoor pool, sauna, gym, tennis court, croquet lawn, course fishery, a snooker room and a new 9-hole golf course, driving range and golf shop. A new leisure spa is due to open in the autumn.

Our inspector loved: *The four-poster and antique beds in this family hotel.*

FIVE LAKES RESORT

COLCHESTER ROAD, TOLLESHUNT KNIGHTS, MALDON, ESSEX CM9 8HX

Set in 320 acres, the superb Five Lakes Resort successfully combines leisure, health and sporting activities with excellent conference and banqueting facilities. Each of the 194 bedrooms are furnished to a high standard offering every comfort and convenience. With two, 18-hole golf courses – one of which, the Lakes Course, was designed by Neil Coles MBE and is used annually for the PGA European Tour - making the Five Lakes one of East Anglia's leading golf venues. Guests can take advantage of the indoor and outdoor championship-standard tennis courts; squash and badminton courts; an indoor pool with spa-bath, steam-room and sauna; gymnasium; jogging trail, snooker and a luxurious Health & Beauty Spa. Two restaurants offer a choice of good food which is complemented by excellent service. Comfortable lounges and 2 bars provide convivial surroundings in which to relax and enjoy a drink. The extensive facilities for conferences, meetings, exhibitions include 18 meeting rooms, a 3,500m² exhibition hall holding over 2,000 guests and a dedicated activity field.

Our inspector loved: The glass staircase and water features in the Atrium style lounge.

Directions: From M25 jct 28 to A12, look for brown signs at Gt Braxted/Silver End exit or A12 from north, look for brown signs at Kelvedon all the way.

Web: www.johansens.com/fivelakes
E-mail: johansens@fivelakes.co.uk
Tel: 0870 381 8524
International: +44 (0)1621 868888
Fax: 01621 869696

Price Guide: (room only)
single £110
double/twin £155
suites £225

Colchester
Stansted Airport
Harlow   Chelmsford
Southend-on-Sea

MAISON TALBOOTH

STRATFORD ROAD, DEDHAM, COLCHESTER, ESSEX CO7 6HN

Directions: Dedham is about a mile from the A12 between Colchester and Ipswich.

Web: www.johansens.com/maisontalbooth
E-mail: maison@milsomhotels.com
Tel: 0870 381 8712
International: +44 (0)1206 322367
Fax: 01206 322752

Price Guide:
single £120–£160
double/twin £165–£225

In the north-east corner of Essex, where the River Stour borders with Suffolk, is the Vale of Dedham, an idyllic riverside setting immortalised in the early 19th century by the paintings of John Constable. One summer's day in 1952, the young Gerald Milsom enjoyed a "cuppa" in the Talbooth tearoom and soon afterwards took the helm at what would develop into Le Talbooth Restaurant. Business was soon booming and the restaurant built itself a reputation as one of the best in the country. In 1969 Maison Talbooth was created in a nearby Victorian rectory, to become, as it still is, a standard bearer for Britain's premier country house hotels. Indeed, in 1982 Gerald Milsom became the founder of the Pride of Britain group. With its atmosphere of opulence, Maison Talbooth has 10 spacious guest suites which all have an air of quiet luxury. Every comfort has been provided. Breakfast is served in the suites. The original Le Talbooth Restaurant is about half a mile upstream on a riverside terrace reached by leisurely foot or courtesy car. The hotel arranges special Constable tours. Maison Talbooth is also available for exclusive use – take over the hotel for your own private house party to celebrate a special occasion or just for an excuse for a 'get together' with family and friends. please call for details. Special short breaks also available.

Our inspector loved: The welcoming greeting on the front steps.

GREENWOODS ESTATE

STOCK ROAD, NEAR CHELMSFORD, ESSEX CM4 9BE

For rest, relaxation and rebuilding energy, few places better this luxury hotel, spa and peaceful retreat situated in the Essex countryside, 40 minutes from London and Stansted Airport. Greenwoods Estate stands on a high point at the edge of the village of Stock, famed for its church belfry whose beams originate from Spanish galleons and is a beautifully restored and extended Grade II listed manor house with a combination of Georgian and Victorian architecture. Located in 42 acres of parkland, Greenwoods has 4 acres of formal gardens including a beautiful sunken herb garden supplying the kitchens with the freshest produce. The highly skilled chef offers an imaginative and creative combination of fine dining and a balanced menu. Guests are offered opulence without intimidation, character, charm and welcoming hospitality. Public areas are lavishly decorated with sumptuous panelling, original fireplaces and comfortable sofas. Bedrooms are individually designed and furnished to the highest standard; most have panoramic views and all premier rooms have antique beds. The spa facilities include over 50 beauty and holistic treatments, 34 qualified therapists, sauna, steam and spa bath facilities, a fully equipped gymnasium and a 20m lap swimming pool. Ideal for weddings, meetings, conferences and teambuilding activities; delegates can enjoy free use of the spa facilities during their stay.

Directions: From the A12 take the B1007.

Web: www.johansens.com/greenwoods
E-mail: info@greenwoodsestate.com
Tel: 0870 381 8575
International: +44 (0)1277 829990
Fax: 01277 829899

Price Guide:
single from £95
double/twin from £125
suite from £125

Our inspector loved: The original hand-painted graphics in the new wing.

THE SWAN HOTEL AT BIBURY

BIBURY, GLOUCESTERSHIRE GL7 5NW

Directions: Bibury is signposted off A40 Oxford–Cheltenham road, on the left hand side. Secure free parking now available next to the hotel.

Web: www.johansens.com/swanhotelatbibury
E-mail: info@swanhotel.co.uk
Tel: 0870 381 8931
International: +44 (0)1285 740695
Fax: 01285 740473

Price Guide:
single £99–£155
double/twin £130–£260

Gloucester
Cheltenham
Cirencester

The Swan Hotel at Bibury in the South Cotswolds, a 17th-century coaching inn, is a perfect base for both leisurely and active holidays which will appeal especially to motorists, fishermen and walkers. The hotel has its own fishing rights and a moated ornamental garden encircled by its own crystalline stream. Bibury itself is a delightful village, with its honey-coloured stonework, picturesque ponds, the trout-filled River Coln and its utter lack of modern eyesores. When Cotswold Inns and Hotels acquired the Swan they gained a distinctive hotel in the English countryside which acknowledges the needs of the sophisticated modern-day traveller. Oak panelling, plush carpets and sumptuous fabrics create the background for the fine paintings and antiques that grace the interiors. The 18 eccentric bedrooms are superbly appointed with luxury bathrooms and comfortable furnishings. Guests may dine in the brassiere for lunch and the magnificent Signet Room or Gallery Restaurant for dinner. Midweek special rates available. The luxurious Swan Sanctuary beauty treatment facility is located next to the hotel.

Our inspector loved: *The lovely new Swan Sanctuary - ideal for a day of pampering.*

NEW

THE DIAL HOUSE

THE CHESTNUTS, HIGH STREET, BOURTON-ON-THE-WATER, GLOUCESTERSHIRE GL54 2AN

Built in 1698 from traditional Cotswold stone, The Dial House is the essence of sophisticated English country style offering guests peace and tranquillity, charm, and a spacious, luxurious interior filled with period furnishings such as large inglenook fireplaces, exposed timber beams, monks' chairs, poor boxes, secret cupboards, water wells and stone arches. Surrounded by a secluded lawned garden, highlighted by aromatic flowers and colourful shrub-filled borders and beds, this privately owned, family-run hotel is idyllically situated in a picturesque and unspoiled village where the little River Windrush flows down the main street under "toy town" low bridges beside trees and lawns. Each of the hotel's 13 bedrooms has every detail and accessory to make a guest's stay comfortable and memorable: hand-painted wallpaper, lavish big beds, deep baths, exquisite fabrics, together with television, video, direct dial telephone and state-of-the-art communication links. Mouth-watering cuisine, created from the finest and freshest of local and national produce, is served in intimate dining rooms whose innovative style and high standards have been recognised by 2 AA Rosettes and plaudits from Egon Ronay. Blenheim Palace, Warwick Castle, the Roman antiquities at Bath and all the delights of Shakespeare country are nearby.

Directions: From the A40 take the A429 north towards Stow-on-the-Wold for approximately 3.5 miles.

Web: www.johansens.com/dialhouse
E-mail: info@dialhousehotel.com
Tel: 0870 381 9296
International: +44 (0)1451 822244
Fax: 01451 810126

Price Guide:
single £57–£89
double £114–£150
suite £175

Our inspector loved: The intimate dining rooms and excellent food.

HOTEL ON THE PARK

EVESHAM ROAD, CHELTENHAM, GLOUCESTERSHIRE GL52 2AH

Directions: The hotel is opposite Pittville Park, a 5-minute walk from the town centre.

Web: www.johansens.com/hotelonthepark
E-mail: stay@hotelonthepark.co.uk
Tel: 0870 381 8623
International: +44 (0)1242 518898
Fax: 01242 511526

Price Guide:
single from £94.25
double/twin from £128.50

Set in the Regency spa town of Cheltenham, this attractive town house hotel combines attentive service of a bygone era with an excellent standard of accommodation in a relaxed atmosphere featuring jovial, quirky touches. The impressive façade, with its grand pillared doorway, invites guests into the elegant interior where a number of resident teddy bears take pride of place in public rooms, each with a unique story of origin and purpose. Bedrooms are individually styled and decorated with interesting antiques and exquisite fabrics with bathrooms featuring Victorian baths and a rubber duck! The Bacchanalian Restaurant, with its high ceilings and hand-detailed cornice work, has glorious views of Pittville Park and serves contemporary British cuisine alongside a comprehensive wine list. The well-appointed Library is an ideal venue for board meetings or seminars. Special occasions, including private banquets and wedding receptions, can be arranged. Synonymous with National Hunt Racing, Cheltenham is particularly popular during the racing season and hosts the Gold Cup. The town's Regency architecture, attractive promenade, exclusive boutiques, historic properties, museums and theatres are a delight. Alternatively, there is golf, horse-riding, rambling and the Cotswolds to explore.

Our inspector loved: *The stylish elegance, comfortable surroundings and friendly staff.*

THE GREENWAY

SHURDINGTON, CHELTENHAM, GLOUCESTERSHIRE GL51 4UG

Set amidst gentle parkland with the rolling Cotswold hills beyond, The Greenway is an Elizabethan country house with a style that is uniquely its own – very individual and very special. Renowned for the warmth of its welcome, its friendly atmosphere and its immaculate personal service, The Greenway is the ideal place for total relaxation. The public rooms with their antique furniture and fresh flowers are elegant and spacious yet comfortable, with roaring log fires in winter and access to the formal gardens in summer. The 21 bedrooms all have private bathrooms and are individually decorated with co-ordinated colour schemes. Eleven of the rooms are located in the main house with a further ten rooms in the converted Georgian coach house immediately adjacent to the main building. The award-winning conservatory dining room overlooks the sunken garden, providing the perfect backdrop to superb cuisine of international appeal complemented by an outstanding selection of wines. Situated in one of Britain's most charming areas, The Greenway is well placed for visiting the spa town of Cheltenham, the Cotswold villages and Shakespeare country.

Our inspector loved: A charming country house with spacious rooms and pretty gardens.

Directions: On the outskirts of Cheltenham off the A46 Cheltenham–Stroud road, 2½ miles from the town centre.

Web: www.johansens.com/greenway
E-mail: greenway@btconnect.com
Tel: 0870 381 8574
International: +44 (0)1242 862352
Fax: 01242 862780

Price Guide:
single from £99
double/twin £150–£240

CHARINGWORTH MANOR

NR CHIPPING CAMPDEN, GLOUCESTERSHIRE GL55 6NS

Directions: Charingworth Manor is on the B4035 between Chipping Campden and Shipston-on-Stour.

Web: www.johansens.com/charingworthmanor
E-mail: charingworthmanor@englishrosehotels.co.uk
Tel: 0870 381 8414
International: +44 (0)1386 593555
Fax: 01386 593353

Price Guide: (including full breakfast)
limited double sole occupancy from £125
double/twin from £180

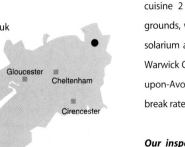

The ancient manor of Charingworth lies amid the gently rolling Cotswold countryside, just a few miles from the historic towns of Chipping Campden and Broadway. Beautiful old stone buildings everywhere recall the flourishing wool trade that gave the area its wealth. The 14th-century manor house overlooks its own 50-acre grounds and offers peace and enthralling views. Inside, Charingworth is a historic patchwork of intimate public rooms with log fires burning during the colder months. There are 26 individually designed bedrooms, including a limited number of non smoking rooms and a new contemporary style suite called the Ebrington Suite, all furnished with antiques and fine fabrics. Outstanding cuisine is regarded as being of great importance and guests at Charingworth are assured of imaginative dishes. Great emphasis is placed on using only the finest produce and the AA has awarded the cuisine 2 Rosettes. There is an all-weather tennis court within the grounds, while inside, a beautiful swimming pool, sauna, steam room, solarium and gym are available, allowing guests to relax and unwind. Warwick Castle, Hidcote Manor Gardens, Batsford Arboretum, Stratford-upon-Avon, Oxford and Cheltenham are all within easy reach. Short break rates are available on request.

Our inspector loved: *The beautiful setting surrounded by Cotswold countryside.*

COTSWOLD HOUSE HOTEL

HIGH STREET, CHIPPING CAMPDEN, GLOUCESTERSHIRE GL55 6AN

Chipping Campden is a nostalgic Cotswold town, unspoilt by the 20th-century, and Cotswold House is a splendid 17th-century mansion facing the town square, impressive with colonnades flanking the front door and built in the lovely soft local stone. The interior has been sensitively decorated and modernised so there is no distraction from the graceful pillared archway and staircase. Lovely antiques, fine paintings and fabrics reminiscent of the Regency era blend easily with comfortable sofas in the elegant drawing room. The bedrooms are very individual, but all are peaceful, decorated in harmonious colours and have country house style furnishings. Cotswold House is deservedly proud of its kitchen, which has won many accolades. The attractive Juliana's Restaurant has a splendid menu and a cellar book of 150 wines. Informal meals are served in Hicks' Brasserie. Private functions and small conferences can be held in the secluded Courtyard Room and The Grammar School Suite. Guests enjoy exploring Chipping Campden's intriguing shops and alleyways. The hotel is a superb base for Stratford-on-Avon and Oxford. The hotel has parking facilities.

Our inspector loved: The old Grammar School Suite - stunning.

Directions: Chipping Campden is 2 miles north-east of A44, on the B4081.

Web: www.johansens.com/cotswoldhouse
E-mail: reception@cotswoldhouse.com
Tel: 0870 381 8449
International: +44 (0)1386 840330
Fax: 01386 840310

Gloucester
Cheltenham
Cirencester

Price Guide:
single from £125
double/twin from £190
four poster from £275
cottage rooms from £325
grammar school 2-bed suite from £595

THE NOEL ARMS HOTEL

HIGH STREET, CHIPPING CAMPDEN, GLOUCESTERSHIRE GL55 6AT

A long tradition of hospitality awaits you at the Noel Arms Hotel. In 1651 the future Charles II rested here after his Scottish army was defeated by Cromwell at the battle of Worcester, and for centuries the hotel has entertained visitors to the ancient and unspoilt, picturesque Cotswold Village of Chipping Campden. Many reminders of the past, fine antique furniture, swords, shields and other mementoes can be found around the hotel. There are 26 en-suite bedrooms in either the main house or in the tastefully constructed new wing, some of which boast luxurious antique four-poster beds and all offering the standards you expect from a country hotel. The Gainsborough restaurant offers an excellent Oriental menu including a seasonal selection of fresh local produce. You may be tempted to choose from the extensive range of bar snacks available in the conservatory or Dovers Bar. The fine selection of wines from around the world are delicious accompaniments to any meal. Try some of the traditional cask ales and keg beers. Browse around the delightful array of shops in Chipping Campden or many of the enchanting honey-coloured Cotswold Villages, Hidcote Manor Gardens, Cheltenham Spa, Worcester, Oxford and Stratford-upon-Avon which are all close by.

Directions: The Noel Arms is in the centre of Chipping Campden, which is on the B4081, 2 miles east of the A44.

Web: www.johansens.com/noelarms
E-mail: reception@noelarmshotel.com
Tel: 0870 381 8763
International: +44 (0)1386 840317
Fax: 01386 841136

Price Guide:
single £90
double £125–£195

Gloucester
Cheltenham
Cirencester

Our inspector loved: The civil war weaponry hanging in the entrance hall.

NEW

BARNSLEY HOUSE

BARNSLEY, CIRENCESTER, GLOUCESTERSHIRE GL7 5EE

Sumptuous guest rooms, interiors of the highest quality, enticing food, discreet and impeccable service. Those were the aims of Tim Haigh and Rupert Pendered when they bought this lovely Cotswold stone dwelling in the centre of the attractive village of Barnsley 2 years ago. They have more than just succeeded: Barnsley House is a real gem, a place to escape to and totally relax time and again. Embellished with a carved-in-stone date of 1697 and the initials BB, this simple, south-east facing building first housed the Squire of Barnsley, Brereton Bouchier, and remained a family home until its conversion to a hotel in July 2003. The grounds are superb and are the perfect example of a traditional English country house lay-out with charming walks, formal lawns, ancient meadows, ungoverned wilderness, a temple and pool garden where guests enjoy a peaceful read and a shady veranda on which to sip a cooling summer drink. The elegantly furnished bedrooms are individually and harmoniously designed for absolute comfort. Guests staying in suites are welcomed with homemade ice cream, chocolates and champagne. Chef Graham Grafton, formerly of London's Caprice, Bibendum and Chez Bruce, creates amazing Italian cuisine and robust, simple, fresh dishes in the charming restaurant and the hotel's own village pub across the road.

Our inspector loved: The fabulous bedrooms and stunning gardens.

Directions: Barnsley is on the B4425 Cirencester-Bilbury-Burford Road, 4 miles north east of Cirencester. From London, exit the M40 at junction 8 and follow the A40 towards Cheltenham. Join the B4425 at Burton roundabout.

Web: www.johansens.com/barnsleyhouse
E-mail: info@barnsleyhouse.com
Tel: 0870 381 9327
International: +44 (0)1285 740000
Fax: 01285 740900

Gloucester
Cheltenham
Cirencester

Price Guide:
single £208–£260
double £208–£356
suite £315–£450

LOWER SLAUGHTER MANOR

LOWER SLAUGHTER, GLOUCESTERSHIRE GL54 2HP

Directions: The Manor is on the right as you enter Lower Slaughter from A429.

Web: www.johansens.com/lowerslaughtermanor
E-mail: info@lowerslaughter.co.uk
Tel: 0870 381 8706
International: +44 (0)1451 820456
Fax: 01451 822150

Price Guide:
single £175–£375
double/twin £200–£400
suite £350–£400

With a history that spans nearly a thousand years, this Grade II listed Manor stands in complete tranquillity within private grounds on the edge of one of the Cotswold's prettiest villages. Visitors are warmly welcomed by a team of dedicated staff, and enjoy elegant, spacious surroundings. All rooms are beautifully furnished, with carefully chosen antiques, fine china and original paintings. Outside the wonderful grounds reveal a croquet lawn and tennis court, and, within the delightful walled garden, a unique 2-storey dovecote dating back to the 15th century when the Manor was a convent. The award-winning cuisine is prepared using the best local and continental ingredients, and an outstanding wine list offers a range of 800 specially selected wines from the Old and New Worlds. An excellent setting for business meetings, The Sir George Whitmore Suite accommodates up to 16 people, and offers phone line, full secretarial services and audio-visual equipment. For more leisurely pursuits, visitors can explore the Cotswolds, Cheltenham, Stratford, and Warwick and Sudeley Castles. Lower Slaughter Manor is a member of The Leading Small Hotels of the World.

Our inspector loved: *A beautiful manor house in one of the Cotswold's most idyllic villages*

WASHBOURNE COURT HOTEL

LOWER SLAUGHTER, GLOUCESTERSHIRE GL54 2HS

Washbourne Court Hotel is in the heart of the tranquil and beautiful Cotswold village of Lower Slaughter, set on the bank of the River Eye. The 4 acres of private gardens have been lovingly re-landscaped with lawns and many delightful features. With just 28 bedrooms, it has parts dating back to the 17th century. The recent additions to the hotel, a spacious new dining room and a further 6 guest rooms with comfortable and elegant furnishings, blend in perfectly with the original building. Always full of freshly picked flowers and planted bowls, the hotel has the feel of a private house with its many personal touches. The modern English cuisine offers an abundance of fresh local produce, concentrating on good textures and intense flavours combined with outstanding presentation. Head chef Sean Ballington now oversees the running of the kitchen. Drinks, light lunches and traditional afternoon tea are also served on the garden terrace during the summer months.

Our inspector loved: The beautiful setting right next to the river.

Directions: The hotel is situated ½ a mile from the main A429 Fosseway between Stow-on-the-Wold and Bourton-on-the-Water (signed To the Slaughters).

Gloucester
Cheltenham

Cirencester

Web: www.johansens.com/washbournecourt
E-mail: info@washbournecourt.co.uk
Tel: 0870 381 8970
International: +44 (0)1451 822143
Fax: 01451 821045

Price Guide: (including dinner)
single from £115
double/twin from £170

BURLEIGH COURT

BURLEIGH, MINCHINHAMPTON, NEAR STROUD, GLOUCESTERSHIRE GL5 2PF

Built in the 18th century, Burleigh Court Hotel is a former gentleman's manor house nestling on the edge of a steep hillside overlooking the Golden Valley in the heart of the Cotswolds. Comfortable surroundings, quality service, the ambience of a bygone era and a tranquil, relaxed atmosphere are combined with 3½ acres of beautifully tended gardens featuring terraces, ponds, pools, hidden pathways and Cotswold stone walls to create an idyllic setting. All the bedrooms are individually and delightfully furnished, with the highest standard of facilities and stunning scenic views. The coach house bedrooms, located by a Victorian plunge pool, and those within the courtyard gardens provide versatile accommodation for families. The elegant restaurant has a reputation for classical cuisine which utilises only the best local produce, whilst an extensive cellar produces a wine list to satisfy the most demanding palate. For special occasions a private dining room overlooking the rear terrace is available. Burleigh Court is perfectly situated to explore the famous honey-stoned villages of the Cotswolds, the market towns of Minchinhampton, Tedbury, Cirencester, Painwick and Bibury and attractions such as Berkely Castle and Chavenage House.

Directions: Leave Stroud on A419 towards Cirencester. After approximately 2½ miles turn right, signposted Burleigh and Minchinhampton. After a further 500 yards turn left and the hotel is signposted.

Web: www.johansens.com/burleighgloucestershire
E-mail: info@burleighcourthotel.co.uk
Tel: 0870 381 8664
International: +44 (0)1453 883804
Fax: 01453 886870

Price Guide:
single £80-£100
double £105-£145
suite £145

Our inspector loved: This comfortable stylish hotel with lovely views.

THE MANOR HOUSE HOTEL

MORETON-IN-MARSH, GLOUCESTERSHIRE GL56 0LJ

This former 16th-century manor house is set in beautiful gardens in the Cotswold village of Moreton-in-Marsh. The Manor House Hotel has been tastefully extended and restored, yet retains many of its historic features. The 38 well-appointed bedrooms have been individually decorated and furnished. The 2 Red Rosettes restaurant offers imaginative and traditional English dishes using only the freshest ingredients, accompanied by an expertly selected wine list. For the guest seeking relaxation, leisure facilities include an indoor heated swimming pool and spa bath. Sports enthusiasts will also find that tennis, golf and riding can be arranged locally. Spacious modern business facilities, combined with the peaceful location, make this an excellent venue for executive meetings. It is also an ideal base for touring, with many attractions nearby, including Stratford-upon-Avon, Warwick and the fashionable centres of Cheltenham, Oxford and Bath.

Our inspector loved: The stylish restaurant overlooking the pretty garden.

Directions: The Hotel is on the A429 Fosse Way near the junction of the A44 and A429 north of Stow, on the Broadway side of the intersection.

Web: www.johansens.com/manorhousemoreton
E-mail: bookings@cotswold-inns-hotels.co.uk
Tel: 0870 381 8717
International: +44 (0)1608 650501
Fax: 01608 651481

Price Guide:
single £115
double/twin £135–£175
suite £210

THE PAINSWICK HOTEL

KEMPS LANE, PAINSWICK, GLOUCESTERSHIRE GL6 6YB

Directions: M5 Jct13. Painswick is on A46 between Stroud and Cheltenham, turn into road by the church and continue round the corner, taking the first right. The hotel is at the bottom of the road on the right hand side.

Web: www.johansens.com/painswick
E-mail: reservations@painswickhotel.com
Tel: 0870 381 8797
International: +44 (0)1452 812160
Fax: 01452 814059

Price Guide:
single from £90
double/twin from £140–£215

The village of Painswick stands high on a hill overlooking the beautiful rolling valleys of the Cotswolds. Dating back to the 14th century, the village was an old wool community; medieval cottages mingle gracefully with elegant Georgian merchants' houses. A feature of the village is the church, with its ancient churchyard graced by 99 Yew trees planted in 1792 and 17th-century table tombs in memory of the wealthy clothiers. Situated majestically within these architectural gems is the Palladian-style Painswick Hotel, built in 1790 and formerly the home of affluent village rectors. Each of the luxury en-suite bedrooms have modern amenities, beautiful fabrics, antique furniture and objets d'art, creating a restful atmosphere and the impression of staying in a comfortable private house. The stylish restaurant, with its pine panelling, offers delicious cuisine with an emphasis upon regional produce such as locally reared Cotswold meat, game, wild Severn salmon and Gloucestershire cheeses. The private Dining Room accommodates quiet dinner parties, wedding occasions and business meetings.

Our inspector loved: *The interesting historic features of this former rectory in such a picturesque village.*

NEW

FOSSE MANOR

FOSSE WAY, STOW-ON-THE-WOLD, GLOUCESTERSHIRE GL54 1JX

Set in the heart of the Cotswolds, just outside Stow-on-the-Wold, this former rectory, set in 5 acres, combines contemporary style with country charm to provide the perfect place to relax and unwind. Set back from the Fosse Way, the ancient roman road from which the hotel takes its name, Fosse Manor is ideally located for visiting the famous Cotswold towns and villages and the Spa town of Cheltenham. The bedrooms are individually designed using natural tones and fabrics and each one features either a DVD player or a Playstation with plenty of films and games to choose from. The restaurant and the more informal Green Room, offer an extensive menu ranging from traditional to contemporary English cuisine using the highest quality local produce and ingredients. As well as a comprehensive wine list, we also offer a selection of wines from the proprietor's cellar. The new conference suite, situated in the garden with views over the rolling countryside can cater for discreet meetings and small parties.

Our inspector loved: *The relaxed atmosphere and beautiful views of the surrounding countryside.*

Directions: Fosse Manor is located adjacent to the A429 just south of Stow-on-the-Wold.

Web: www.johansens.com/fossemanor
E-mail: enquiries@fossemanor.co.uk
Tel: 0870 381 9324
International: +44 (0)1451 830354
Fax: 01451 832486

Price Guide:
single £95
double £130–£225

THE GRAPEVINE HOTEL

SHEEP STREET, STOW-ON-THE-WOLD, GLOUCESTERSHIRE GL54 1AU

Directions: Sheep Street is part of A436 in the centre of Stow-on-the-Wold.

Web: www.johansens.com/grapevine
E-mail: enquiries@vines.co.uk
Tel: 0870 381 8564
International: +44 (0)1451 830344
Fax: 01451 832278

Price Guide:
single from £80
double/twin from £130

Set in the pretty town of Stow-on-the-Wold, regarded by many as the jewel of the Cotswolds, The Grapevine Hotel has an atmosphere which makes visitors feel welcome and at ease. The outstanding personal service provided by a loyal team of staff is perhaps the secret of the hotel's success. This, along with the exceptionally high standard of overall comfort and hospitality, earned The Grapevine the 1991 Johansens Hotel Award for Excellence – a well-deserved accolade. Beautifully furnished bedrooms, including 6 superb garden rooms across the courtyard, offer every facility. Visitors can linger over imaginative cuisine in the relaxed and informal atmosphere of the Conservatory Restaurant. Awarded 1 AA Rosette for food, the restaurant, like all of the bedrooms, is non-smoking. Whether travelling on business or pleasure, guests will wish to return to The Grapevine again and again. The local landscape offers unlimited scope for exploration, whether to the numerous picturesque villages in the Cotswolds or to the towns of Oxford, Cirencester and Stratford-upon-Avon. Nature enthusiasts must visit the beautiful gardens of Hidcote, Kifsgate and Barnsley House nearby. Open over Christmas.

Our inspector loved: *The attractive restaurant with ancient vine canopy.*

THE UNICORN HOTEL

SHEEP STREET, STOW-ON-THE-WOLD, GLOUCESTERSHIRE GL54 1HQ

Low oak-beamed ceilings and large stone fireplaces pay tribute to The Unicorn's lengthy past. Over the last 300 years, the inn has changed its standards of accommodation, incorporating the latest modern facilities, yet many vestiges of the former centuries remain. The recently refurbished interior is decorated in a stylish manner featuring Jacobean furniture and antique artefacts whilst log fires abound. Enhanced by floral quilts and comfortable armchairs, the 20 en-suite bedrooms are simple yet charming. Fine paintings adorn the walls of the public rooms and the cosy bar offers hand-carved wooden chairs and rich carpets. Modern British cooking is served in the elegant surroundings of the Georgian restaurant from an imaginative à la carte menu. The hotel is well frequented on Sundays by guests wishing to indulge in the delicious lunchtime roast. Local leisure facilities include horse riding and the golf course. Shooting and fishing are popular outdoor pursuits. Many historic buildings and castles are within easy reach including the magnificent Blenheim Palace and Warwick Castle. Nature enthusiasts will be delighted with the splendid gardens at Sudeley Castle.

Our inspector loved: The friendly welcome.

Directions: The nearest motorway is the M40 junction 10. Then take the A44 or the A436 in the direction of Stow-on-the-Wold. The hotel is located on the A429.

Gloucester
Cheltenham
Cirencester

Web: www.johansens.com/unicorn
E-mail: reception@birchhotels.co.uk
Tel: 0870 381 8960
International: +44 (0)1451 830257
Fax: 01451 831090

Price Guide:
single £65–£75
double/twin £105–£125

LORDS OF THE MANOR HOTEL

UPPER SLAUGHTER, NR BOURTON-ON-THE-WATER, GLOUCESTERSHIRE GL54 2JD

Directions: Upper Slaughter is 2 miles west of the A429 between Stow-on-the-Wold and Bourton-on-the-Water.

Web: www.johansens.com/lordsofthemanor
E-mail: enquiries@lordsofthemanor.com
Tel: 0870 381 8704
International: +44 (0)1451 820243
Fax: 01451 820696

Price Guide:
single from £100
double/twin £160–£310

Situated in the heart of the Cotswolds, on the outskirts of one of England's most unspoilt and picturesque villages, stands the Lords of the Manor Hotel. Built in the 17th century of honeyed Cotswold stone, the house enjoys splendid views over the surrounding meadows, stream and parkland. For generations the house was the home of the Witts family, who historically had been rectors of the parish. It is from these origins that the hotel derives its distinctive name. Charming, walled gardens provide a secluded retreat at the rear of the house. Each bedroom bears the maiden name of one of the ladies who married into the Witts family; each room is individually and imaginatively decorated with period furniture. The reception rooms are magnificently furnished with fine antiques, paintings, traditional fabrics and masses of fresh flowers. Log fires blaze in cold weather. The heart of this English country house is its dining room, where truly memorable dishes are created from the best local ingredients. Nearby are Blenheim Palace, Warwick Castle, the Roman antiquities at Bath and Shakespeare country.

Our inspector loved: *The beautiful views of the lake and parkland from the front of the manor.*

134

THE BEAR OF RODBOROUGH

RODBOROUGH COMMON, STROUD, NR CIRENCESTER, GLOUCESTERSHIRE GL5 5DE

This 17th-century former coaching inn offers comfortable accommodation in an area of outstanding beauty. Nestling on the top of a steep hill, The Bear of Rodborough is situated in the verdant landscape of the western Cotswolds, described by the author, Laurie Lee, as "vegetative virginity". The hotel has undergone a careful and precise restoration, yet many of its past features such as the original archway entrance have been retained. The refurbished bedrooms are exquisite, adorned with plush carpets and beautiful fabrics. All have en-suite facilities and several thoughtful extras. The superb bar, popular with the locals, is renowned for its large selection of traditional beers. Elegantly furnished, the 2 Rosette restaurant is enhanced by the ceiling beams with a "running bear" design. Specialities include cuisine, made with fresh local produce, whilst the light luncheons must also be savoured.

Our inspector loved: The friendly welcome and comfy feel.

Directions: The nearest motorway is the M5, junction 13.

Web: www.johansens.com/bearofrodborough
E-mail: info@bearofrodborough.info
Tel: 0870 381 8348
International: +44 (0)1453 878522
Fax: 01453 872523

Price Guide:
single £75–£95
double/twin £120–£130
suite £195

CALCOT MANOR

NEAR TETBURY, GLOUCESTERSHIRE GL8 8YJ

Directions: From Tetbury, take the A4135 signposted Dursley; Calcot Manor is on the right after 3½ mile

Web: www.johansens.com/calcotmanor
E-mail: reception@calcotmanor.co.uk
Tel: 0870 381 8398
International: +44 (0)1666 890391
Fax: 01666 890394

Price Guide:
double/twin £175–£215
family room £215
family suite £250

This delightful hotel, built of Cotswold stone, offers guests tranquillity amidst acres of rolling countryside. Situated in the southern Cotswolds close to the historic town of Tetbury, the building dates back to the 15th century and was a farmhouse until 1983. Its beautiful stone barns and stables include one of the oldest tithe barns in England, built in 1300 by the Cistercian monks from Kingswood Abbey. These buildings form a quadrangle and the stone glistening in the dawn or glowing in the dusk is quite a spectacle. Professional service is complemented by cheerful hospitality without any hint of over-formality. Excellent facilities for families include a number of family suites complete with bunk beds and baby listening devices. A play facility to keep older children entertained with Playstation, X boxes and a small cinema, and a full-day care crèche for younger children is open 7 days a week. Parents can escape to the state-of-the-art spa with 16-metre pool, steam room and sauna, gym and outdoor hot tub. The spa also offers a full range of beauty treatments. In the elegant conservatory restaurant dinner is very much the focus of a memorable stay and the congenial Gumstool Bistro and Bar offers a range of simpler traditional food and local ales. A discreet conference facility is available.

Our inspector loved: A perfect retreat for grown-ups, with an abundance of entertainment for the children.

CORSE LAWN HOUSE HOTEL

CORSE LAWN, NR TEWKESBURY, GLOUCESTERSHIRE GL19 4LZ

Although only 6 miles from the M5 and M50, Corse Lawn is a completely unspoilt, typically English hamlet in a peaceful Gloucestershire backwater. The hotel, an elegant Queen Anne listed building set back from the village green, stands in 12 acres of gardens and grounds and still displays the charm of its historic pedigree. Visitors can be assured of the highest standards of service and cooking: Baba Hine is famous for the dishes she produces, while Denis Hine, of the Hine Cognac family, is in charge of the wine cellar. The service here, now in the hands of son Giles, is faultlessly efficient, friendly and personal. As well as the renowned restaurant, there are 3 comfortable drawing rooms, a large lounge bar, a private dining-cum-conference room for up to 45 persons and a similar, smaller room for up to 20. A tennis court, heated indoor swimming pool and croquet lawn adjoin the hotel and most sports and leisure activities can be arranged. Corse Lawn is ideal for exploring the Cotswolds, Malverns and Forest of Dean. Short break rates are always available.

Our inspector loved: The beautiful setting, excellent food and personal, friendly service.

Directions: Corse Lawn House is situated on the B4211 between the A417 (Gloucester–Ledbury road) and the A438 (Tewkesbury–Ledbury road).

Web: www.johansens.com/corselawn
E-mail: enquiries@corselawn.com
Tel: 0870 381 8448
International: +44 (0)1452 780479/771
Fax: 01452 780840

Price Guide:
single £85
double/twin £130
four-poster £150

HATTON COURT

UPTON HILL, UPTON ST LEONARDS, NR CHELTENHAM, GLOUCESTERSHIRE GL4 8DE

Tucked away behind a bank of mature trees, Hatton Court sits on the edge of the Cotswold escarpment, between the cathedral city of Gloucester and the glorious village of Painswick. A former splendid private home, the hotel has its own extensive grounds encompassing magnificent gardens and terraced areas, ideal for summer parties. The pace is unhurried, relaxation and comfort are foremost. On arrival guests are welcomed into the reception area which is more of a lounge, with armchairs, magazines, and an open fireplace. The sumptuous ambience is extended in to the bedrooms, all of which are individually decorated and boast en-suite facilities. Executive rooms are available with four-poster bed, mini-bar and whirlpool. . The restaurant combines efficient, friendly service with an elegant, warm setting. Guests can enjoy breathtaking views over the Malvern Hills, Forest of Dean and the Severn Estuary whilst savouring delicious cuisine. The restaurant is complemented by an exceptional wine shop, a unique and unusual feature of this hotel. Visitors to Hatton Court have use of the Health Suite, complete with sauna, whirlpool, and mini gym, while in warmer weather a game of croquet on the lawn makes for relaxing afternoon. This is the perfect location to explore the glorious Cotswold countryside, the Rococo Gardens in Painswick and the "Regency" Cheltenham Spa.

Directions: Leave M5 at Jct 12, A38 towards Gloucester, then B4073 towards Upton St Leonards and Painswick. Hatton Court is located on this road. From North leave M5 at Jct 11a, take A417 towards Cirencester, following signs for A46 Cheltenham/Stroud. At the roundabout take the third exit towards Stroud until you reach Painswick. Turn right onto B4073 towards Upton St Leonards.

Web: www.johansens.com/hattoncourt
E-mail: res@hatton-court.co.uk
Tel: 0870 381 8773
International: +44 (0)1452 617412
Fax: 01452 612945

Gloucester
Cheltenham
Cirencester

Price Guide:
single £80–£100
double/twin £115–£196

Our inspector loved: The lovely views over the Cotswold countryside.

THORNBURY CASTLE

THORNBURY, SOUTH GLOUCESTERSHIRE BS35 1HH

Built in 1511 by Edward Stafford, third Duke of Buckingham, Thornbury Castle was later owned by Henry VIII, who stayed here in 1535 with Anne Boleyn. Today it stands in 15 acres of regal splendour with its vineyard, high walls and the oldest Tudor garden in England. Rich furnishings are displayed against the handsome interior features, including ornate oriel windows, panelled walls and large open fireplaces. The 25 carefully restored bedchambers retain many period details. Thornbury Castle has received many accolades for its luxurious accommodation and excellent cuisine, which includes delights such as Gloucestershire Old Spot pork, Isle of Skye scallops, Goosnargh duckling, Scotch beef, local vegetables, regional cheeses, local organic free-range eggs and you will often see the chef picking fresh herbs from the Castle garden. The Castle also provides peaceful and secluded meeting facilities. Thornbury is an ideal base from which to explore Bath, Wales and the Cotswolds. Personally guided tours are available to introduce guests to the little-known as well as the famous places which are unique to the area. In addition, golf may be enjoyed locally and day clay pigeon shooting and archery can be arranged locally.

Our inspector loved: A unique property with an abundance of historic features and charm.

Directions: The entrance to the Castle is left of the Parish Church at the lower end of Castle Street.

Web: www.johansens.com/thornburycastle
E-mail: info@thornburycastle.co.uk
Tel: 0870 381 8944
International: +44 (0)1454 281182
Fax: 01454 416188

Price Guide:
single from £110
double/twin from £130
suite from £295

ESSEBORNE MANOR

HURSTBOURNE TARRANT, ANDOVER, HAMPSHIRE SP11 0ER

Directions: Midway between Newbury and Andover on the A343, 1½ miles north of Hurstbourne Tarrant.

Web: www.johansens.com/essebornemanor
E-mail: info@essebornemanor.com
Tel: 0870 381 8506
International: +44 (0)1264 736444
Fax: 01264 736725

Price Guide:
single £95–£135
double/twin £100–£180

Esseborne Manor is small and unpretentious, yet stylish. The present house was built at the end of the 19th century and carries the name used to record details of the local village in the Domesday Book. It is set in a pleasing garden amid the rich farmland of the North Wessex Downs in a designated area of outstanding natural beauty. Ian and Lucilla Hamilton, who own the house, have established the restful atmosphere of a private country home where guests can unwind and relax. There are just 15 comfortable bedrooms, some reached via a courtyard. Two doubles and a delightful suite are in converted cottages with their own patio overlooking the main gardens. The pretty sitting room and cosy library are comfortable areas in which to relax. Dave Morris's fine 2 Rosette cooking is set off to advantage in the new dining room and adjoining bar. There is now a spacious meeting and function facility. In the grounds there is a herb garden, an all-weather tennis court, a croquet lawn and plenty of good walking beyond. Nearby Newbury racecourse has a busy programme of steeple-chasing and flat racing. Places to visit include Highclere Castle, Stonehenge, Salisbury, Winchester and Oxford.

Our inspector loved: The hospitality at this increasingly popular country house.

TYLNEY HALL

ROTHERWICK, HOOK, HAMPSHIRE RG27 9AZ

Approaching this hotel in the evening, with its floodlit exterior and forecourt fountain, it is easy to imagine arriving for a party in a private stately home. Grade II listed and set in 66 acres of ornamental gardens and parkland, Tylney Hall typifies the great houses of a bygone era. Apéritifs are taken in the wood-panelled library bar; haute cuisine is served in the glass-domed Oak Room restaurant. The hotel holds RAC and AA food awards and also AA 4 Red Stars and RAC Gold Ribbon. The health and leisure facilities include a heated pool and whirlpool, solarium, fitness studio, beauty and hairdressing, sauna, tennis, croquet and snooker, whilst hot-air ballooning, archery, clay pigeon shooting, golf and riding can be arranged. Surrounding the hotel are wooded trails ideal for jogging. Functions for up to 100 people are catered for in the Tylney Suite or Chestnut Suite; more intimate gatherings are available in one of the other 10 private banqueting rooms. Tylney Hall is licenced to hold wedding ceremonies on-site. The cathedral city of Winchester and Stratfield Saye House are nearby. Legoland and Windsor Castle are a 40-minute drive away.

Our inspector loved: Coming up the winding drive, through the stately trees into 66 acres of garden and to a wonderful welcome.

Directions: M4/jct 11 towards Hook and Rotherwick, follow signs to the hotel. M3/jct 5, A287 towards Newnham, over the A30 into Old School Road. Left for Newnham then right onto Ridge Lane. Hotel is on the left after 1 mile.

Web: www.johansens.com/tylneyhall
E-mail: reservations@tylneyhall.com
Tel: 0870 381 8958
International: +44 (0)1256 764881
Fax: 01256 768141

Price Guide:
single £135–£400
double/twin £165–£220
suite £285–£430

THE MONTAGU ARMS HOTEL

BEAULIEU, NEW FOREST, HAMPSHIRE SO42 7ZL

Directions: The village of Beaulieu is well signposted and the hotel commands an impressive position at the foot of the main street.

Web: www.johansens.com/montaguarms
E-mail: reservations@montaguarmshotel.co.uk
Tel: 0870 381 8743
International: +44 (0)1590 612324
Fax: 01590 612188

Price Guide: (inclusive terms available)
single £100–£145
double/twin £160–£190
suites £190–£210

An AA top 200 hotel with 3 Red Stars, in the heart of the New Forest, close to the M27, The Montagu Arms is a delightful hotel that takes great pride in its outstanding service. With just 23 beautifully decorated bedrooms and suites, the hotel is a small oasis of luxury, recently winning the AA's Courtesy and Care Award England 2003/2004 for its attentive levels of service. Available for exclusive use, the hotel lends itself ideally to both weddings and conferences, able to cater for anything between 10 and 100 people. The Terrace Restaurant overlooks the beautiful and secluded gardens, and head chef Adrian Coulthard is happy to cater for specific occasions and tastes, whilst the Oakwood and Paris Rooms can provide a more intimate setting for both board meetings, family celebrations or private dining. The New Forest is well known for both sailing on the Solent and for good riding in the forest; both of these activites are easily arranged by the hotel. The Montagu Arms has its own fully-crewed luxury 84ft yacht that can take up to 12 guests for a day's sail, possibly reaching Cowes on the Isle of Wight or the famous Needles. The hotel also has strong links with a number of nearby estates to be able to provide clay pigeon shooting, fishing, and other country pursuits.

Our inspector loved: *The lovely village setting and the timeless*

CAREYS MANOR HOTEL & SENSPA

BROCKENHURST, NEW FOREST, HAMPSHIRE SO42 7RH

Careys Manor dates from 1888 and is built on the site of a royal hunting lodge used by Charles II. Situated close to the glorious New Forest countryside, the hotel is proud of the personal welcome and care it extends to its visitors. The bedrooms are comfortably appointed and furnished in a range of styles. In the modern Garden wing some of the rooms have balconies and others open directly onto lawns and borders. The restaurant offers a hearty breakfast and an English and French influenced cuisine at dinner. The superb new Oriental Spa is set within the grounds and linked to the hotel through charming corridors. The spa offers a variety of treatments performed by Eastern and Western therapists and features a state-of-the-art hydrotherapy pool with several experience rooms and showers, which include amongst others, a mud room, blizzard shower, ice room, tepidarium, laconium and Vichy shower. Windsurfing, riding and sailing can all be enjoyed locally, whilst Stonehenge, Beaulieu, Broadlands, Salisbury and Winchester are a short distance away. Business interests can be catered for; there are comprehensive self-contained conference facilities.

Our inspector loved: The comprehensive range of treatments available in the vast and impresssive new leisure facility.

Directions: From the M27, junction 1, follow the A337 signed to Lymington. Careys Manor is on the left after the 30 mph sign at Brockenhurst.

Web: www.johansens.com/careysmanor
E-mail: stay@careysmanor.com
Tel: 0870 381 8405
International: +44 (0)1590 623551
Fax: 01590 622799

Price Guide:
double/twin £129–£199

LE POUSSIN AT WHITLEY RIDGE

BEAULIEU ROAD, BROCKENHURST, NEW FOREST, HAMPSHIRE SO42 7QL

Directions: M27 junction 1. Situated on the B3055, Brockenhurst – Beaulieu

Web: www.johansens.com/poussinwhitleyridge
E-mail: whitleyridge@brockenhurst.co.uk
Tel: 0870 381 8994
International: +44 (0)1590 622354
Fax: 01590 622856

Price Guide:
single from £65
double £110–£140
suite £140–£150

Set in 5 acres of secluded parkland in the heart of the New Forest, this privately owned Georgian house was once a Royal hunting lodge visited by the Queen Mother. Today it has the ambience of a true country house with the accent on relaxation. The bedrooms are individually decorated, and most have lovely views over open forest. The public rooms are similarly luxurious and elegant and log fires burn on cool evenings. Internationally acclaimed chef patron Alex Aitken has re-located his famous Le Poussin restaurant, awarded a Michelin Star and 3 AA Rosettes, in to Whitley Ridge whilst nearby Parkhill undergoes extensive refurbishment and expansion; his innovative, imaginative cuisine is a joy not to be missed. Guests can relax in the grounds or enjoy a game of tennis. Some of the country's best woodland walks are directly accessible from the gardens. Whichever pastime you choose, Whitley Ridge guarantees a restful and enjoyable stay. A number of stately homes, including Broadlands and Wilton House, are within easy reach. Lord Montague's Motor Museum, Buckler's Hard and historic Stonehenge are also within driving distance

Our inspector loved: *The very tranquil setting at the heart of the New Forest. Attention to detail is a keynote here.*

NEW PARK MANOR

LYNDHURST ROAD, BROCKENHURST, NEW FOREST, HAMPSHIRE SO42 7QH

Escape from the pressures of a hectic lifestyle in this Grade II listed former hunting lodge of Charles II which dates from the 16th century. The house stands within its own clearing in the heart of the New Forest, yet is easily accessed from the main Lyndhurst/Lymington road. All bedrooms boast fine views of the surrounding parklands and forest and are individually decorated, in keeping with the historic nature of the house. The New Forest rooms are contemporary in style and even have LCD TV screens in the bathrooms! Wandering ponies and wild deer can be viewed from the hotel and on the many walks and paths that run through the forest. The hotel has its own Equestrian Centre, with BHS trained stable crew, heated outdoor pool and tennis court. It affords a perfect starting point from which to explore the surrounding countryside and to visit the nearby coast and sailing of the Solent. The lively Polo Bar offers a light menu throughout the day whilst the romantic restaurant provides a more extensive menu serving traditional British cuisine with a continental twist. The views from the New Forest room, with its picture windows, provides a wonderful setting for parties and functions, which are tailor-made to suit personal requirements.

Our inspector loved: The wonderful opportunity for riding in the New Forest from the hotels' own stables.

Directions: New Park Manor is ½ mile off the A337 between Lyndhurst and Brockenhurst, easily reached from the M27 junction 1.

Web: www.johansens.com/newparkmanor
E-mail: info@newparkmanorhotel.co.uk
Tel: 0870 381 8761
International: +44 (0)1590 623467
Fax: 01590 622268

Price Guide:
single from £90
double/twin from £120
four poster from £210

145

PASSFORD HOUSE HOTEL

MOUNT PLEASANT LANE, LYMINGTON, HAMPSHIRE SO41 8LS

Set in 9 acres of picturesque gardens and rolling parkland, the Passford House Hotel lies midway between the charming New Forest village of Sway and the Georgian splendour of Lymington. Once the home of Lord Arthur Cecil, it is steeped in history and the traditions of leisurely country life. Pleasantly decorated bedrooms include a number of superior rooms, whilst comfort is the keynote in the 4 public lounges. The hotel prides itself on the standard and variety of cuisine served in its delightful restaurant and the extensive menu aims to give pleasure to the most discerning of palates. Meals are complemented by a speciality wine list. The hotel boasts a compact leisure centre, catering for all ages and activities. In addition to 2 heated swimming pools, there is a multi-gym, sauna, pool table, croquet lawn, pétanque and tennis court. Just a short drive away are Beaulieu, the cathedral cities of Winchester and Salisbury and ferry ports to the Isle of Wight and France. The New Forest has numerous golf courses, riding and trekking centres, cycling paths, beautiful walks, and of course sailing on the Solent. Milford-on-Sea, 4 miles away, is the nearest beach.

Directions: Exit 1/M27, A337 to Brockenhurst. After railway bridge and mini roundabout, right at Tollhouse Pub and bear right into Mount Pleasant Lane. Hotel is 1 mile past garden centre.

Web: www.johansens.com/passfordhouse
E-mail: sales@passfordhousehotel.co.uk
Tel: 0870 381 8804
International: +44 (0)1590 682398
Fax: 01590 683494

Price Guide:
single from £80
double/twin from £130

Basingstoke

Winchester

Southampton

Portsmouth

Lymington

Our inspector loved: *Every year another improvement - guests' pleasure is at the heart of this hotel.*

CHEWTON GLEN

NEW MILTON, NEW FOREST, HAMPSHIRE BH25 6QS

Voted Best Country House Hotel in the World by Gourmet magazine, Chewton Glen is set in 130 acres of gardens, woodland and parkland on the edge of the New Forest, close to the sea. Owners Martin and Brigitte Skan have created a haven of tranquillity, luxury and comfort. The wonderful setting of the restaurant, which overlooks the landscaped gardens, adds to the sublime culinary experience created by head chef Luke Matthews, who uses fresh local produce to create surprising and delicious dishes, complemented by an impressive wine list. The 58 sumptuous bedrooms, all individually designed with carefully chosen fabrics, are the ultimate in luxury with fantastic marble bathrooms, cosy bathrobes and views over the surrounding parkland. The stunning Spa opened in spring 2002. In addition to the magnificent 17.5m pool, there are now improved changing rooms with their own steam room and sauna, more treatment rooms, larger gym, hydrotherapy pool and a totally new lounge, buffet and bar with a conservatory and sun terrace. There are indoor and outdoor tennis courts, a 9-hole par 3 golf course and an outdoor swimming pool. Fishing, shooting and riding can be arranged locally.

Our inspector loved: *The spacious, superbly styled ambience of the stunningly beautiful spa – here is your opportunity for total indulgence.*

Directions: Take A35 from Lyndhurst towards Bournemouth. Turn left at Walkford, then left before roundabout. The hotel is on the right.

Web: www.johansens.com/chewtonglen
E-mail: reservations@chewtonglen.com
Tel: 0870 381 8427
International: +44 (0)1425 275341
Fax: 01425 272310

Price Guide: (room only)
double £205–£445
suites £445–£780

CHILWORTH MANOR

CHILWORTH, SOUTHAMPTON, HAMPSHIRE SO16 7PT

Directions: Take the M3 and exit at junction 14. At the roundabout take the third exit towards Romsey (A27). Chilworth Manor is on the left after Clump Inn.

Web: www.johansens.com/chilworth
E-mail: sales@chilworth-manor.co.uk
Tel: 0870 381 9057
International: +44 (0)23 8076 7333
Fax: 023 8076 6392

Price Guide:
single from £47.50
double £95-£135
suite £160

A long, sweeping, tree-lined drive leads visitors to this imposing Edwardian manor house situated in 12 landscaped acres of glorious Hampshire countryside. The mellow, cream coloured stone exterior is highlighted by tall, slim, sparkling wide sash windows and an attractive balustrade. Heavy, dark oak-front doors open into a magnificent galleried hall, which sets the pattern for a rich and gracious interior overhung with a wealth of historical ambience, charm and comfort. There are 26 bedrooms with panoramic estate views in the Manor and 69 in the Garden Wing; all have been refurbished to a high standard, are pleasantly decorated and have every comfort, including 24-hour room service. Dining in the elegant restaurant is a delight, to be sampled leisurely whilst enjoying views over and beyond manicured lawns and colourful flower beds. The hotel's cuisine is innovative and imaginative and complemented by an extensive international wine list. For the energetic there is a jogging route within the grounds and a hard tennis court. Southampton's splendid shopping facilities and nightlife are within easy reach, as is Portsmouth and the cathedral city of Winchester. Extensive purpose-built conference and meeting facilities are available.

Our inspector loved: *Its lovely grounds and its surprising proximity to the town of Romsey and the urban and maritime delights of Portsmouth and Southampton.*

HOTEL DU VIN & BISTRO

SOUTHGATE STREET, WINCHESTER, HAMPSHIRE SO23 9EF

Relaxed, charming and unpretentious are words which aptly describe the stylish and intimate Hotel du Vin & Bistro. This elegant hotel is housed in one of Winchester's most important Georgian buildings, dating back to 1715. It was the first of this successful group's properties and established an entirely new approach to what hotels are all about. The 23 individually decorated bedrooms feature superb beds made up with crisp Egyptian cotton and offer every modern amenity, including trouser press, mini bar and CD players. Each bedroom is sponsored by a wine house whose vineyard features in its decorations. Bathrooms boasting power showers, oversized baths and fluffy towels and robes add to guests' sense of luxury and comfort. Quality food cooked simply with fresh ingredients is the philosophy behind the Bistro, where, as you would expect, an outstanding and reasonably priced wine list is available. There are also 2 function rooms for special occasions. The welcoming and enthusiastic staff cater for every need. The hotel is a perfect base for exploring England's ancient capital, famous for its cathedral, its school and antique shops. The New Forest is a short drive away.

Our inspector loved: The exciting bustle of this town centre haven of good living.

Directions: Take the M3 to Winchester. Southgate Street leads from the city centre to St Cross.

Web: www.johansens.com/hotelduvinwinchester
E-mail: reception@winchester.hotelduvin.com
Tel: 0870 381 8615
International: +44 (0)1962 841414
Fax: 01962 842458

Price Guide: (room only)
double/twin £115–£185
suite £190–£230

THE GROVE HOTEL

CHANDLER'S CROSS, HERTFORDSHIRE WD3 4TG

Directions: From M25 clockwise junction 19, anti-clockwise junction 20.

Web: www.johansens.com/thegrove
E-mail: info@the grove.co.uk
Tel: 0870 381 8646
International: +44 (0)1923 807807
Fax: 01923 221008

Price Guide: (excluding VAT)
single £240–£320
double/twin £240–£320
suite £450–£900

This magnificent 18th-century former home of the Earls of Clarendon stands in 300 acres of Hertfordshire countryside and has been painstakingly restored and transformed into an impressive cosmopolitan country estate just 45 minutes from the centre of London. The Grove brings together the best of 21st-century living with all that makes a memorable past era so beguiling and attractive: the peace of the countryside, a friendly, personal welcome, a sense of sanctuary and refuge. The attention to detail and quality is balanced with the ethos of pleasure and the wellbeing of guests. The Grove has character, feel and style. Its gardens, grounds and woodland walks are superb; its food, wine, and staff are excellent. The interior is gorgeous and grand with antiques set against contemporary elegance, fine pictures and quirky little effects. Guest rooms and suites are luxuriously appointed. Many have balconies or terraces, some boast working fireplaces, and all offer panoramic garden and parkland views. There are 3 bars, 3 restaurants and a spa with 13 treatment rooms, a saltwater vitality pool, fitness and exercise studios, plus an indoor and outdoor swimming pool, tennis courts and 18-hole golf course.

Our inspector loved: The diverse elements that both surprise and delight.

DOWN HALL COUNTRY HOUSE HOTEL

HATFIELD HEATH, NEAR BISHOP'S STORTFORD, HERTFORDSHIRE CM22 7AS

Set in 110 acres of parkland, this Italianate mansion is the perfect choice for those wishing to escape the pressures of everyday life. A peaceful ambience pervades this tastefully restored country house hotel. The well-appointed bedrooms all feature period furnishings; and afford picturesque views across the grounds. Gastronomes will be pleased with the excellent cuisine served in the Downham and the new Ibbetsons 2 AA Rosette restaurant. Here, English and French dishes are prepared with only the finest fresh ingredients. The superb on-site sporting facilities include croquet lawn, swimming pool, sauna and whirlpool. Clay pigeon shooting, horse-riding and golf can be arranged nearby. Day excursions include visits to Cambridge, horse racing at Newmarket, Constable Country and the old timbered village of Thaxted. This is an ideal venue for board meetings, conferences, award dinners and corporate hospitality in a secluded environment. The rooms accommodate from 10 delegates boardroom style, up to 180 theatre style and a maximum of 500 for a dinner dance. An executive shuttle is available to and from Stansted Airport.

Our inspector loved: *The "wow factor" of the book-lined lift.*

Directions: The hotel is 14 miles from the M25, 7 miles from the M11 and Bishop's Stortford Station. Heathrow Airport is 60 miles away; Stansted is 9 miles. There is ample free parking.

Colchester
Stansted Airport
Harlow   Chelmsford
Southend-on-Sea

Web: www.johansens.com/downhall
E-mail: sales@downhall.co.uk
Tel: 0870 381 8489
International: +44 (0)1279 731441
Fax: 01279 730416

Price Guide:
single £140
double/twin £175
suite £235

SOPWELL HOUSE COUNTRY CLUB & SPA

COTTONMILL LANE, SOPWELL, ST ALBANS, HERTFORDSHIRE AL1 2HQ

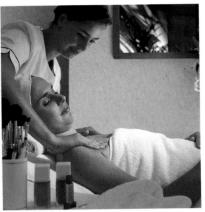

Once the country home of Lord Mountbatten, surrounded by a peaceful and verdant 12-acre estate, Sopwell House is an oasis just minutes away from the motorways. The classic reception rooms reflect its illustrious past and the grand panelled ballroom opens out onto the terraces and gardens. The bedrooms, some with four-posters, are spacious and well-equipped. Beautifully designed Mews Suites are ideal for long-stay executives and bridal parties. Superb English and international cuisine and fine wines are served in the enchanting 2 AA Rosette Magnolia Restaurant amidst the trees after which it is named, whilst Bejerano's Brasserie offers an informal ambience. The conference and banqueting suites, overlooking the splendid gardens and terrace, are popular venues for weddings and special events. A Business Centre provides guests with facilities such as photocopier, fax and e-mail. The Country Club & Spa, dedicated to health and relaxation, has a full range of fitness facilities and highly qualified beauty therapists, using ESPA and Clarins products.

Directions: Close to M25, M1, M10, A1(M). 28m from Heathrow Airport. From M25 or A414 take A1081 to St Albans. Turn left at Grillbar. Cross mini-roundabout. Hotel is ¼ mile on left.

Web: www.johansens.com/sopwellhouse
E-mail: enquiries@sopwellhouse.co.uk
Tel: 0870 381 8898
International: +44 (0)1727 864477
Fax: 01727 844741/845636

Price Guide: (room only)
single £99–£129
double/twin £169–£185
suites from £217

Our inspector loved: The huge entrance lobby with sofas and open fire set in a French cheateâu fireplace.

 GYM SPA

ST MICHAEL'S MANOR

ST MICHAEL'S VILLAGE, FISHPOOL STREET, ST ALBANS, HERTFORDSHIRE AL3 4RY

Owned and run by the Newling Ward family for the past 37 years, St Michael's Manor is a rare gem – peaceful, intimate, and set in delightful landscaped grounds. It is also within the historic village of St Michael's and a stone's throw from the magnificent St Albans Abbey. Each of the 22 bedrooms has been individually designed – some have four-poster beds and some are sitting-room suites – and all have an elegance and charm. Many of the bedrooms overlook the award-winning grounds, set in 5 acres, with wide sweeping lawns and a beautiful lake that hosts a variety of wildlife. The Georgian lounge and the award-winning conservatory dining room also overlook the gardens and make a wonderful setting for a tantalising dinner. There is also an excellent variety of vegetarian dishes. Coffee may be served in the Oak Lounge, which dates from 1586, with its fine panelled walls and original Elizabethan ceiling. Hatfield House and the Roman remains of Verulamium are within easy reach, as is London, which is only 20 minutes away by train. Weekend rates from £60 per person are available.

Our inspector loved: The gardens and the lake; they are wonderful.

Directions: Easy access to the M1, junction 6/7, M25, junction 21a - 10 minutes; M4/M40 - 25 minutes; Luton Airport - 20 minutes.

Web: www.johansens.com/stmichaelsmanor
E-mail: reservations@stmichaelsmanor.com
Tel: 0870 381 8906
International: +44 (0)1727 864444
Fax: 01727 848909

Stevenage   Stansted
             Bishop's
             Stortford
             Hertford
St Albans

Price Guide:
single £125–£195
double/twin £160–£260
suite £245–£320

THE PENDLEY MANOR HOTEL

COW LANE, TRING, HERTFORDSHIRE HP23 5QY

Directions: Leave the M25 at junction 20 and take the new A41. Take the exit marked "Tring". At the roundabout take the A4251, then 1st right turn into Cow Lane.

Web: www.johansens.com/pendleymanor
E-mail: sales@pendley-manor.co.uk
Tel: 0870 381 8812
International: +44 (0)1442 891891
Fax: 01442 890687

Price Guide:
single £110
double/twin £130–£150
suites £160

The Pendley Manor was commissioned by Joseph Grout Williams in 1872. His instructions, to architect John Lion, were to build it in the Tudor style, reflecting the owner's interest in flora and fauna on the carved woodwork and stained-glass panels. The bedrooms are attractively furnished and well equipped and the restaurant boasts AA and RAC awards. Pendley Manor offers flexible conference facilities for up to 350 people. 9 purpose-built conference suites and 8 syndicate rooms, all with natural daylight, are available. Team-building and multi-activity days within the grounds can be arranged as well as marquee events. On the estate, which lies at the foot of the Chiltern Hills, sporting facilities include tennis courts, gymnasium, a snooker room with full-size table, games rooms, buggy riding, laser shooting, archery and hot-air balloon rides. The hotel's new health and leisure facilities include an indoor heated swimming pool, Jacuzzi, sauna and solarium. The beauty spa now offers a full range of Clarins treatments Places of interest nearby include Woburn, Winslow Hall, Chenies Manor, Tring Zoological Museum and Dunstable Downs.

Our inspector loved: The sophisticated swimming pool and the diversity of the special events, such as the annual flower show with Charlie Dimmock and the outdoor Shakespeare festival.

THE PRIORY BAY HOTEL

PRIORY DRIVE, SEAVIEW, ISLE OF WIGHT PO34 5BU

From decades gone by this beautiful site has been built upon by Medieval monks, Tudor farmers and Georgian gentry. Now its medley of buildings has been sympathetically restored and brought to life as a splendid hotel. Situated in a gorgeous open coastal setting to the south of Seaview, the Priory Bay overlooks its own private beach. Everything about it is stylish and elegant, from the impressive arched stone entrance with magnificent carved figures to the delightful, flower-filled gardens with their shady corners and thatched roofed tithe barns. The public rooms are a delight, exquisitely and comfortably furnished, with tall windows framed by rich curtains and liberally filled with vases of flowers. Log fires blaze in open fireplaces during colder months. Each of the 18 comfortable bedrooms is individually decorated and has picturesque views over the gardens. The dining room is establishing a reputation for first-class gastronomy, complemented by a fine wine list. Guests can relax under shady umbrellas in the garden or on the surrounding terraces. For the more energetic guest, there is an outdoor pool and the hotel's adjoining 9-hole golf course. The islands' coastal paths for walking and riding passes the gate, Carisbrooke Castle and Osborne House are nearby.

Our inspector loved: This totally relaxing destination - families are especially welcome here.

Directions: Ferry from Portsmouth, Lymington or Southampton to Fishbourne, Yarmouth. Ryde, East or West Cowes. The hotel is on the B3330.

Web: www.johansens.com/priorybayiow
E-mail: reception@priorybay.co.uk
Tel: 0870 381 8839
International: +44 (0)1983 613146
Fax: 01983 616539

Price Guide:
single £80–£220
double/twin £150–£260

EASTWELL MANOR

BOUGHTON LEES, NEAR ASHFORD, KENT TN25 4HR

Directions: M20, junction 9. Turn left into Trinity Road over 4 roundabouts turn left onto the A251. The hotel is 1 mile, on the left.

Web: www.johansens.com/eastwellmanor
E-mail: enquiries@eastwellmanor.co.uk
Tel: 0870 381 8498
International: +44 (0)1233 213000
Fax: 01233 635530

Price Guide:
single From £190
double/twin £220–£310
suites £265–£395

Set in the "Garden of England", Eastwell Manor has a past steeped in history dating back to the 16th century when Richard Plantagenet, son of Richard III, lived on the estate. Surrounded by impressive grounds it encompasses a formal Italian garden, scented rose gardens and attractive lawns and parkland. The magnificent exterior is matched by the splendour of the interior. Exquisite plasterwork and carved oak panelling adorn the public rooms whilst throughout the Manor interesting antique pieces abound. The individually furnished bedrooms and suites, some with fine views across the gardens, feature every possible comfort. There are 19 courtyard apartments giving 39 more bedrooms, all with en-suite facilities. The new health and fitness spa features an indoor and outdoor heated 20m pool, hydrotherapy pool, sauna, steam room, Technogym gymnasium and 15 beauty treatment rooms. Guests can enjoy a choice of dining experiences, fine British cuisine in the Manor Restaurant, and a similar standard of food at the less formal Brasserie. Nearby attractions include the cathedral city of Canterbury, Leeds Castle and several charming market towns. Situated near Ashford Eurostar station, Eastwell is perfect for trips to Paris and Brussels.

Our inspector loved: *The topiary walks and gardens - a perfect setting for this magnificent ancient building.*

ROWHILL GRANGE HOTEL AND SPA

WILMINGTON, DARTFORD, KENT DA2 7QH

An unexpected find on the outer edge of London bordering on the Kent countryside, Rowhill Grange nestles in 9 acres of woodlands and mature gardens descending to a picturesque lake. A combination of top service and friendliness makes Rowhill Grange the perfect venue for everything from weekend breaks to special occasions such as weddings and anniversaries. All the luxurious bedrooms boast individual character and decoration, with a full range of facilities available to ensure maximum comfort and convenience for guests. The à la carte Restaurant is supplemented with the delightful Brasserie. From late spring and through the summer months guests may take dinner on the terrace, sharing a scenic view with the swans and ducks. For special occasions, business meetings or dinners, private dining rooms are available. The Clockhouse Suite is a self- contained functions annexe with a dining/dancing area, comfortable lounge and a bar. The Utopia Health and Leisure Spa is outstanding with all the latest equipment for women and for men including the UK's first therapy pool of its kind.

Our inspector loved: *The Spa Brasserie - always filled with activity - and the stunning bedrooms.*

Directions: M20 junction 1/M25 junction 3. Take the B2173 into Swanley and B258 north at Superstore roundabout. After Hextable Green the entrance is almost immediately on the left.

Web: www.johansens.com/rowhillgrange
E-mail: admin@rowhillgrange.com
Tel: 0870 381 8870
International: +44 (0)1322 615136
Fax: +44 (0)1322 615137

Price Guide: (room only)
single £155–£190
double/twin £180–£220
suite £200–£330

CHILSTON PARK

SANDWAY, LENHAM, NR MAIDSTONE, KENT ME17 2BE

This magnificent Grade I listed mansion, one of England's most richly decorated hotels, was built in the 13th century and remodelled in the 18th century. Now sensitively refurbished, the hotel's ambience is enhanced by the lighting, at dusk each day, of over 200 candles. The drawing room and reading room offer guests an opportunity to relax and to admire the outstanding collection of antiques. The entire hotel is a treasure trove full of many interesting objets d'art. The opulently furnished bedrooms are fitted to a high standard and many have four-poster beds. Good, fresh English cooking features on outstanding menus supported by an excellent wine list. Several intimate and delightful rooms afford wonderful opportunities for private dining parties. In keeping with the traditions of a country house, a wide variety of sporting activities are available, golf and riding nearby, fishing in the natural spring lake and punting.

Directions: Take junction 8 off the M20, then A20 towards Lenham. Turn left into Boughton Road. Go over the crossroads and M20; Chilston Park is on the left.

Our inspector loved: The astonishing collections of object d,art.

Web: www.johansens.com/chilstonpark
E-mail: chilstonpark@handpicked.co.uk
Tel: 0870 381 8428
International: +44 (0)1622 859803
Fax: 01622 858588

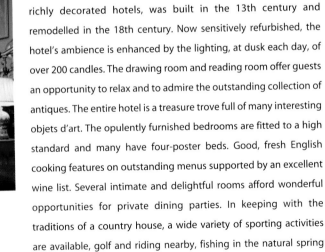

Price Guide:
single from £90
double/twin from £130
suite from £295

HOTEL DU VIN & BISTRO

CRESCENT ROAD, ROYAL TUNBRIDGE WELLS, KENT TN1 2LY

Set in the historic town of Tunbridge Wells, this Grade II sandstone mansion dates back to 1762 and although in the centre, it enjoys spectacular views over Calverley Park. An inviting ambience is present throughout the property, from the convivial bar to the sunny terrace. The 35 en suite bedrooms have been individually decorated and are enhanced by superb Egyptian linen, CD players and satellite television. The spacious bathrooms feature power showers, large baths and fluffy robes and towels. The hotel takes great pride in its excellent bistro cuisine and the outstanding wine list. The imaginative dishes are prepared using the freshest local ingredients and are exceptionally good value. Fine wine dinners are often held at the hotel, whilst private tastings may be organised given prior notice. There are many castles, gardens and stately homes within the vicinity, such as Chartwell, Groombridge Place and Hever Castle. Guests can work up their appetites by rambling through the orchards and hop fields, perusing the shops and boutiques in the Pantiles or playing golf nearby.

Our inspector loved: The ambience: this is such a relaxed and comfortable hotel, entirely at ease with its place in the scheme of things.

Directions: From the M25 take the A21 south in the direction of Hastings to Tunbridge Wells. The hotel is within the town centre and has parking facilities.

Web: www.johansens.com/hotelduvintunbridge
E-mail: info@tunbridgewells.hotelduvin.com
Tel: 0870 381 8614
International: +44 (0)1892 526455
Fax: 01892 512044

Price Guide: (room only)
double from £89
large double from £120
suite from £195

THE SPA HOTEL

MOUNT EPHRAIM, ROYAL TUNBRIDGE WELLS, KENT TN4 8XJ

The Spa Hotel was originally built in 1766 as a country mansion with its own landscaped gardens and 3 beautiful lakes. A hotel for over a century now, it retains standards of service reminiscent of life in Georgian and Regency England. All the bedrooms are individually furnished and many offer spectacular views. Above all else, The Spa prides itself on the excellence of its cuisine. The grand, award-winning Chandelier restaurant features the freshest produce from Kentish farms and London markets complemented by a carefully selected wine list. Within the hotel is Sparkling Health, a magnificent health and leisure centre, which is equipped to the highest standards. Leisure facilities include an indoor heated swimming pool, a fully equipped state-of-the-art gymnasium, cardio-vascular gymnasium, steam room, sauna, beauty and hairdressing salons, floodlit hard tennis court and ½ mile jogging track. The newly established stables include gentle trails and safe paddocks for children to enjoy pony-riding under expert guidance. Special half-board weekend breaks are offered, for a minimum 2-night stay, with rates from £91 per person per night – full details available upon request.

Directions: The hotel faces the common on the A264 in Tunbridge Wells.

Web: www.johansens.com/spahotel
E-mail: reservations@spahotel.co.uk
Tel: 0870 381 8901
International: +44 (0)1892 520331
Fax: 01892 510575

Price Guide: (room only)
single £94–£104
double/twin £119–£180

Our inspector loved: The newly created top floor suites - more space than ever.

        SPA

NORTHCOTE MANOR

NORTHCOTE ROAD, LANGHO, BLACKBURN, LANCASHIRE BB6 8BE

Large, redbrick and typically Victorian, this attractive and externally decorative hotel stands in the foothills of the Ribble Valley amidst some of Lancashire's most spectacular countryside. Excellently run by joint proprietors Craig Bancroft, a wine connoisseur, and Nigel Haworth, an award-winning chef, Northcote Manor has been an esteemed restaurant with rooms since 1983. Its high standards of hospitality, comfort, décor and food has earned it the prestigious award of "The Independent Hotel of the Year" by the Caterer and Hotelkeeper. Nigel, proud member of the Academy of Culinary Arts, trained in Switzerland and London and his gourmet cuisine has received innumerable accolades, including a Michelin Star and Egon Ronay's 1995 Chef of the Year distinction. His superb local and creative International dishes are presented with professionalism and aplomb in a delightful restaurant. Each meal is complemented by a superb wine list that is 400 bin strong. The hotel has 14 beautifully furnished, en-suite bedrooms that offer every comfort. Nearby are the Trough of Bowland and the Roman town of Ribchester, and 4 golf courses are within a 10 mile radius. The Yorkshire Dales and Lake District are within easy reach.

Our inspector loved: The delicious cuisine featuring local and home grown produce.

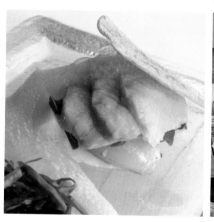

Directions: From M6 junction 31 take A59 towards Glitheroe. After 8 miles turn left into Northcote Road, immediately before the Langho roundabout.

Web: www.johansens.com/northcotelancs
E-mail: sales@northcotemanor.com
Tel: 0870 381 8766
International: +44 (0)1254 240555
Fax: 01254 246568

Price Guide:
single £110–£145
double/twin £140–£175

NEW

THE PINES HOTEL

CLAYTON–LE–WOODS, CHORLEY, LANCASHIRE PR6 7ED

Directions: Take junction 28 off the M6 then the B5256 towards Chorley. At the roundabout turn right onto the A6 towards Chorley and the hotel is immediately on the left.

Web: www.johansens.com/thepines
E-mail: mail@thepineshotel.co.uk
Tel: 0870 381 9274
International: +44 (0)1772 338551
Fax: 01772 629002

Price Guide:
single £75–£100
double/twin £85–£110
suite £110–£140

Built in 1895, this Victorian-style hotel proudly stands within landscaped gardens and mature woodlands. Owner and managing director, Betty Duffin, takes an active role in the day-to-day running of the hotel to ensure that each guest is guaranteed an enjoyable and comfortable stay. Each of the 37 guest rooms has en suite facilities and are individually decorated. De luxe rooms boast Jacuzzi showers, Jacuzzi baths and 4-poster beds whilst telephone, Internet access and voice mail are standard in all bedrooms. Before adjourning to haworth's bar & grill or the more intimate Crystal Room, which is perfect for private dining, guests are welcome to relax in the lounge and visit the well-equipped bar and sample many of the 150 bottles of wine on offer. The highly respected kitchen brigade creates a varied à la carte menu and creates imaginative daily specials. Private dinners, parties and weddings can be accommodated in the Dixon Suite with attentive staff on-hand to provide support; weekly cabaret and dinner dances are also very popular. Haydock Park Race Course and Blackpool are nearby.

Our inspector loved: The relaxed and informal atmosphere in haworth's bar & grill.

THE GIBBON BRIDGE HOTEL

NR CHIPPING, FOREST OF BOWLAND, LANCASHIRE PR3 2TQ

This award-winning hotel in the heart of Lancashire in the Forest of Bowland is a welcoming and peaceful retreat. The area, a favourite of the Queen, is now officially recognised as the Centre of the Kingdom! Created in 1982 by resident proprietor Janet Simpson and her late Mother Margaret, the buildings combine traditional architecture with interesting Gothic masonry. Individually designed and equipped to the highest standard, the 7 bedrooms and 22 suites include four-posters, half-testers, Gothic brass beds and whirlpool baths. The restaurant overlooks the garden and is renowned for traditional and imaginative dishes incorporating home-grown vegetables and herbs. The garden bandstand is perfect for musical repertoires or civil wedding ceremonies. Elegant rooms, lounges and a unique al fresco dining area are available for private dinner parties and wedding receptions. For executive meetings and conference facilities the hotel will offer that "something a bit different". Leisure facilities include beauty studio, gymnasium, solarium, steam room, all-weather tennis court and outdoor activities.

Our inspector loved: *The spectacular landscaped gardens surrounding the bandstand.*

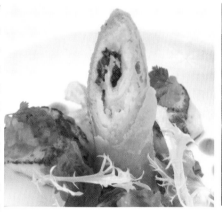

Directions: From the south: M6 Exit 31A, follow signs for Longridge. From the north: M6 Exit 32, follow A6 to Broughton and B5269 to Longridge. At Longridge follow signs for Chipping for approx 3 miles, then follow Gibbon Bridge brown tourism signs.

Lancaster

Blackpool

Preston Blackburn

Web: www.johansens.com/gibbonbridge
E-mail: reception@gibbon–bridge.co.uk
Tel: 0870 381 8544
International: +44 (0)1995 61456
Fax: 01995 61277

Price Guide:
single £80–£120
double/twin £120
suite £150–250

QUORN COUNTRY HOTEL

66 LEICESTER ROAD, QUORN, LEICESTERSHIRE LE12 8BB

Directions: Situated just off the A6 Leicester to Derby main road, in the bypassed village of Quorn (Quorndon), 5 miles from Jct 23 of the M1 from North, Jct 21A from South, East and West.

Web: www.johansens.com/quorncountry
E-mail: reservations@quorncountryhotel.co.uk
Tel: 0870 381 8847
International: +44 (0)1509 415050
Fax: 01509 415557

Burton-Upon-Trent
Melton Mowbray
Leicester
Hinckley

Price Guide: (room only)
single £82–£105
double/twin £95–£145
suite £130– £155

Originally Leicestershire's most exclusive private club, created around the original 17th-century listed building, this award-winning 4-star hotel is set in 4 acres of landscaped gardens. For the tenth consecutive year the hotel has received all 3 RAC merit awards for excellence in cuisine, hospitality and comfort and was also a recipient of a second AA Rosette Award in 1997. The bedrooms are equipped to the very highest standard with attention given to every detail. Suitable for both the business traveller or for weekend guests seeking those extra touches, which help create the ideal peaceful retreat. Ladies travelling alone can feel reassured that their special needs are met and indeed exceeded. Particular emphasis is given to the enjoyment of food with a declared policy of using, whenever possible, the freshest local produce. Guests' stay will be enhanced by the choice of two different dining experiences. They can choose between the Shires Restaurant with its classical cuisine with a modern style or the Orangery Brasserie with its changing selection of contemporary dishes.

Our inspector loved: *The peaceful River Soar at the end of the garden by the rose walk.*

STAPLEFORD PARK HOTEL, SPA, GOLF & SPORTING ESTATE

NR. MELTON MOWBRAY, LEICESTERSHIRE LE14 2EF

A stately home and sporting estate where casual luxury is the byword. This 16th-century house was once coveted by Edward, Prince of Wales, but his mother Queen Victoria forbade him to buy it for fear that his morals would be corrupted by the Leicestershire hunting society! Today, Stapleford Park offers guests and club members a "lifestyle experience" to transcend all others in supreme surroundings with views over 500 acres of parkland. Stapleford was voted Top UK Hotel for Leisure Facilities by Condé Nast Traveller, Johansens Most Excellent Business Meeting Venue 2000 and holds innumerable awards for its style and hospitality. Individually designed bedrooms and a 4-bedroom cottage have been created by famous names such as Mulberry, Wedgwood, Zoffany and Crabtree & Evelyn. The British with European influences cuisine is carefully prepared to the highest standards and complemented by an adventurous wine list. Sports include fishing, shooting, falconry, riding, tennis and an 18-hole championship golf course designed by Donald Steel. The luxurious Clarins Spa with indoor pool, Jacuzzi, sauna and fitness room offers an array of health therapies. 11 elegant function and dining rooms are suited to private dinners, special occasions and corporate hospitality.

Our inspector loved: *The grandeur and the magnificence of the building and the stunning grounds.*

Directions: By train Kings Cross/Grantham in 1 hour. Take the A1 north to Colsterworth then the B676 via Saxby.

Web: www.johansens.com/staplefordpark
E-mail: reservations@stapleford.co.uk
Tel: 0870 381 8912
International: +44 (0)1572 787 522
Fax: 01572 787 651

Price Guide:
double/twin £205–£359
suites from £488

THE ANGEL AND ROYAL HOTEL

HIGH STREET, GRANTHAM, LINCOLNSHIRE NG31 6PN

Directions: From the A1 follow the town centre signs.

Web: www.johansens.com/angelandroyal
E-mail: enquiries@angelandroyalhotel.co.uk
Tel: 0870 381 9164
International: +44 (0)1476 565816
Fax: 01476 567149

Price Guide:
single £75–£115
double/twin £115–£165

With a history spanning 800 years and a reputation as the oldest inn in England, The Angel and Royal is a fascinating and memorable place to stay. The "Angel" was a medieval sign illustrating the connection between religious houses and travellers' inns, but despite visitations by 7 kings over the centuries, it wasn't until a visit from Edward VII in 1866 that "Royal" was added to create the existing name. The main façade was built 600 years ago, although the site had already been an inn for 200 years, and the ancient cellars and tunnels date back to the 9th century. Since undergoing a recent £2-million refurbishment, the present owners have successfully combined the enthralling history of The Angel and Royal with every contemporary comfort and convenience. The centre-piece of the Angel Bar must be its impressive 9ft x 6ft medieval fireplace, whilst the Kings Restaurant features original carved stone panelling, oriel windows and a spiral staircase leading to the turret. Both make excellent venues for private functions. A perfect blend of luxury and elegance, the bedrooms feature sophisticated bathrooms and novel extras. Local attractions include Belvoir Castle, Rutland Water, the historic town of Stamford, Belton House and Lincoln with its magnificent cathedral.

Our inspector loved: The newly refurbished bedrooms - choose from modern elegance or truly traditional styles.

NEW

THE LINCOLN HOTEL

EASTGATE, LINCOLN LN2 1PN

Historic Lincoln, with its Roman remains, second largest cathedral in England, Norman castle, Medieval buildings and cobbled streets surround this extremely modern hotel, with its subtle décor and 21st-century freshness that delights the senses. The Lincoln Hotel is situated opposite the majestic, triple-towered 12th-century cathedral with views of its 365ft high, honey-coloured stone walls from the comfortable lounge and brasserie. Carefully selected furnishings and the finest of fabrics have been judiciously chosen to enrich the hotel's appeal and big beds together with chic bathrooms feature prominently in the spacious bedrooms. Excellent cuisine, incorporating the freshest Lincolnshire produce, can be enjoyed in the coolly elegant restaurant or informal brasserie while pre and after dinner drinks, mid-morning coffee and afternoon tea can be taken in the small, tranquil garden set within Roman walls; a scenic setting for a special celebration. In addition to sightseeing and shopping in the city there are many delightful villages to explore in the nearby area and numerous historic properties such as the Elizabethan Manor House, Doddington Hall and the Norman Boothby Park Manor. There is motor racing at Cadwell Park and horse racing at Market Rasen.

Our inspector loved: The shark in the lounge - is it Jaws?

Directions: From the A1 take the A46 at Newark and follow signs to the historic city centre.

Web: www.johansens.com/lincolnhotel
E-mail: sales@lincolnhotel.com
Tel: 0870 381 9288
International: +44 (0)1522 520348
Fax: 01522 510780

Price Guide:
single £75–£95
double £80–£110

Scunthorpe

Louth

Lincoln

Grantham

Stamford

167

THE GEORGE OF STAMFORD

ST MARTINS, STAMFORD, LINCOLNSHIRE PE9 2LB

Directions: Stamford is a mile from the A1 on the B1081. The George is in the town centre opposite the gallows sign. Car parking is behind the hotel.

Web: www.johansens.com/georgeofstamford
E-mail: reservations@georgehotelofstamford.com
Tel: 0870 381 8543
International: +44 (0)1780 750750
Fax: 01780 750701

Price Guide:
single from £78–£120
double/twin from £110–£225
suite £150–£170

The George, a beautiful, 16th-century coaching inn, retains the charm of its long history, as guests will sense on entering the reception hall with its oak travelling chests and famous oil portrait of Daniel Lambert. Over the years, The George has welcomed a diverse clientèle, ranging from highwaymen to kings – Charles I and William III were both visitors. At the heart of the hotel is the lounge, its natural stone walls, deep easy chairs and softly lit alcoves imparting a cosy, relaxed atmosphere, whilst the blazing log fire is sometimes used to toast muffins for tea! The flair of Julia Vannocci's interior design is evident in all the expertly styled, fully appointed bedrooms. Exotic plants, orchids, orange trees and coconut palms feature in the Garden Lounge, where a choice of hot dishes and an extensive cold buffet are offered. Guests may also dine al fresco in the courtyard garden. The more formal, oak-panelled restaurant serves imaginative but traditional English dishes and an award-winning list of wines. Superb facilities are incorporated in the Business Centre, converted from the former livery stables. Special weekend breaks available.

Our inspector loved: *The delightful recently completed bas - relief frieze by Jenny Bell, depicting the legend of St George and the dragon.*

THE GORING

BEESTON PLACE, LONDON SW1W 0JW

Founded by O R Goring, the present owner's grandfather, in 1910, The Goring is the oldest family-owned and run hotel in London. Its close proximity to Buckingham Palace has virtually made it an "annexe" to the Palace, frequently accommodating British and foreign royalty on State occasions. A warm welcome and outstanding personal service are the hallmarks of this friendly hotel, which was built in Edwardian Baroque style and was the first in the world to offer central heating and en-suite bathrooms. Each of the luxuriously appointed bedrooms is individually designed and decorated; many overlook the private garden – the largest, and quietest, of any central London hotel. Traditional English cuisine with a few continental touches and superb wines can be enjoyed in the elegant dining room, acclaimed as one of the best restaurants in London, whilst the delightful Garden Bar is the ideal venue for a pre-dinner drink and chat. Private dining, larger functions, weddings and meetings can be catered for, and the hotel is happy to help organise a multitude of events. Guests receive free membership of the fully equipped local health club, which is only a short stroll away. The City and London's major attractions are all within easy reach.

Our inspector loved: The very pretty garden bar overlooking the hotel's private garden.

Directions: The hotel is a 5-minute walk from Victoria Station with direct rail links to Gatwick and Heathrow airports.

Web: www.johansens.com/goring
E-mail: reception@goringhotel.co.uk
Tel: 0870 381 9328
International: +44 (0) 20 7396 9000
Fax: 020 7834 4393

Price Guide: (excluding breakfast & VAT)
double/twin £210–£340
suite £340–£395

Enfield

Central London

Richmond

Croydon

41

41 BUCKINGHAM PALACE ROAD, LONDON SW1W 0PS

Directions: Victoria Station and Underground links are within minutes' walk; Gatwick Express 30 minutes; Heathrow 40 minutes.

Web: www.johansens.com/41buckinghampalaceroad
E-mail: book41@rchmail.com
Tel: 0870 381 8300
International: +44 (0)20 7300 0041
Fax: 020 7300 0141

Price Guide:
king bedded £295
junior suite £495
master suite £695

This small and intimate, AA 5 Red Star Hotel is quietly situated, overlooking the Royal Mews and Buckingham Palace Gardens. Adjacent also to St James's Park it is perfectly positioned for access to the City and West End. The hotel reflects a remarkable attention to detail, from its discreet and secluded guest entrance and magnificent architectural features to the beautiful furniture and club-like qualities of its superb day rooms. The 18 de luxe bedrooms and 2 split-level suites are furnished with traditional mahogany and black leather décor. With affordable 5-star service, continental breakfast and a variety of tasty snacks are served in the Executive Lounge. Flooded with natural daylight and comfortable chairs, the Lounge is the perfect place to read, meet or just take a moment to unwind. "41" has the world's most comfortable, handmade English mattresses and pure wool carpets throughout, bathrooms are in marble with bespoke bath and beauty products. Every room features an interactive entertainment centre with DVD/CD players and full high speed Internet/e-mail facilities. A state-of-the-art boardroom offers ISDN teleconferencing and private dining. 41 offers secretarial support, chauffeur driven cars, butler and chef services. Trafalgar Square, the Houses of Parliament and West End theatres are all nearby.

Our inspector loved: The striking room décor and intimate feel to the hotel.

DRAYCOTT HOUSE APARTMENTS

10 DRAYCOTT AVENUE, CHELSEA, LONDON SW3 3AA

Draycott House is an attractive period town house, standing in a quiet, tree-lined avenue in the heart of Chelsea. Housed in an attractive period building, the apartments have been designed in traditional styles to provide the ideal surroundings and location for a leisure or business visit, combining comfort, privacy and security with a convenient location. All are spacious, luxury suites with a kitchen and a wonderful alternative to a hotel, with 1, 2 or 3 bedrooms. Some have private balconies, a roof terrace and overlook the private courtyard garden. Each apartment is fully equipped with all home comforts; cable television, video, DVD, CD/hi-fi, private direct lines for own telephone/fax/answer machine/data, provisions/continental breakfast on arrival. A complimentary membership to an exclusive nearby health club, maid service, covered garage parking and laundry service. Additional services include airport transfers, transport, catering, travel, theatre tickets, dry cleaning/laundry, childminding and secretarial services. The West End and the City are within easy reach. Knightsbridge within walking distance. Long term reservations may attract preferential terms.

Our inspector loved: These well appointed apartments, which are perfect for a long stay in London.

Directions: Draycott House is situated on the corner of Draycott Avenue and Draycott Place, close to Sloane Square.

Web: www.johansens.com/draycotthouseapartments
E-mail: sales@draycotthouse.co.uk
Tel: 0870 381 8490
International: +44 (0)20 7584 4659
Fax: 020 7225 3694

Price Guide: (excluding VAT)
£188–£235 per night
£1178–£2948 per week

THE MAYFLOWER HOTEL

26-28 TREBOVIR ROAD, LONDON SW5 9NJ

Directions: Between Earls Court Road and Warwick Road. The nearest underground station is Earls Court.

Web: www.johansens.com/mayflower
E-mail: info@mayflower-group.co.uk
Tel: 0870 381 9195
International: +44 (0)20 7370 0991
Fax: 020 7370 0994

Price Guide:
single £79
double £109
family room £130

This recently renovated hotel is located in 2 Edwardian town houses conveniently situated in central London. The interior has been designed in a unique style – a fusion of eastern influences with serene and spacious modern luxury. Pale stone and wood floors, rich, vibrant fabrics with Indian and oriental antiques abound in 48 individually decorated bedrooms, 4 of which have balconies. The elegant light rooms have high ceilings and fans, enhanced by beautiful hand-carved wardrobes and bedside tables with ornate beds covered in luxurious Andrew Martin fabrics. All rooms offer state-of-the-art technology with Internet access, wide-screen televisions, CD players, safes and tea and coffee making facilities. The en-suite bathrooms are stylish and sparkling in marble and chrome with superb walk-in showers. Guests can enjoy a complimentary continental buffet breakfast before venturing out to explore the nearby fashionable shopping areas of Knightsbridge and Chelsea or visit the V&A and The Natural History and Science Museum. The Mayflower's proximity to the famous Earl's Court Exhibition Centre makes it perfectly located to suit business travellers and corporate events. Earl's Court underground station is only a minute's walk away and provides direct access to Heathrow Airport, the City and the West End.

Our inspector loved: This gem of a hotel with the emphasis on design - a great find!.

WEST LODGE PARK COUNTRY HOUSE HOTEL

COCKFOSTERS ROAD, HADLEY WOOD, BARNET, HERTFORDSHIRE EN4 0PY

West Lodge Park is a country house hotel which stands in 34 acres of green belt parklands and gardens. These include a lake and an arboretum with hundreds of mature trees. Run by the Beale family for over 50 years, West Lodge Park was originally a gentleman's country seat, rebuilt in 1838 on the site of an earlier keeper's lodge. In the public rooms, antiques, original paintings and period furnishings create a restful atmosphere. All the bright and individually furnished bedrooms, many of which enjoy country views, have a full range of modern amenities. Well presented cuisine is available in the elegant restaurant. Beauty rooms feature Elemis products. Residents enjoy free membership and a free taxi to the nearby leisure centre, which has excellent facilities. Hatfield House and St Albans Abbey are a 15-minute drive away. The hotel is credited with AA 4 stars and 2 Rosettes, RAC 4 stars plus 3 merit awards. Enquire about special offers available.

Our inspector loved: *The stunning arboretum and the diverse programme of special events.*

Directions: The hotel is on the A111, 1 mile north of Cockfosters underground station and 1 mile south of junction 24 on the M25.

Web: www.johansens.com/westlodgepark
E-mail: westlodgepark@bealeshotels.co.uk
Tel: 0870 381 8978
International: +44 (0)20 8216 3900
Fax: 020 8216 3937

Price Guide:
single £90–£160
double/twin from £115–£180

KENSINGTON HOUSE HOTEL

15-16 PRINCE OF WALES TERRACE, KENSINGTON, LONDON W8 5PQ

Directions: The nearest underground station is High Street Kensington.

Web: www.johansens.com/kensingtonhouse
E-mail: reservations@kenhouse.com
Tel: 0870 381 8648
International: +44 (0)20 7937 2345
Fax: 020 7368 6700

Price Guide:
single £150
double/twin £175-£195
junior suites £215

This attractive hotel with its architecturally splendid tall, ornate windows and pillared entrance stands grandly on a 19th-century site long associated with style and elegance. Just off Kensington High Street, this charming town house is an ideal base from which to explore London's attractions. Views cover delightful mews houses, leafy streets and out across the City rooftops. The emphasis is on providing informal, professional service in an atmosphere of relaxation and comfort. Each of the 41 intimate bedrooms offers en-suite facilities. Rooms are bright and airy with modern furniture and fittings adding to the fresh, contemporary treatment of a classic design. Home-from-home comforts include crisp linen, duvets and bathrobes. Other features offered: courtesy tray, ceiling fan, voicemail, modem connection and in-room safe. The 2 junior suites can convert into a family room. The stylish Tiger Bar is a popular venue for coffee or cocktails prior to enjoying a delicious dinner, with a menu that draws on a range of influences offering both traditional and modern dishes. The serenity of Kensington Gardens is just a gentle stroll away and some of the capital's most fashionable shops, restaurants and cultural attractions are within walking distance. Weekend rates are available.

Our inspector loved: *The fresh contemporary feel to this hidden away town house hotel.*

THE MILESTONE HOTEL & APARTMENTS

1 KENSINGTON COURT, LONDON W8 5DL

The beautifully appointed Condé Nast Johansens award winning Milestone Hotel is situated opposite Kensington Palace with views over Kensington Gardens and the Royal parklands. A Victorian showpiece, this unique hotel has been carefully restored to its original splendour whilst incorporating every modern facility. The 57 bedrooms include 12 suites and 6 apartments; all are individually designed with antiques, elegant furnishings and some have private balconies. Guests may relax in the comfortable, panelled Park Lounge which, in company with all other rooms, provides a 24-hour service. The hotel's restaurant, Cheneston's, the early spelling of Kensington, has an elaborately carved ceiling, original fireplace and ornate windows. The Windsor Suite is a versatile function room, perfect for private dining and corporate meetings. The health and fitness centre offers guests the use of a Jacuzzi, sauna, new resistance pool and gymnasium. The traditional bar, Stables, on the ground floor as well as the bright and airy conservatory are ideal for meeting and entertaining friends. The Milestone is within walking distance of some of the finest shopping in Kensington and in Knightsbridge such as Harrods and is a short taxi ride to the West End, the heart of London's Theatreland. The Royal Albert Hall and all the museums in Exhibition Road are nearby.

Our inspector loved: *The Prince Albert suite, regency elegance at its very best.*

Directions: At the end of Kensington High Street, at the junction with Princes Gate.

Web: www.johansens.com/milestone
E-mail: bookms@rchmail.com
Tel: 0870 381 8732
International: +44 (0)020 7917 1000
Fax: 020 7917 1010

Enfield

Central London

Richmond

Croydon

Price Guide:
single from £280
double/twin £280–£470
suites £570–£820

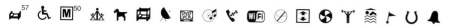

Twenty Nevern Square

20 NEVERN SQUARE, LONDON SW5 9PD

A unique experience in hospitality awaits guests at this elegant 4-star town house hotel. Sumptuously restored, the emphasis is on natural materials and beautiful hand-carved beds and furniture. The hotel overlooks a tranquil garden square and has its own delightful restaurant, Café Twenty, which is also available for small dinner and cocktail parties. Each of the 20 intimate bedrooms provides white marble, compact en-suite facilities, and is individually designed echoing both Asian and European influences. You can choose the delicate silks of the Chinese Room or a touch of opulence in the Rococo Room. The grandeur of the Pasha Suite, complete with four-poster bed and balcony, makes an ideal setting for a special occasion. All rooms have full modern facilities including wide-screen digital TV, CD player, private safe and a separate telephone and Internet/fax connection. Gym facilities are available by arrangement. The location is ideal – close to Earl's Court and Olympia exhibition centres and the tube. The Picadilly Line brings guests arriving at Heathrow in just over 30 minutes. Guests are a mere 10 minutes from London's most fashionable shopping areas, restaurants, theatres and cultural attractions such as the V&A and Science Museums.

Directions: 2 minutes from Earls Court station.

Web: www.johansens.com/twentynevernsquare
E-mail: hotel@twentynevernsquare.co.uk
Tel: 0870 381 8957
International: +44 (0)20 7565 9555
Fax: 020 7565 9444

Price Guide:
single £99–£130
double/twin £130–£165
suite £275

Our inspector loved: This very friendly townhouse hotel with its luxurious Eastern fabrics and furniture in all the rooms.

WARREN HOUSE

WARREN ROAD, COOMBE, KINGSTON-UPON-THAMES, SURREY KT2 7HY

This impressive 19th-century redbrick house with its York stone door surrounds, balustrades and tall chimneys stands in 4 acres of landscaped gardens. It is ideally situated for the business visitor, just 5 miles from central London, within easy reach of Heathrow and Gatwick airports and on the doorstep of Surrey's sweeping countryside and attractions. For some years Warren House has been an outstanding meeting venue with an unparalleled range of technology and equipment. Built in 1884, the house has been sensitively restored to its original style with the addition of 21st-century facilities. The en-suite bedrooms and suites are individually designed, tastefully decorated and furnished to the highest standard, including desk, television, direct dial telephone and modem connection. Chef Paul Bellingham prides himself on his international cuisine, attentively served in an elegant restaurant featuring an Oriental tiled fireplace. There is a spacious lounge, well-stocked library and excellent leisure facilities including a heated swimming pool and gymnasium. Richmond Park and 2 golf courses are close by with Hampton Court, Kew Gardens, Windsor, Sandown Park, Epsom and Kempton racecourses within easy reach.

Our inspector loved: *All of the outstanding features that made this hotel winner of Condé Nast Johansens Most Excellent Business Meetings Venue.*

Directions: From M25 Jct 10 follow A3 north to Robin Hood roundabout. Turn left onto A308 to Kingston Hill. At the top turn left after 2nd zebra crossing into Warren Road.

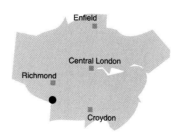

Web: www.johansens.com/warren
E-mail: info@warrenhouse.com
Tel: 0870 381 8969
International: +44 (0)20 8547 1777
Fax: 020 8547 1175

Price Guide:
single from £188
double/twin from £240

BEAUFORT HOUSE

45 BEAUFORT GARDENS, KNIGHTSBRIDGE, LONDON SW3 1PN

Directions: Beaufort Gardens leads off Brompton Road near Knightsbridge underground station. There is a 24hr car park nearby.

Web: www.johansens.com/beauforthouseapartments
E-mail: info@beauforthouse.co.uk
Tel: 0870 381 8350
International: +44 (0)20 7584 2600
Fax: 020 7584 6532

Price Guide: (excluding VAT)
£230–£650

Situated in Beaufort Gardens, a quiet tree-lined Regency cul-de-sac in the heart of Knightsbridge, 250 yards from Harrods, Beaufort House is an exclusive establishment comprising 21 self-contained fully serviced luxury apartments. All the comforts of a first-class hotel are combined with the privacy, discretion and relaxed atmosphere of home. Accommodation ranges in size from an intimate 1- bedroom to a spacious 4-bedroom apartment. Each apartment has been individually and traditionally decorated to the highest standard. All apartments have direct dial telephones with voice mail, personal safes, satellite television, DVD players and high speed Internet access. Some apartments benefit from balconies or patios. The fully equipped kitchens include washer/dryers and many have dishwashers. A daily maid service is included at no additional charge. Full laundry/dry cleaning services are available. A dedicated Guests Services team provides 24 hours coverage and will be happy to organise tours, theatre tickets, restaurant bookings, taxis or chauffeur driven limousines and other services. Complimentary membership at Aquilla's Health Club is offered to all guests during their stay. Awarded 5 stars by the English Tourism Council.

Our inspector loved: The stylish comfortable apartments which are perfect for the long stay guest in an ideal location.

NEW

THE CARLTON TOWER

ON CADOGAN PLACE, LONDON SW1X 9PY

In the heart of Knightsbridge, overlooking the private, leafy gardens of Cadogan Place, this 5-star luxury hotel successfully combines ultra modern convenience and facilities with traditional hospitality. The ideal city venue for the leisure and business visitor alike, Harrods and some of the capital's most fashionable shops are within walking distance and the bright lights of the West End and the financial areas of The City can be reached by a short taxi ride or tube journey. Beautifully furnished and decorated, an understated elegance pervades the hotel. The stylish and spacious bedrooms, including 59 suites and a Presidential Suite on the 18th floor, are equipped with every amenity and comfort expected from a leading hotel, such as air conditioning, modem access and fax machine. All rooms offer memorable London views. Arguably London's finest, the 184m^2 Presidential Suite offers unmatched accommodation and boasts a private sauna, enhanced security and the highest level of personalized service. The hotel is proud of its eclectic mix of restaurants and bars: the Rib Room & Oyster Bar is an acknowledged gourmet delight for those who enjoy the finest steaks. Extensive facilities at the rooftop health club include a tropical, glass-domed, 20m, stainless steel swimming pool.

Our inspector loved: *The superb tropical swimming pool and health club.*

Directions: A 3-minute walk from Knightsbridge tube station (Piccadilly Line). Take Sloane Street/Brompton Road station exit, turn right down Sloane Street then left into Cadogan Place.

Enfield

Central London

Richmond

Croydon

Web: www.johansens.com/carltontower
E-mail: contact@carltontower.com
Tel: 0870 381 9326
International: +44 (0)20 7235 1234
Fax: +44 (0)20 7235 9129

Price Guide: (excluding VAT)
single £335
double/twin £335
suites from £435

 SPA

THE LOWNDES HOTEL

21 LOWNDES STREET, KNIGHTSBRIDGE, LONDON SW1X 9ES

Directions: The nearest underground tube stations are Knightsbridge, Hyde Park Corner and Sloane Square.

Web: www.johansens.com/lowndes
E-mail: contact@lowndeshotel.com
Tel: 0870 381 9285
International: +44 (0)20 7823 1234
Fax: 020 7235 1154

Price Guide: (room only, excluding VAT)
double £260-£280
suite £360-£460

The Lowndes Hotel is a stylish, discreet boutique town house hotel overflowing with character situated in residential Belgravia, just minutes from Hyde Park; in the heart of the stylish Sloane Street and Duke of York Square shops. Classical English décor combines effortlessly with modern comforts; rich fabrics, antique furniture and open fireplaces create a homely and inviting atmosphere, complemented by personal recognition from a team of friendly and attentive staff. Ideal for business or leisure travellers alike. Many of the bedrooms have balconies overlooking the famous, fashionable Halkin Arcade. Exquisite gourmet cuisine is served in the contemporary Citronelle, an informal all-day restuarant featuring a terrace for al fresco dining. Alternatively, guests can dine in The Carlton Tower, The Lowndes' sister hotel. Each guest receives temporary membership to Montes, a private members' club with a fabulous Mediterranean restaurant, relaxing bar area and nightclub. First-class leisure facilities include a magnificent indoor pool, spa treatments, sauna, steam and Jacuzzi as well as a lavish ballroom. There is also The Peak rooftop health club, set under a vast canopy of glass. The hotel's central location enables easy access by foot, public transport or taxi to London's major tourist attractions, West End and City.

Our inspector loved: The view of Lowndes Square from the terrace.

NEW

THE ROYAL PARK

3 WESTBOURNE TERRACE, LANCASTER GATE, HYDE PARK, LONDON W2 3UL

Situated on the doorstep of Hyde Park, this exquisite hotel comprises of 3 Grade II listed Georgian town houses, lovingly restored to their 1840's elegance. There are 48 charming bedrooms, decorated in stunning Regency colours that truly enhance the antique furniture, luxurious linens and handmade beds. Each room boasts a splendid antique writing desk, as well as the latest technology including flatscreen television and broadband Internet access. The hotel is adorned with delightful Georgian and Victorian antique pieces, carefully selected by Jonty Hearnden of "The Antiques Roadshow." Upon arrival, guests enter the glorious marble chequered reception with roaring log fire and receive a complimentary glass of sherry or whiskey. Although there is no restaurant, an excellent room service menu is available and breakfast can be served in guests' rooms or in the drawing room. Complimentary traditional English tea is served in the afternoon and a glass of champagne, with canapés, may be enjoyed in the evening. For small meetings the Green Room can accomodate 10 people. Oxford Street and Notting Hill are both within walking distance.

Our inspector loved: The beautifully designed bedrooms with their handmade four poster beds and exquisite linens.

Directions: The nearest underground tube station is Lancaster Gate. The hotel is a 2-minute walk from the Heathrow Express at Paddington Station.

Enfield

Central London

Richmond

Croydon

Web: www.johansens.com/royalpark
E-mail: info@theroyalpark.com
Tel: 0870 381 9289
International: +44 (0)20 7479 6600
Fax: 020 7479 6601

Price Guide: (weekend rates incl VAT)
single £110–£165
double £135–£190
suite £210–£270

THE LEONARD

15 SEYMOUR STREET, LONDON W1H 7JW

Directions: The Leonard is north of Marble Arch off Portman Square and just around the corner from Oxford Street and Selfridges. Parking in Bryanston Street.

Web: www.johansens.com/leonard
E-mail: the.leonard@dial.pipex.com
Tel: 0870 381 8688
International: +44 (0)20 7935 2010
Fax: 020 7935 6700

Price Guide: (excl VAT)
double £170–£220
suites £280– £550

4 late 18th-century Georgian town houses set the character of this relaxing Johansens award-winning property. Superbly located off Portman Square, which celebrated its 7th anniversary in 2003, The Leonard has become popular very quickly with discerning travellers and celebrities alike. Imaginative reconstruction has created 11 rooms and 21 suites decorated individually to a very high standard, with a further 12 rooms and a small roof garden completed in 2002. All rooms are fully air-conditioned and include private safe, mini-bar, hi-fi system, provision for fax/modem and within the reception area complimentary access to the Internet. Bathrooms are finished in marble, and some of the larger suites have a butler's pantry or fully-fitted kitchen. The first-floor Grand suites are particularly impressive, and the Café Bar offers breakfast and light meals throughout the day. For physical fitness and stress reduction there is a compact exercise room. With professional, friendly "Can-do" staff, The Leonard is the epitome of casual luxury in the heart of London's West End. Available opposite, also part of the hotel, The Leonard Residence offers 5 serviced apartments which are available for longer stays.

Our inspector loved: *The rooftop patio garden.*

DORSET SQUARE HOTEL

39 DORSET SQUARE, MARYLEBONE, LONDON NW1 6QN

This little gem of a hotel is in a prime location for all that the west end of London has to offer. Set in a leafy square that was the original site for Thomas Lord's cricket ground, this Regency town house has been lovingly restored and designed to offer the ultimate in comfort and charm with a chic London edge. Each of the 37 bedrooms has been perfectly appointed to offer the latest amenities such as air conditioning, modem ports, and the marble bathrooms are equipped to an extremely high standard. The Potting Shed restaurant is a delight – light and airy and exuding character with an array of terracotta pots along one wall. The cuisine is a selection of modern British. For those who prefer to remain in the luxury of their bedrooms there is also the wonderful "bedroom picnic" – a basket laden with cold meats, fresh fruits, cheeses and pastries and chilled champagne. The Business Center with large plasma screen, natural daylight and air condition rooms is ideal for small meetings of up to 10 people. Madame Tussauds, the Planetarium and Regent's Park zoo are all within 2 minutes walk, and the shops of Oxford Street, Baker Street and even Bond Street are not far away. Theatreland is only a few minutes away, and the city is easily accessible by tube.

Our inspector loved: The devine Potting Shed restaurant.

Directions: Left from Marylebone tube or right from Baker street tube – the hotel is just minutes from each.

Web: www.johansens.com/dorsetsquare
E-mail: info@dorsetsquare.co.uk
Tel: 0870 381 8488
International: +44 (0)20 7723 7874
Fax: 020 7724 3328

Enfield

Central London

Richmond

Croydon

Price Guide: (excluding VAT)
double £210
twin/king £250
suite/four poster £300

47 PARK STREET

MAYFAIR, LONDON W1K 7EB

Directions: The nearest underground tube station is Marble Arch. Valet parking is available.

Web: www.johansens.com/parkstreet
E-mail: reservations@47parkstreet.com
Tel: 0870 381 9282
International: +44 (0)20 7491 7282
Fax: 020 7491 7281

Price Guide:
suite £325 – £595

Passing through the grand, twin-pillared entranceway and tall, double-opening doors it is evident that this is a luxurious, discrete and intimate hotel, an exclusive residence for those wishing to avail themselves of the best that London can offer. In a superb location on the edge of Park Lane and Hyde Park, the hotel is surrounded by lovely Georgian terraces, leafy squares and the quiet back streets of Mayfair. The fashionable shopping areas of Bond Street, Knightsbridge and Oxford Street are a short walk away and the West End is easily accessible. Built in 1929 as a private home for the first Baron Milford, beautifully appointed accommodation has been combined with a sense of intimacy and belonging. Each of the one and two-bedroomed spacious and comfortably furnished guest suites feature restful décor, elegant drapes, antique furniture, fully-equipped kitchen, generous dining area and lounge, marble bathroom with power shower, satellite television, DVD and 3 telephone lines. Exceptional services on offer include: a discreet and uncompromising Concierge team, 24-hour reception, twice daily maid service, grocery pre-stocking, in-house florist, personal shopping service and limousine service. An abundance of prestigious restaurants are nearby, including the renowned Le Gavroche, whilst 24-hour room service enables friends or business associates to be entertained in style and privacy.

Our inspector loved: *The exclusive and luxurious surroundings.*

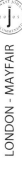

THE DORCHESTER

PARK LANE, MAYFAIR, LONDON W1A 2HJ

Built in 1931, this grand hotel successfully combines ultra-modern convenience with traditional service and atmosphere. All 250 rooms, including 55 suites, have air conditioning, an entertainment and business system, video on demand (up to 60 films), direct Internet access and Microsoft Word, Excel and Powerpoint operated via an infrared keyboard on the TV. These individually decorated, supremely comfortable English country house style bedrooms also boast a fax, scanner, copier, DVD and CD player, with a music library of 4,100 tracks available in all the rooms, 90 of which have 42" plasma screens. All the rooms have recently undergone a multi million pound refurbishment programme. A variety of cuisine is on offer; from traditional British food in The Grill Room, Cantonese in The Oriental Restaurant, Italian cooking in The Dorchester Bar and an award-winning traditional afternoon tea in The Promenade. The fully air-conditioned banqueting rooms can be hired independently. There is a highly regarded day spa, offering a wide range of treatments. Personalised care is a pillar of The Dorchester's fine reputation. Year round packages are available.

Our inspector loved: *The sheer timeless elegance of the suites combined with contemporary touches.*

Directions: Towards Hyde Park Corner/Piccadilly end of Park Lane.

Web: www.johansens.com/thedorchester
E-mail: reservations@dorchesterhotel.com
Tel: 0870 381 8485
International: +44 (0)20 7629 8888
Fax: 020 7409 0114

Enfield

Central London

Richmond

Croydon

Price Guide: (incl service, excl VAT & breakfast)
single £275–£365
double/twin £355–£465
suite £550–£2,125

250   M450   DVD/VCR   SPA

PEMBRIDGE COURT HOTEL

34 PEMBRIDGE GARDENS, LONDON W2 4DX

This gracious Victorian town house has been lovingly restored to its former glory whilst providing all the modern facilities demanded by today's discerning traveller. The 20 rooms, all of which have air conditioning, are individually decorated with pretty fabrics and the walls adorned with an unusual collection of framed fans and Victoriana. The charming and tranquil sitting room is as ideal for a quiet drink and light snacks as it is for a small informal meeting. There is also a small boardroom and sitting room on the lower ground floor. The Pembridge Court is renowned for the devotion and humour with which it is run. Its long serving staff and its famous cat "Churchill" assure you of a warm welcome and the very best in friendly, personal service. Over the years the hotel has built up a loyal following amongst its guests, many of whom regard it as their genuine "home from home" in London. The Pembridge is situated in quiet tree-lined gardens in Londons' trendy Notting Hill Gate. The area is colourful and full of life with lots of great pubs and restaurants and the biggest antiques market in the world at nearby Portobello Road.

Directions: Pembridge Gardens is a small turning off Notting Hill Gate/Bayswater Road, just 2 minutes from Portobello Road Antiques Market.

Web: www.johansens.com/pembridgecourt
E-mail: reservations@pemct.co.uk
Tel: 0870 381 8808
International: +44 (0)20 7229 9977
Fax: 020 7727 4982

Price Guide:
(inclusive of English breakfast & VAT)
single £130–£170
double/twin £190–£200

Our inspector loved: *The cosy "at home" feel of the sitting room and the collection of Victorian fans.*

THE ATHENAEUM HOTEL & APARTMENTS

116 PICCADILLY, LONDON W1J 7BJ

Set in a superb location, the stylish Athenaeum Hotel & Apartments is extremely welcoming with friendly staff and highly personalised service. Comfortable and luxurious décor adorns the cosy, secluded Windsor Lounge and the public areas. Lovely airy and bright bedrooms, some with views over Green Park, have fresh colour schemes, double, twin or king-size beds and all modern conveniences to create a contemporary yet traditional ambience. Housed in Edwardian town houses adjacent to the hotel, the spacious and elegantly furnished 1 and 2-bedroom apartments have a private entrance and kitchen facilities. Modern British cuisine using the finest seasonal ingredients is served in the highly acclaimed Bullochs restaurant, whose warm and intimate surroundings feature a floor of imported Jerusalem stone. For the energetic or those wishing to be pampered, the Spa offers a well-equipped gym, Jacuzzi, steam room, sauna, beauty therapy and massage. With its central location, the Athenaeum is ideal for business, leisure and shopping. Buckingham Palace, Hyde Park, Bond Street and the theatre district are a short walk away, whilst Harrods, Covent Garden, Westminster, Kensington Palace and Soho are only a few minutes by taxi or underground.

Our inspector loved: The park views, dedicated staff and fabulous apartments.

Directions: The nearest underground station is Green Park.

Web: www.johansens.com/athenaeum
E-mail: info@athenaeumhotel.com
Tel: 0870 381 8329
International: +44 (0)20 7499 3464
Fax: 020 7493 1860

Price Guide: (excl VAT)
single from £265
double/twin from £295
suite/apartment from £415

NEW

THE RITZ

150 PICCADILLY, LONDON W1J 9BR

Directions: The Ritz is less than a minute's walk from Green Park underground station .

Web: www.johansens.com/theritz
E-mail: enquire@theritzlondon.com
Tel: 0870 381 9308
International: +44 (0)20 7493 8181
Fax: 020 7493 2687

Price Guide: (excluding VAT)
single from £310
double from £370
suite from £800

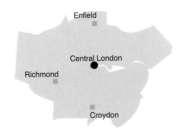

One of London's most famous and beloved landmarks, The Ritz first opened in 1906 and soon established an unparalleled reputation for sophistication, glamour and elegance. The hotel today retains the ambience of a French château and has been lovingly refurbished to restore the smallest details of the Louis XVI style. Every room and suite is exquisitely and individually decorated in the distinctive Ritz colour schemes of blue, peach, pink and yellow, and range from junior suites through to superior king and queen-sized rooms with modern facilities and exceptional standards of comfort. The popular 1-bedroom Piccadilly Suites have views along Piccadilly toward the Royal Academy, while as the name suggests, the Green Park Suites overlook one of London's most picturesque parks and skylines. Located on the 7th floor, the Berkeley Suite is the jewel in the crown, and is simply magnificent with its marble floor lobby, 2 bedrooms and dining area that can accommodate up to 10 people. The Ritz Restaurant offers classical cuisine with contemporary influences and impeccable service, and afternoon tea in the spectacular Palm Court is an institution. During warmer months luncheons and receptions can be held on the private terrace, and the art deco Rivoli Bar provides an informal area to dine and enjoy a drink.

Our inspector loved: *The timeless elegance of this majestic hotel.*

THE RICHMOND GATE HOTEL AND RESTAURANT

RICHMOND HILL, RICHMOND-UPON-THAMES, SURREY TW10 6RP

This former Georgian country house stands on the crest of Richmond Hill close to the Royal Park and Richmond Terrace with its commanding views over the River Thames. The 68 stylishly furnished en-suite bedrooms combine every comfort of the present with the elegance of the past and include several luxury four-poster rooms and suites. Exceptional and imaginative cuisine, complemented by an extensive wine list offering over 100 wines from around the world is served in the sophisticated surroundings of the Gates On The Parks Restaurant. Weddings, business meetings and private dining events can be arranged in a variety of rooms. The beautiful Victorian walled garden provides for summer relaxation. Cedars Health and Leisure Club is accessed through the hotel and includes a 20-metre pool, 6-metre spa, sauna, steam room, aerobics studio, cardiovascular and resistance gymnasia and a health and beauty suite. Richmond is close to London and the West End yet in a country setting. The Borough offers a wealth of visitor attractions, including Hampton Court Palace, Syon House and Park and the Royal Botanic Gardens at Kew.

Our inspector loved: Its unique location at the gates of Richmond Park - acres of open parkland where deer still graze beneath the trees.

Directions: Opposite the Star & Garter Home at the top of Richmond Hill.

Web: www.johansens.com/richmondgate
E-mail: richmondgate@corushotels.com
Tel: 0870 381 8855
International: +44 (0)20 8940 0061
Fax: 020 8332 0354

Price Guide:
single from £120
double/twin from £150
suite from £225

THE CRANLEY

10 BINA GARDENS, SOUTH KENSINGTON, LONDON SW5 0LA

Directions: The nearest underground stations are Gloucester Road and South Kensington.

Web: www.johansens.com/cranley
E-mail: info@thecranley.com
Tel: 0870 381 8456
International: +44 (0)20 7373 0123
Fax: 020 7373 9497

Price Guide:
single £180
double/twin £220
suite £350

Standing in a quiet, tree-lined street in the heart of Kensington, this charming and sophisticated Victorian town house is an ideal city venue for the leisure and business visitor alike, blending traditional style and service with 21st-century technology. Furnished with beautiful antiques and hand-embroidered linen fabrics, The Cranley has an understated elegance. Striking colour combinations and stone used throughout the bedrooms and reception areas are derived from the original floor in the entrance hall. Recently completely refurbished, The Cranley's bedrooms are now among some of the most comfortable in the Capital. All are delightfully decorated and have king-sized, four-poster or half-tester canopied beds. Each room is light, air-conditioned and has facilities ranging from antique desk, 2 direct dial telephone lines and voicemail to broadband connection. The luxury bathrooms have traditional Victorian-style fittings combined with a lavish use of warm limestone. Guests can enjoy copious continental breakfasts, complimentary English afternoon tea and an evening help-yourself apéritif with canapés. Many of London's attractions are within easy walking distance, including the shops and restaurants of Knightsbridge and the Kings Road.

Our inspector loved: *The beautifully decorated rooms and gorgeous antique furniture.*

NUMBER SIXTEEN

16 SUMNER PLACE, LONDON SW7 3EG

Freshly refurbished behind an immaculate pillared façade, Number Sixteen, winner of Condé Nast Johansens Most Excellent London Hotel in 2004, and situated in the heart of South Kensington, is surrounded by some of London's best restaurants, bars, shops and museums. Harrods, Knightsbridge shopping, Hyde Park and the Victoria & Albert Museum are all just a short walk away. Although the area has a buzzy, cosmopolitan character, the hotel is a haven of calm and seclusion. In winter an open fire and honesty bar in the drawing room entices with its warmth, whilst in summer the conservatory opens onto an award-winning private garden. The library is ideal for greeting friends or holding an informal business meeting. The 42 bedrooms are individually designed and decorated in a modern English style complete with crisp Frette bedlinen and white, hand-embroidered bedspreads. Each is appointed with facilities expected by the modern traveller, including mini-bar, personal safe and direct dial telephone with voice mail and modem point. Staff are friendly and attentive ensuring that guests are looked after almost as if they were staying in a private home. South Kensington underground station is just a two-minute walk away, providing easy access to the West End and the City and a direct link to Heathrow Airport.

Our inspector loved: The divine fabrics and design of all the rooms.

Directions: Sumner Place is off the Old Brompton Road near Onslow Square.

Web: www.johansens.com/numbersixteen
E-mail: sixteen@firmdale.com
Tel: 0870 381 8771
International: +44 (0)20 7589 5232
Fax: 020 7584 8615

Price Guide: (excluding VAT)
single from £95
double/twin from £170

SOFITEL ST JAMES

6 WATERLOO PLACE, LONDON SW1Y 4AN

Directions: The nearest underground station is Piccadilly Circus.

Web: www.johansens.com/stjames
E-mail: H3144@accor.com
Tel: 0870 381 9185
International: +44 (0)20 7747 2200
Fax: +44 (0) 20 7747 2210

Price Guide:
single from £275
double from £320
suite £430-£1,200

Located on the corner of Waterloo Place and Pall Mall, this imposing Grade II listed building is the former home of the Cox's and King's bank and has been carefully renovated to create an elegant 5-star hotel. Sofitel acquired the majority of the original artwork from the bank, which is now proudly displayed and balanced out by contemporary design. Bedrooms and suites are sophisticated and equipped with ultra-modern technology, and in the bathrooms black and white marble harmonises with granite tops and chrome fittings. The elegant Rose Lounge is the ideal place for a traditional afternoon tea amidst an eclectic mix of colours and styles, whilst the St James Bar offers the largest selection of Champagnes and cigars in London. French flair and refined cuisine are the hallmark of the buzzing Brasserie Roux. Guests can enjoy a pampering session in the hotel's fitness and massage centre complete with treatment rooms and steam room. The hotel's conference and banqueting facilities comprise of 8 rooms including a state-of-the-art boardroom with private dining room as well as a banqueting suite for up to 170 people. Numerous of London's major attractions, such as Trafalgar Square, Piccadilly Circus and the theatre district, are just around the corner.

Our inspector loved: *The grand marble entrace with its skilful mix of original and contemporary features.*

DOLPHIN SQUARE HOTEL

DOLPHIN SQUARE, CHICHESTER STREET, LONDON SW1V 3LX

Centrally located in large, exquisite gardens bordered by the River Thames and Westminster this quiet oasis is decorated with contemporary style and offers discreet service. The 148 suites offer a classical or modern décor with subtle colour co-ordinated design. Most suites have a compact, well-equipped kitchen, yet 24-hour room service and full hotel facilities are available. Guests can enjoy delicious international cuisine in the informal Brasserie and the Clipper Bar is a fun and stylish venue for a drink and chat. The hotel's restaurant, Allium, is an exciting new venue under the direction of internationally renowned chef patron Anton Edelmann (formerly of The Savoy). The menu features contemporary European cuisine with an emphasis placed on flavours and simplicity in a relaxed but sophisticated atmosphere. A selection of Anton Edelmann's menus are also available for private dining. A variety of shops in Dolphin Square provide for guests' every need, including a newsagent, chemist, hair salon and travel agent. The hotel's heated swimming pool and health club include a fully-equipped gym, tennis courts, squash courts, croquet lawn, sauna, steam room and numerous beauty and health treatments. There are superb facilities for celebrations of any size and excellent business and corporate services.

Our inspector loved: The large indoor swimming pool and great health spa.

Directions: The closest underground station is Pimlico.

Web: www.johansens.com/dolphinsquare
E-mail: reservations@dolphinsquarehotel.co.uk
Tel: 0870 381 8483
International: +44 (0)20 7834 3800
Fax: 020 7798 8735

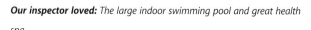

Price Guide:
studio suite double/twin £175–£195
1 bedroom suite £190–£400
2 bedroom suite £320
3 bedroom suite £450

51 BUCKINGHAM GATE

51 BUCKINGHAM GATE, WESTMINSTER, LONDON SW1E 6AF

Directions: The nearest underground stations are St James's Park and Victoria.

Web: www.johansens.com/buckinghamgate
E-mail: info@51-buckinghamgate.co.uk
Tel: 0870 381 8301
International: +44 (0)20 7769 7766
Fax: 020 7828 5909

Price Guide:
suites £405–£975

Close to Buckingham Palace, St James's Park and the Houses of Parliament, 51 Buckingham Gate is contemporary style and luxury on a grand scale. This attractive Victorian town house offers everything the discerning guest could wish for: privacy, relaxation and superb service delivered by multilingual staff which includes a team of Ivor Spencer trained butlers. Guests have a choice of dining options: Quilon, offering southern coastal Indian cuisine, Bank Westminster, Zander Bar and The Library. There are 82 suites and apartments, ranging from junior suites to the 5-bedroom Prime Minister's Suite, which combine contemporary interior design with luxury hotel facilities. De luxe suites offer award-winning bathrooms, whilst designated Ivor Spencer Suites have 16-hour personal butler service, limousine pick-up and an exclusive range of special amenities. Each suite provides sophisticated technology including 2-line speaker telephones, voicemail, dataport, fax/copier/printer, CD and DVD player. Fully equipped kitchens as well as 24-hour room service are available. A team of talented chefs is also at hand to prepare private dinners. Guests can enjoy treatments at the exclusive spa and a fully equipped gymnasium at the Club at St James Court.

Our inspector loved: *The hotel's secret location, a stone's throw from Buckingham Palace, and the magnificent Prime Minister's Suite.*

CANNIZARO HOUSE

WEST SIDE, WIMBLEDON COMMON, LONDON SW19 4UE

Cannizaro House, an elegant Georgian country house, occupies a tranquil position on the edge of Wimbledon Common, yet is only 18 minutes by train from London Waterloo and the Eurostar terminal. Cannizaro House restored as a superb hotel has, throughout its history, welcomed Royalty and celebrities such as George III, Oscar Wilde and William Pitt. The 18th century is reflected in the ornate fireplaces and mouldings, gilded mirrors and many antiques. All the hotel's 45 bedrooms are individually designed, with many overlooking beautiful Cannizaro Park. All of the 17 executive rooms have air conditioning. Several intimate rooms are available for meetings and private dining, including the elegant Queen Elizabeth Room – a popular venue for wedding ceremonies. The Viscount Melville Suite offers air-conditioned comfort for up to 100 guests. There is a spacious south-facing summer terrace as ideal for afternoon tea and receptions as it is for evening cocktails. The award-winning kitchen produces the finest modern and classical cuisine, complemented by an impressive list of wines.

Our inspector loved: *The south facing lavender filled terrace overlooking the extensive grounds.*

Directions: The nearest tube and British Rail station is Wimbledon.

Web: www.johansens.com/cannizarohouse
E-mail: cannizarohouse@thistle.co.uk
Tel: 0870 381 8402
International: +44 (0)208 879 1464
Fax: 020 8970 2753

Price Guide: (room only):
double/twin from £156
feature room from £184

DIDSBURY HOUSE

DIDSBURY PARK, DIDSBURY VILLAGE, MANCHESTER M20 5LJ

Directions: Exit the M56 at junction 1 and take the A34 towards Manchester. At the traffic lights turn left onto the A5145 towards Didsbury. At the 2nd set of traffic lights turn right into Didsbury Park. The hotel is on the left.

Web: www.johansens.com/didsburyhouse
E-mail: enquiries@didsburyhouse.co.uk
Tel: 0870 381 8481
International: +44 (0)161 448 2200
Fax: 0161 448 2525

Price Guide:
single £124–£180
double/twin £160–£220
suite £226–£380

This stylish and contemporary small boutique hotel, in a leafy south Manchester suburb, is a careful refurbishment and extension of a Grade II listed, mid-19th-century Victorian villa and coach house. It is the second town house hotel concept to be opened in the city by Eamonn and Sally O'Loughlin, the first being the acclaimed Eleven Didsbury Park. Their new hotel, just 100 yards away, is double the size and twice as stunning. It seduces guests immediately as they enter its beautiful hallway. The superb original carved wooden staircase carries the eye up to a magnificent stained-glass window. Ornate ceilings and architraves, polished wooden floors and warm décor dominate the luxurious public rooms. The exquisite and romantic attic suite has separate his and hers cast-iron roll-top baths and his and hers seats in a huge shower and steam cubicle, whilst in every gorgeous en-suite bedroom the bath fits 2. A top floor footbridge spans a central atrium and a charming lounge with ostrich-egg sized lights and pewter bar leads onto a secluded courtyard furnished with a restful and imaginative combination of steel, bamboo and water features. Gym, steam room and face, body and holistic treatments are available in the SO Spa. Breakfast and a room service menu are available in the evenings, but complimentary transport is provided for dining out.

Our inspector loved: *The original 18th-century staircase set in front of the stained-glass window.*

ETROP GRANGE

THORLEY LANE, MANCHESTER AIRPORT, GREATER MANCHESTER M90 4EG

Hidden away near Manchester Airport lies Etrop Grange, a beautiful country house hotel and restaurant. The original house was built in 1780 and more than 200 years on has been lovingly restored. Today, the hotel enjoys a fine reputation for its accommodation, where the luxury, character and sheer elegance of the Georgian era are evident in every feature. The magnificent award-winning restaurant offers a well balanced mix of traditional and modern English cuisine, complemented by an extensive selection of fine wines. Attention to detail ensures personal and individual service. In addition to the obvious advantage of having an airport within walking distance, the location of Etrop Grange is ideal in many other ways. With a comprehensive motorway network and InterCity stations minutes away, it is accessible from all parts of the UK. Entertainment for visitors ranges from the shopping, sport and excellent nightlife offered by the city of Manchester to golf, riding, clay pigeon shooting, water sports and outdoor pursuits in the immediate countryside. Cheshire also boasts an abundance of stately homes, museums and historical attractions.

Our inspector loved: *The complimentary chauffeured Jaguar to Manchester Airport.*

Directions: Leave M56 at junction 5 towards Manchester Airport. Follow signs for Terminal 2. Go up the slip road. At roundabout take first exit, take immediate left and hotel is 400yds on the right.

Web: www.johansens.com/etropgrange
E-mail: etropgrange@corushotels.com
Tel: 0870 381 8507
International: +44 (0)161 499 0500
Fax: 0161 499 0790

Price Guide:
single £137–£145
double/twin £175–£205
suites £199

CONGHAM HALL

GRIMSTON, KING'S LYNN, NORFOLK PE32 1AH

Dating from the mid-18th century, this stately manor house is set in acres of parkland, orchards and gardens. The conversion from country house to luxury hotel in 1982 was executed with care to enhance the elegance of the classic interiors. The hotel's renowned herb garden grows over 700 varieties of herb, many are used by the chef to create modern English dishes with the accent on fresh local produce and fish from the local Norfolk markets. The hotel's hives even produce the honey for your breakfast table. The beautiful flower displays, homemade pot pourri and roaring log fires blend together to create a welcoming and relaxing atmosphere. Congham Hall is the ideal base from which to tour the spectacular beaches of the north Norfolk coastline, Sandringham, Burnham Market and Holkham Hall.

Directions: Go to the A149/A148 interchange northeast of King's Lynn. Follow the A148 towards Sandringham/Fakenham/ Cromer for 100 yards. Turn right to Grimston. The hotel is then 2 miles on the left

Our inspector loved: *The wonderful herb garden.*

Web: www.johansens.com/conghamhall
E-mail: info@conghamhallhotel.co.uk
Tel: 0870 381 8443
International: +44 (0)1485 600250
Fax: 01485 601191

Price Guide:
single from £105
double/twin from £165
suites from £250

PARK FARM COUNTRY HOTEL & LEISURE

HETHERSETT, NORWICH, NORFOLK NR9 3DL

Park Farm Hotel & Leisure occupies a secluded location in beautifully landscaped grounds south of Norwich, once the second greatest city in England. There are executive rooms for additional comfort, with four-poster beds and Jacuzzi baths. Additional bedrooms have been sympathetically converted from traditional and new buildings to reflect the style of the 4 rooms available in the main house. A superb leisure complex to suit all ages has been carefully incorporated alongside the original Georgian house to include heated swimming pool, sauna, steam room, solarium, spa bath, gymnasium, aerobics studio and a beauty therapy area. The delightful restaurant is renowned for its high standards of cuisine and service, with a wide selection of dishes and fine choice of wines. Conference facilities cater for up to 120 candidates (24-hour and daily delegate rates available). This is an ideal location for wedding receptions. The Norfolk broads, the coast, Norwich open market, castle museum and cathedral are nearby. A self-catering apartment, "Tumbrils," with private walled garden, is situated within the grounds.

Our inspector loved: *The friendly atmosphere and "buzz" in the conservatory and bar.*

Directions: By road, just off the A11 on the B1172. 8 miles from Norwich Airport, 6 miles from Norwich rail station and 5 miles from Norwich bus station.

Web: www.johansens.com/parkfarm
E-mail: enq@parkfarm–hotel.co.uk
Tel: 0870 381 8800
International: +44 (0)1603 810264
Fax: 01603 812104

Price Guide:
single £92-£130
double/twin £118-£170
suites £170-£180

199

FAWSLEY HALL

FAWSLEY, NEAR DAVENTRY, NORTHAMPTONSHIRE NN11 3BA

Directions: Fawsley Hall can be reached by the M40, junction 11 or the M1, junction16. Both are 10 miles from the hotel.

Web: www.johansens.com/fawsleyhall
E-mail: reservations@fawsleyhall.com
Tel: 0870 381 8516
International: +44 (0)1327 892000
Fax: 01327 892001

Price Guide:
single from £140
double/twin from £190
suite from £340

Market Harborough

Northampton

Towcester

Set in the beautiful Northamptonshire countryside and surrounded by acres of rolling parkland with lakes, landscaped by Capability Brown, Fawsley Hall combines the charm and character of a gracious manor with the facilities and comforts of a modern hotel. The original Tudor Manor House opened as a hotel in 1998 but many traces of its illustrious past have been retained, such as the vaulted hall and Queen Elizabeth I chamber. 43 wonderfully decorated rooms offer a range of Tudor, Georgian, Victorian and "classic modern"styles, many of which include four-poster beds. The Knightley Restaurant has established a reputation as being the finest in Northamptonshire and the Old Laundry Bar provides delicious light meals at lunchtime. The hotel's spa in the Georgian cellar includes a beauty salon, fitness studio, steam, sauna and spa bath. 6 conference and syndicate rooms can accommodate up to 80 delegates and the attractive Salvin Suite can seat up to 140 for a private banquet or wedding reception. Places of historic interest include: Sulgrave Manor, ancestral home of George Washington; Althorp; Canons Ashby; Blenheim Palace; Silverstone; Towcester Racecourse; an Elizabethan manor house and Warwick Castle. Oxford and Stratford-upon-Avon are nearby.

Our inspector loved: *The Great Hall with its paintings, fireplace and fine furnishings.*

WHITTLEBURY HALL

WHITTLEBURY, NEAR TOWCESTER, NORTHAMPTONSHIRE NN12 8QH

Whittlebury Hall is a modern building where the elegance of classic Georgian architecture has been complemented by contemporary furnishings and fabrics to create a truly fabulous hotel. The spacious bedrooms have all been elegantly decorated with a host of modern touches and thoughtful extras, whilst 3 superbly appointed, individually styled suites have a whirlpool spa bath and shower. The Silverstone Bar is aptly named with a host of motor racing memorabilia adorning the walls whilst Bentleys offers Italian pizza, pasta and salad. Astons Restaurant provides a relaxed atmosphere with menus blending classic and contemporary cuisine. By contrast Murrays Restaurant provides the latest in food trends and fashion boasting 2 AA Rosettes for fine food. The management training centre offers 14 suites, 35 syndicate rooms, 6 meeting rooms and a lecture room for up to 500 delegates. Guests can relax and unwind at the Spa, where over 60 treatments are available in the health and beauty treatment suite. There is a 19-metre swimming pool, whirlpool spa, steam room, sauna, relaxation and a 42-station StairMaster® gym, whilst the adjacent Whittlebury Park golf course offers preferred rates for guests. Motor racing enthusiasts can enjoy racing action at nearby Silverstone. Warwick Castle, Towcester racecourse and Oxford are all within a easy drive.

Directions: 11 miles from M1, junction 15A. 18 miles from M40, junction 10.

Web: www.johansens.com/whittleburyhall
E-mail: sales@whittleburyhall.co.uk
Tel: 0870 381 8995
International: +44 (0)1327 857857
Fax: 01327 857867

Market Harborough

Northampton

Towcester

Price Guide:
single £130
double/twin £160
suite £265

Our inspector loved: The spacious relaxing main lounge.

MARSHALL MEADOWS COUNTRY HOUSE HOTEL

BERWICK-UPON-TWEED, NORTHUMBERLAND TD15 1UT

Directions: A1 heading North, take Berwick by-pass and at Meadow House roundabout, head towards Edinburgh. After 300 yards, turn right, indicated by white sign – hotel is at end of small side road.

Web: www.johansens.com/marshallmeadows
E-mail: stay@marshallmeadows.co.uk
Tel: 0870 381 8721
International: +44 (0)1289 331133
Fax: 01289 331438

Price Guide:
single £90–£100
double/twin £110–£160
suite £150–£160

Berwick-upon-Tweed

Alnwick

Morpeth

Hexham

Marshall Meadows can truly boast that it is England's most northerly hotel, just a quarter of a mile from the Scottish border, an ideal base for those exploring the rugged beauty of Northumberland. A magnificent Georgian mansion standing in 15 acres of woodland and formal gardens, Marshall Meadows today is a luxurious retreat, with a country house ambience – welcoming and elegant. It has a burn and small waterfall with attractive woodland walks. This is not a large hotel; there are just 19 bedrooms, each individually designed. Restful harmonious colour schemes, comfortable beds and the tranquillity of its surroundings ensure a good night's sleep! The lounge is delightful, with traditional easy chairs and sofas, overlooking the patio. Ideal for summer afternoon tea. The congenial Duck & Grouse Bar stocks a range of whiskies, beers and fine wines. Marshall Meadows has a galleried restaurant where diners enjoy local game, fresh seafood and good wine. Private dining facilities are also available. Excellent golf, fishing and historic Berwick-on-Tweed are nearby. Short breaks are available throughout the year.

Our inspector loved: *The peaceful country setting in close proximity to the sea and its coastal walks.*

TILLMOUTH PARK

CORNHILL-ON-TWEED, NEAR BERWICK-UPON-TWEED, NORTHUMBERLAND TD12 4UU

This magnificent mansion house, built in 1882 using stones from nearby Twizel Castle, offers the same warm welcome to visitors today as when it was an exclusive private house. Tillmouth Park is situated in 15 acres of mature parkland gardens above the river Till. The generously sized bedrooms are individually designed with period and antique furniture, and are fully appointed with bathrobes, toiletries, hairdryer and trouser press. Most bedrooms offer spectacular views of the surrounding countryside. The wood-panelled, 2 AA Rosette, restaurant serves a fine table d'hôte menu offering contemporary British cuisine, whilst the Bistro is less formal. A well-chosen wine list and a vast selection of malt whiskies complement the cuisine. The elegant, galleried main hall offers country house comfort with open log fires. Tillmouth Park is ideally situated for country pursuits, with fishing on the Tweed and Till and clay shooting available on the grounds. The area also abounds in fine golf courses. Coldstream and Kelso are within easy reach; the Northumbrian coast and Berwick are 15 minutes away, and Flodden Field, Lindisfarne and Holy Island are nearby. There are many stately homes to visit in the area including Floors, Manderston, Paxton and the spectacular Alnwick Garden Project.

Our inspector loved: The magnificent galleried main hall.

Directions: Tillmouth Park is on the A698 Coldstream to Berwick-upon-Tweed road.

Berwick-upon-Tweed

Alnwick

Morpeth

Hexham

Web: www.johansens.com/tillmouthpark
E-mail: reception@tillmouthpark.f9.co.uk
Tel: 0870 381 8948
International: +44 (0)1890 882255
Fax: 01890 882540

Price Guide:
single £60–£140
twin/double £145–£190

203

MATFEN HALL

MATFEN, NEWCASTLE-UPON-TYNE, NORTHUMBERLAND NE20 0RH

Directions: From A1 take A69 towards Hexham. At Heddon on the Wall take B6318 towards Chollerford, travel 7 miles and turn right to Matfen.

Web: www.johansens.com/matfenhall
E-mail: info@matfenhall.com
Tel: 0870 381 8724
International: +44 (0)1661 886500
Fax: 01661 886055

Price Guide:
single from £102–£147
double from £140–£250

Berwick-upon-Tweed

Alnwick

Morpeth

Hexham

Originally built in 1830 by Sir Edward Blackett, Matfen Hall has been carefully restored by Sir Hugh and Lady Blackett. This magnificent family seat lies in the heart of some of Northumberland's most beautiful countryside. Recently awarded Small Hotel of the Year in the Excellence in England awards, Matfen Hall offers splendid facilities for conferences, weddings and leisure breaks. The Great Hall is awe-inspiring with its stained glass windows, massive pillars and stone floors, whilst each of the 53 bedrooms has its own individual character, combining modern features with traditional opulence. A huge open fireplace adds charm to the elegantly furnished Drawing Room and the unique Library and Print Room restaurant serves contemporary English cuisine and has been awarded 2 AA rosettes for the highest standard of cuisine and service. Matfen Hall enjoys stunning views over its own championship golf course, laid out on a classic parkland landscape with manicured greens and fairways flanked by majestic trees. Rated as one of the finest in the North East, it provides a pleasurable test for players of all abilities. There is also a 9-hole par 3 golf course. A new swimming pool, beauty and leisure spa opened in the spring of 2004. Scenic coastal, rural and ancient sites are within comfortable driving distance. Newcastle-upon-Tyne is only 20 minutes away. Special breaks available.

Our inspector loved: Having a relaxing pamper day in the new leisure spa.

    SPA

NEW

HART'S HOTEL

STANDARD HILL, PARK ROW, NOTTINGHAM, NOTTINGHAMSHIRE NG1 6FN

Modern and stylish, Hart's opened in 2003 in a quiet cul-de-sac just a 5-minute walk from Nottingham's bustling centre. On one side there is a charming courtyard and guest car park spaces. On the other, a delightful, secluded, tree-shaded garden where coffee, tea and cool drinks can be sipped over social chit-chat whilst enjoying views over the city. Owner Tim Hart also runs the luxurious Hambleton Hall in Rutland, home to one of the region's outstanding gourmet restaurants. His aim in Nottingham has been to apply equally high standards of hospitality and cooking in a contemporary, comfortable and affordable environment; he has succeeded. Bedrooms are light and airy with open views, chic décor and a high standard of 21st-century comforts and facilities. These include Egyptian cotton bed linen, goose down stuffed pillows and duvet, DDI phone line, modem connection and charging point for laptop or mobile phone. The fashionable and sophisticated Park Bar, with its soft, flush ceiling lighting, cool wall tints, colourful prints, shiny wood floor and bright red leather armchairs, offers champagne by the glass and a selection of light meals and snacks as an alternative to eating at the hotel's acclaimed restaurant located in a separate building 20m away.

Our inspector loved: Having breakfast on the private terrace garden with its panoramic views over the city.

Directions: Follow signs for city centre and Nottingham Castle. Going north on Maid Marion Way, turn left after the Gala Casino and left again at the top of a slight hill.

Worksop

Mansfield

Nottingham

Web: www.johansens.com/hartshotel
E-mail: ask@hartshotel.co.uk
Tel: 0870 381 9330
International: +44 (0)115 988 1900
Fax: 0115 947 7600

Price Guide:
single £115
double £115–£155
garden £140–£155

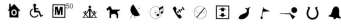

NEW

LACE MARKET HOTEL

29-31, HIGH PAVEMENT, THE LACE MARKET, NOTTINGHAM, NOTTINGHAMSHIRE NG1 1HE

Occupying a prime location in Nottingham's city centre, just yards from the most fashionable shopping area and the National Arena, this privately owned boutique hotel offers guests outstanding hospitality and service. The property has a large clientele from amongst the music industry and celebrity A-list, which is not surprising since the Lace Market boasts luxurious accommodation, stylish conference rooms, a gastro pub, an upmarket brasserie and chic cocktail bar all under one roof. The 42 bedrooms are individually designed and furnished with sumptuous bedding, unique artwork and indulgent en-suite facilities carefully selected to create a calming ambience in which to unwind. Serving classic French brasserie fayre, the sophisticated Merchants brasserie provides a delectable dining experience and guests may continue their evening with drinks in the trendy Saint Bar. Although this property is centrally based, arriving by car is not a problem with free, on-street overnight parking available and a convenient multi-storey car park located in the neighbouring road. Whilst visitors to Lace Market will find plenty to do in and around Nottingham they can also enjoy complimentary access to nearby Holmes Place Health Club with indoor pool, full gym facilities and fitness classes.

Directions: Head for the city centre and use Stoney Street NCP car park.

Web: www.johansens.com/lacemarkethotel
E-mail: reservations@lacemarkethotel.co.uk
Tel: 0870 381 9325
International: +44 (0)115 852 3232
Fax: 0115 852 3223

Price Guide:
small single £90
double/twin £110–£135
superior £175
studios £225

Worksop

Mansfield

Nottingham

Our inspector loved: The Cock & Hoop traditional pub with its range of real ales, and Merchants Restaurant, recently restored by David Collins.

 42 M 35

LANGAR HALL

LANGAR, NOTTINGHAMSHIRE NG13 9HG

Set in the Vale of Belvoir, mid-way between Nottingham and Grantham, Langar Hall is the family home of Imogen Skirving. It was built in 1837 on the site of a great historic house, the home of Admiral Lord Howe. It stands in quiet seclusion overlooking gardens, where sheep graze among the ancient trees in the park. Below the croquet lawn lies a romantic network of medieval fishponds stocked with carp. Epitomising "excellence and diversity", Langar Hall combines the standards of good hotel-keeping with the hospitality and style of country house living. The popular neighbourhood restaurant serves English dishes of local meat, poultry, game, fish and shell fish with garden vegetables in season. The en-suite bedrooms are individually designed and comfortably appointed, whilst the public rooms feature fine furnishings and most rooms afford beautiful views of the garden, park and moat. Langar Hall is an ideal venue for small boardroom meetings. It is also an ideal base from which to visit Belvoir Castle, see cricket at Trent Bridge, visit students at Nottingham University and to see Robin Hood's Sherwood Forest. Dogs can be accommodated by arrangement.

Our inspector loved: The friendly relaxing home-from-home atmosphere.

Directions: Langar is accessible via Bingham on the A52, or via Cropwell Bishop from the A46 (both signposted). The house adjoins the church and is hidden behind it.

Worksop

Mansfield

Nottingham

Web: www.johansens.com/langarhall
E-mail: langarhall–hotel@ndirect.co.uk
Tel: 0870 381 8676
International: +44 (0)1949 860559
Fax: 01949 861045

Price Guide:
single £65–£97.50
double/twin £130–£185
suite £185

BIGNELL PARK HOTEL & RESTAURANT

CHESTERTON, BICESTER, OXFORDSHIRE OX26 1UE

Directions: From M40, junction 9, follow A41 towards Bicester. After approximately 1½ miles turn left to Chesterton and then take A4095.

Web: www.johansens.com/bignellpark
E-mail: enq@bignellparkhotel.co.uk
Tel: 0870 381 8362
International: +44 (0)1869 326550
Fax: 01869 322729

Price Guide:
single £70–£90
double/twin £90–£110
four poster £135

In the lovely setting of the pretty village Chesterton, this friendly and welcoming Cotswold stone hotel combines traditional old-world charm with the grace of a delightfully run country home. Originally an 18th-century farmhouse, Bignell Park stands in 2½ acres of secluded, lawned gardens and orchard. Close by is the distinguished Kirtlington Polo Club and the historic market town and important hunting centre of Bicester. It is an ideal location for those wishing to explore a succession of enchanting, honey-coloured Cotswold villages and enjoy the attractions of Stratford-Upon-Avon, Warwick Castle, Oxford and Blenheim Palace, ancestral home to the Dukes of Marlborough. The tastefully refurbished en-suite bedrooms, which include 3 four-posters, are spacious, attractively decorated and provide every facility to make visiting a pleasure. During winter months guests can relax before a roaring log fire in the comfortable and elegant drawing room which looks out over the garden. The candle-lit restaurant, with wood-beamed ceiling, minstrels' gallery and open fire, has gained a deserved reputation. Head Chef Stuart Turvey and his team carefully prepare imaginative and varied English/French menus to suit all tastes.

Our inspector loved: *The contemporary yet classic style.*

THE BAY TREE HOTEL

SHEEP STREET, BURFORD, OXON OX18 4LW

The Bay Tree has been expertly refurbished so that it retains all its Tudor splendour whilst offering every modern facility. The oak-panelled rooms have huge stone fireplaces and a galleried staircase leads upstairs from the raftered hall. All the bedrooms are en suite, three of them furnished with four-poster beds and 2 of the 5 suites have half-tester beds. In the summer, guests can enjoy the delightful walled gardens, featuring landscaped terraces of lawn and flower beds. A relaxing atmosphere is enhanced by the staff's attentive service in the flagstoned dining room where the head chef's creative cuisine is complemented by a comprehensive selection of fine wines. Light meals are served in a country-style bar. Burford, often described as the gateway to the Cotswolds, is renowned for its assortment of antique shops and the Tolsey Museum of local history. The Bay Tree Hotel makes a convenient base for day trips to Stratford-upon-Avon, Stow-on-the-Wold and Blenheim Palace. Golf, clay pigeon shooting and riding can be arranged locally.

Our inspector loved: *The garden rooms - and the delicious crème brûlée.*

Directions: Burford is on the A40 between Oxford and Cheltenham. Proceed halfway down the hill into Burford, turn left into Sheep Street and The Bay Tree Hotel is 30 yards on your right.

Banbury

Oxford

Henley-on-Thames

Web: www.johansens.com/baytree
E-mail: info@baytreehotel.info
Tel: 0870 381 8347
International: +44 (0)1993 822791
Fax: 01993 823008

Price Guide:
single £119
double/twin £155–£185
suite £195–£230

PHYLLIS COURT CLUB

MARLOW ROAD, HENLEY-ON-THAMES, OXFORDSHIRE RG9 2HT

Directions: M40, junction 4 to Marlow or M4, junction 8/9 then follow signposts to Henley-on-Thames.

Web: www.johansens.com/phylliscourt
E-mail: enquiries@phylliscourt.co.uk
Tel: 0870 381 8822
International: +44 (0)1491 570500
Fax: 01491 570528

Price Guide:
single £112
twin/double £131

Founded in 1906 by the owner of the house and a group of friends and London businessmen, the Club has an intriguing history spanning 6 centuries and involving royal patronage. Phyllis Court occupies an unrivalled position on the banks of the Thames and overlooking the Henley Royal Regatta course. Phyllis Court prides itself on retaining the traditions of its illustrious past, whilst guests today who now stay in this fine historic residence can enjoy the highest standards of up-to-date hospitality. Oliver Cromwell slept here and he built the embankment wall; and it was here that William II held his first Royal Court. Years later, when the name Henley became synonymous with rowing, they came as patrons of the Royal Regatta: Prince Albert, King George V and Edward, Prince of Wales. The character of the place remains unaltered in its hallowed setting, but the comfortable bedrooms, the restaurant, the "cellar" and the entire complement of amenities are of the latest high quality. Residents become temporary members as the dining room and bar are open to members only. Likely to be fully booked far ahead during the season. Ideal for meetings, functions and wedding parties.

Our inspector loved: *The view along the Regatta course - The Thames.*

THE COTSWOLD LODGE HOTEL

66A BANBURY ROAD, OXFORD OX2 6JP

Situated in a quiet conservation area just ½ mile away from Oxford is this picturesque Victorian building, which has been restored in the style of a stately manor house. An ideal location for tourists and those on business, the hotel offers a comfortable and relaxed environment. The Scholars bar is ideal for a light lunch or pre-dinner drink, and during winter, log fires enhance the cosy ambience. The elegant Sixty Six A restaurant serves outstanding seasonal menus, with high-quality ingredients a priority. Fresh fish and lobster come from Cornwall, sausages are made specially for the hotel, wild salmon is delivered from Scotland, and local lamb and game are used extensively. An impressive wine list ensures that there is something to suit all tastes and complement every meal. The tastefully furnished en-suite bedrooms differ in size and style. The Cotswold Lodge happily caters for conferences on a daily or residential basis, and over the years has become renowned for its superb reputation in hosting wedding receptions. Staff are on hand to provide their expertise and tailor arrangements to suit individual requirements. The Banquet room accommodates up to 100 people and has access to a patio with fountain and walled garden.

Our inspector loved: The warmth of welcome and attention to detail.

Directions: From M40 junction 8, take A40 for Oxford; or junction 9, take A34; or from M4, junction 13, take A34 for Oxford.

Web: www.johansens.com/cotswoldlodge
E-mail: info@cotswoldlodgehotel.co.uk
Tel: 0870 381 8450
International: +44 (0)1865 512121
Fax: 01865 512490

Banbury

Oxford

Henley-on-Thames

Price Guide:
single £125
double/twin £175
suite from £295

HAWKWELL HOUSE

CHURCH WAY, IFLEY VILLAGE, OXFORD OX4 4D2

Directions: From Oxford, take the A34 south, then A4142 east. Iffley is signed on your left.

Web: www.johansens.com/hawkwell
E-mail: info@hawkwellhouse.co.uk
Tel: 0870 381 8326
International: +44 (0)1865 749988
Fax: 01865 748525

Price Guide:
single from £90
double from £130
suite from £150

A secluded, quintessentially English country garden with 3 acres of lush lawns, shady trees, deep beds of mature shrubs and colourful flowers surround this imposing, white-fronted hotel in the leafy village of Iffley, just 2 miles from the centre of Oxford. Next door is the 12th-century Norman Church of St Mary, noted for its carvings, rich decorations and splendid west front. Hawkwell House is a homely environment providing total tranquillity in a sleepy Thamesside setting. It offers comfort, charm and style with 66 individually designed, en-suite bedrooms and suites that provide luxurious solace and an abundance of modern facilities. The elegant, award-winning Arezzo restaurant overlooks an attractive fountain patio and serves seasonal menus of highly individual dishes, with quality ingredients a high priority. An impressive wine list ensures that there is something to suit all tastes. More informal dining can be enjoyed in Barezzo, a conservatory-style bar with distinctive décor, where talented kitchen staff provide everything from a tasty tiffin to an exotic 3-course meal. The hotel happily caters for conferences for up to 200 delegates and banquets for 180. Blenheim Palace, Woodstock and the Cotswolds are within easy reach and the attractions of Oxford are to hand.

Our inspector loved: *The secluded garden.*

FALLOWFIELDS

KINGSTON BAGPUIZE WITH SOUTHMOOR, OXON OX13 5BH

Fallowfields, once the home of Begum Aga Khan, dates back more than 300 years. It has been updated and extended over past decades and today boasts a lovely early Victorian Gothic southern aspect. The house is set in 2 acres of gardens, surrounded by 10 acres of grassland. The guests' bedrooms, which offer a choice of four-poster or coroneted beds, are large and well appointed and offer every modern amenity to ensure maximum comfort and convenience. During the winter months, there are welcoming log fires in the elegant main reception rooms. The cuisine is mainly British, awarded 3 RAC dining awards, imaginative in style and presentation and there is a good choice of menus available. The walled kitchen garden provides most of the vegetables and salads for the table and locally grown and organic produce is otherwise used wherever possible. Fallowfields is close to Stratford, the Cotswolds, Stonehenge, Bath and Bristol to the west, Oxford, Henley on Thames, the Chilterns and Windsor to the east. Heathrow airport is under an hour away.

Our inspector loved: The wonderful collection of elephants!

Directions: Take the Kingston Bagpuize exit on the A420 Oxford to Swindon. Fallowfields is at the west end of Southmoor, just after the Longworth sign.

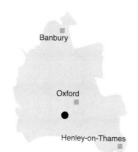

Banbury

Oxford

Henley-on-Thames

Web: www.johansens.com/fallowfields
E-mail: stay@fallowfields.com
Tel: 0870 381 8513
International: +44 (0)1865 820416
Fax: 01865 821275

Price Guide:
single £115–£145
double £122–£170

WESTON MANOR

WESTON-ON-THE-GREEN, OXFORDSHIRE OX25 3QL

Directions: From the M40, exit at junction 9 onto the A34 towards Oxford. Leave the A34 at the first junction, towards Middleton Stoney. At the mini roundabout turn right onto the B430. The hotel is approx 500m on the left.

Web: www.johansens.com/westonmanor
E-mail: lesliewood@westonmanor.co.uk
Tel: 0870 381 8981
International: +44 (0)1869 350621
Fax: 01869 350901

Price Guide:
single from £99
double/twin from £124
suite from £195

Banbury

Oxford

Henley-on-Thames

Imposing wrought-iron gates flanked by sculptured busts surmounting tall grey stone pillars lead into the impressive entrance to this delightful old manor house, the showpiece of the lovely village of Weston-on-the-Green since the 11th century. The ancestral home of the Earls of Abingdon and Berkshire, and once the property of Henry VIII, Weston Manor stands regally in 12 acres of colourful gardens. Restored as a exceptional country house hotel, wonderful accommodation and impeccable service are on offer in this peaceful retreat from which visitors can discover the delights of the nearby Cotswold countryside and of Oxford, Woodstock, Blenheim Palace and Broughton Castle. Many of the charming bedrooms, including 4 in a cottage and 16 in the coach-house, retain antique furniture and all have garden views, and private bathrooms. There is a croquet lawn and a secluded, heated outdoor swimming pool. The restaurant, a magnificent vaulted and oak-panelled Baronial Hall serves delectable, 2 AA Rosette award-winning cuisine; dining in such historic splendour is very much the focus of a memorable stay. There are 7 versatile meeting rooms, including the Baronial Hall, with natural daylight, ideal for exclusive use, conferences and team building events. The elegant surroundings provide a beautiful backdrop for weddings.

Our inspector loved: The Baronial Hall restaurant and Minstrel Gallery.

THE SPREAD EAGLE HOTEL

CORNMARKET, THAME, OXFORDSHIRE OX9 2BW

The historic market town of Thame with its mile-long main street is a delightful town just 6 miles from the M40 and surrounded by beautiful countryside speckled with tiny, charming villages, many of them with cosy thatched cottages. The Spread Eagle has stood tall, square and imposingly in the heart of Thame since the 16th century and over the years has played host to Charles II, French prisoners from the Napoleonic wars, famous politicians and writers such as Evelyn Waugh. The former proprietor John Fothergill introduced haute cuisine to the provinces and chronicled his experiences in the best seller, "An Innkeeper's Diary". The book is still available at The Spread Eagle and the brasserie is named after him. It serves excellent English and French cuisine made with the freshest local produce. Seasonal changing menus are complemented by a well-balanced wine list which includes some superb half-bottles of unusual vintages. Guests have 33 bedrooms to choose from, comprising 2 suites, 23 doubles, 3 twins and 5 singles. All are en suite, well equipped and in the style expected of a coaching inn hotel. Conference facilities are available. The Spread Eagle is ideally situated for visits to many fascinating historic places such as Blenheim Palace and Waddesdon Manor.

Our inspector loved: The new brasserie.

Directions: Exit M40 at junction 6. Take B4009 to Chinnor and then B4445 to Thame. The hotel is on the left after the roundabout at the west end of Upper High Street.

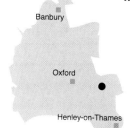

Web: www.johansens.com/spreadeaglethame
E-mail: enquiries@spreadeaglethame.co.uk
Tel: 0870 381 8902
International: +44 (0)1844 213661
Fax: 01844 261380

Price Guide:
single from £98
double/twin from £115

THE SPRINGS HOTEL & GOLF CLUB

NORTH STOKE, WALLINGFORD, OXFORDSHIRE OX10 6BE

Directions: From the M40 take exit 6 onto B4009, through Watlington to Benson; turn left onto A4074 towards Reading. After 2 miles go right onto B4009. The hotel is ½ mile further on the right.

Web: www.johansens.com/springshotel
E-mail: info@thespringshotel.com
Tel: 0870 381 8904
International: +44 (0)1491 836687
Fax: 01491 836877

Price Guide:
single from £95
double/twin from £110
suite from £155

The Springs is a grand old country house which dates from 1874 and is set deep in the heart of the beautiful Thames Valley. One of the first houses in England to be built in the Mock Tudor style, it stands in 6 acres of grounds. The hotel's large south-facing windows overlook a spring-fed lake, from which it takes its name. Many of the luxurious bedrooms and suites offer beautiful views over the lake and lawns, whilst others overlook the quiet woodland that surrounds the hotel. Private balconies provide patios for summer relaxation. The Lakeside restaurant has an intimate atmosphere inspired by its gentle décor and the lovely view of the lake. The award-winning restaurant's menu takes advantage of fresh local produce and a well-stocked cellar of international wines provides the perfect accompaniment to a splendid meal. Leisure facilities include a 18-hole par 72 golf course, clubhouse and putting green, a swimming pool, sauna and touring bicycles. Oxford, Blenheim Palace and Windsor are nearby and the hotel is conveniently located for racing at Newbury and Ascot and the Royal Henley Regatta.

Our inspector loved: *The newly renovated rooms and dining room.*

THE FEATHERS HOTEL

MARKET STREET, WOODSTOCK, OXFORDSHIRE OX20 1SX

The Feathers is a privately owned and run town house hotel, situated in the centre of Woodstock, a few miles from Oxford. Woodstock is one of England's most attractive country towns, constructed mostly from Cotswold stone and with some buildings dating from the 12th century. The hotel, built in the 17th century, was originally four separate houses. Antiques, log fires and traditional English furnishings lend character and charm. There are 20 bedrooms, all of which have private bathrooms and showers. Public rooms, including the drawing room and study, are intimate and comfortable. The small garden is a delightful setting for a light lunch or afternoon tea and guests can enjoy a drink in the cosy courtyard bar, which has an open fire in winter. The antique-panelled restaurant is internationally renowned for its fine cuisine, complemented by a high standard of service and 3 AA Rosettes. The menu changes frequently and offers a wide variety of dishes, using the finest local ingredients. Blenheim Palace, seat of the Duke of Marlborough and birthplace of Sir Winston Churchill, is just around the corner. The Cotswolds and the dreaming spires of Oxford are a short distance away.

Our inspector loved: *The newly decorated bar and secluded courtyard gardens.*

Directions: From London leave the M40 at junction 8; from Birmingham leave at junction 9. Take A44 and follow the signs to Woodstock. The hotel is on the left.

Web: www.johansens.com/feathers
E-mail: enquiries@feathers.co.uk
Tel: 0870 381 8519
International: +44 (0)1993 812291
Fax: 01993 813158

Price Guide:
single £115
double/twin £130–£185
suite £235–£290

217

HAMBLETON HALL

HAMBLETON, OAKHAM, RUTLAND LE15 8TH

Winner of Johansens Most Excellent Country Hotel Award 1996, Hambleton Hall, originally a Victorian mansion, became a hotel in 1980. Since then its renown has continually grown. It enjoys a spectacular lakeside setting in a charming and unspoilt area of Rutland. The hotel's tasteful interiors have been designed to create elegance and comfort, retaining individuality by avoiding a catalogue approach to furnishing. Delightful displays of flowers, an artful blend of ingredients from local hedgerows and the London flower markets colour the bedrooms. In the Michelin-Starred restaurant, chef Aaron Patterson and his enthusiastic team offer a menu which is strongly seasonal. Grouse, Scottish ceps and chanterelles, partridge and woodcock are all available at just the right time of year, accompanied by the best vegetables, herbs and salads from the Hall's garden. The Croquet Pavilion, a 2-bedroom suite with living room and breakfast room is a luxurious addition to the accommodation options. For the energetic there are lovely walks around the lake and opportunities for tennis and swimming, golf, riding, bicycling, trout fishing, and sailing. Burghley House and Belton are nearby, as are the antique shops of Oakham, Uppingham and Stamford. Hambleton Hall is a Relais & Châteaux member.

Directions: In the village of Hambleton, signposted from the A606, 1 mile east of Oakham.

Web: www.johansens.com/hambletonhall
E-mail: hotel@hambletonhall.com
Tel: 0870 381 8582
International: +44 (0)1572 756991
Fax: 01572 724721

Price Guide:
single from £165
double/twin £190–£355
suite £600

Oakham

Stamford

Uppingham

Our inspector loved: *Breakfasting on the terrace of the detached 2-bedroom Croquet Pavilion overlooking the gardens and views of Rutland Water.*

THE LAKE ISLE

16 HIGH STREET EAST, UPPINGHAM, RUTLAND LE15 9PZ

This small personally run restaurant and town house hotel is situated in the pretty market town of Uppingham, dominated by the famous Uppingham School and close to Rutland Water. The entrance to the building, which dates back to the 18th century, is via a quiet courtyard where a wonderful display of flowering tubs and hanging baskets greets you. In winter, sit in the bar where a log fire burns or relax in the upstairs lounge which overlooks the High Street. In the bedrooms, each named after a wine growing region in France and all of which are en suite, guests will find fresh fruit, homemade biscuits and a decanter of sherry. Those in the courtyard are cottage-style suites. Under the personal direction of chef Stuart Mead, the restaurant offers seasonal changing menus using fresh ingredients. There is an extensive wine list of more than 200 wines ranging from regional labels to old clarets. Special "Wine Dinners" are held throughout the year, enabling guests to appreciate this unique cellar. Burghley House, speedway in Rockingham and Belvoir Castle are within a short drive.

Our inspector loved: *The spacious home from home that is the "Petrus" cottage.*

Directions: Uppingham is near the intersection of A47 and A6003. The hotel is on the High Street and is reached on foot via Reeves Yard and by car via Queen Street.

Oakham

Stamford

Uppingham

Web: www.johansens.com/lakeisle
E-mail: info@lakeislehotel.com
Tel: 0870 381 8670
International: +44 (0)1572 822951
Fax: 01572 824400

Price Guide:
single £55–£70
double/twin £70–£85
suite £80–£100

*S*cotland is famed for its brooding hills and **SENSATIONAL** views. It's also home to an **EXTRAORDINARILY** *diverse range of whiskies. One of the finest is* Talisker,® *a* **POWERFUL** *single malt whisky imbued with the distinctive and* **UNCOMPROMISING** *character of its birthplace — the Isle of Skye.*

DO YOU HAVE A TASTE FOR THE FINER THINGS IN LIFE?

If so, we think you'll appreciate Spirit. It's a gateway to experiencing some of the world's most delightful drinks, designed to broaden the horizons of all connoisseurs of the good life. You'll find Spirit brings you real insights, because it's been created by makers of fine spirits including **Talisker** single malt whisky, **Johnnie Walker**® **Black Label**® Scotch whisky and **Tanqueray**® gin.

All you have to do to register with Spirit is visit
www.spirit-taste.co.uk

And if you would like to find out about purchasing a wide range of Scotch whiskies, please visit
www.malts.com

For more information about Spirit — or for any trade enquiries — you can contact us on
+44 (0) 121 472 9040

SPIRIT

The Talisker, Johnnie Walker Black Label and Tanqueray words are trade marks © Diageo 2004

DINHAM HALL

LUDLOW, SHROPSHIRE SY8 1EJ

Tall, square, solid and stylish Dinham Hall is the epitome of a grand, late 18th-century family home. Now an elegant hotel, it stands prestigiously in the centre of the historic market town of Ludlow, just a short stroll from the ruins of a great sandstone castle built by Roger Montgomery, Earl of Shrewsbury, in 1085. An enviable location that provides guests with ready access to the town's broad streets, narrow lanes, graceful buildings and mellow beauty. Dinham offers a comfortable and relaxing atmosphere. Lounges are restful and warmed by open fires in winter and each of the 12 bedrooms offers modern facilities with period design. Some have four-posters and 2 of the bedrooms are within a cottage in the garden grounds. Dinham has gained the deserved reputation as Ludlow's latest gastronomic delight. The restaurant serves innovative, modern British cuisine with an Italian influence prepared by talented new chef, P. J. McGregor; only the highest quality of local and seasonal produce is used. While dining, guests can enjoy superb views over the walled garden and open countryside towards the Whitcliffe hills and Mortimer forests or when taking tea on the hotel terrace during summer months. As well as browsing in the town's famed antique shops guests can delight in visiting Ludlow races and take lovely river walks.

Our inspector loved: The care and willingness to create a hostelry in the true sense.

Directions: Ludlow is approached via the A49. Dinham Hall is in the centre of town overlooking the castle.

Web: www.johansens.com/dinhamhall
E-mail: info@dinhamhall.co.uk
Tel: 0870 381 8482
International: +44 (0)1584 876464
Fax: 01584 876019

Price Guide:
single £95–£250
double/twin £130–£280

Chester

Oswestry

Shrewsbury   Wolverhampton

● Bridgnorth

MADELEY COURT

TELFORD, SHROPSHIRE TF7 5DW

Directions: 4 miles from Jct 4 off M54; follow A442 then B4373. Signposted Dawley then Madeley.

Web: www.johansens.com/madeleycourt
E-mail: enquires@hotels-telford.com
Tel: 0870 381 8711
International: +44 (0)1952 680068
Fax: 01952 684275

Price Guide: (incl breakfast & priory dinner)
executive £79.95 per night
historic £79.95 per night
based on 2 guests sharing
minimum stay 2 days

Chester

Oswestry

Shrewsbury ● Wolverhampton

Bridgnorth

Situated deep in its own estate of Shropshire countryside in a beautiful lakeside setting, this unique 16th-century country house has been skilfully transformed into one of the county's premier hotels. As you drive along the tree lined driveway you are met by the original Grade 1 listed Elizabethan Gatehouse, the first historical visual delight that awaits you. Madeley Court, once a monastery and former local gentry's residence, is steeped in history and has many a tale to tell in its original quarters of the house. With its individual accommodation located throughout the grounds, the hotel offers the perfect opportunity to relax in style and elegance, whether on business or pleasure. Still abiding by traditional rules of service and standards, the unique and stunning restaurants are situated in the oldest and most historic parts of the house, with the elegant Priory Restaurant occupying the original Hall and Le Rendezvous, a French provincial Brasserie situated in the cellarage of the house, both offering a tempting and unforgettable dining experience. The friendly and helpful staff are always happy to impart their in-depth local knowledge of nearby attractions, such as historic Ironbridge, Buildwas Abbey, Weston Park and the market towns of Shrewsbury and Bridgenorth.

Our inspector loved: *The changes made to Madeley Court this year.*

STON EASTON PARK

STON EASTON, BATH, SOMERSET BA3 4DF

The internationally renowned hotel at Ston Easton Park is a Grade I Palladian mansion of notable distinction. A showpiece for some exceptional architectural and decorative features of its period, it dates from 1739 and has recently undergone extensive restoration, offering a unique opportunity to enjoy the opulent splendour of the 18th century. A high priority is given to the provision of friendly and unobtrusive service. The hotel has won innumerable awards for its décor, service and food. Jean Monro, an acknowledged expert on 18th-century decoration, supervised the design and furnishing of the interiors, complementing the original features with choice antiques, paintings and objets d'art. Fresh, quality produce, delivered from all parts of Britain, is combined with herbs and vegetables from the Victorian kitchen garden to create English and French dishes. To accompany your meal, a wide selection of rare wines and old vintages is stocked in the house cellars. The grounds, landscaped by Humphry Repton in 1793, consist of romantic gardens and parkland. The 17th-century Gardener's Cottage, close to the main house on the wooded banks of the River Norr, provides private suite accommodation.

Our inspector loved: *The feeling of a bygone era and the peace and seclusion at this magnificent location.*

Directions: 11 miles south of Bath on the A37 between Bath and Wells.

Web: www.johansens.com/stoneastonpark
E-mail: info@stoneaston.co.uk
Tel: 0870 381 8916
International: +44 (0)1761 241631
Fax: 01761 241377

Price Guide:
single from £120
double/twin £150–£395
four-poster £210–£395

223

DANESWOOD HOUSE HOTEL

CUCK HILL, SHIPHAM, NEAR WINSCOMBE, SOMERSET BS25 1RD

Directions: Shipham is signposted from the A38 Bristol-Bridgwater road. Go through the village towards Cheddar and the hotel is on the left.

Web: www.johansens.com/daneswoodhouse
E-mail: info@daneswoodhotel.co.uk
Tel: 0870 381 8475
International: +44 (0)1934 843145
Fax: 01934 843824

Bath

Taunton   Yeovil

Price Guide:
single £89.50–£99.50
double/twin £105–£150
suites £150

This tall, pebble-dashed Edwardian house nestles on the slopes of the Mendip Hills commanding spectacular views over the Somerset countryside towards the Bristol Channel and South Wales. Originally a homeopathic health hydro, it is now a hotel of distinction which has been in the enthusiastic ownership of David and Elise Hodges for almost 25 years. They have created a homely, welcoming and relaxing atmosphere and their continual pursuit of excellence has earned the hotel a reputation for comfort, culinary delights and service. The generous en-suite bedrooms are individually designed, delightfully furnished and have every facility. The Honeymoon Suite boasts a 7ft king-size bed whilst the Victorian Room has a Queen Anne four-poster. Some bedrooms open out onto the 5 acres of grounds and have private patios. Hotel guests with dogs are allowed in garden rooms. Great emphasis is placed on using fresh produce and local meat and poultry for the superb dishes served in the period dining room, which has been awarded 2 AA Rosettes. Breakfast is in the sunny conservatory. Conference facilities. The hotel grounds offer direct access to the Mendip Walkway. Nearby are 5 18-hole golf courses, trout fishing, riding and several National Trust houses.

Our inspector loved: *The newly presented restaurant and menu's created by the new team of chefs.*

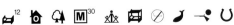

MOUNT SOMERSET COUNTRY HOUSE HOTEL

HENLADE, TAUNTON, SOMERSET TA3 5NB

This elegant Regency residence, awarded 2 Rosettes and 3 stars, stands high on the slopes of the Blackdown Hills, overlooking miles of lovely countryside. The Hotel is rich in intricate craftsmanship and displays fine original features. Its owners have committed themselves to creating an atmosphere in which guests can relax, confident that all needs will be catered for. The bedrooms are sumptuously furnished and many offer views over the Quantock Hills. All of the bedrooms have luxurious bathrooms and some have spa baths. Light lunches, teas, coffees and home-made cakes can be enjoyed in the beautifully furnished drawing room, whilst in the restaurant the finest food and wines are served. A team of chefs work together to create dishes which exceed the expectations of the most discerning gourmet. Places of interest nearby include Glastonbury Abbey, Wells Cathedral and the vibrant city of Exeter.

Our inspector loved: *The tastefully refurbished bedrooms and the wonderful relaxing atmosphere.*

Directions: At the M5 exit at junction 25, join the A358 towards Ilminster. Just past Henlade turn right at the sign for Stoke St. Mary. At the T-junction turn left, the Hotel drive is 150 yards on the right.

Web: www.johansens.com/mountsomerset
E-mail: info@mountsomersethotel.co.uk
Tel: 0870 381 8750
International: +44 (0)1823 442500
Fax: 01823 442900

Price Guide:
single from £95–£105
double/twin from £145–£170
suites £195–£210

225

BINDON COUNTRY HOUSE HOTEL

LANGFORD BUDVILLE, WELLINGTON, SOMERSET TA21 0RU

Directions: 15 minutes from M5/J26, drive to Wellington take B3187 to Langford Budville, through village, right towards Wiveliscombe, then right at junction. Pass Bindon Farm and after 450 yards turn right.

Web: www.johansens.com/bindoncountryhouse
E-mail: stay@bindon.com
Tel: 0870 381 8364
International: +44 (0)1823 400070
Fax: 01823 400071

Price Guide:
single from £95
double/twin £115–£215
suite from £145

Occupying a glorious location in 7 acres of tranquil gardens and woodland, this property offers guests a peaceful retreat from a hectic life. Bindon really is the quintessential country house hotel with croquet on the lawn, a delightful rose garden and a rediscovered Victorian orangery. Some parts of the building date back to the 17th century and when current owners Mark and Lynn Jaffa purchased the property in 1996 they undertook a painstaking restoration process to create the wonderful hotel that stands today. The 12 luxurious bedrooms are light, airy and spacious, each with its own character, yet enjoying the same sumptuous fabrics, exquisite linens and pampering bathrooms. Scott Dickson, head chef at the acclaimed Wellesley restaurant, has trained in some of Scotland's finest hotels including Cameron House and Skibo Castle. The dishes he creates are an exciting blend of French and English cuisine for both the à la carte and tasting menus. After a satisfying meal guests may adjourn to the oak-panelled Wellington Bar to enjoy drinks in front of the cosy open fire. Local places of interest include Exmoor, Exeter, Wells, Dartmoor, Bath and Glastonbury with Langford Heath Nature Reserve just a 5-minute walk away. Short breaks from £150, including dinner are available. Exclusive use of the hotel can be arranged.

Our inspector loved: *The peaceful location, warm welcome and total comfort.*

HOLBROOK HOUSE HOTEL & SPA

WINCANTON, SOMERSET BA9 8BS

Holbrook House is a quiet and easily accessible hotel surrounded by 17 acres of gardens, lush meadows, unspoilt woodland, abundant wildlife and deep, clear rivers on the borders of Somerset and Dorset. Comfortable, exquisitely furnished rooms exude warmth and cosiness with open fires, beautiful antique furniture and warm, attractive décor. En-suite bedrooms are extremely spacious and overlook the gorgeous grounds. Dining at the hotel is a pleasure with exceptionally imaginative and delicious seasonal dishes to tempt any discerning palate together with an extensive cellar and first-class service. An indoor heated pool, sauna, steam rooms, gymnasium, solarium and beauty studio are available for guests' complete relaxation, and outdoor enthusiasts will appreciate the beautifully calm river (perfect for fishing). There is also hiking, horse riding, cycling, shooting and a wealth of excellent golf courses nearby. For the more energetic there is a specially dedicated lawn on which guests can play tennis, croquet, badminton or volleyball. Leisure and spa breaks are available. Nearby tourist attractions include Longleat, Stourhead, Salisbury and Glastonbury as well as the beautiful cities of Wells and Bath. The beautiful Exmoor countryside with wild ponies and idyllic villages is within easy reach.

Directions: Leave the A303 at Wincanton slip road and join the A371 towards Castle Cary at the first roundabout. Continue over 3 more roundabouts and the hotel driveway is immediately on the right.

Web: www.johansens.com/holbrookhouse
E-mail: enquiries@holbrookhouse.co.uk
Tel: 0870 381 9174
International: +44 (0)1963 824466
Fax: 01963 32681

Price Guide:
single £107– £135
double/twin £135–£175
suite £245

Bath

Taunton   Yeovil

Our inspector loved: The so many first-class facilities to enjoy.

HOAR CROSS HALL SPA RESORT

HOAR CROSS, NR YOXALL, STAFFORDSHIRE DE13 8QS

Directions: From Lichfield turn off the A51 onto the A515 towards Ashbourne. Go through Yoxall and turn left to Hoar Cross.

Web: www.johansens.com/hoarcrosshall
E-mail: info@hoarcross.co.uk
Tel: 0870 381 8598
International: +44 (0)1283 575671
Fax: 01283 575652

Price Guide: (fully inclusive price including some treatments per person)
single £150-£170
double/twin £150-£170

Stoke-on-Trent

Stafford

Cannock

The only spa resort in a stately home in England. Surrounded by 80 acres of beautiful countryside, lakes and exquisite formal gardens with water features, exotic plants and beautiful flowers, Hoar Cross Hall is a secluded haven and the perfect venue for those who want a peaceful environment in which to be pampered. Oak panelling, tapestries, rich furnishings and paintings adorn the interior. A stunning Jacobean staircase leads to luxurious bedrooms, all with crown tester or four-poster beds and elegant design. Penthouses have private saunas and balconies overlooking the treetops. Breathtaking gilded ceilings and William Morris wallpaper in the original ballroom set the scene for the dining room, where a superb à la carte menu is offered. A tasty breakfast and buffet lunch is served in the Plantation Restaurants overlooking the pools. There are unlimited ways in which visitors can de-stress at Hoar Cross Hall; yoga, meditation, tai chi, aqua-aerobics and dance classes are all available and outdoor pursuits include tennis, croquet, archery and a fantastic golf academy. Trained professionals are ready to assist and the spa consists of hydrotherapy baths, flotation therapy, saunas, a gymnasium, steam rooms, water grotto, saunarium, aromatherapy room and aerobics.

Our inspector loved: *The balance of excellent meals and welcoming restaurant combined with serious facilities. Relaxed but so professional. Something for everyone - especially happiness.*

BRUDENELL HOTEL

THE PARADE, ALDEBURGH, SUFFOLK IP15 5BU

This delightful hotel is the epitome of a charming contemporary seaside hideaway with a light, airy and relaxed ambience. Informal décor and comfortable furnishings complement the occasional piece of driftwood, and welcoming staff attend to your every need. The AA Rosette awarded restaurant is situated immediately on the seafront and has the feel of an ocean liner. Fresh fish and grills is the speciality. The interior has been cleverly arranged so that the majority of guests can enjoy a stunning panoramic sea view. Decorated in a fresh modern style the spacious bedrooms are well-equipped and many offer either a sea, marsh or river view. Aldeburgh has something for everybody - scenic walks past pastel-coloured houses and fishermen's huts, superb boutique shopping, highly acclaimed restaurants and the annual Aldeburgh Festival. Thorpeness is an unusual and interesting village to explore and also has a splendid golf course. For those interested in history, there are many historic buildings, castles and an abbey in the area. The marshes are a haven for wading birds and birdwatchers or for the more adventurous there is horse riding, archery and rally karting. Access to the hotel is very easy for the less mobile and there is a lift.

Our inspector loved: *Watching the sun glistening on the waves from so many windows.*

Directions: Take the M25, junction 28 onto the A12, then take the A1094 to Aldeburgh. The hotel is on the seafront at the south end of town.

Web: www.johansens.com/brudenell
E-mail: info@brudenellhotel.co.uk
Tel: 0870 381 9182
International: +44 (0)1728 452071
Fax: 01728 454082

Bury St Edmunds
Newmarket
Sudbury
Ipswich
Colchester

Price Guide:
single £65-£93
double £101-£198

♨⁴² ♿ ⚒ 🐕 🦅 ☎ ⊘ ⬍ ♪ ⌐ ↺

229

ANGEL HOTEL

BURY ST EDMUNDS, SUFFOLK IP33 1LT

Directions: Follow the signs to Historic Centre.

Web: www.johansens.com/angelburysted
E-mail: sales@angel.co.uk
Tel: 0870 381 8315
International: +44 (0)1284 714000
Fax: 01284 714001

Price Guide:
single from £85
double/twin from £119
suite from £165

Being the most historic coaching inn in East Anglia, the hotel was immortalised by Charles Dickens, and has welcomed King Louis Phillippe of France and more recently Pierce Brosnan. On one of the prettiest squares in England, visitors will have the immediate impression of a hotel that is loved and nurtured by its owners. In the public rooms, guests will appreciate the carefully chosen ornaments and pictures, fresh flowers and log fires. The hotel has numerous suites and four-poster bedrooms, some with air conditioning. All bedrooms are individually furnished and decorated and all have en-suite bathrooms. The elegant dining room has been awarded 2 Rosettes by the AA for excellent food and service. Overlooking the ancient abbey, the restaurant serves classic English cuisine, including local speciality dishes and succulent roasts. The Angel can offer a wide range of quality conference and banqueting facilities catering for private dinners, meetings and weddings from 10–60 persons. The hotel is within an hour of the east coast ferry ports and 45 minutes from Stansted Airport. Nearby there is racing at Newmarket and several golf courses within easy reach. Bury St Edmunds is an interesting and historic market town and an excellent centre for touring the surrounding area.

Our inspector loved: The dining room, dramatic yet elegant, which complements this historic building.

RAVENWOOD HALL COUNTRY HOTEL & RESTAURANT

ROUGHAM, BURY ST EDMUNDS, SUFFOLK IP30 9JA

Nestling within 7 acres of lovely lawns and woodlands deep in the heart of Suffolk lies Ravenwood Hall. Now an excellent country house hotel, this fine Tudor building dates back to 1530 and retains many of its original features. The restaurant, still boasting the carved timbers and huge inglenook from Tudor times, creates a delightfully intimate atmosphere in which to enjoy imaginative cuisine. The menu is a combination of adventurous and classical dishes, featuring some long forgotten English recipes. The Hall's extensive cellars are stocked with some of the finest vintages, along with a selection of rare ports and brandies. A cosy bar offers a less formal setting in which to enjoy some unusual meals. Comfortable bedrooms are furnished with antiques, reflecting the historic tradition of the Hall, although each is equipped with every modern facility. A wide range of leisure facilities is available for guests, including a croquet lawn and heated swimming pool. There are golf courses and woodland walks to enjoy locally; hunting and shooting can be arranged. Places of interest nearby include the famous medieval wool towns of Lavenham and Long Melford; the historic cities of Norwich and Cambridge are within easy reach, as is Newmarket, the home of horseracing.

Our inspector loved: *The huge inglenook fireplaces and the informal reminders of a private country estate.*

Directions: 2 miles east of Bury St Edmunds off the A14.

Web: www.johansens.com/ravenwoodhall
E-mail: enquiries@ravenwoodhall.co.uk
Tel: 0870 381 8849
International: +44 (0)1359 270345
Fax: 01359 270788

Price Guide:
single £80.50–£109
double/twin £105.50–£149

SALTHOUSE HARBOUR HOTEL

1 NEPTUNE QUAY, IPSWICH, SUFFOLK IP4 1AS

Directions: From the A14 take the A137 and head towards Ipswich town centre. Keep to the outside lane in the one-way system and follow tourist signs to hotel.

Web: www.johansens.com/salthouse
E-mail: staying@salthouseharbour.co.uk
Tel: 0870 381 9196
International: +44 (0)1473 226789
Fax: 01473 226927

Price Guide:
single £90–£115
double/twin £100–£125
suite £155–£180

This newly opened hotel is situated in a unique and historic waterfront location on the bustling and sophisticated Ipswich marina, stylishly transformed from the town's wet dock. The hotel owes its name to the building's former function as a 19th-century store for salt. Salt was kept here before being shipped to Yarmouth for the herring trade, once one of the largest in Europe. Throughout the hotel, Victorian architecture, natural materials, subdued colours and contemporary design combine to form an intriguing and elegant blend, and the hotel's own collection of contemporary artwork is displayed to complement the original style of the industrial structure. All 43 bedrooms, some of which with balconies, are cleverly arranged to offer beautiful views, above all the 2 spectacular penthouse suites with their large panoramic windows. Details such as the original carved bed heads reflect earlier trade with distant places. Guests can enjoy culinary delights in the hotel's bustling brasserie and bar, or explore this exciting new part of the town. Conferences can be arranged in the nearby Custom House. A Thames sailing barge and boat trips down the Orwell River and beyond are available from the quay, whilst the more active guest can enjoy the facilities of a nearby ski centre as well as sailing and windsurfing.

Our inspector loved: The dramatic "Red Lady" in the restaurant – the inspiration for the staff uniforms.

HINTLESHAM HALL

HINTLESHAM, IPSWICH, SUFFOLK IP8 3NS

The epitome of grandeur, Hintlesham Hall is a house of evolving styles: its splendid Georgian façade belies its 16th-century origins, to which the red-brick Tudor rear of the hall is a testament. The Stuart period also left its mark, in the form of a magnificent carved oak staircase leading to the north wing of the hall. The combination of styles works extremely well, with the lofty proportions of the Georgian reception rooms contrasting with the timbered Tudor rooms. The décor throughout is superb – all rooms are individually appointed in a discriminating fashion. Iced mineral water, toiletries and towelling robes are to be found in each of the comfortable bedrooms. The herb garden supplies many of the flavours for the well-balanced menu which will appeal to the gourmet and the health-conscious alike, complemented by a 300-bin wine list. Bounded by 175 acres of rolling countryside, leisure facilities include an associated 18-hole championship golf course. The Health Club offers a new state-of-the-art gymnasium, sauna, steam room, spa bath, tennis and croquet. A full range of E'spa products and services are available in the beauty suite by arrangement. Guests can also explore Suffolk's 16th-century wool merchants' villages, its pretty coast, Constable country and Newmarket

Our inspector loved: The great cookery days and wine dinners.

Directions: Hintlesham Hall is 4 miles west of Ipswich on the A1071 Sudbury road.

Web: www.johansens.com/hintleshamhall
E-mail: reservations@hintleshamhall.com
Tel: 0870 381 8595
International: +44 (0)1473 652334
Fax: 01473 652463

Price Guide:
single £110–£195
double/twin £120–£250
suite £250–£350

233

THE SWAN HOTEL

HIGH STREET, LAVENHAM, SUDBURY, SUFFOLK CO10 9QA

Directions: From the A14 at Bury St Edmunds, take the A134 towards Sudbury. Turn onto the A1141 for Lavenham.

Web: www.johansens.com/theswanlavenham
E-mail: info@theswanlavenham.co.uk
Tel: 0870 381 9280
International: +44 (0)1787 247477
Fax: 01787 248286

Price Guide: (per person)
single £55–£60
double/twin £55–£80
suite £80–£90

Welcoming travellers since 1400 this medieval hotel stands within the heart of the Tudor village of Lavenham. Modern luxury sits comfortably alongside the 15th-century oak beams, panelled walls, flagged floors, log fires and inglenook fires, and the discovery of Medieval wall paintings have influenced the style of the interior, which features mementoes of England's early history hanging on the walls, such as the oldest surviving map of England, circa 1250. Each of the 51 en suite bedrooms has been decorated in calming colour schemes, with natural fabrics evoking the town's wool trade history. Lounge areas invite guests to relax in a soothing atmosphere surrounded by peace and traquillity and the Old Bar, with its brick floor, provides a welcoming retreat. The friendly and refined dining room prides itself on serving imaginative cuisine, created from fresh Suffolk and Norfolk produce accompanied by a comprehensive wine list. During the summer months guests may wish to dine al fresco in the courtyard. 3 large rooms can accommodate executive conferences and are equipped with state-of-the-art facilities and an experienced conference team are on-hand to help. Weddings can also be catered for. The Swan Hotel is a perfect base from which to enjoy an abundance of history, culture and unspoilt countryside.

Our inspector loved: *The Medieval wall paintings.*

BLACK LION HOTEL & RESTAURANT

CHURCH WALK, THE GREEN, LONG MELFORD, SUFFOLK CO10 9DN

One of Long Melford's oldest Inns The Black Lion glories in its superb position overlooking the green, and the village with its elegant broad street and imposing church. Having been in existence for over 300 years, the hotel recently entered a fresh era in its illustrious history. Under owner Craig Jarvis a transformation has taken place, with rich colours, comfortable antique furniture and welcoming open fires all creating a charming country house ambience. Flanked by the stately homes of Kentwell and Melford Hall, good sized bedrooms are furnished with antiques and offer individual design plus modern facilities; some have picturesque views. The menu, based on traditional dishes with a modern approach, may be sampled casually in the Lounge Bar or more formally in the Rosette-awarded Restaurant, each providing superb presentation and excellent food. The Victorian walled garden is an ideal setting to enjoy summer barbecues. A prolifery of antique emporiums, interesting shops, picturesque country walks and stately homes are within walking distance of the hotel. Racegoers will find The Black Lion a perfect base from which to attend Newmarket, whilst those simply longing to get away from it all could not wish for a more peaceful and inviting country retreat. Nominated for the best service award by Condé Nast Johansens.

Our inspector loved: The Yquem Room with its new romantic and sumptous Arabic styling.

Directions: From A14 take A134 in direction of Sudbury. Hotel overlooks Long Melford village green.

Web: www.johansens.com/blacklion
E-mail: enquiries@blacklionhotel.net
Tel: 0870 381 8366
International: +44 (0)1787 312356
Fax: 01787 374557

Price Guide:
single £85–£106
double/twin £109–£120
suite from £146

THE HOTEL VICTORIA

KIRKLEY CLIFF, LOWESTOFT SUFFOLK NR33 0BZ

Directions: Located in the south beach area of Lowestoft. From London take the A12 or the A146 from Norwich. Alternatively, the hotel is just a 2-minute taxi ride from Lowestoft Station.

Web: www.johansens.com/hotelvictoria
E-mail: info@hotelvictoria.freeserve.co.uk
Tel: 0870 381 9293
International: +44 (0)1502 574433
Fax: 01502 501529

Price Guide:
single £85
double £115-£135
suite £150

Situated in an enviable position overlooking the golden sands of one of the best beaches in Britain, this highly acclaimed hotel combines glorious Victorian features with modern comforts. A friendly and enthusiastic atmosphere extends throughout the hotel with attentive staff and relaxing rooms. Luxurious bedrooms, some with balconies, have excellent bathrooms and sweeping cliff-top views of the coast, promenade and pier. Tempting flavours of the Mediterranean are served in the Salute Restaurant, which is informal and airy, reflecting the healthy pleasures of an outdoor holiday. The well stocked bar offers a selection of wines from around the world, freshly brewed coffees and light meals throughout the day. Bird and nature enthusiasts will love to explore the miles of award-winning sandy beaches of the Suffolk Heritage Coast and North Norfolk Coast. The Hotel Victoria is also an ideal base for experiencing the unique beauty of the Norfolk Broads, an area steeped in history and heritage surrounded by rolling countryside and delightful villages. Lowestoft is a bustling market town that offers all the facilities one would expect, including shopping, cinema, restaurants and ten pin bowling.

Our inspector loved: The guest rooms with a balcony.

SWYNFORD PADDOCKS HOTEL AND RESTAURANT

SIX MILE BOTTOM, NEAR NEWMARKET, SUFFOLK CB8 0UE

This classical white mansion standing in glorious gardens and idyllic countryside, with racehorses grazing its pastures, has a romantic history. In 1813 it was the scene of a passionate love affair between Lord Byron and the wife of the owner, Colonel George Leigh. Swynford was converted into a hotel 20 years ago. It has a country house atmosphere with open fires and attention to detail of times gone by. Each individually decorated, en suite bedroom has colour television, clock radio alarm, telephone and many other amenities. Silks conservatory overlooks the gardens whilst the elegantly refurbished dining room offers an imaginative menu, changed regularly to incorporate the season's fresh produce. The award-winning restaurant has been awarded 2 RAC Dining Awards and an AA Rosette. Conference facilities are available and a luxury marquee for private and special functions. Tennis, croquet and a few games for children are within the grounds and guided tours of Newmarket with a look at the horseracing world can be arranged. Helicuisine: for a special occasion guests are chauffeur driven in a limousine to Cambridge Airport for a helicopter aerial view of the surrounding towns, then land for a superb lunch at the hotel.

Our inspector loved: *The Silks conservatory – just the place for morning coffee, informal lunch or afternoon tea.*

Directions: From the M11, exit at junction 9 and take the A11 towards Newmarket. After 10 miles join the A1304 signed Newmarket. The hotel is on left after ¾ of a mile.

Web: www.johansens.com/swynfordpaddocks
E-mail: info@swynfordpaddocks.com
Tel: 0870 381 8935
International: +44 (0)1638 570234
Fax: 01638 570283

Price Guide:
single £110
double/twin £135–£155
suite £175

237

THE SWAN HOTEL

MARKET PLACE, SOUTHWOLD, SUFFOLK IP18 6EG

Rebuilt in 1659, following the disastrous fire that destroyed most of the town, The Swan Hotel was remodelled in the 1820s, with further additions made in 1938. The hotel provides all modern amenities required by today's discerning traveller and an extensive refurbishment programme has ensured that a modern, stylish sophistication exudes throughout the hotel. This refined yet relaxed environment together with the friendly staff on-hand guarantees a most comfortable stay. Many of the bedrooms in the main hotel offer a glimpse of the sea, whilst the contemporary designed garden rooms are clustered around the old bowling green. The elegant Drawing Room is perfect for quiet relaxation; the Reading Room and Southwold Room are also ideal for private functions. The daily menu offers dishes ranging from simple, delicious fare through the English classics to the chef's personal specialities as well as a full à la carte menu. An exciting selection of wines is offered. Southwold is bounded on 3 sides by creeks, marshes and the River Blyth, making it a paradise for birdwatchers and nature lovers. Little has changed in the town for a century, built around a series of greens; there is a fine church, lighthouse and golf course close by. Music lovers flock to nearby Snape Maltings for the Aldeburgh Festival. Dr Hauschka beauty therapy treatments are now available at the hotel.

Directions: Southwold is off the A12 Ipswich–Lowestoft road. The Swan Hotel is in the town centre.

Web: www.johansens.com/swansouthwold
E-mail: swan.hotel@adnams.co.uk
Tel: 0870 381 8929
International: +44 (0)1502 722186
Fax: 01502 724800

Price Guide:
single £75
double/twin £130
suite £190

Our inspector loved: The quirky chicken pictures in one of the bedrooms.

SECKFORD HALL

WOODBRIDGE, SUFFOLK IP13 6NU

Seckford Hall dates from 1530 and it is said that Elizabeth I once held court here. Furnished as a private house with many fine period pieces, the panelled rooms, beamed ceilings, carved doors and great stone fireplaces are set against the splendour of English oak. Local delicacies such as the house speciality, lobster, feature on the à la carte menu. The original minstrels gallery can be viewed in the banqueting hall, which is now a conference and function suite designed in-keeping with the general style. The Courtyard area was converted from a giant Tudor tithe barn, dairy and coach house; it now incorporates 10 charming cottage-style suites and a modern leisure complex, which includes a heated swimming pool, exercise machines, spa bath and beauty salon. Alternatively, guests may use the Internet Café where Internet access and office equipment is available. Set in 34 acres of tranquil parkland with sweeping lawns and a willow-fringed lake, guests may stroll about the grounds or simply relax in the attractive terrace garden. Equipment can be hired for the 18-hole golf course or a gentle walk along the riverside to picturesque Woodbridge, with its tide mill, antique shops and yacht harbours can be enjoyed. Visit the Sutton Hoo burial ship site and new museum and the Constable country and Suffolk coast nearby.

Our inspector loved: Being inspired at the first sight of this beautiful Tudor building.

Directions: Remain on the A12 Woodbridge bypass until the blue and white hotel sign.

Web: www.johansens.com/seckfordhall
E-mail: reception@seckford.co.uk
Tel: 0870 381 8890
International: +44 (0)1394 385678
Fax: 01394 380610

Price Guide:
single £85–£130
double/twin £130–£200
suite £170–£200

PENNYHILL PARK HOTEL

LONDON ROAD, BAGSHOT, SURREY GU19 5EU

Directions: From the M3, exit 3, take A322 towards Bracknell. Turn left on to A30 signposted to Camberley. ¾ mile after Bagshot; turn right 50 yards past the Texaco garage.

Web: www.johansens.com/pennyhillpark
E-mail: enquiries@pennyhillpark.co.uk
Tel: 0870 381 8815
International: +44 (0)1276 471774
Fax: 01276 473217

Price Guide:
single from £212
double/twin from £230
suite from £412

Egham
Kingston upon Thames
Epsom
Guildford
Gatwick

Surrounded by 120 acres of peaceful parkland and a challenging 9-hole golf course this carefully restored Victorian manor house offers guests a unique atmosphere and the intimacy of a private country estate with a level of luxury, service and facilities equal to those found in some of the world's best hotels. Built in 1849, Pennyhill Park Hotel is an imposing and prestigious sight with the deep green and russet colours of summer and autumn ivy highlighting the majesty of its exterior walls and beautifully framing lead-paned, pillared windows. The hotel exudes dignity and elegance and, as befits its original intent of the 19th-century era, a friendly and welcoming intimacy. Every guest room blends the refined character of the past with the comfort of the present. Individually and uniquely designed, they have soft, warm-toned, traditional décor enhanced with fine antiques and paintings. Tantalising cuisine is served in the cosy Laymer restaurant with its low beamed ceiling and huge York stone fireplace and in the St James restaurant ,which features a marble floor, tall centrepiece statue and dual aspect views. Imaginative menus are essentially English with a French influence. Outdoor activities include clay pigeon shooting, fishing in the hotel lake, archery, tennis and croquet. There is also a Roman-style heated swimming pool.

Our inspector loved: *The stunning 120-acre setting of the is exceptional luxury experience.*

GREAT FOSTERS

STROUDE ROAD, EGHAM, SURREY TW20 9UR

Probably built as a Royal hunting lodge in Windsor Forest, very much a stately home since the 16th century, today Great Fosters is a prestigious hotel within half an hour of both Heathrow Airport and central London. Its past is evident in the mullioned windows, tall chimneys and brick finials, whilst the Saxon moat – crossed by a Japanese bridge – surrounds 3 sides of the formal gardens, complete with topiary, statuary and a charming rose garden. Inside are fine oak beams and panelling, Jacobean chimney pieces, superb tapestries and a rare oakwell staircase leading to the Tower. Some of the guest rooms are particularly magnificent – one Italian styled with gilt furnishings and damask walls, others with moulded ceilings, beautiful antiques and Persian rugs. Guests relax in the bar before enjoying good English and French cooking and carefully selected wines in The Oak Room. Celebrations, meetings and weddings take place in the elegant Orangery and impressive Tithe Barn. Great Fosters is close to polo in Windsor Great Park, racing at Ascot, golf at Wentworth, boating in Henley and pageantry at Windsor Castle, Runnymede and Hampton Court.

Our inspector loved: The magnificent modern tapestry in the dining room so perfectly complementing the outstanding architectural details of this ancient building.

Directions: M25/J13, head for Egham and watch for brown Historic Buildings signs.

Web: www.johansens.com/greatfosters
E-mail: enquiries@greatfosters.co.uk
Tel: 0870 381 8569
International: +44 (0)1784 433822
Fax: 01784 472455

Price Guide:
single from £120
double/twin from £155
suite from £280

LANGSHOTT MANOR

LANGSHOTT, HORLEY, SURREY RH6 9LN

Directions: From the A23 at Horley take Ladbroke Road immediately north of the Chequers Hotel roundabout. The Manor is ¾ of a mile (1 kilometre) on the right.

Web: www.johansens.com/langshottmanor
E-mail: admin@langshottmanor.com
Tel: 0870 381 8680
International: +44 (0)1293 786680
Fax: 01293 783905

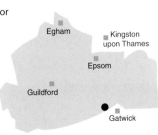

Price Guide:
single from £165
double/twin from £185
suite £290

The peace and seclusion of this beautiful Manor House, tucked away down a quiet country lane amidst 3 acres of lovely garden, belies its proximity to London's Gatwick Airport, only 10 minutes away by car. Retaining the essential feel of a fine Elizabethan house, Langshott has recently been sympathetically expanded to encompass an attractive new dining room with views over ponds and gardens. Additional to the main house, superb bedrooms have been created in both the Coach House Mews and the Moat Mews. The Manor prides itself on outstanding levels of hospitality, service, cuisine and comfort acknowledged by 3 AA Red Stars and an RAC Gold Ribbon. Each of the bedrooms is decorated in individual style and offers exceptional standards of provision exemplified by luxurious towelling robes and comfy slippers. There are Egyptian cotton sheets on the beds, hot water bottles to go in the beds and homemade cookies beside the beds. There are romantic and honeymoon breaks, and if you are flying from Gatwick special arrangements include 2 weeks car parking and a chauffeured car to the airport.

Our inspector loved: *This extremely stylish house and its immaculate garden setting.*

LYTHE HILL HOTEL & SPA

PETWORTH ROAD, HASLEMERE, SURREY GU27 3BQ

Cradled by the Surrey foothills in a tranquil setting is the enchanting Lythe Hill Hotel & Spa. It is an unusual cluster of ancient buildings – parts of which date from the 14th century. While most of the beautifully appointed accommodation is in the more recently converted part of the hotel, there are 5 charming bedrooms in the Tudor House, including the Henry VIII room with a four-poster bed dated 1614. There are 2 delightful restaurants: the Auberge de France offers classic French cuisine in the oak-panelled room which overlooks the lake and parklands, and the 'Dining Room' has the choice of imaginative English fare. An exceptional wine list offers over 200 wines from more than a dozen countries. The hotel boasts a splendid leisure facility called Amarna (which was voted hotel spa of the year) within the grounds of the hotel. It has a 16 x 8 metre swimming pool, steam room and sauna, gym, hairdressing, treatment rooms and a nail bar. National Trust hillside adjoining the hotel grounds provides interesting walks and views over the surrounding countryside. The area is steeped in history, with the country houses of Petworth, Clandon and Uppark to visit as well as racing at Goodwood and polo at Cowdray Park. Brighton and the south coast are only a short drive away.

Our inspector loved: The setting and the wonderful new spa facility.

Directions: Lythe Hill lies about 1½ miles from the centre of Haslemere, east on the B2131.

Web: www.johansens.com/lythehill
E-mail: lythe@lythehill.co.uk
Tel: 0870 381 8709
International: +44 (0)1428 651251
Fax: 01428 644131

Price Guide: (room only)
standard from £125
superior from £150
suite from £170

FOXHILLS

STONEHILL ROAD, OTTERSHAW, SURREY KT16 0EL

Directions: From M25 Jct 11, follow signs to Woking. After a dual carriageway, turn left into Guildford Road. 3rd exit at roundabout and immediately right into Foxhills Road. Turn left at the end of the road, Foxhills is on the right.

Web: www.johansens.com/foxhills
E-mail: reservations@foxhills.co.uk
Tel: 0870 381 8530
International: +44 (0)1932 704500
Fax: 01932 874762

Price Guide: (room only)
double/twin from £170
suite from £225

This magnificent 400-acre estate is a delightful environment for any discerning traveller, whatever their interests may be. Named after the 18th-century foreign secretary, Charles James Fox, Foxhills comprises a large Manor House, elegant suites, 3 golf courses, numerous tennis courts, indoor and outdoor swimming pools, 2 restaurants and a host of health and fitness facilities including a gymnasium and beauty salon. The 42 bedrooms, located in a superb courtyard setting, are the essence of comfort; elegantly furnished and offering all the latest amenities, they are designed in a number of styles; some have gardens whilst others are on 2 floors. The 2 restaurants pride themselves on their culinary excellence. Inside the Manor itself, the award-winning restaurant serves fine cuisine and is renowned for the Sunday buffet – a gourmet's delight! The sport and health facilities at Foxhills are particularly impressive and with 20 qualified instructors on hand, guests may wish to acquire a new skill such as racquetball or T'ai Chi. Those wishing to be pampered will enjoy the sauna, steam room and the fine beauty salon. Awarded 4-stars by the AA.

Our inspector loved: *The rare combination of a fine country house set amidst such expansive sporting provision.*

OATLANDS PARK HOTEL

146 OATLANDS DRIVE, WEYBRIDGE, SURREY KT13 9HB

Records of the Oatlands estate show that Elizabeth I and the Stuart kings spent time in residence in the original buildings. The present mansion dates from the late 18th century and became a hotel in 1856: famous guests included Émile Zola, Anthony Trollope and Edward Lear. The hotel stands in acres of parkland overlooking Broadwater Lake, with easy access to Heathrow, Gatwick and central London. Although it caters for the modern traveller, the hotel's historic character is evident throughout. The accommodation ranges from superior rooms to large de luxe rooms and suites. The elegant, high-ceilinged Broadwater Restaurant is the setting for creative à la carte menus with dishes to suit all tastes. A traditional roast is served every Sunday lunchtime. The 6 air-conditioned meeting rooms and 6 syndicate rooms offer up-to-date facilities and are complemented by the professional conference team. Many sporting and leisure activities are offered including a 9 hole, par 27 golf course and tennis court.

Our inspector loved: The sheer size - everything here is on a grand scale.

Directions: From M25 junction 11, follow signs to Weybridge. Follow A317 through High Street into Monument Hill to mini-roundabout. Turn left into Oatlands Drive; hotel is 50 yards on left.

Web: www.johansens.com/oatlandspark
E-mail: info@oatlandsparkhotel.com
Tel: 0870 381 8779
International: +44 (0)1932 847242
Fax: 01932 842252

Price Guide: (room only)
single £80–£202
double/twin £113–£224
suite from £150–£230

WHITE LODGE COUNTRY HOUSE HOTEL

SLOE LANE, ALFRISTON, EAST SUSSEX BN26 5UR

Directions: Alfriston is on the B2108 between the A27/A259. The hotel is well signed from the village centre.

Web: www.johansens.com/whitelodgecountryhouse
E-mail: sales@whitelodge-hotel.com
Tel: 0870 381 8990
International: +44 (0)1323 870265
Fax: 01323 870284

Price Guide:
single from £47.50
double/twin from £95
suite from £125

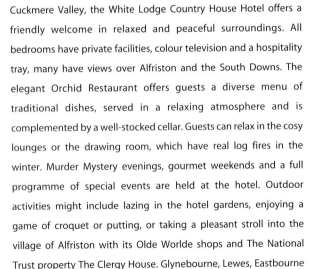

Nestled in 5 acres of landscaped grounds in the heart of the Cuckmere Valley, the White Lodge Country House Hotel offers a friendly welcome in relaxed and peaceful surroundings. All bedrooms have private facilities, colour television and a hospitality tray, many have views over Alfriston and the South Downs. The elegant Orchid Restaurant offers guests a diverse menu of traditional dishes, served in a relaxing atmosphere and is complemented by a well-stocked cellar. Guests can relax in the cosy lounges or the drawing room, which have real log fires in the winter. Murder Mystery evenings, gourmet weekends and a full programme of special events are held at the hotel. Outdoor activities might include lazing in the hotel gardens, enjoying a game of croquet or putting, or taking a pleasant stroll into the village of Alfriston with its Olde Worlde shops and The National Trust property The Clergy House. Glynebourne, Lewes, Eastbourne and Brighton are only a short drive away.

Our inspector loved: *The village setting and stunning views over the South Downs.*

THE POWDERMILLS

POWDERMILL LANE, BATTLE, EAST SUSSEX TN33 0SP

The PowderMills is an 18th-century listed country house skilfully converted into an elegant hotel. Originally the site of a famous gunpowder works, reputed to make the finest gunpowder in Europe during the Napoleonic wars, the beautiful and tranquil grounds are set amidst 150 acres of parks, lakes and woodlands, and feature a 7-acre specimen fishing lake. Wild geese, swans, ducks, kingfishers and herons abound. Situated close to the historic town of Battle, the hotel adjoins the famous battlefield of 1066, and guests can enjoy a leisurely walk through woodlands and fields to the Abbey. The hotel has been carefully furnished with locally acquired antiques and paintings, and on cooler days log fires burn in the entrance hall and drawing room. There is a range of 40 individually decorated en-suite bedrooms and junior suites in keeping with the style of the house, many with four-poster beds. Fine classical cooking by chef James Penn is served in the Orangery Restaurant, whilst light meals and snacks are available in the library and conservatory. The location is an ideal base from which to explore the beautiful Sussex and Kent countryside.

Our inspector loved: *Always something new here - this year there's an antique barge on the upper lake.*

Directions: From centre of Battle take the Hastings road south. After ¼ mile turn right into Powdermill Lane. After a sharp bend, the entrance is on the right; cross over the bridge and lakes to reach the hotel.

Web: www.johansens.com/powdermills
E-mail: powdc@aol.com
Tel: 0870 381 8835
International: +44 (0)1424 775511
Fax: 01424 774540

Uckfield
Hastings
Brighton
Eastbourne

Price Guide:
single from £95
double/twin £120–£190

HOTEL DU VIN & BISTRO

SHIP STREET, BRIGHTON BN1 1AD

Directions: Take the A23 to Brighton city centre. Follow signposts to the sea front, at the roundabout turn right and pass Ship Street. Turn right into Middle Street and right again into Ship Street. The hotel is at the end of the road.

Web: www.johansens.com/hotelduvinbrighton
E-mail: info@brighton.hotelduvin.com
Tel: 0870 381 8617
International: +44 (0)1273 718588
Fax: 01273 718599

Price Guide: (room only)
double/twin from £125
suite from £230

Since 1994, the Hotel du Vin group has successively excited visitors and residents of Winchester, Tunbridge Wells, Harrogate, Bristol and Birmingham with its alternative hotel style; it arrived in Brighton during the autumn of 2002. A well-located but neglected area has been completely transformed to introduce the south coast to their very individual formula of relaxed eating, fine wines and supremely comfortable bedrooms in a stunning building. Immediately off the sea front and adjacent to the famous Lanes, with its myriad of inviting little shops, this is a real treat. Inside, the various public areas provide several choices for relaxing; the fine wine bar offers 16 wines by the glass and bourbon as the featured drink, the main bistro opens onto the pavement and on sunny days, lunch in the inner courtyard is available. The cellar dining room is one of 2 private dining areas and the original wine cellar can be visited; tastings are on offer as well as tours of the walk-in cigar humidor. Brighton positively explodes with exhilarating, sophisticated, quirky, colourful and vibrant things to see and do; enjoy the exotic beauty of The Royal Pavilion, visit the Regency Town House or experience how the Edwardians lived at Preston Manor. The Brighton Festival each May is the biggest Arts Fiesta in England.

Our inspector loved: *The vibrant "club" atmosphere around the bar on weekend nights.*

THE GRAND HOTEL

KING EDWARD'S PARADE, EASTBOURNE, EAST SUSSEX BN21 4EQ

The Grand Hotel is a fine property, steeped in history, which evokes the charm and splendour of the Victorian era. The majestic façade complements the elegant interior whilst the reception rooms are beautifully appointed with rich fabrics and ornaments. Many of the 152 bedrooms are of vast proportions: all being refurbished to include every comfort with attractive bathrooms. The hotel has numerous areas in which to relax and a good choice of restaurants and bars. The Mirabelle in particular achieves exceptional standards of fine dining. The array of new leisure facilities includes both indoor and outdoor pools, gymnasium, sauna, solarium, spa bath, steam room, snooker tables and a hair salon and 8 beauty rooms. Guests may choose to try the nearby racquet and golf clubs. For the meeting organiser, the hotel offers an impressive range of rooms which can cater for a number of business purposes from a board meeting for 12 to a larger conference for up to 300 delegates. Those seeking a peaceful retreat will be pleased with the tranquil atmosphere of Eastbourne. Pastimes include walks along the Downs, sea fishing and trips to the 2 nearby theatres.

Our inspector loved: *The welcoming provision for every member of the family - children are made especially "at home".*

Directions: A22 from London. A259 from East or West. Hotel is at the western end of the seafront.

Web: www.johansens.com/grandeastbourne
E-mail: reservations@grandeastbourne.com
Tel: 0870 381 8560
International: +44 (0)1323 412345
Fax: 01323 412233

Price Guide:
single £135–£325
double/twin £165–£285
suite £220–£430

Uckfield
Hastings
Brighton
Eastbourne

ASHDOWN PARK HOTEL AND COUNTRY CLUB

WYCH CROSS, FOREST ROW, EAST SUSSEX RH18 5JR

Directions: East of A22 at Wych Cross traffic lights on road signposted to Hartfield.

Web: www.johansens.com/ashdownpark
E-mail: reservations@ashdownpark.com
Tel: 0870 381 8325
International: +44 (0)1342 824988
Fax: 01342 826206

Price Guide:
single £135–£325
double/twin £165–£220
suite £285–£355

Ashdown Park is a grand, rambling 19th-century mansion overlooking almost 200 acres of landscaped gardens to the forest beyond. Built in 1867, the hotel is situated within easy reach of Gatwick Airport, London and the South Coast and provides the perfect backdrop for every occasion, from a weekend getaway to a honeymoon or business convention. The hotel is subtly furnished throughout to satisfy the needs of escapees from urban stress. The 107 en-suite bedrooms are beautifully decorated – several with elegant four-poster beds, all with up-to-date amenities. The Anderida restaurant offers a thoughtfully compiled menu and wine list, complemented by discreetly attentive service in soigné surroundings. Guests seeking relaxation can retire to the indoor pool and sauna, pamper themselves with a massage, before using the solarium, or visiting the beauty salon. Alternatively, guests may prefer to amble through the gardens and nearby woodland paths; the more energetic can indulge in tennis, croquet or use the Fitness Studio and Beauty Therapy. There is also an indoor driving range, a lounge/bar and an 18-hole par 3 golf course with an outdoor driving range.

Our inspector loved: *The exceptional level of customer service throughout the hotel.*

HORSTED PLACE COUNTRY HOUSE HOTEL

LITTLE HORSTED, EAST SUSSEX TN22 5TS

Horsted Place enjoys a splendid location amid the peace of the Sussex Downs. This magnificent Victorian Gothic Mansion, which was built in 1851, overlooks the East Sussex National golf course and boasts an interior predominantly styled by the celebrated Victorian architect, Augustus Pugin. In former years the Queen and Prince Philip were frequent visitors. Guests today are invited to enjoy the excellent service offered by a committed staff. Since the turn of 2001, and under new management, the bedrooms have been refurbished to provide luxurious décor and every modern comfort, whilst all public areas have been refurbished and upholstered. Dining at Horsted is guaranteed to be a memorable experience. Chef Allan Garth offers a daily fixed price menu as well as the seasonal à la carte menu. The Terrace Room is an elegant and airy private function room, licenced for weddings for up to 100 guests. The smaller Morning Room and Library are ideal for boardroom-style meetings and intimate dinner parties, and the self-contained management centre offers privacy and exclusivity for business meetings in a contemporary setting. Places of interest nearby include Royal Tunbridge Wells, Lewes and Glyndebourne. For golfing enthusiasts there is the East Sussex National Golf Club, one of the finest golf complexes in the world.

Directions: The hotel entrance is on the A26 just short of the junction with the A22, 2 miles south of Uckfield and signposted towards Lewes.

Web: www.johansens.com/horstedplace
E-mail: hotel@horstedplace.co.uk
Tel: 0870 381 8609
International: +44 (0)1825 750581
Fax: 01825 750459

Price Guide:
double/twin from £130
suite from £220

Our inspector loved: The value offered by this fine house in the country.

Newick Park

NEWICK, NEAR LEWES, EAST SUSSEX BN8 4SB

Directions: The nearest motorway is the M23, jct 11.

Web: www.johansens.com/newickpark
E-mail: bookings@newickpark.co.uk
Tel: 0870 381 8762
International: +44 (0)1825 723633
Fax: 01825 723969

Price Guide:
single from £115
double/twin from £165

This magnificent Grade II listed Georgian country house, set in over 200 acres of breathtaking parkland and landscaped gardens, overlooks the Longford River and lake and the South Downs. Whilst situated in a convenient location near to the main road and rail routes and only 30 minutes away from Gatwick Airport, Newick Park maintains an atmosphere of complete tranquillity and privacy. The en-suite bedrooms are decorated in a classic style and contain elegant antique furnishings. The exquisite dining room offers a wide choice of culinary delights, carefully devised by the Head Chef, Chris Moore. The convivial bar complements the restaurant with its delicate style and understated elegance. The friendly staff ensure that guests receive a warm welcome and an outstanding level of comfort. The house and grounds are ideal for weddings or conferences and may be hired for exclusive use by larger groups. The Dell gardens, planted primarily in Victorian times, include a rare collection of Royal Ferns. Vibrant and diverse colours saturate the lawns during the changing seasons, courtesy of the various flowers and shrubs encompassing the gardens. The activities on the estate itself include fishing, shooting and tennis, whilst nearby distractions include the East Sussex Golf Club, racing at Goodwood and Glyndebourne Opera House.

Our inspector loved: *The peace and tranquillity of this country house.*

DALE HILL

TICEHURST, NEAR WADHURST, EAST SUSSEX TN5 7DQ

Situated in over 350 acres of fine grounds, high on the Kentish Weald, the newly refurbished Dale Hill combines the best in golfing facilities with the style and refinement desired by discerning guests. The décor is enhanced by soft coloured fabrics and carpets, creating a summery impression throughout the year. Golfers have the choice of 2 18-hole courses, a gently undulating 6,093 yards par 70 and a new, challenging championship standard course designed by former US Masters champion Ian Woosnam. Just a 20-minute drive away, under the same ownership as the hotel, is the Nick Faldo designed Chart Hills course hailed as "the best new course in England". Packages allow guests to play both championship courses. Diners enjoy glorious views in a choice of restaurants where traditional award-winning cuisine is complemented by a fine wine list and service. The fully equipped health club features a heated swimming pool and a range of health, beauty and fitness facilities. Dale Hill is only a short drive from Tunbridge Wells and its renowned Pantiles shopping walk. Also nearby are medieval Scotney Castle, which dates back to 1380, Sissinghurst, a moated Tudor castle with gardens and Bewl Water, renowned for fly-fishing and water sports.

Our inspector loved: The new stylish décor - the hotel has been transformed.

Directions: From the M25, junction 5, follow the A21 to Flimwell. Then turn right onto the B2087. Dale Hill is on the left.

Web: www.johansens.com/dalehill
E-mail: info@dalehill.co.uk
Tel: 0870 381 8471
International: +44 (0)1580 200112
Fax: 01580 201249

Price Guide:
single £90–£110
double/twin £110–£180
suites £170-£210

AMBERLEY CASTLE

AMBERLEY, NEAR ARUNDEL, WEST SUSSEX BN18 9LT

Directions: Amberley Castle is on the B2139, off the A29 between Bury and Storrington. Look out for the Union flag, which clearly marks the driveway.

Web: www.johansens.com/amberleycastle
E-mail: info@amberleycastle.co.uk
Tel: 0870 381 8312
International: +44 (0)1798 831992
Fax: 01798 831998

Price Guide: (room only)
double/twin £155–£375
suite £285–£375

Winner of the Johansens Award for Outstanding Excellence and Innovation, Amberley Castle boasts an amazing history spanning over 900 years. Set between the rolling South Downs and the peaceful expanses of the Amberley Wildbrooks, its towering battlements give breathtaking views and massive 14th-century curtain walls and the mighty portcullis bear silent testimony to a fascinating past. Proprietors, Joy and Martin Cummings, have transformed this medieval fortress into a unique country castle hotel. They offer a warm, personal welcome and their hotel provides the ultimate in contemporary luxury, whilst retaining an atmosphere of timelessness. 5 distinctive suites were added recently in the Bishopric by the main gateway. Each room is individually designed and has its own Jacuzzi bath. The exquisite 12th-century Queen's Room is the perfect setting for the creative cuisine of head chef James Peyton and his team. Amberley Castle is a natural first choice for romantic or cultural weekends, sporting breaks or confidential executive meetings. Roman ruins, antiques, stately homes, castle gardens, horse-racing and history "everywhere" you look, all within a short distance. It is easily accessible from London and the major air and channel ports.

Our inspector loved: *The thrill of approaching the ancient and massive stone walls. Amberley never disappoints.*

BAILIFFSCOURT HOTEL & HEALTH SPA

CLIMPING, WEST SUSSEX BN17 5RW

Bailiffscourt is a perfectly preserved "medieval" house, built in the 1930s using authentic material salvaged from historic old buildings. Gnarled 15th-century beams and gothic mullioned windows combine to recreate a home from the Middle Ages. Set in 30 acres of beautiful pastures and walled gardens, this is a wonderful sanctuary in which to relax or work. Bedrooms are individually decorated and luxuriously furnished, many offer four-poster beds, open log fires and beautiful views over the surrounding countryside. The restaurant serves a varied menu and summer lunches can be taken al fresco in a rose-clad courtyard or in the walled garden; a list of well-priced wines accompanies meals. Private dining rooms are available for weddings, conferences and meetings, and companies can hire the hotel as their "country house" for 2 or 3 days. Bailiffscourt is surrounded by tranquil pastureland and an award-winning health spa featuring an outdoor Californian hot tub, indoor spa pool, sauna, steam room, gym, hammocks and 6 beauty therapy rooms offering 50 Mediterranean treatments. 2 tennis courts and a croquet lawn completes the on-site leisure facilities, whilst a private pathway leads 100yds down to Climping beach, ideal for windsurfing and morning walks. Arundel Castle and Chichester and Goodwood are nearby for classic car driving.

Directions: 3 miles south of Arundel, off the A259.

Web: www.johansens.com/bailiffscourt
E-mail: bailiffscourt@hshotels.co.uk
Tel: 0870 381 8333
International: +44 (0)1903 723511
Fax: 01903 723107

Price Guide:
single from £175
double £195–£305
suite £345–£460

Our inspector loved: The spa building built from green oak.

THE MILLSTREAM HOTEL

BOSHAM, NR CHICHESTER, WEST SUSSEX PO18 8HL

Directions: South of the A259 between Chichester and Havant.

Web: www.johansens.com/millstream
E-mail: info@millstream–hotel.co.uk
Tel: 0870 381 8739
International: +44 (0)1243 573234
Fax: 01243 573459

Price Guide:
single £85–£115
double/twin £135–£169
suite £185–£199

A village rich in heritage, Bosham is depicted in the Bayeux Tapestry and King Harold is thought to be buried, alongside King Canute's, daughter in the local Saxon church. Moreover, sailors from the world over navigate their way to Bosham, which is a yachtsman's idyll on the banks of Chichester Harbour. The Millstream, just 300 yards from the harbour, consists of a restored 18th-century malthouse and adjoining cottages linked to The Grange, a small English manor house. Individually furnished bedrooms are complemented by chintz fabrics and pastel décor. The bar, drawing room and the restaurant are all most stylishly refurbished. A stream meanders past the front of the beautiful gardens. Cross the bridge to the 2 delightful new suites in "Waterside" the thatched cottage. Whatever the season, care is taken to ensure that the composition and presentation of the dishes reflect high standards. An appetising luncheon menu is offered and includes local seafood specialities such as: dressed Selsey crab, the Millstream's own home-smoked salmon and grilled fresh fillets of sea bass. During the winter, good-value "Hibernation Breaks" are available.

Our inspector loved: *The commitment to ever improving standards in the restaurant and bedrooms.*

OCKENDEN MANOR

OCKENDEN LANE, CUCKFIELD, WEST SUSSEX RH17 5LD

Set in 9 acres of grounds in the centre of the Tudor village of Cuckfield on the Southern Forest Ridge, this hotel is an ideal base from which to discover Sussex and Kent, the Garden of England. First recorded in 1520, Ockenden Manor has become a hotel of great charm and character. The bedrooms all have their own individual identity: climb your private staircase to Thomas or Elizabeth, look out across the glorious Sussex countryside from Victoria's bay window or choose Charles, with its handsome four-poster bed. The elegant wood-panelled restaurant with its beautiful handpainted ceiling is the perfect setting in which to enjoy the chef's innovative cooking. An outstanding, extensive wine list offers, for example, a splendid choice of first-growth clarets. Spacious and elegantly furnished, the Ockenden Suite welcomes private lunch and dinner parties. A superb conservatory is part of the Ockenden Suite, this opens on to the lawns, where marquees can be set up for summer celebrations. The gardens of Nymans, Wakehurst Place and Leonardslee are nearby, as is the opera at Glyndebourne.

Our inspector loved: The instant feeling of welcome as you step across the threshold of this very beautiful country house.

Directions: In the centre of Cuckfield on the A272. Less than 3 miles east of the A23.

Web: www.johansens.com/ockendenmanor
E-mail: ockenden@hshotels.co.uk
Tel: 0870 381 8780
International: +44 (0)1444 416111
Fax: 01444 415549

Price Guide:
single from £105
double/twin from £155
suite from £290

ALEXANDER HOUSE HOTEL

EAST STREET, TURNER'S HILL, WEST SUSSEX RH10 4QD

Directions: Alexander House lies on the B2110 road between Turner's Hill and East Grinstead, 6 miles from junction 10 of the M23.

Web: www.johansens.com/alexanderhouse
E-mail: info@alexanderhouse.co.uk
Tel: 0870 381 8308
International: +44 (0)1342 714914
Fax: 01342 717328

Price Guide:
single from £125
double/twin from £155
junior suite from £295

A previous winner of the Johansens Most Excellent Service Award, Alexander House Hotel is a magnificent mansion with its own secluded 175 acres of parkland, including a gently sloping valley, which forms the head of the River Medway. Records trace the estate from 1332 when a certain John Atte Fen made it his home. Alexander House is now a modern paragon of good taste and excellence. Spacious rooms throughout this luxurious hotel are splendidly decorated to emphasise their many original features and the bedrooms are lavishly furnished to the highest standards of comfort. The house is renowned for its delicious classic English and French cuisine, rare wines and vintage liqueurs. Music recitals and garden parties feature among a full programme of special summer events and the open fires and cosy atmosphere make this the ideal place to pamper oneself in winter. Antique shops, National Trust properties, museums and the Royal Pavilion in Brighton are nearby. Gardens close by include Wakehurst Place, Nymans and Leonardslee. Gatwick Airport is less than 15 minutes away by car.

Our inspector loved: A real comfortable country house composed of many intimate areas; the décor is stunning.

SOUTH LODGE HOTEL

LOWER BEEDING, NR HORSHAM, WEST SUSSEX RH13 6PS

South Lodge is a magnificent country house hotel, which has successfully captured the essence of Victorian elegance. With one of the most beautiful settings in rural Sussex, unrivalled views may be enjoyed over the South Downs from the hotel's elevated position. The mansion was originally built by Frederick Ducane Godman, a 19th-century botanist and explorer, and the hotel's wonderful 93 acre grounds are evidence of his dedication. Many original features have been preserved, wood panelling throughout the hotel and open fires in the reception rooms. The 45 individually designed bedrooms are luxuriously equipped with every modern requirement. There is also a beautiful cottage within the grounds – The Bothy, with 3 double and 2 single rooms, kitchen, bathrooms, lounge, conservatory and dining room. It is set in its own garden and can be used for leisure and conference purposes. The Camellia Restaurant has seasonally changing menus complemented by an international wine list. A variety of leisure facilities include a fitness centre, snooker room, croquet, tennis and clay pigeon shooting (shooting and archery by prior arrangement), as well as golf at South Lodge's two 18-hole championship courses.

Our inspector loved: The exquisite architectural features and the lovely garden setting of one of our finest hotels.

Directions: On A281 at Lower Beeding, south of Horsham. Gatwick airport 12 miles. Nearest motorway M23 Jct11.

Web: www.johansens.com/southlodge
E-mail: enquiries@southlodgehotel.co.uk
Tel: 0870 381 8900
International: +44 (0)1403 891711
Fax: 01403 891766

Price Guide: (room only)
single from £115
double/twin £185–£320
suite/premier rooms from £360

THE ANGEL HOTEL

NORTH STREET, MIDHURST, WEST SUSSEX GU29 9DN

Directions: From the A272, the hotel is on the left as the town centre is approached from the east.

Web: www.johansens.com/angelmidhurst
E-mail: info@theangelmidhurst.co.uk
Tel: 0870 381 8314
International: +44 (0)1730 812421
Fax: 01730 815928

Price Guide:
single £80–£115
double/twin £110–£150

The Angel Hotel is a stylishly restored 16th century coaching inn which has earned widespread praise from its guests, the national press and guidebooks. Sympathetically renovated to combine contemporary comfort with original character, The Angel bridges the gap between town house bustle and country house calm. To the front, a handsome Georgian façade overlooks the High Street, while at the rear, quiet rose gardens lead to the parkland and ruins of historic Cowdray Castle. There are 28 bedrooms, all offering private bathrooms and modern amenities. Individually furnished with antiques, many rooms feature original Tudor beams. The newly created Bistro style restaurant offers an excellent value contemporary menu. For corporate guests the hotel offers two attractive meeting rooms, a business suite, presentation aids and secretarial services. Racegoers will find it very convenient for Goodwood and theatregoers for the internationally acclaimed Chichester Festival Theatre. The historic market town of Midhurst is well placed for visits to Petworth House, Arundel Castle and the South Downs.

Our inspector loved: The bustle of locals lunching.

THE SPREAD EAGLE HOTEL & HEALTH SPA

SOUTH STREET, MIDHURST, WEST SUSSEX GU29 9NH

Dating from 1430, when guests were first welcomed here, The Spread Eagle Hotel is one of England's oldest hotels and is steeped in history; rich in charms, retaining many period features. Those wishing to be pampered will enjoy the superb fitness facilities and excellent standard of service. Located in either the main building or the market house, the 39 en-suite bedrooms, some with four-poster beds, are well-appointed with soft furnishings and fine ornaments. A roaring log fire attracts guests into the historic lounge bar, ideal for relaxing in the afternoons or enjoying an apéritif. Sumptuous modern British cuisine may be savoured in the candle-lit restaurant, complemented by an extensive wine list. Weddings, banquets and meetings are held in the Jacobean Hall and Polo Room. The Aquila Health Spa is an outstanding facility featuring a blue tiled swimming pool as its centrepiece. A Scandinavian sauna, Turkish steam room, hot tub, fitness centre and a range of beauty treatments, aromatherapy and massage are also offered. The stately homes at Petworth, Uppark and Goodwood are all within a short drive, with Chichester Cathedral, the Downland Museum and Fishbourne Roman Palace among the many local attractions. Cowdray Park Polo Club is only 1 mile away.

Our inspector loved: The ambience of this historic old inn combines with the up-to-date spa provisions.

Directions: Midhurst is on the A286 between Chichester and Milford.

Web: www.johansens.com/spreadeaglemidhurst
E-mail: spreadeagle@hshotels.co.uk
Tel: 0870 381 8903
International: +44 (0)1730 816911
Fax: 01730 815668

Gatwick
East Grinstead
Midhurst
Chichester
Brighton

Price Guide:
single £85–£195
double/twin £99–£235

NEW

GHYLL MANOR

HIGH STREET, RUSPER, NEAR HORSHAM, WEST SUSSEX RH12 4PX

Directions: Leave M23 at junction 11 and follow A264 to Horsham. Turn off at roundabout signed Faygate and Rusper

Web: www.johansens.com/ghyllmanor
E-mail: ghyll.manor@csma.uk.com
Tel: 0870 381 9331
International: +44 (0)845 345 3426
Fax: 01293 871419

Price Guide:
single £120
double/twin £140–£180

Set in a pretty village in the heart of deepest Sussex countryside and surrounded by 50 acres of gardens and parkland, this elegant 17th-century manor is the ideal location for a relaxing break. The hotel consists of the original manor house, the more modern converted Stable Mews, 2 cottage suites and 8 beautifully furnished luxury bedrooms. All rooms are individually decorated; many boast traditional features including beamed ceilings and four-poster beds, and one room even has a tester bed with canopy. Superb food prepared, with only the freshest of local produce, is served in the Benedictine restaurant, winner of the Les Routiers Gold Key of Excellence for 4 consecutive years. Just 20 minutes from Gatwick Airport, Ghyll Manor, with its choice of 3 meeting rooms and first-class service, is the ideal location for conferences, whilst a dedicated team is on-hand to co-ordinate weddings. Guests can enjoy numerous walks such as the South Downs Way, and visit a number of fascinating National Trust properties and internationally renowned gardens such as Leonardslee and Wakehurst Place. London is only an hour's train journey away, as is the bustling city of Brighton with its mix of historical attractions, infamous piers and great shopping.

Our inspector loved: *This characterful hotel, right in the high street of this delightful village yet backing onto expansive grounds and open country.*

THE VERMONT HOTEL

CASTLE GARTH, NEWCASTLE-UPON-TYNE, TYNE & WEAR NE1 1RQ

The Vermont is Newcastle's only 4-star independent hotel, located next to the Castle, overlooking the Cathedral and the Tyne and Millennium Bridges. This impressive 12 storey, Manhattan-style tower boasts an unrivalled city centre position; a short walk to the main shopping centre, theatres, galleries, universities and main railway station. It has direct access to the Quayside and on site complimentary car parking. The 101 bedrooms and suites are a combination of classical and modern design with 24-hour service expected from a luxury hotel. 7 luxuriously appointed meeting rooms are available for special business occasions and private dining. The Bridge Restaurant is located at the Castle Garth level with spectacular views of the Tyne Bridge, alternatively there is the Redwood Bar, with its fireplace and sofas, open until very late. For those wishing to sample the atmosphere of the famous Quayside, Martha's Bar & Courtyard on the ground floor is the entrance to Newcastle's nightlife. The Vermont is the ideal base from which to explore Newcastle's excellent shops as well as the surrounding areas of Northumberland, Durham and The Borders

Our inspector loved: Peaceful luxury next to the castle in the centre of Newcastle.

Directions: Close to the A1(M), and 7 miles from Newcastle International Airport.

Web: www.johansens.com/vermont
E-mail: info@vermont-hotel.co.uk
Tel: 0870 381 8962
International: +44 (0)191 233 1010
Fax: 0191 233 1234

Whitley Bay

Newcastle upon Tyne

Sunderland

Price Guide:
single from £125
double from £125
suites £240–£550

NAILCOTE HALL

NAILCOTE LANE, BERKSWELL, NEAR SOLIHULL, WARWICKSHIRE CV7 7DE

Directions: Situated 6 miles south of Birmingham International Airport/ NEC on the B4101 Balsall Common–Coventry road.

Web: www.johansens.com/nailcotehall
E-mail: info@nailcotehall.co.uk
Tel: 0870 381 8752
International: +44 (0)2476 466174
Fax: 02476 470720

Price Guide:
single £165
double/twin £175
suite £195–£275

Nuneaton

Leamington Spa

Stratford-upon-Avon

Nailcote Hall is a charming Elizabethan country house hotel set in 15 acres of gardens and surrounded by Warwickshire countryside. Built in 1640, the house was used by Cromwell during the Civil War and was damaged by his troops prior to the assault on Kenilworth Castle. Ideally located in the heart of England, Nailcote Hall is within 15 minutes' drive of the castle towns of Kenilworth and Warwick, Coventry Cathedral, Birmingham International Airport/Station and the NEC. Situated at the centre of the Midlands motorway network, Birmingham city centre, the ICC and Stratford-upon-Avon are less than 30 minutes away. Leisure facilities include indoor swimming pool, gymnasium, solarium and sauna. Outside there are all-weather tennis courts, pétanque, croquet, a challenging 9-hole par-3 golf course and putting green (host to the British Championship Professional Short Course Championship). In the intimate Tudor surroundings of the Oak Room restaurant, chef will delight guests with superb cuisine, whilst the cellar boasts an extensive choice of international wines. En-suite bedrooms offer luxury accommodation and elegant facilities are available for conferences, private dining and corporate hospitality.

Our inspector loved: The glorious façade of the building.

NUTHURST GRANGE

HOCKLEY HEATH, WARWICKSHIRE B94 5NL

The most memorable feature of this friendly country house hotel is its outstanding restaurant. David Randolph and his head chef have won many accolades for their imaginative menus, described as "English, cooked in the light French style". Diners can enjoy their superb cuisine in one of the 3 adjoining rooms which comprise the restaurant and form the heart of Nuthurst Grange. The rest of the house is no less charming – the spacious bedrooms have a country house atmosphere and are appointed with extra luxuries such as an exhilarating air-spa bath, a trouser press, hairdryer and a safe for valuables. For special occasions there is a room furnished with a four-poster bed and a marble bathroom. There are fine views across the 7½ acres of landscaped gardens. Executive meetings can be accommodated at Nuthurst Grange – within a 12 mile radius of the hotel lie central Birmingham, the NEC, Stratford-upon-Avon, Coventry and Birmingham International Airport. Sporting activities available nearby include golf, canal boating and tennis.

Our inspector loved: *The beautiful grounds.*

Directions: From M42 exit 4 take A3400 signposted Hockley Heath (2 miles, south). Entrance to Nuthurst Grange Lane is ¼ mile south of village. Also, M40 (exit 16 – southbound only), take first left, entrance 300 yards.

Nuneaton

Leamington Spa

Stratford-upon-Avon

Web: www.johansens.com/nuthurstgrange
E-mail: info@nuthurst-grange.com
Tel: 0870 381 8776
International: +44 (0)1564 783972
Fax: 01564 783919

Price Guide:
single £139
double/twin £159–£179
suite £189

MALLORY COURT

HARBURY LANE, BISHOPS TACHBROOK, LEAMINGTON SPA, WARWICKSHIRE CV33 9QB

Surrounded by 10 acres of attractive gardens, Mallory Court boasts a truly stunning backdrop across the beautiful Warwickshire countryside and is just a stone's throw away from Stratford-upon-Avon and Warwick Castle. Offering every home comfort, arriving guests are enveloped by the welcoming and tranquil ambience. Guests may begin their evening sipping champagne on the terrace before setting off to visit the Royal Shakespeare Theatre. During the winter season, afternoon tea may be enjoyed in the comfortable lounges beside the burning log fires. The 29 luxurious rooms are enhanced by thoughtful finishing touches and stunning views across the grounds. Modern, English-style dishes are served in the elegant restaurant where chef is happy to create tailor-made menus. Diners may begin with roasted Skye scallops chicken with Avruga caviar with marinated cucumber and oyster jus followed by braised shoulder and roasted fillet of Lighthorne lamb with Provençal vegetables ending with a hot passion fruit soufflé. This is an ideal venue for weddings and business meetings. Luxury leisure breaks and exclusive use of the hotel are available.

Directions: 2 miles south of Leamington Spa on Harbury Lane, just off the B4087 Bishops Tachbrook-Leamington Spa Road. Harbury Lane runs from the B4087 towards Fosse Way. M40, Jct13 from London/Jct14 from Birmingham.

Web: www.johansens.com/mallorycourt
E-mail: reception@mallory.co.uk
Tel: 0870 381 8713
International: +44 (0)1926 330214
Fax: 01926 451714

Nuneaton

Leamington Spa

Stratford-upon-Avon

Price Guide:
double (single occupancy) from £135
double from £155
master rooms from £250

Our inspector loved: *The impeccable gardens and the sheer luxury and style of the interior furnishings and bedrooms.*

ALVESTON MANOR

CLOPTON BRIDGE, STRATFORD-UPON-AVON, WARWICKSHIRE CV37 7HP

Legend has it that the first performance of Shakespeare's A Midsummer's Night Dream was given under the ancient cedar tree standing in the grounds of this historic and charming hotel. Alveston Manor is conveniently situated on the south side of the River Avon a short walk from the town centre. With its wood-framed façade, leaded windows, pointed roof peaks and tall, ornate chimneys it is an imposing sight to visitors and passing travellers. The interior is enhanced by tasteful décor, rich furnishings, antiques, fine pictures and striking floral displays. There is also a delightful, delicate aroma created by years of polish on original oak panelling and an Elizabethan staircase. The en-suite bedrooms are fitted to a high standard, with many of the bedrooms being situated in the adjoining modern Warwick and Charlecote Wings. A selection of suites and feature rooms are located in the original Manor House. Pre-dinner apéritifs can be sipped in an intimate cocktail bar before the enjoyment of a superbly prepared dinner. Guests can relax in total peace and enjoy an appealing period charm that sympathetically encompasses every modern day comfort or take advantage of the hotel's Vital Health, Fitness & Beauty Club which features an indoor pool, gymnasium, sauna, steam room and 6 beauty treatment rooms.

Our inspector loved: The elegant antique sundial on the Georgian stable block.

Directions: Exit the M40, junction 15 and take the A46 and A439 towards Stratford. Join the one-way system towards Banbury and Oxford. Alveston Manor is at the junction of A422/A3400

Nuneaton

Leamington Spa

Stratford-upon-Avon

Web: www.johansens.com/alvestonmanor
E-mail: sales.alvestonmanor@macdonald-hotels.co.uk
Tel: 0870 381 8310
International: +44 (0)1789 205478
Fax: 01789 414095

Price Guide:
single from £65
double/twin from £130
suite from £180

BILLESLEY MANOR

BILLESLEY, ALCESTER, NR STRATFORD-UPON-AVON, WARWICKSHIRE B49 6NF

This magnificent 4-star 16th-century Manor House is set in 11 acres of its own private parkland and has a unique topiary garden and sun terrace. Centuries of history and tradition with Shakespearian connection welcome guests to this beautiful hotel. Billesley Manor has 71 beautiful bedrooms, including four-poster rooms and suites, all of which are en suite and many with stunning gardens views. Cuisine of the highest standard is served in the Stuart restaurant, awarded 2 AA Rosettes. A selection of rooms for private dining are available for family, friends or business guests. The Cedar Barns offer a new dimension in conference facilities incorporating state-of-the-art equipment in unique and impressive surroundings. New spa incorporating an impressive indoor heated swimming pool, gym, beauty treatment rooms, sauna, steam room, solarium and healthy eating bistro. Tennis courts, croquet lawn and activity field are also available. The organisation of corporate events such as clay pigeon shooting, archery and quad biking are also on offer. Weekend breaks are available – ideal for visiting the Royal Shakespeare Theatre, Warwick Castle, Ragley Hall and the Cotswolds. Situated in the heart of England, minutes away from Shakespeare's Stratford-upon-Avon and only 23 miles from Birmingham International Airport, the hotel can be easily accessed by air, rail and road.

Directions: Leave M40 at exit 15, follow A46 towards Evesham and Alcester. 4 miles beyond Stratford-upon-Avon turn right to Billesley.

Web: www.johansens.com/billesley
E-mail: bookings@billesleymanor.co.uk
Tel: 0870 381 8363
International: +44 (0)1789 279955
Fax: 01789 764145

Price Guide:
single £115
double/twin £170
suite £220

Our inspector loved: The wonderful topiary garden.

ETTINGTON PARK

ALDERMINSTER, STRATFORD-UPON-AVON, WARWICKSHIRE CV37 8BU

The foundations of Ettington Park date back at least 1000 years. Mentioned in the Domesday Book, Ettington Park rises majestically over 40 acres of Warwickshire parkland, surrounded by terraced gardens and carefully tended lawns, where guests can wander at their leisure to admire the pastoral views. The interiors are beautiful, their striking opulence enhanced by flowers, beautiful antiques and original paintings. Amid these elegant surroundings guests can relax totally, pampered with every luxury. On an appropriately grand scale, the 48 bedrooms and superb leisure complex, comprising an indoor heated swimming pool, spa bath, and sauna, make this a perfect choice for the sybarite. The menu reflects the best of English and French cuisine, served with panache in the dining room, with its elegant 18th-century rococo ceiling and 19th-century carved family crests. The bon viveur will relish the fine wine list. Splendid conference facilities are available: the panelled Long Gallery and 12th-century chapel are both unique venues. Clay pigeon shooting, archery and fishing can be arranged on the premises.

Our inspector loved: *The stunning neo-gothic building and its grounds.*

Directions: From M40 junction 15 (Warwick) take A46, A439 signposted Stratford, then left-hand turn onto A3400. Ettington Park is 5 miles south of Stratford-upon-Avon off the A3400.

Nuneaton

Leamington Spa

Stratford-upon-Avon

Web: www.johansens.com/ettingtonpark
E-mail: ettingtonpark@handpicked.co.uk
Tel: 0870 381 8508
International: +44 (0)1789 450123
Fax: 01789 450472

Price Guide:
single from £125
double/twin from £158
suite from £238

THE GLEBE AT BARFORD

CHURCH STREET, BARFORD, WARWICKSHIRE CV35 8BS

Directions: M40 exit Junction 15 A429 signed Barford & Wellesbourne. Turning left at mini-roundabout, the hotel is on the right just past the church.

Web: www.johansens.com/glebeatbarford
E-mail: sales@glebehotel.co.uk
Tel: 0870 381 8548
International: +44 (0)1926 624218
Fax: 01926 624625

Price Guide:
single £105
double/twin £125
suite £160

Nuneaton

Leamington Spa
Stratford-upon-Avon

"Glebe" means belonging to the Church, which explains why this beautiful Georgian country house is in a unique and quiet position next to the church in Barford, an attractive village in Warwickshire. It is a Grade II listed building, dating back to 1820, with an unusual central atrium and surrounded by gardens. The bedrooms are spacious, comfortable and peaceful. They have all the accessories expected by today's travellers. The restaurant is in an elegant, conservatory, green plants adding cool colour. There are excellent table d'hôte and à la carte menus and the wine list has been carefully selected to complement the dishes. The Glebe is an ideal venue for private celebrations and corporate events as it has several well-equipped conference rooms – the Bentley Suite seats 120 people for a banquet and the Directors Suite, with leather armchairs, is ideal for a discreet strategy meeting. Those wishing to be pampered will be pleased with the beauty and sunbed room. Guests appreciate the Glebe Leisure Club with a pool, gymnasium, sauna, steam room and spa facilities. They can play tennis and golf nearby. Ideally situated for Warwick and Stratford races.

Our inspector loved: *The splendid Cedar tree dominating the gravelled forecourt.*

ARDENCOTE MANOR HOTEL, COUNTRY CLUB & SPA

LYE GREEN ROAD, CLAVERDON, NR WARWICK, WARWICKSHIRE CV35 8LS

Under private ownership, this former Gentlemen's residence, which was built around 1860, has been sympathetically refurbished and substantially extended to provide a luxury hotel with all modern amenities and comforts, whilst retaining its traditional elegance and appealing intimacy. Set in 42 acres of landscaped grounds in the heart of Shakespeare country, it offers beautifully appointed en-suite accommodation – many rooms have glorious views of the lake and gardens – fine cuisine and extensive sports and leisure facilities, including indoor pool and spa bath, outdoor whirlpool, sauna and steamrooms, squash and tennis courts, fully equipped gymnasia and a 9-hole golf course. The Ardencote Spa is also at the disposal of guests, offering an extensive range of relaxing and holistic treatments. Ardencote Manor's award-winning restaurant, the lakeside Lodge, offers an exciting and innovative menu. Places of interest nearby include the NEC, Warwick Castle (discounted tickets available through hotel), Stratford-upon-Avon and the Cotswolds. Weekend breaks available.

Our inspector loved: The light and air and the restful lake.

Directions: From M40 follow signs to Henley-in-Arden. Lye Green Road is off A4189 Henley-in-Arden/Warwick Road at Claverdon Village Green.

Web: www.johansens.com/ardencote
E-mail: hotel@ardencote.com
Tel: 0870 381 8320
International: +44 (0)1926 843111
Fax: 01926 842646

Nuneaton

Leamington Spa

Stratford-upon-Avon

Price Guide:
single £105
double £150

WROXALL ABBEY ESTATE

BIRMINGHAM ROAD, WROXALL, NR.WARWICK, WARWICKSHIRE CV35 7NB

Wroxall Abbey Estate, once the home of Sir Christopher Wren, is a collection of listed buildings including Wroxall Court and Wroxall Mansion and nestles in 27 acres of beautiful landscaped gardens. The hotel offers unrivalled service and quality for both business and pleasure amidst the peace and tranquillity of glorious Warwickshire countryside. Wroxall Court's 22 individually designed bedrooms are furnished with stylish fabrics and boast every modern comfort one would expect from such a unique venue. Delicious, imaginative cuisine is served in the Bistro which has an inviting, informal atmosphere, whilst Tapestries is ideal for receptions and Christmas parties. A fabulous historic clock tower tops the Court. Within the gardens are the ruins of the Abbey and Wren's Chapel which date back to c.1141; the latter displays breathtaking stained glass and a brick tower. Services are held in the Chapel every Sunday and it is a romantic place to exchange wedding vows. Sonnets is Wroxall Mansion's fine dining restaurant and seats up to 80 guests. A further 48 spacious bedrooms and suites, function rooms, Wren's Bar and Vaults, panelled snooker room and bar, spa and indoor pool have undergone a complete refurbishment. Guests can enjoy nearby Warwick and its castle, with Stratford-upon-Avon and the Cotswolds only a short distance away.

Directions: From the M42, exit at jct 5 onto the A4141 to Knowle. Continue towards Warwick for about 10 miles. Drive through Chadwick End and the entrance to Wroxall Abbey Estate is approx 2 miles further on, on the right.

Web: www.johansens.com/wroxallcourt
E-mail: info@wroxallestate.com
Tel: 0870 381 9013
International: +44 (0)1926 484470
Fax: 01926 485206

Price Guide:
single £79–£150
double/twin £99–£399

Our inspector loved: *The bedrooms - what an amazing range and variety of shapes, sizes, styles and décor.*

THE MANOR HOUSE HOTEL & GOLF CLUB

CASTLE COMBE, NEAR BATH, WILTSHIRE SN14 7HR

Nestling in the heart of one of England's prettiest villages deep in the Southern Cotswolds, the 14th-century Manor House at Castle Combe is one of Britain's most architecturally beautiful and idyllically set country house hotels. Ivy-clad stone walls and mullioned windows, oak panelling, log fires and antique furniture blend sympathetically with the individually designed bedrooms, many of which feature four poster beds, original beams and exposed walls. Cottage style simpler rooms are found in the Mews Cottages. Set in the 365-acre estate of wooded valley and downland is the Peter Alliss and Clive Clark 6340 yard, par 73, championship golf course, one of the most spectacular and challenging courses in the South of England. Delightful walks in the surrounding countryside or a stroll through the estate, unchanged for almost 200 years, are a magical experience. With its enchanting gardens and parkland, a gently flowing trout stream and the romance of a terraced Italian garden, the Manor House provides peace and tranquillity, together with a friendly atmosphere and award-winning cuisine and hospitality.

Our inspector loved: *The wonderful hi-tech Lordsmeer suite in the main house.*

Directions: A 15-minute drive from junctions 17 and 18 of the M4, or 20 minutes from the M5/M4 intersection. 12 miles from the beautiful Georgian city of Bath and only a 2-hour drive from central London. Approached directly from the A420 and B4039.

Web: www.johansens.com/manorhousecastlecombe
E-mail: enquiries@manor-housecc.co.uk
Tel: 0870 381 8718
International: +44 (0)1249 782206
Fax: 01249 782159

Price Guide: (room only)
single/double/twin from £145
suite £265–£600

THE OLD BELL

ABBEY ROW, MALMESBURY, WILTSHIRE SN16 0AG

Directions: Near the market cross in the centre of Malmesbury.

Web: www.johansens.com/oldbell
E-mail: info@oldbellhotel.com
Tel: 0870 381 9209
International: +44 (0)1666 822344
Fax: 01666 825145

Price Guide:
single from £85
double/twin £110–£170

The Old Bell was established by the Abbot of Malmesbury during the reign of King John as a place to refresh guests who came to consult the Abbey's library. Situated at the edge of the Cotswolds, this Grade I listed building may well be England's most ancient hotel, including features such as a medieval stone fireplace in the Great Hall. A classic and imaginative, 2 Rosettes awarded, menu exemplifies the best in English cooking, with meals ranging from 4-course dinners complemented by fine wines served in the Edwardian dining room, to innovative snacks in the Great Hall. In the main house rooms are decorated and furnished with an individual style and character. The Coach House features bedrooms styled on an oriental theme. Now under new ownership a comprehensive refurbishment programme has begun. The entire ground floor is complete, and all the bedrooms will now be attended to. The Bell is ideal for peaceful breaks, country walks, garden visits, Sunday papers and afternoon teas; quintessentially English! Malmesbury is only 30 minutes from Bath and is close to a number of other beautiful villages such as Castle Combe, Bourton-on-the-Water and Lacock. Other places of interest include the mysterious stone circle at Avebury and Westonbirt Arboretum.

Our inspector loved: The huge stone fireplaces and interesting character throughout.

HOWARD'S HOUSE

TEFFONT EVIAS, SALISBURY, WILTSHIRE SP3 5RJ

Tucked away in the depths of rural Wiltshire and surrounded by 2 acres of beautiful gardens the fragrance of jasmine exudes through the open windows of the House and the tinkling of the fountain in the lily pond can be gently heard. This charming small country house hotel, run by Noële Thompson, is located in the quintessential English hamlet of Teffon Evias, just 9 miles from Stonehenge. Howard's House is a haven of tranquillity for those seeking to escape the noise and stress of the modern world. The bedrooms are delightfully appointed, with additional touches of fresh fruit, homemade biscuits, plants and up-to-date magazines. The 3 Rosettes awarded restaurant is the height of elegance and serves modern British cuisine providing dishes of national acclaim. Cooked with flair and imagination and using home-grown and the best local produce, alfresco dining can be enjoyed during the summer. During winter guests may curl up by the genuine log fire with a good book and a glass of vintage port. Whatever the time of year you are guaranteed the ultimate in country house hospitality. Howard's House is ideally situated for visiting Stonehenge, Old Sarum, Salisbury Cathedral, Wilton House and Stourhead Gardens.

Our inspector loved: A lovely house in an idyllic location with beautiful gardens.

Directions: From London, turn left off A303. 2 miles after the Wylye intersection follow signs to Teffont and on entering the village join the B3089. Howard's House is signposted.

Web: www.johansens.com/howardshouse
E-mail: enq@howardshousehotel.com
Tel: 0870 381 8627
International: +44 (0)1722 716392
Fax: 01722 716820

Price Guide:
single £105
double/twin £165–£185

THE PEAR TREE AT PURTON

CHURCH END, PURTON, SWINDON, WILTSHIRE SN5 4ED

Dedication to service is the hallmark of this excellent honey-coloured stone hotel nestling in the Vale of the White Horse between the Cotswolds and Marlborough Downs. Owners Francis and Anne Young are justly proud of its recognition by the award of the RAC's Blue Ribbon for excellence. Surrounded by rolling Wiltshire farmland, The Pear Tree sits majestically in 7½ acres of tranquil grounds on the fringe of the Saxon village of Purton, famed for its unique twin towered Parish Church and the ancient hill fort of Ringsbury Camp. Each of the 17 individually and tastefully decorated bedrooms and suites is named after a character associated with the village, such as Anne Hyde, mother of Queen Mary II and Queen Anne. All are fitted to a high standard and have digital television, hairdryer, trouser press, a safe and a host of other luxuries. The award-winning conservatory restaurant overlooks colourful gardens and is the perfect setting in which to enjoy good English cuisine prepared with style and flair. Cirencester, Bath, Oxford, Avebury, Blenheim Palace, Sudeley Castle and the Cotswolds are all within easy reach.

Directions: From M4 exit 16 follow signs to Purton and go through the village until reaching a triangle with Spar Grocers opposite. Turn right up the hill and the Pear Tree is on the second left after the Tithe Barn.

Web: www.johansens.com/peartree
E-mail: relax@peartreepurton.co.uk
Tel: 0870 381 8806
International: +44 (0)1793 772100
Fax: 01793 772369

Price Guide:
single £110
double/twin £110–£135
suites £135

Our inspector loved: The light newly refurbished restaurant overlooking the lovely garden.

BISHOPSTROW HOUSE

WARMINSTER, WILTSHIRE BA12 9HH

Bishopstrow House is the quintessential Georgian mansion. It combines the intimacy of a grand country hotel retreat with all the benefits of modern facilities and the luxury of the Ragdale Spa, which offers a superb range of beauty, fitness and relaxation therapies in addition to Michaeljohn's world famous hair styling. A Grade II listed building, Bishopstrow House was built in 1817 and has been sympathetically extended to include indoor and outdoor heated swimming pools, a gymnasium and a sauna. The attention to detail is uppermost in the library, drawing room and conservatory with their beautiful antiques and Victorian oil paintings. The bedrooms are grandly furnished; some have opulent marble bathrooms and whirlpool baths. Skilfully prepared modern British food is served in the Mulberry Restaurant, with lighter meals available in the Mulberry Bar and the conservatory which overlooks 27 acres of gardens. There is fly fishing on the hotel's private stretch of the River Wylye, golf at 5 nearby courses, riding, game and clay pigeon shooting. Longleat House, Wilton House, Stourhead, Stonehenge, Bath, Salisbury and Warminster are within easy reach.

Our inspector loved: *The comfortable, relaxing and informal atmosphere.*

Directions: Bishopstrow House is south east of Warminster on the B3414 from London via the M3.

Web: www.johansens.com/bishopstrowhouse
E-mail: enquiries@bishopstrow.co.uk
Tel: 0870 381 8365
International: +44 (0)1985 212312
Fax: 01985 216769

Price Guide:
single £99
double/twin £160–£245
suite from £330

THE ELMS

ABBERLEY, WORCESTERSHIRE WR6 6AT

Directions: From M5, exit at jct 5 (Droitwich) or jct 6 (Worcester) then A443 towards Tenbury Wells. The Elms is 2 miles after Great Witley. Do not take Abberley village turning.

Web: www.johansens.com/elmsworcester
E-mail: info@theelmshotel.com
Tel: 0870 381 8304
International: +44 (0)1299 896666
Fax: 01299 896804

Price Guide:
single £100–£120
double/twin £140–£180
coach house £130

Built in 1710 by a pupil of Sir Christopher Wren, and converted into a country house hotel in 1946, The Elms has achieved an international reputation for excellence spanning the past half century. Standing impressively between Worcester and Tenbury Wells, this fine Queen Anne mansion is surrounded by beautiful meadows, woodland, hop fields and orchards of cider apples and cherries of the Teme Valley, whose river runs crimson when in flood from bank-side soil tinged with red sandstone. Each of the 16 main house and 5 coach house bedrooms has its own character and provides magnificent views across the landscaped gardens. Guests can enjoy pre-dinner drinks in a comfortable, panelled bar before adjourning to the handsomely furnished restaurant, awarded 2 Rosettes, to be served with sophisticated and imaginative dishes prepeared by Head Chef Daren Bale, complemented by fine wines. The surrounding countryside is ideal for walking, fishing, shooting, golf and horse racing. Within easy reach are the attractions of the market town of Tenbury Wells, Hereford with meppa murdi (oldest map in the world), Witley Court, Bewdley and the ancient city of Worcester with its cathedral, county cricket ground and porcelain factory.

Our inspector loved: *The cosy wood-panelled bar with open log fire and the abundance of fresh flowers throughout the hotel.*

THE BROADWAY HOTEL

THE GREEN, BROADWAY, WORCESTERSHIRE WR12 7AA

The Broadway Hotel stands proudly in the centre of the picturesque Cotswold village of Broadway where every stone evokes memories of Elizabethan England. Once used by the Abbots of Pershore, the hotel was formerly a 16th-century house, as can be seen by its architecture which combines the half timbers of the Vale of Evesham with the distinctive honey-coloured and grey stone of the Cotswolds. It epitomises a true combination of Old World charm and modern day amenities with friendly, efficient service. All bedrooms provide television, telephone and tea and coffee making facilities. Traditional English dishes and a peaceful ambience are offered in the beamed Courtyard Restaurant. There is an impressive variety of à la carte dishes complemented by good wines. The congenial Jockey Club bar is a pleasant place to enjoy a drink. The hotel overlooks the village green at the bottom of the main street where guests can browse through shops offering an array of fine antiques. On a clear day, 13 counties of England and Wales can be viewed from Broadway Tower. Snowhill, Burford, Chipping Campden, Bourton-on-the-Water, Stow-on-the-Wold and Winchcombe as well as larger Cheltenham, Worcester and Stratford are within easy reach.

Our inspector loved: The minstrels gallery above the atmospheric dining room.

Directions: From London M40 to Oxford, A40 to Burford, A429 through Stow-on-the-Wold, then A44 to Broadway.

Web: www.johansens.com/broadwayworcestershire
E-mail: info@broadwayhotel.info
Tel: 0870 381 8381
International: +44 (0)1386 852401
Fax: 01386 853879

Price Guide:
single £80–£90
double £130–£150

DORMY HOUSE

WILLERSEY HILL, BROADWAY, WORCESTERSHIRE WR12 7LF

This former 17th-century farmhouse has been beautifully converted into a delightful hotel which retains much of its original character. With its oak beams, stone-flagged floors and honey-coloured local stone walls it imparts warmth and tranquillity. Dormy House provides a wealth of comforts for the most discerning guest. Each bedroom is individually decorated – some are furnished with 4-poster beds – and suites are available. Head chef, Alan Cutler, prepares a superb choice of menus and the dining room offers an extensive wine list with a diverse range of half bottles. The versatile Dormy Suite is an ideal venue for conferences, meetings or private functions – professionally arranged to individual requirements. The hotel has its own leisure facilities, which include a games room, gym, sauna/steam room, croquet lawn and putting green. Mountain bikes are available for hire. Broadway Golf Club is adjacent. The locality is idyllic for walkers. Stratford-upon-Avon, Cheltenham Spa, Hidcote Manor Garden and Sudeley Castle are all within easy reach. Closed 2 days at Christmas.

Our inspector loved: The character of the building and tastefully designed bedrooms in a tranquil location.

Directions: The hotel is ½ mile off the A44 between Moreton-in-Marsh and Broadway. Take the turning signposted Saintbury, the hotel is the first building on the left passed the picnic area.

Web: www.johansens.com/dormyhouse
E-mail: reservations@dormyhouse.co.uk
Tel: 0870 381 8487
International: +44 (0)1386 852711
Fax: 01386 858636

Price Guide:
single £115
double/twin £155–£170
suite from £200

Kidderminster

Worcester

Evesham

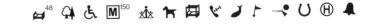

THE LYGON ARMS
BROADWAY, WORCESTERSHIRE WR12 7DU

The Lygon Arms, a magnificent 16th-century building with numerous historical associations, stands in Broadway, acclaimed by many as the prettiest village in England, in the heart of the North Cotswolds. Over the years much restoration has been carried out, emphasising the outstanding period features, such as original 17th-century oak panelling and an ancient hidden stairway. All the bedrooms are individually and tastefully furnished and offer guests every modern luxury, combined with the elegance of an earlier age. The Great Hall, complete with a 17th-century minstrels' gallery and the smaller private dining rooms provide a fine setting for a well-chosen and imaginative menu. Conference facilities including the state-of-the-art Torrington Room are available for up to 80 participants. Guests can enjoy a superb range of leisure amenities in The Lygon Arms Spa, including all-weather tennis, indoor pool, spa bath, gymnasium, billiard room, beauty salons, steam room and saunas. Golf can be arranged locally. The many Cotswold villages, Stratford-upon-Avon, Oxford and Cheltenham are nearby, whilst Broadway itself is a paradise for the antique collector.

Our inspector loved: The extensive spa and leisure facilities.

Directions: Set in the heart of Broadway.

Web: www.johansens.com/lygonarms
E-mail: info@the-lygon-arms.co.uk
Tel: 0870 381 9190
International: +44 (0)1386 852255
Fax: 01386 858611

Price Guide:
single from £119
double/twin from £179
suite from £279

Kidderminster

Worcester

Evesham

BROCKENCOTE HALL

CHADDESLEY CORBETT, NR KIDDERMINSTER, WORCESTERSHIRE DY10 4PY

Directions: Exit 4 from M5 or exit 1 from M42 (southbound). Brockencote Hall is set back from A448 at Chaddesley Corbett between Bromsgrove and Kidderminster.

Web: www.johansens.com/brockencotehall
E-mail: info@brockencotehall.com
Tel: 0870 381 8382
International: +44 (0)1562 777876
Fax: 01562 777872

Price Guide:
single £88–£140
double/twin £116–£180

The Brockencote estate consists of 70 acres of landscaped grounds surrounding a magnificent hall. There is a gatehouse, half-timbered dovecote, lake, some fine European and North American trees and an elegant conservatory. The estate dates back over three centuries and the style of the building reflects the changes which have taken place in fashion and taste. The hotel has been awarded 3 AA Red Stars, 4 RAC dining awards and is Heart of England Tourist Board Midlands Hotel of the Year silver award 2002. At present, the interior combines classical architectural features with contemporary creature comforts. As in most country houses, each of the bedrooms is different: all have their own character, complemented by tasteful furnishings and décor. The friendly staff provide a splendid service under the supervision of owners Alison and Joseph Petitjean. The Hall specialises in traditional French cuisine with occasional regional and seasonal specialities. Brockencote Hall is an ideal setting for those seeking peace and quiet in an unspoilt corner of the English countryside. Located a few miles south of Birmingham, it is convenient for business people and sightseers alike and makes a fine base for touring historic Worcestershire. Special rates available Sunday to Saturday.

Our inspector loved: *The spacious and tastefully decorated bedrooms and the breathtaking setting in the heart of the English countryside .*

        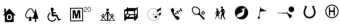

THE EVESHAM HOTEL

COOPER'S LANE, OFF WATERSIDE, EVESHAM, WORCESTERSHIRE WR11 1DA

It is the somewhat unconventional atmosphere at the Evesham Hotel that stays in the memory. Originally a Tudor farmhouse, the hotel was extended and converted into a Georgian mansion house in 1809. Unusually, it combines an award-winning welcome for families with the relaxed but efficient style required by business users. For the past quarter of a century it has been successfully run by the Jenkinson family. Each of the 40 en-suite bedrooms is furnished complete with a teddy bear and a toy duck for the bath. The restaurant offers delicious cuisine from a very imaginative and versatile menu, accompanied by a somewhat unique "Euro-sceptic" wine list (everything but French and German!). The drinks selection is an amazing myriad. The indoor swimming pool has a seaside theme. The peace of the 2½ acre garden belies the hotel's proximity to the town – a 5-minute walk away. In the gardens are 6 300-year-old mulberry trees and a magnificent cedar of Lebanon, planted in 1809. The hotel is a good base from which to explore the Cotswolds, Stratford-upon-Avon and the Severn Valley. Closed at Christmas.

Our inspector loved: *This family orientated hotel with its quirky features.*

Directions: Cooper's Lane lies just off Waterside (the River Avon).

Web: www.johansens.com/evesham
E-mail: reception@eveshamhotel.com
Tel: 0870 381 8510
International: +44 (0)1386 765566
Fax: 01386 765443

Price Guide:
single £75–£87
double/twin £118
family £176

WOOD NORTON HALL

WOOD NORTON, EVESHAM, WORCESTERSHIRE WR11 4YB

Directions: The hotel stands on the A44 Worcester Road, 3 miles north of the town centre.

Web: www.johansens.com/woodnortonhall
E-mail: info@wnhall.co.uk
Tel: 0870 381 9154
International: +44 (0)1386 425780
Fax: 01386 425781

Price Guide:
single £85-135
double/twin £130-£200
suite £145-£230

Wood Norton Hall is a glorious Grade II listed Victorian country house standing in 170 acres of beautiful Worcestershire countryside. A short drive from the historic market town of Evesham, 8 miles from Broadway and the Cotswolds with Stratford-upon-Avon only 15 miles away. French connections date back to 1872 and culminated in the wedding of Princess Louise of Orléans and Prince Charles of Bourbon in 1907. Original fleur-de-lys carved oak panelling lines the walls; grand fireplaces, elegant furniture and beautiful tapestries add comfort and colour. The en-suite rooms are furnished to the highest standards. The ground floor public rooms reflect the grandeur of the Victorian era with voluptuous window drapes framing views to the Vale of Evesham and the River Avon. The award-winning Le Duc's Restaurant provides the perfect ambience to savour a fine culinary tradition. The hall has 8 rooms suitable for conferences and private banquets and is an ideal venue for incentive programmes. Extensive leisure facilities include a billiard room, fitness suite and golf at a nearby international course.

Our inspector loved: *The original Victorian carved oak panelling throughout the main building and the glorious views from the house set in 170 acres of beautiful countryside.*

THE COTTAGE IN THE WOOD

HOLYWELL ROAD, MALVERN WELLS, WORCESTERSHIRE WR14 4LG

The Malvern Hills, once the home and inspiration for England's most celebrated composer, Sir Edward Elgar, are the setting for The Cottage in the Wood. With its spectacular outlook across the Severn Valley plain, this unique hotel won acclaim from the Daily Mail for the best view in England. The main house was originally the Dower House to the Blackmore Park estate and accommodation is offered here and in Beech Cottage, an old scrumpy house – and the magnificent new building, "the Pinnacles", named after the hill that rises above, which houses 19 of the traditional-styled bedrooms, many with patio's or balcomies and giving the best view of all. Owned and run by 2 generations of the Pattin family, the atmosphere is genuinely warm and relaxing. A regularly changing modern English menu is complemented by an almost obsessional wine list of 600 bins. If this causes any over-indulgence, guests can walk to the tops of the Malvern Hills direct from the hotel grounds. Nearby are the Victorian spa town of Great Malvern, the Three Counties Showground and the Cathedral cities of Worcester, Gloucester and Hereford.

Our inspector loved: Its wonderful location with breathtaking views.

Directions: 3 miles south of Great Malvern on A449, turn into Holywell Road by post box and hotel sign. Hotel is 250 yards on right.

Web: www.johansens.com/cottageinthewood
E-mail: proprietor@cottageinthewood.co.uk
Tel: 0870 381 8452
International: +44 (0)1684 575859
Fax: 01684 560662

Price Guide:
single £79–£110
double/twin £99–£185

WILLERBY MANOR HOTEL

WELL LANE, WILLERBY, HULL, EAST YORKSHIRE HU10 6ER

Originally the home of the Edwardian shipping merchant, Sir Henry Salmon, Willerby Manor was bought in the early 1970s by John Townend, a Wine Merchant from Hull. The elegance of the hotel, as it, stands today, is testament to the careful work of the Townend family over the years. Furnished in a stylish manner, the public rooms are the essence of comfort. The 51 bedrooms are beautifully decorated with colour co-ordinated fabrics and soft furnishings. Every modern amenity is provided as well as an array of thoughtful extras such as fresh floral arrangements. Restaurant Icon serves modern English food, which is complemented by an extensive well-chosen wine list from the House of Townend. A more informal ambience pervades the Everglades Brasserie where guests may savour bistro-style meals and beverages. Fitness enthusiasts will be delighted with the well-equipped Health Club which includes a 19 metre swimming pool, spacious gymnasium, whirlpool spa bath, an exercise studio with daily classes and a beauty treatment room. The hotel is in a convenient location for those wishing to explore the cities of Hull and York.

Directions: Take the M62 towards Hull, which runs into the A63, turn off onto the A164 in the direction of Beverley. Follow the signs to Willerby and then Willerby Manor.

Web: www.johansens.com/willerbymanor
E-mail: willerbymanor@bestwestern.co.uk
Tel: 0870 381 8998
International: +44 (0)1482 652616
Fax: 01482 653901

Price Guide:
single £50–£91
double/twin £80–£129

Bridlington
York
Beverley
● *Hull*

Our inspector loved: *Having a relaxing swim in the large pool before dinner.*

THE DEVONSHIRE ARMS COUNTRY HOUSE HOTEL

BOLTON ABBEY, SKIPTON, NORTH YORKSHIRE BD23 6AJ

The Devonshire reflects its charming setting in the Yorkshire Dales: a welcome escape from a busy and crowded world, peace and quiet, beautiful countryside – the perfect place in which to relax. The hotel is owned by the Duke and Duchess of Devonshire and is set in rolling parkland on their 30,000-acre Bolton Abbey Estate in the Yorkshire Dales National Park. The Dowager Duchess of Devonshire personally supervises the decoration of the interiors which include antiques and paintings from their family home at Chatsworth. Fine dining led by Michelin Star Executive Head Chef Michael Wignall in the elegant Burlington Restaurant is complemented by an outstanding award-winning wine list. Alternatively there is the less informal atmosphere of The Devonshire Brasserie and Bar with its lively décor and contemporary art. The Devonshire Club housed in a converted 17th-century barn offers a full range of leisure, health and beauty therapy facilities. There is plenty to do and see on the hotel's doorstep from exploring the ruins of the 12th-century Augustinian Bolton Priory to fly fishing on the river Wharfe. Managing Director, Jeremy Rata, together with General Manager Eamonn Elliott, lead an enthusiastic team committed to providing a high standard of service and hospitality.

Our inspector loved: The unique glass-fronted wine rooms offering a choice of over 2000 bins of fine and rare wines.

Directions: Off the A59 Skipton–Harrogate road at junction with the B6160

Web: www.johansens.com/devonshirearms
E-mail: reservations@thedevonshirearms.co.uk
Tel: 0870 381 8480
International: +44 (0)1756 718111
Fax: 01756 710564

Price Guide:
single £160–£360
double/twin £220–£360
suite £380

GRANTS HOTEL

SWAN ROAD, HARROGATE, NORTH YORKSHIRE HG1 2SS

Directions: Swan Road is in the centre of Harrogate, off the A61 to Ripon.

Web: www.johansens.com/grants
E-mail: enquiries@grantshotel-harrogate.com
Tel: 0870 381 8562
International: +44 (0)1423 560666
Fax: 01423 502550

Price Guide:
single £99–£115
double/twin £110–£160
suites £168

Towards the end of the last century, Harrogate became fashionable among the gentry, who came to "take the waters" of the famous spa. Today's visitors have one advantage over their Victorian counterparts – they can enjoy the hospitality of Grants Hotel, the creation of Pam and Peter Grant. Their friendly welcome, coupled with high standards of service, ensures a pleasurable stay. All bedrooms are attractively decorated and have en-suite bathrooms. Downstairs, guests can relax in the comfortable lounge or take refreshments out to the terrace gardens. Drinks and light meals are available at all times from Harry Grant's Bar and dinner is served in the French café-style Chimney Pots Bistro, complete with brightly coloured check blinds and cloths and lots of humorous Beryl Cook pictures. Cuisine is basically traditional rustic with a smattering of Oriental influence complemented by the mouth-watering home-made puddings. Located less than 5 minutes' walk from Harrogate's Conference and Exhibition Centre, Grants offers its own luxury meeting and syndicate rooms, the Herriot Suite. The Royal Pump Room Museum and the Royal Baths Assembly Rooms are nearby. Guests have free use of The Academy Health and Leisure Club. Super value breaks available.

Our inspector loved: The Beryl Cook pictures in the Bistro.

HOTEL DU VIN & BISTRO

PROSPECT PLACE, HARROGATE, NORTH YORKSHIRE HG1 1LB

Opened in September 2003 following an extensive renovation programme, Hotel du Vin Harrogate was built from an existing hotel property, the Harrogate Spa Hotel, and delights visitors and residents of this famous Yorkshire spa town alike. It is the 6th venture of the Hotel du Vin group, which since 1994 has opened successful venues in Winchester, Tunbridge Wells, Bristol, Brighton and Birmingham. The 43 classically decorated bedrooms, 4 of which are large "loft suites", offer all the Hotel du Vin trademarks such as superb beds, fine linens, fantastic showers and oversized baths. The Bistro with its leather banquettes and antique tables serves high-quality food, which can be enjoyed al fresco in the private courtyard during the warmer months. The wine cellar boasts over 600 bins, whilst the Champagne & Claret bar is a popular venue to mingle, and a walk-in cigar humidor, billiard room and cellar "snug" create a cosy ambience. 2 private dining rooms are available accommodating up to 60. The hotel also has a small but superbly equipped gym. Guests can enjoy Harrogate's fantastic shopping, whilst the Pump Room, the famous Betty's Tea Room and the Harrogate International Centre are all just a few minutes' walk away.

Our inspector loved: Viewing the collection of wines in the innovative glass wine cellar.

Directions: From the A1M - take A59 to Harrogate. Town centre - at Prince of Wales rounabout take 3rd exit towards town centre, the hotel is on the right

Web: www.johansens.com/duvinharrogate
E-mail: reservations@harrogate.hotelduvin.com
Tel: 0870 381 8493
International: +44 (0)1423 856800
Fax: 01423 856801

Price Guide: (room only)
double/twin £95–£140
suite £145–£250

RUDDING PARK HOTEL & GOLF

RUDDING PARK, FOLLIFOOT, HARROGATE, NORTH YORKSHIRE HG3 1JH

Rudding Park's award-winning hotel is just 2 miles from Harrogate town centre. Its setting is superb, surrounded by 230 acres of parkland. The hotel has an elegant façade and entrance, approached by a sweeping driveway. The Regency period house offers fine conference and banqueting rooms, whilst the adjoining hotel has been brilliantly designed and built to harmonise with the original mansion. A warm welcome awaits guests in the pleasant foyer, with its big fireplace and easy chairs. The bedrooms are spacious, with contemporary cherry wood furniture, relaxing colour schemes, many modern accessories and lovely views over the estate. Guests can relax in the Mackaness Drawing Room. The stylish 2 AA Rosette Clocktower Restaurant and Bar are inviting and on sunny days they extend onto the terrace. The food is delicious and the wine list extensive. Leisure facilities are excellent – there is an 18-hole par 72 parkland golf course which has played host to the PGA Mastercard tour series. The golf academy and driving range are ideal for lessons and practice. Hotel guests are welcome to use a local award-winning gym and health club.

Directions: Rudding Park is accessible from the A1 north or south, via the A661, just off the A658.

Web: www.johansens.com/ruddingpark
E-mail: sales@ruddingpark.com
Tel: 0870 381 8879
International: +44 (0)1423 871350
Fax: 01423 872286

Price Guide:
single £135–£155
double/twin £165–£185
suite from £300

Our inspector loved: The enthusiastic and helpful staff with their attention to detail.

HOB GREEN HOTEL AND RESTAURANT

MARKINGTON, HARROGATE, NORTH YORKSHIRE HG3 3PJ

Set in 870 acres of farm and woodland this charming "country house" hotel is only a short drive from the spa town of Harrogate and the ancient city of Ripon. The restaurant has an excellent reputation locally with only the finest fresh local produce being used, much of which is grown in the hotel's own garden. The interesting menus are complemented by an excellent choice of sensibly priced wines. All 12 bedrooms have been individually furnished and tastefully equipped to suit the most discerning guest. The drawing room and hall, warmed by log fires in cool weather, are comfortably furnished with the added attraction of fine antique furniture, porcelain and pictures. Situated in the heart of some of Yorkshire's most dramatic scenery, the hotel offers magnificent views of the valley beyond from all the main rooms. York is only 23 miles away. There is a wealth of cultural and historical interest nearby with Fountains Abbey and Studley Royal water garden and deer park a few minutes' drive. The Yorkshire Riding Centre is in Markington Village. Simply relax in this tranquil place where your every comfort is catered for. Special breaks available.

Our inspector loved: *Strolling around the large lovingly tended Victorian walled herb, vegetable and cutting flower garden.*

Directions: Turn left signposted Markington off the A61 Harrogate to Ripon road, the hotel is 1 mile after the village on the left.

Web: www.johansens.com/hobgreen
E-mail: info@hobgreen.com
Tel: 0870 381 8600
International: +44 (0)1423 770031
Fax: 01423 771589

Price Guide:
single £85–£115
double/twin £100–£145
suite £135–£155

THE BOAR'S HEAD HOTEL

THE RIPLEY CASTLE ESTATE, HARROGATE, NORTH YORKSHIRE HG3 3AY

Imagine relaxing in a luxury hotel at the centre of a historic, private country estate in England's incredibly beautiful North Country. The Ingilby family who have lived in Ripley Castle for 28 generations invite you to enjoy their hospitality at The Boar's Head Hotel. There are 25 luxury bedrooms, individually decorated and furnished, most with king-sized beds. The restaurant's menu is outstanding, presented by a creative and imaginative kitchen brigade and complemented by a wide selection of reasonably priced, good quality wines. There is a welcoming bar serving traditional ales straight from the wood and popular bar meal selections. When staying at The Boar's Head, guests can enjoy complimentary access to the delightful walled gardens and grounds of Ripley Castle, which include the lakes and a deer park. A conference at Ripley is a different experience – using the idyllic meeting facilities available in the Castle, organisers and delegates alike will appreciate the peace and tranquillity of the location, which also offers opportunities for all types of leisure activity in the Deer Park.

Our inspector loved: *The historic Ripley Castle and the pretty village of Ripley.*

Directions: Ripley is very accessible, just 10 minutes from the conference town of Harrogate, 20 minutes from the motorway network and Leeds/Bradford Airport, and 40 minutes from the City of York.

Web: www.johansens.com/boarsheadharrogate
E-mail: reservations@boarsheadripley.co.uk
Tel: 0870 381 8370
International: +44 (0)1423 771888
Fax: 01423 771509

Price Guide:
single £105–£125
double £125–£150

SIMONSTONE HALL

HAWES, NORTH YORKSHIRE DL8 3LY

Fine cuisine, comfort, peace and tranquillity combine with breathtaking scenery to make any stay at Simonstone Hall totally memorable. This former 18th-century hunting lodge has been lovingly restored and furnished with antiques to create an idyllic retreat for its guests. The hall stands in 5 acres of beautiful landscaped gardens with an adjacent 14,000 acres of grouse moors and upland grazing. Many period features have been retained such as the panelled dining room, mahogany staircase with ancestral stained glass windows and a lounge with ornamental fireplace and ceilings. The bedrooms are of the highest standards and offer every modern comfort including four-poster and sleigh beds. In the restaurant, guests savour the freshest local produce presented with flair and imagination, whilst enjoying stunning views across Upper Wensleydale. An excellent wine list is available to complement any dish. Traditional and Thai cuisine is served in the Game Tavern and The Orangery which provide a particularly warm and informal atmosphere. Simonstone Hall, with its fine views, is the perfect base for enjoying and exploring the hidden Yorkshire Dales. The area abounds with ancient castles, churches and museums. Hardraw Force, England's highest single drop waterfall, which can be heard from the gardens, is only a walk away.

Our inspector loved: The wonderful setting with stunning views across Upper Wensleydale.

Directions: Hawes is on A684. Turn north on Buttertubs Pass towards Muker. Simonstone Hall is ½ mile on the left.

Web: www.johansens.com/simonstonehall
E-mail: email@simonstonehall.demon.co.uk
Tel: 0870 381 8895
International: +44 (0)1969 667255
Fax: 01969 667741

Price Guide:
single £50–£100
double/twin £100–£180

THE FEVERSHAM ARMS HOTEL

HELMSLEY, NORTH YORKSHIRE YO62 5AG

Directions: From A1 take A64, then take the York north bypass (A1237) and then B1363. Alternatively, from A1 take A168 signposted Thirsk, then A170.

Web: www.johansens.com/fevershamarms
E-mail: stay@fevershamarmshotel.com
Tel: 0870 381 9283
International: +44 (0)1439 770766
Fax: 01439 770346

Ripon   Scarborough

Harrogate   York

Price Guide:
single £110–£140
double/twin £120–£150
suite £180–£190

This former mid-19th-century coaching inn, standing in the heart of an attractive market town nestling beneath the southern rim of the North Yorkshire moors, has been carefully redeveloped and furnished to create a relaxing retreat. The highest standards of hospitality and service are provided in a casual ambience where elements of the inn's past and present mingle in complete harmony. Mousey Thompson furniture and traditional soft leather sofas and armchairs feature comfortably next to Julia Burns' contemporary paintings. The 17 en suite bedrooms, including 5 suites, are individually decorated and have every home-from-home facility. Dining is an experience: each dish is presented with flair and imagination, with the emphasis on game, lamb and the freshest of seafood from nearby Whitby. Guests can enjoy their meals in the lovely conservatory restaurant, in front of open fires in either of the delightfully decorated lounges or, on fine summer days, on the poolside terrace. As well as the outdoor pool the hotel has a tennis court and a fully equipped health and fitness club. Places of interest nearby include Byland and Rievaulx Abbeys, Helmsley Castle, Castle Howard and Nunnington Hall.

Our inspector loved: *The unique dining experience in the conservatory restaurant, which overlooks the swimming pool and tennis court.*

THE PHEASANT

HAROME, HELMSLEY, NORTH YORKSHIRE YO62 5JG

The Pheasant, rich in oak beams and open log fires, offers 2 types of accommodation, some in the hotel and some in a charming, 16th-century thatched cottage. The Binks family, who built the hotel and now own and manage it, have created a friendly atmosphere which is part of the warm Yorkshire welcome that awaits all guests. The bedrooms and suites are brightly decorated in an attractive cottage style, and are all complete with en-suite facilities. Traditional English cooking is the speciality of the restaurant; many of the dishes are prepared using fresh fruit and vegetables. During summer, guests may relax on the terrace overlooking the pond. An indoor heated swimming pool is an added attraction. Other sporting activities available locally include swimming, riding, golf and fishing. York is a short drive away, as are a host of historic landmarks including Byland and Rievaulx Abbeys and Castle Howard of Brideshead Revisited fame. Also nearby is the magnificent North York Moors National Park. Dogs by arrangement. Closed Christmas, January and February.

Our inspector loved: *The friendly and relaxed ambience in this family-run hotel.*

Directions: From Helmsley, take the A170 towards Scarborough; after ¼ mile turn right for Harome. The hotel is near the church in the village.

Web: www.johansens.com/pheasanthelmsley
Tel: 0870 381 8821
International: +44 (0)1439 771241
Fax: 01439 771744

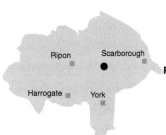

Price Guide: (including 5-course dinner)
single £70–£78
double/twin £138–£155

HAZLEWOOD CASTLE HOTEL

PARADISE LANE, HAZLEWOOD, TADCASTER, NR LEEDS & YORK, NORTH YORKSHIRE LS24 9NJ

Directions: Off the A64 east of the A1 Leeds/York intersection.

Web: www.johansens.com/hazlewoodcastle
E-mail: info@hazlewood-castle.co.uk
Tel: 0870 381 8589
International: +44 (0)1937 535353
Fax: 01937 530630

Price Guide:
single from £120
double/twin £140–£190
suites £255–£320

Behind the restored 13th-century façade of this fascinating castle lies a vibrant and professional hotel, where outstanding cuisine and flawless hospitality are offered in magnificent surroundings. Famed for its gourmet food, the hotel offers a masterclass, where John Benson-Smith, formerly a Masterchef Judge, gives lively demonstrations when guests can join in. The hotel has 2 excellent restaurants, the informal Prickly Pear and the chic Restaurant 1086, as well as a range of facilities for private dining. A distinct panache is lent to the atmosphere of a banquet set in the Old Dining Room and State Drawing Rooms, and Restaurant 1086, the signature restaurant of John Benson-Smith, can be hired to add charismatic zest to a dinner party. Hazlewood Castle is well designed to accommodate corporate or private events, whilst providing a sense of privilege and individuality for its guests. Its fortified buildings include the impressive Great Hall and the Chapel of St Leonards, ideal for musical occasions, amongst its many convivial reception rooms. The beautifully decorated bedrooms reflect the perfect balance of tradition and design that is evident throughout the hotel. Numerous activities include golf and clay pigeon shooting. Special weekend breaks available.

Our inspector loved: *The Victoria room, which has gold wallpaper from Queen Victoria's private bathroom at the Great Exhibition in 1851.*

SWINTON PARK

MASHAM, NEAR RIPON, NORTH YORKSHIRE HG4 4JH

Swinton Park, with its battlement-topped turrets and round tower, coloured green with climbing ivy, is a Grade II listed castle dating from the late 1600s. The heart of the building is essentially Regency style but heavily disguised by a Victorian influence, with the addition of turrets and castellations. Sold by the Earl of Swinton in 1980, but recently bought back by the family and extensively refurbished, this luxurious hotel offers every comfort and up-to-date facility. Rising picturesquely against the skyline, it is set in 200 acres of deer-stocked parkland and formal gardens, surrounded by a 20,000-acre family estate, ½ mile from Masham. Ground floor rooms enjoy sweeping views over the parkland, lake and gatehouse and feature antiques and family portraits. The guest rooms, on the first and second floors, are individually designed with 4 suites and the turret room on 3 circular floors with a free-standing rain bath. Superb British cuisine, with an emphasis on produce from the walled garden, is served in the elegant dining room, which features a gold leaf ceiling and sumptuous décor. Enjoy country pursuits including falconry, off-road driving and fishing. Rosemary Shrager, the celebrity chef, runs her cooking school in the converted Georgian stables with residential and day courses throughout the year. VisitBritain Hotel of the Year 2004 at The Excellence in England Awards.

Directions: Masham is off the A6108 between Leyburn and Ripon.

Web: www.johansens.com/swintonpark
E-mail: enquiries@swintonpark.com
Tel: 0870 381 8934
International: +44 (0)1765 680900
Fax: 01765 680901

Price Guide:
single £120–£250
double/twin £120–£250
suites £250–£350

Our inspector loved: The attentive service in this family ancestral home.

    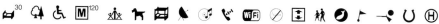

THE ROYAL HOTEL

ST NICHOLAS STREET, SCARBOROUGH, NORTH YORKSHIRE YO11 2HE

The Royal Hotel has had a long and colourful history since its construction during the peak of Regency elegance in the 1830s, and remains a centrepiece overlooking the South Bay in England's oldest resort town. Many illustrious guests have passed through its doors including Winston Churchill, Charles Laughton and the playwright Alan Ayckbourn, all of whom have suites named after them. Offering a wide range of comfortable comtemporary accommodation, en suite rooms combine the modern and traditional and some have wonderful views over the harbour and the bay. A varied table d'hôte menu, with à la carte options, is served in the grand setting of the Dining Room, whilst traditional teas and light refreshments are on offer in the extensive lounges and Theatre Bar. A new continental-style café, Café Bliss, means visitors can enjoy a selection of delicacies indoors or al fresco. Once a spa town, Scarborough is close to the North Yorkshire Moors National Park and provides an excellent base for touring the local area, as well as enjoying its own features such as the Victorian Spa Complex.

Directions: From the A1/M1 take A64, continue to the town on Seamer Road. Turn onto Falsgrave towards the town centre. Turn right at the railway station then left at traffic lights and roundabout. The hotel is before the Town Hall.

Web: www.johansens.com/royalscarborough
E-mail: royalhotel@englishrosehotels.co.uk
Tel: 0870 381 9277
International: +44 (0)1723 364333
Fax: 01723 371780

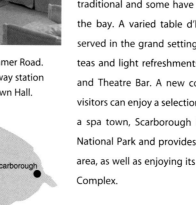

Price Guide:
single £60-£80
double £120-£185
suite £175-£320

Our inspector loved: *The original Regency Atrium with its elegant main staircase.*

HACKNESS GRANGE

NORTH YORK MOORS NATIONAL PARK, SCARBOROUGH, NORTH YORKSHIRE YO13 0JW

The attractive Georgian Hackness Grange country house lies at the heart of the dramatic North York Moors National Park – miles of glorious countryside with rolling moorland and forests. Set in acres of private grounds, overlooking a tranquil lake, home to many species of wildlife, Hackness Grange is a haven of peace and quiet for guests. There are charming bedrooms in the gardens, courtyard and the main house. For leisure activities, guests can enjoy 9-hole pitch 'n' putt golf, tennis and an indoor heated swimming pool. Hackness Grange is an ideal meeting location for companies wishing to have exclusive use of the hotel for VIP gatherings. The attractive Derwent Restaurant with its quality décor, is the setting for lunch and dinner. Here you will enjoy creatively prepared delicious cuisine, which is partnered by a wide choice of international wines. When you choose to stay at Hackness Grange you will find you have chosen well – a peaceful and relaxing location with so much to see and do: for example, visit Great Ayton, birthplace of Captain Cook.

Our inspector loved: The ducks and wildlife around the lake.

Directions: Take A64 York road until left turn to Seamer on to B1261, through to East Ayton and Hackness.

Web: www.johansens.com/hacknessgrange
E-mail: hacknessgrange@englishrosehotels.co.uk
Tel: 0870 381 8578
International: +44 (0)1723 882345
Fax: 01723 882391

Price Guide:
single from £65
double/twin £125–£180
suite from £190

WREA HEAD COUNTRY HOTEL

SCALBY, NR SCARBOROUGH, NORTH YORKSHIRE YO13 0PB

Directions: Follow the A171 north from Scarborough, past the Scalby Village, until the hotel is signposted. Follow the road past the duck pond and then turn left up the drive.

Web: www.johansens.com/wreaheadcountry
E-mail: wreahead@englishrosehotels.co.uk
Tel: 0870 381 9012
International: +44 (0)1723 378211
Fax: 01723 355936

Price Guide:
single from £65
double/twin £95–£195
suite from £195

Wrea Head Country Hotel is an elegant, beautifully refurbished Victorian country house built in 1881 and situated in 14 acres of wooded and landscaped grounds on the edge of the North York Moors National Park, just 3 miles from Scarborough. The house is furnished with antiques and paintings, and the oak-panelled front hall with its inglenook fireplace with blazing log fires in the winter, is very welcoming. All the bedrooms are individually decorated to the highest standards, with most having delightful views of the gardens. The elegant Four Seasons Restaurant is renowned for serving the best traditional English fare using fresh local produce and has a reputation for outstanding cuisine. There are attractive meeting rooms, each with natural daylight, ideal for private board meetings and training courses requiring privacy and seclusion. Scarborough is renowned for its cricket, music and theatre. Wrea Head is a perfect location from which to explore the glorious North Yorkshire coast and country, and special English Rose breaks are offered throughout the year.

Our inspector loved: The large collection of Pietro Annigoni paintings in the main hall.

JUDGES COUNTRY HOUSE HOTEL

KIRKLEVINGTON HALL, KIRKLEVINGTON, YARM, NORTH YORKSHIRE TS15 9LW

Stunningly located within 31 acres of idyllic landscaped gardens and woodlands, this gracious country house hotel is a haven of peace. Its charm and welcoming atmosphere create a sense of intimacy, whilst the warmth of the hotel's opulent interior design makes it perfect for relaxing and unwinding from the stresses of daily life. Beautiful public rooms are elegantly decorated with opulent fabrics, and guests are surrounded by books, stunning paintings and antiques. Sumptuous bedrooms are the ultimate in comfort some with Jacuzzi baths, evening turndowns, foot spas and goldfish. Attention to detail and expertly chosen décor enhance the feeling of luxury. A mouth-watering 6-course meal is served in the Conservatory Restaurant, accompanied by the finest of wines. Private dining is available, perfect for parties or the family. The hotel's location makes it ideal for exploring the North East, whilst local attractions include the historic city of Durham, various castles and museums, the races at York and Sedgefield and walking in the Cleveland Hills. Various adventure activities can also be organised including horse riding, canoeing, cycling, go karting, off roading, quad biking as well as many others.

Our inspector loved: *The friendly, attentive staff and goldfish in every bedroom.*

Directions: From A19 - Take the A67 Yarm exit, Judges is 1½ miles along A67 on the left after Kirklevington village.

Web: www.johansens.com/judges
E-mail: enquiries@judgeshotel.co.uk
Tel: 0870 381 9165
International: +44 (0)1642 789000
Fax: 01642 782878

Price Guide:
single £127–£140
double/twin £155–£165

THE GRANGE HOTEL

1 CLIFTON, YORK, NORTH YORKSHIRE YO30 6AA

Set near the ancient city walls, just a short walk from the world-famous Minster, this sophisticated Regency town house has been carefully restored and its spacious rooms richly decorated. Beautiful stone-flagged floors lead to the classically styled reception rooms. The flower-filled Morning Room is welcoming, with its deep sofas and blazing fire in the winter months. Double doors between the panelled library and drawing room can be opened up to create a dignified venue for parties, wedding receptions, meetings or business entertaining. Prints, antiques and English chintz in the bedrooms reflect the proprietor's careful attention to detail. The Ivy Restaurant has an established reputation for first-class gastronomy, incorporating the best in modern British and European cuisine. The Seafood Bar has two murals depicting racing scenes. The Brasserie is open for lunch Monday to Saturday and dinner every night until after the theatre closes most evenings. For conferences, a computer and fax are available as well as secretarial services. Brimming with history, York's list of attractions includes the National Railway Museum, the Jorvik Viking Centre and the medieval Shambles.

Directions: The Grange Hotel is on the A19 York–Thirsk road, 400 yards from the city centre.

Web: www.johansens.com/grangeyork
E-mail: info@grangehotel.co.uk
Tel: 0870 381 8561
International: +44 (0)1904 644744
Fax: 01904 612453

Price Guide:
single £110–£165
double/twin £140–£200
suite £250

Our inspector loved: The stunning orchid arrangement in the York stone-paved front hall.

MIDDLETHORPE HALL HOTEL, RESTAURANT & SPA

BISHOPTHORPE ROAD, YORK, NORTH YORKSHIRE YO23 2GB

Middlethorpe Hall is a delightful William III house, built in 1699 for Thomas Barlow, a wealthy merchant and was for a time the home of Lady Mary Wortley Montagu, the 18th-century diarist. The house has been immaculately restored by Historic House Hotels, who have decorated and furnished it in its original style and elegance. There are beautifully designed bedrooms and suites in the main house and the adjacent 18th-century courtyard and a health and fitness spa with pool and treatment rooms. The restaurant, which has been awarded 3 Rosettes from the AA, offers the best in contemporary English cooking. Middlethorpe Hall, which was awarded Yorkshire Life Hotel of the Year 2004, stands in 26 acres of parkland and overlooks York Racecourse yet is only 1½ miles from the medieval city of York with its fascinating museums, restored streets and world-famous Minster. From Middlethorpe you can visit Yorkshire's famous country houses, like Castle Howard, Beningbrough and Harewood, the ruined Abbeys of Fountains and Rievaulx and explore the magnificent Yorkshire Moors. Helmsley, Whitby and Scarborough are nearby. Special breaks available.

Our inspector loved: The Spa which is situated in the adjacent cottages and the organic walled garden.

Directions: Take A64 (T) off A1 (T) near Tadcaster, follow signs to York West, then smaller signs to Bishopthorpe.

Web: www.johansens.com/middlethorpehall
E-mail: info@middlethorpe.com
Tel: 0870 381 8731
International: +44 (0)1904 641241
Fax: 01904 620176

Price Guide:
single £124–£180
double/twin £195–£310
suite from £260–£400

303

ALDWARK MANOR

ALDWARK, NR ALNE, YORK, NORTH YORKSHIRE YO61 1UF

Directions: A1 Jct 47 - A59 towards York. After 3 miles, left onto theB6265. Cont. until signpost to Aldwark Manor. Left at T-junction over the bridge and right into Boat Lane. Continue over the toll bridge and take next turn right.

Web: www.johansens.com/aldwark
E-mail: aldwark@marstonhotels.com
Tel: 0870 381 8491
International: +44 (0)1347 838146
Fax: 01347 838867

Price Guide:
single £99–£244
double/twin £134–£278
suite £210–£278

Aldwark Manor is set in 120 acres of natural parkland in the Vale of York with the River Ure meandering through its grounds. Originally commissioned in 1865 by Lord Walsingham as a gift to his daughter, it has since undergone extensive refurbishment and upgrading to create an eclectic and harmonious blend of a bygone age and contemporary-style architecture. Ornate traditional bedrooms, antiques and artworks in the original manor provide a stunning visual contrast to the crisp minimalism of the restaurant and leisure areas with their striking colour schemes and light, spacious feel. Delicious and imaginative meals are created in the hotel's fine restaurant, which has been awarded 2 AA Rosettes and the golfers bistro-style bar restaurant for a more informal meal. On warm summer days guest can relax on the terrace patio whilst admiring the picturesque and challenging 18-hole golf course that surrounds the hotel. For leisure visitors may test their golfing skills or use the luxurious leisure centre, which has an indoor heated pool, spa, steam room, solarium, gymnasium, aerobics studio, beauty salon and treatment rooms. The hotel is close to York with its many shops and interesting historic buildings.

Our inspector loved: The views across the golf course on either side of the River Ure.

         SPA

THE WORSLEY ARMS HOTEL

HOVINGHAM, NEAR YORK, NORTH YORKSHIRE YO62 4LA

The Worsley Arms is an attractive stone-built Georgian spa hotel in the heart of Hovingham, a pleasant and unspoilt Yorkshire village with a history stretching back to Roman times. The hotel, which overlooks the village green and is set amid delightful gardens, was built in 1841 by the baronet Sir William Worsley and is now owned and personally run by Anthony and Sally Finn. Hovingham Hall, home of the Worsley family and birthplace of the Duchess of Kent, is nearby. Elegant furnishings and open fires create a welcoming atmosphere. The spacious sitting rooms are an ideal place to relax over morning coffee or afternoon tea. The award-winning restaurant offers creatively prepared dishes, including game from the estate, cooked and presented with flair. Guests can visit the wine cellar to browse or choose their wine for dinner. The Cricketers bar provides a more informal setting to enjoy modern cooking at its best. The en-suite bedrooms range in size and have recently all been redecorated. There is plenty to do nearby, including tennis, squash, jogging, golf and scenic walks along nature trails. Guests can explore the beautiful Dales, the North Yorkshire Moors and the spectacular coastline or discover the abbeys, stately homes and castles nearby. Special breaks available.

Our inspector loved: *Walking around the wine cellar choosing the wine for dinner.*

Directions: Hovingham is on the B1257, 8 miles from Malton and Helmsley. 20 minutes north of York.

Web: www.johansens.com/worsleyarms
E-mail: worsleyarms@aol.com
Tel: 0870 381 9011
International: +44 (0)1653 628234
Fax: 01653 628130

Price Guide:
single £75–£95
double/twin £100–£180

305

MONK FRYSTON HALL HOTEL

MONK FRYSTON, NORTH YORKSHIRE LS25 5DU

Directions: The Hall is 3 miles off the A1, on the A63 towards Selby in the centre of Monk Fryston.

Web: www.johansens.com/monkfrystonhall
E-mail: reception@monkfryston-hotel.co.uk
Tel: 0870 381 8741
International: +44 (0)1977 682369
Fax: 01977 683544

Price Guide:
single £88–£161
double/twin £112–£172

A short distance from the A1 and almost equal distance from Leeds and York, this mellow old manor house hotel, built in 1740, is ideal for tourists, business people and those looking for an invitingly secluded spot for a weekend break. The mullioned and transom windows and the family coat of arms above the doorway are reminiscent of Monk Fryston's fascinating past. In 1954 the Hall was acquired by the late Duke of Rutland, who has created an elegant contemporary hotel, whilst successfully preserving the strong sense of heritage and tradition. The bedrooms, ranging from cosy to spacious, have private en-suite bathrooms and are appointed to a high standard. A generous menu offers a wide choice of traditional English dishes with something to suit all tastes. From the Hall, the terrace leads down to an ornamental Italian garden which overlooks a lake and is a delight to see at any time of year. Wedding receptions are held in the oak-panelled Haddon Room with its splendid Inglenook fireplace. The Rutland Room provides a convenient venue for meetings and private parties. York is 17 miles, Leeds 13 miles and Harrogate 18 miles away.

Our inspector loved: The oak-panelled front hall and bar with open fires in the winter.

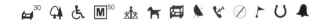

HELLABY HALL HOTEL

OLD HELLABY LANE, NR ROTHERHAM, SOUTH YORKSHIRE S66 8SN

The impressive 17th-century façade of Hellaby Hall has been an unmistakable feature of the South Yorkshire skyline since 1692, when it was built by Ralph Fretwell on his return from Barbados. Today this award-winning hotel continues to nurture its excellent reputation, combining historic charm with luxurious and modern facilities. All 90 bedrooms are tastefully furnished in a variety of styles, including the romantic four-poster suite with its magnificent bed, private lounge and dining area. Elsewhere, guests can relax in the oak-panelled lounge where friendly staff are on hand to ensure that any stay is as comfortable as possible. The light and spacious Attic Restaurant is perfect for intimate celebrations or business lunches. A selection of rooms can host corporate meetings or dining events and some are now licensed to hold civil wedding ceremonies. The Hotel also comprises of Bodyscene, a £2 million state-of-the-art health and leisure club with swimming pool and steam room, a large fitness suite and dedicated gym instructor and beauty team.

Our inspector loved: The large health and leisure club and swimming pool.

Directions: From the M18, exit at junction 1 and take the A631 towards Bawtry. The Hotel is ½ mile on the left.

Web: www.johansens.com/hellabyhall
E-mail: sales@hellabyhallhotel.co.uk
Tel: 0870 381 8592
International: +44 (0)1709 702701
Fax: 01709 700979

Price Guide:
single £45–£148
double/twin £79–£148
suite £165–£190

CHARNWOOD HOTEL

10 SHARROW LANE, SHEFFIELD, SOUTH YORKSHIRE S11 8AA

The Charnwood Hotel is a listed Georgian mansion dating from 1780. Originally owned by John Henfrey, a Sheffield Master Cutler, it was later acquired by William Wilson of the Sharrow Snuff Mill. Restored in 1985, this elegant "country house in town" is tastefully furnished, with colourful flower arrangements set against attractive décor. The non-smoking bedrooms are all individually decorated and the Woodford suite is designed specifically to meet the requirements of a family. Brasserie Leo has a relaxed atmosphere serving traditional English and French cuisine. The Library and Henfrey's are ideal for private dining or small meetings and larger functions are catered for in the Georgian Room and Coach House. Also there are 19 self-catering apartments nearby. While approximately a mile from Sheffield city centre, with its concert hall, theatre and hectic night-life, Charnwood Hotel is also convenient for the Peak District National Park. Meadowhall shopping centre and Sheffield Arena are a short ride away.

Directions: Sharrow Lane is near the junction of London Road and Abbeydale Road, 1½ miles from city centre. Junction 33 from the M1.

Web: www.johansens.com/charnwood
E-mail: reception@charnwoodhotel.co.uk
Tel: 0870 381 8417
International: +44 (0)114 258 9411
Fax: 0114 255 5107

Price Guide:
single £68–£93
double/twin £83–£110

Our inspector loved: The lively atmosphere in Brasserie Leo.

WHITLEY HALL HOTEL

ELLIOTT LANE, GRENOSIDE, SHEFFIELD, SOUTH YORKSHIRE S35 8NR

Carved into the keystone above one of the doors is the date 1584, denoting the start of Whitley Hall's lengthy country house tradition. In the bar is a priest hole, which may explain the local belief that a tunnel links the house with the nearby 11th-century church. In the 18th century, the house was a prestigious boarding school, with Gothic pointed arches and ornamentation added later by the Victorians. Attractively refurbished, Whitley Hall is now a fine hotel with all the amenities required by today's visitors. Stone walls and oak panelling combine with richly carpeted floors and handsome decoration. A sweeping split staircase leads to the bedrooms, all of which have en-suite bathrooms. Varied yet unpretentious cooking is served in generous portions and complemented by a wide choice from the wine cellar, including many clarets and ports. Peacocks strut around the 30 acre grounds, which encompass rolling lawns, mature woodland and 2 ornamental lakes. Banquets and private functions can be held in the conference suite.

Our inspector loved: The peacocks fanning their tails in the garden.

Directions: Leave M1 at junction 35, following signs for Chapeltown (A629), go down hill and turn left into Nether Lane. Go right at traffic lights, then left opposite Arundel pub, then immediately right into Whitley Lane. At fork turn right into Elliott Lane; hotel is on left.

Web: www.johansens.com/whitleyhall
E-mail: reservations@whitleyhall.com
Tel: 0870 381 8993
International: +44 (0)114 245 4444
Fax: 0114 245 5414

Price Guide:
single £70–£105
double/twin £92–£120

HOLDSWORTH HOUSE HOTEL & RESTAURANT

HOLDSWORTH, HALIFAX, WEST YORKSHIRE HX2 9TG

Directions: From M1 Jct42 take M62 west to Jct26. Follow A58 to Halifax (ignore signs to town centre). At Burdock Way roundabout take A629 to Keighley; after 1½ miles go right into Shay Lane; hotel is a mile on right.

Web: www.johansens.com/holdsworthhouse
E-mail: info@holdsworthhouse.co.uk
Tel: 0870 381 8603
International: +44 (0)1422 240024
Fax: 01422 245174

Price Guide:
single £95–£135
double/twin £130 –£180
suite £135–£190

Holdsworth House is a beautiful grade II Jacobean manor house, 3 miles north of Halifax in the heart of Yorkshire's West Riding. Built in 1633, it was acquired by the Pearson family over 40 years ago. With care, skill and professionalism they have created a hotel and restaurant of considerable repute. The interior, with its polished oak panelling and open fireplaces, has been carefully preserved and embellished with fine antiques and paintings. The comfortable lounge opens onto a pretty courtyard and overlooks the parterre and gazebo. The restaurant, with its 2 AA Rosettes, comprises 3 beautifully furnished rooms, ideal for private dinner parties. Exciting modern English and continental cuisine is meticulously prepared and presented using local produce, complemented by a thoughtfully compiled wine list. Each cosy bedroom has its own style, from the split-level suites to the interconnecting rooms for families. This is the perfect base from which to explore the Pennines, the Yorkshire Dales and Haworth, home of the Brontë family. Weekend breaks available.

Our inspector loved: The cosy, oak-panelled, award-winning restaurant.

HALEY'S HOTEL & RESTAURANT

SHIRE OAK ROAD, HEADINGLEY, LEEDS, WEST YORKSHIRE LS6 2DE

Just 2 miles from Leeds City Centre, yet set in a quiet leafy lane in the Headingley conservation area close to the cricket ground and the university, Haley's is truly the country house hotel in the city. Each of the 28 guest rooms offers the highest levels of comfort and is as individual as the fine antiques and rich furnishings which grace the hotel. A new addition to the existing accommodation is Bedford House, the elegant Victorian Grade II listed building next door which contains 7 outstandingly furnished and beautifully equipped modern bedrooms, including 2 suites, one with its own private entrance. The Bramley Room and Library are popular venues for private meetings, lunch or dinner parties. Haley's Restaurant has an enviable reputation, holding 2 AA Rosettes. An imaginative menu of modern English cuisine is accompanied by a fine wine list. Leeds offers superb shopping (including Harvey Nichols) and the Victorian Arcades. Opera North and the theatres combine with Haley's superb accommodation and food to provide entertaining weekends. Special weekend breaks are available.

Our inspector loved: *This elegant and peaceful retreat in the leafy suburbs of Leeds.*

Directions: 2 miles north of Leeds city centre off the main A660 Otley Road – the main route to Leeds/Bradford Airport, Ilkley and Wharfedale.

Web: www.johansens.com/haleys
E-mail: info@haleys.co.uk
Tel: 0870 381 8579
International: +44 (0)113 278 4446
Fax: 0113 275 3342

Price Guide:
single from £125
double/twin from £150
suite from £250

311

42 THE CALLS

42 THE CALLS, LEEDS, WEST YORKSHIRE LS2 7EW

42 the Calls is a remarkable, award-winning hotel situated in the heart of Leeds, yet peacefully set in a quiet location alongside the river. Originally a corn mill, this unique hotel takes advantage of many of the original features of the mill, incorporating impressive beams, girders and old machinery into the décor. Each of the 41 bedrooms is imaginatively decorated in an individual style using beautiful fabrics and expert interior design to create a wonderful sense of harmony. Handmade beds and armchairs, a plethora of eastern rugs and extremely lavish bathrooms enhance the feeling of comfort and luxury. There is an excellent choice of restaurants in the vicinity, including the world renowned Michelin starred Pool Court at 42 next door and the stylish Brasserie 44. The hotel does offer round the clock room service or guests may dine in 6 of the city's restaurants and simply sign their lunch or dinner to their hotel bill. Shops, offices, galleries and theatres are all within a few minutes' walk from the hotel.

Directions: M621, jct 3. Follow City Centre and West Yorkshire Playhouse signs then turn left after Tetley's Brewery then left again onto the City Centre Loop, following City signs. Take jct 15 and The Calls is immediately ahead.

Web: www.johansens.com/42thecalls
E-mail: hotel@42thecalls.co.uk
Tel: 0870 381 8737
International: +44 (0)113 244 0099
Fax: 0113 234 4100

Price Guide:
single £130–£190
double/twin £163–£225
suite from £285

Our inspector loved: The innovative design of the hotel and the privacy hatches for room service.

NEW

WOODLANDS

GELDERD ROAD, GILDERSOME, LEEDS, WEST YORKSHIRE LS27 7LY

Built in 1871 as a family mansion home for a local textile owner, this imposing, typical Yorkshire building stands in the heart of extensive landscaped grounds on the outskirts of Leeds. Sympathetic, skillful and careful renovation over an 18-month period has restored the house to its original glory and created a luxury hotel of growing repute. Behind solid stone walls is a stylish interior that combines classic elegance with modern lines, enhanced with 21st-century quality facilities, comfort and friendly, 24-hour service. In-keeping with Woodlands' history the individually designed guest rooms are named after luxurious or unusual fabrics such as cambric and pashmine. All are superbly decorated, furnished and fitted with high standard amenities and state-of-the-art sound, vision and communication systems. 3 large ground-floor rooms have French windows opening onto the garden terrace. A second-floor penthouse suite has a king-size leather sleigh bed, dressing room and lounge with gas fire. Tasty traditional and modern British cuisine, complemented by an extensive wine list, can be enjoyed in a quintessentially English restaurant, which has 3 elegant yet informal dining rooms that seat up to 70 guests, and have picturesque views over the gardens. Woodlands is an ideal and convenient base for enjoying the superb shopping, dining and entertainment attractions of Leeds.

Our inspector loved: This new, innovative hotel on the outskirts of Leeds.

Directions: Exit the M62 at junction 27 and take the A62 towards Leeds. Woodlands is 2 miles on the right.

Web: www.johansens.com/woodlandleeds
E-mail: enquiries@woodlandleeds.co.uk
Tel: 0870 381 9356
International: +44 (0)113 238 1488
Fax: 0113 253 6773

Price Guide:
single £80–£225
double £100–£225
suite £400

313

CHEVIN COUNTRY PARK HOTEL

YORKGATE, OTLEY, WEST YORKSHIRE LS21 3NU

Directions: From A658 between Bradford and Harrogate, take the Chevin Forest Park road, then left into Yorkgate for Chevin Park.

Web: www.johansens.com/chevinlodge
E-mail: reception@chevinlodge.co.uk
Tel: 0870 381 8426
International: +44 (0)1943 467818
Fax: 01943 850335

Price Guide:
single £65–£140
double/twin £110–£165

A quite unique hotel – you would probably need to travel to Scandinavia to discover a similar hotel to Chevin Park. Built entirely of Finnish logs and surrounded by birch trees, it is set in 50 acres of lake and woodland in the beauty spot of Chevin Forest Park. The spacious, carefully designed bedrooms are tastefully furnished with pine and some have patio doors leading to the lakeside gardens. In addition, there are several luxury lodges tucked away in the woods, providing alternative accommodation to the hotel bedrooms. Imaginative and appetising meals are served in the beautiful balconied restaurant, which overlooks the lake. Chevin Lodge offers conference facilities in the Woodlands Suite which is fully equipped for all business requirements. The Leisure Club has a 11 x 7 metres swimming pool, spa bath, sauna, solarium and gym. There is also a games room, all- weather tennis court and jogging trails that wind through the woods. Leeds, Bradford and Harrogate are within 20 minutes' drive. Special weekend breaks are available.

Our inspector loved: This small piece of Finland set in Yorkshire.

WOOD HALL

TRIP LANE, LINTON, NR WETHERBY, WEST YORKSHIRE LS22 4JA

Off the A1/M1 link about 15 miles due west of York, built of stone from the estate, Wood Hall, part of the Handpicked Hotel Group, is an elegant Georgian country house overlooking the River Wharfe. Its grounds, over 100 acres in all, are approached along a private drive that winds through a sweep of parkland. Wood Hall has had a complete transformation after an extensive refurbishment, and now offers a modern, light and luxurious haven, which combines traditional hospitality. The sumptuously furnished drawing room and the oak-panelled bar, with its gentlemen's club atmosphere, lead off the grand entrance hall. Gastronomes will relish the excellent menu, which combines contemporary Anglo-French style with attractive presentation. The mile-long private stretch of the Wharfe offers up trout and barbel to the keen angler, while miles of walks and jogging paths encompass the estate. There is a spa including a swimming pool, spa bath, steam room, gymnasium and treatment salon. Near to the National Hunt racecourse at Wetherby, York, Harrogate, Leeds, the Dales and Harewood House are only a short distance away. Special breaks available.

Our inspector loved: *The stunning view of the hotel as you drive up the long driveway.*

Directions: From Wetherby, take the A661 towards Harrogate. Take turning for Sicklinghall and Linton, then left for Linton and Wood Hall. Turn right opposite the Windmill public house; hotel is 1½ miles further on.

Web: www.johansens.com/woodhall
E-mail: woodhall@handpicked.co.uk
Tel: 0870 381 9004
International: +44 (0)1937 587271
or 0800 9 177 877
Fax: 01937 584353

Price Guide:
single from £110
double/twin from £170

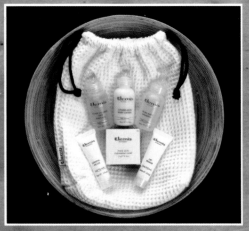

For further information on the Channel Islands, please contact:

Visit Guernsey
PO Box 23, St Peter Port, Guernsey GY1 3AN
Tel: +44 (0)1481 723552
Internet: www.visitguernsey.com

Jersey Tourism
Liberation Square, St Helier, Jersey JE1 1BB
Tel: +44 (0)1534 500777
Internet: www.jtourism.com

Sark Tourism
Harbour Hill, Sark, Channel Islands GY9 0SB
Tel: +44 (0)1481 832345
Internet: www.sark.info

Herm Tourist Office
The White House Hotel, Herm Island via Guernsey GY1 3HR
Tel: +44 (0)1481 722377
Internet: www.herm-island.com

or see pages 412-414 for details of
local attractions to visit during your stay.

Images from www.britainonview.com

CHÂTEAU LA CHAIRE

ROZEL BAY, JERSEY JE3 6AJ

Directions: The hotel is signposted off the main coastal road to Rozel Bay, 6 miles north-east of St Helier.

Web: www.johansens.com/chateaulachaire
E-mail: res@chateau-la-chaire.co.uk
Tel: 0870 381 8420
International: +44 (0)1534 863354
Fax: 01534 865137

Price Guide:
single from £100
double/twin from £132
suites from £231

When the Victorians sought a stunning location to build a gracious château home on the island of Jersey they discovered the wonderful wooded valley of Rozel. Today, nestling on its sunny slopes and surrounded by beautiful gardens, is Château La Chaire, recognised by both the AA and RAC as one of the finest small hotels in the British Isles. The AA include it in their Top 200 Hotels whilst the RAC has awarded the hotel their coveted Gold Ribbon. Built in 1843, the château has been enhanced and transformed into a luxurious hotel offering a superb blend of comfort, service and cuisine. Each of the spacious, beautifully proportioned bedrooms has been furnished to the highest standards and offers an impressive array of personal comforts; many en-suite bathrooms feature Jacuzzis. Both adventurous and traditional dishes and, above all, seafood, can be enjoyed in the oak-panelled La Chaire restaurant. 2 AA Rosettes and 3 RAC dining awards acknowledge the excellence of the food and service. A few minutes away is the picturesque Rozel Bay, a bustling fishing harbour with safe beaches close by. St Helier is just 6 miles away. Spectacular cliff top walks, golf, fishing and riding are among the many leisure activities guests can enjoy during their stay.

Our inspector loved: *The wonderful "wedding cake" plasterwork, polished panelling and the intimate setting.*

THE ATLANTIC HOTEL

LE MONT DE LA PULENTE, ST BRELADE, JERSEY JE3 8HE

This is a stunning luxury hotel that offers elegance, grace, comfort, exquisite cuisine and impeccable service. It is excellent in every way, from majestic interior pillars and magnificent wood panelling to sumptuous furnishings, warm décor and perfect location. The Atlantic stands regally in 3 acres of private grounds alongside La Moye Golf Course overlooking the 5-mile sweep of St Ouen's Bay. A multi-million pound refurbishment of the hotel including the enlargement of bedrooms and remodelling of the building's exterior to give a marine flavour, has resulted in even more venue quality and the hotel's elevation to 5-Sun status by Jersey Tourism. No expense has been spared in refurnishing the bedrooms, suites and garden studios. Tastefully decorated, they offer occupants the highest standard of facilities and comfort together with splendid views of the sea or the golf course. Most prestigious and stylish is the spacious Atlantic Suite with its own entrance hall, living room, guest cloakroom and service pantry in addition to the en suite master bedroom. The delightful, award-winning restaurant overlooks the open-air swimming pool and sun terrace. Excellent and imaginative menus showcase the Modern British cuisine with the emphasis on seafood and fresh local produce.

Our inspector loved: The coastal views, the impeccable service and the splendidly fat Koi carp, which swim serenely at the foot of the staircase.

Directions: From the airport turn right at the roundabout towards St Brelade. At the traffic lights turn right towards St Ouen's Bay then right into La Rue de la Sergente. Look out for the hotel sign at the top of Le Mont de la Pulente.

Web: www.johansens.com/atlantic
E-mail: info@theatlantichotel.com
Tel: 0870 381 8330
International: +44 (0)1534 744101
Fax: 01534 744102

Price Guide:
single £145–£175
double/twin £190–£275
suite £260–£455

www.hildon.com

Recommendations in Ireland appear on pages 322-338

For further information on Ireland, please contact:

The Irish Tourist Board
(Bord Fáilte Éireann)
Baggot Street
Dublin 2
Tel: +353 (0)1 602 4000
Internet: www.ireland.ie

Northern Ireland Tourist Information
Belfast Welcome Centre
47 Donegall Place
Belfast, BT1 5AD
Tel: +44 (0)28 9024 6609
Internet: www.gotobelfast.com

or see pages 412-414 for details of
local attractions to visit during your stay.

Images from Fáilte Ireland

NEW

BUSHMILLS INN HOTEL

9 DUNLUCE ROAD, BUSHMILLS, CO ANTRIM, BT57 8QG, NORTHERN IRELAND

Directions: Situated 2 miles from Giant's Causeway on the A2 in the village of Bushmills as you cross the river.

Web: www.johansens.com/bushmills
E-mail: mail@bushmillsinn.com
Tel: 0870 381 9315
International: +44 (0)28 2073 3000
Fax: +44 (0)28 2073 2048

Price Guide:
Mill House double/twin £138–£248
Coaching Inn
small single £68
double/twin £88–£98

With the oldest part dating back to the 1600s, Bushmills was originally an old coaching inn - the last stop for weary travelers on their way to the Giant's Causeway, now a world heritage site. It was here they would stop to sample the whiskey that made the village internationally famous - the original licence to distill dates back to 1608 making Bushmills the world's oldest distillery. In the late 1890s, the inn fell into disrepair and was used as a bicycle factory and a residence for chickens! Now refurbished and extended this fabulous hotel has received numerous awards and epitomises the true spirit of Ulster hospitality. Public rooms are varied and cosy with stripped pine and peat fires. A magnificent wooden staircase leads to a gallery displaying stunning paintings of the Causeway Coast by a world renowned local artist. In the old hay loft, with its original oak beams there's a snug, complete with stove fire and comfortable chairs, where books are tucked into the nooks and crannies. The adjoining Mill House accommodates most of the bedrooms, all imaginatively designed in traditional style with discretely hidden modern conveniences. Explore the rugged staggered coastline with its wide sandy beaches, picturesque harbours, craggy cliffs and ruined castles. The area boasts seven quality golf courses including the classic dunes setting at Royal Portrush, consistently ranked amongst the world's top 10 courses.

Our inspector loved: The authenticity and uniqueness of this lovely inn.

DROMOLAND CASTLE

NEWMARKET-ON-FERGUS, SHANNON AREA, CO CLARE

Dating from the 16th century, Dromoland Castle is one of the most famous baronial castles in Ireland. Dromoland was the ancestral seat of the O'Briens, direct descendants of Irish King Brian Boru. Reminders of its past are everywhere: in the splendid wood and stone carvings, magnificent panelling, oil paintings and romantic gardens. The 100 en-suite guest rooms and suites are all beautifully furnished. Stately halls and an elegant dining room are all part of the Dromoland experience. The Dromoland International Centre is one of Europe's most comprehensive conference venues, hosting groups of up to 450. Classical cuisine is prepared by award-winning chef David McCann. Dromoland's 18-hole golf course, designed by Ron Kirby & JB Carr, this over 6850-yard championship course roams through woodland and around lakes with subtlety and sensitivity. Fishing, clay pigeon shooting and full Health and Beauty Centre are all available on the estate, whilst activities nearby include horse riding and golf on some of Ireland's other foremost courses. The castle is an ideal base from which to explore this breathtakingly beautiful area. Member of Preferred Hotels & Resorts World Wide.

Our inspector loved: The unique Dromoland experience in a stunning setting.

Directions: Take the N18 to Newmarket-on-Fergus, go 2 miles beyond the village and the hotel entrance is on the right-hand side. 8 miles from Shannon Airport

Web: www.johansens.com/dromolandcastle
E-mail: sales@dromoland.ie
Tel: 00 353 61 368144
Fax: 00 353 61 363355

Price Guide: (room only)
single/double €225–€573
suite €471–€955

HARVEY'S POINT

LOUGH ESKE, DONEGAL TOWN, CO DONEGAL, IRELAND

Directions: From Killybegs travel to Donegal Town. At the roundabout take the third exit towards Donegal Town. After 300m take the road on the left and follow the signs to Harvey's Point (7km).

Web: www.johansens.com/harveyspoint
E-mail: info@harveyspoint.com
Tel: 00 353 74 972 2208
Fax: 00 353 74 972 2352

Price Guide:
single €170
double/twin €290
suite €310

Carndonagh

Ballybofey

Donegal

Nestling on the edge of Lough Eske against the backdrop of the beautiful Blue Stack Mountains, Harvey's Point is a serene idyll where guests come to unwind and rejuvenate. The architecture blends perfectly with the magnificent surroundings, providing luxurious accommodation and every modern convenience as well as plenty of fresh air and breathtaking scenery. Peaceful, airy bedrooms are elegantly decorated with pure relaxation in mind. Wooden floors and classic furniture create a harmonious atmosphere and lovely French doors open out onto rolling lawns and pretty gardens that stretch all the way to the shores of the loch. Only the splashing of trout and singing of birds break the silence. Some rooms have four-poster beds and the honeymoon suite has a fabulous tub. Harvey's Point is renowned for its superb cuisine: recipient of the prestigious AA 2 Rosette Award and the RAC Blue Ribbon Award for Excellence. Delicious French dishes are wonderfully imaginative and served with an impressive list of international wines with the finest vintages. The bar is ideal for enjoying a quiet drink whilst the resident pianist enhances the soothing ambience. Donegal is a charming old town with magnificent examples of ancient architecture, stunning gardens, golf courses and arts. Enjoy an energetic hill-walking holiday or merely to relax and enjoy the surroundings.

Our inspector loved: *This piece of Switzerland in Ireland.*

NEW

RATHMULLAN HOUSE

RATHMULLAN, LETTERKENNY, CO DONEGAL, IRELAND

Delightfully situated above the shores of peaceful Lough Swilly this large and attractive former manor is a sanctuary of comfort and relaxation, and an ideal base for exploring the wild and beautiful county of Donegal. Built as a summer house for a Belfast banking family in the 1800s and excellently run as a country hotel by Robin and Bob Wheeler since 1963, Rathmullan House has all the charm, graciousness, gentility and good taste of the 19th-century era. Prize-winning, tree-shaded gardens, leading to a clean sandy beach, provide total serenity and the opportunity to breath fresh Irish air whilst absorbing the dramatic surrounding scenery. Inside are 3 elegant sitting-rooms with tall ceilings, marble fireplaces, deep and soft sofas and chairs, fine antiques, oil paintings and overflowing bookcases. The bedrooms vary in décor and facilities, ranging from simple garret rooms for families to luxurious superior rooms with balconies overlooking the garden and Lough Swilly. The pavilion-like dining room, with unusual tented ceiling, is renowned for good food and generous, award-winning breakfasts. Leisure facilities include an indoor heated swimming pool and steam rooms, 2 all-weather tennis courts and a croquet lawn. Nearby are 4 challenging golf course, deep sea and wreck fishing, boat trips, sailing, horse riding, mountain climbing and miles of beaches to stroll along.

Our inspector loved: The warmth of welcome to children.

Directions: From Dublin take the N2 and A5. From Belfast take the A6. Drive to Letterkenny and take the road to Ramelton. At the bridge in Ramelton turn right towards Rathmullan. Go through the village and head north. The entrance to the hotel is just beyond the chapel .

Carndonagh

Ballybofey

Donegal

Web: www.johansens.com/rathmullanhouse
E-mail: info@rathmullanhouse.com
Tel: 00 353 74 915 8188
Fax: 00 353 74 915 8200

Price Guide:
single from €80
double/twin from €160
suite from €200

RENVYLE HOUSE HOTEL

CONNEMARA, CO GALWAY, IRELAND

Directions: On the N59 from Galway turn right at Recess, take the Letterfrack turning to Tully Cross and Renvyle is signposted.

Web: www.johansens.com/renvylehouse
E-mail: info@renvyle.com
Tel: 00 353 95 43511
Fax: 00 353 95 43515

Price Guide:
single from €30
double/twin from €60

Renvyle House Hotel has occupied its rugged, romantic position on Ireland's west coast for over 4 centuries. Set between mountains and sea on the unspoilt coast of Connemara, this hardy, beautiful building with its superlative views over the surrounding countryside is just an hour's drive from Galway or Sligo. Originally constructed in 1541, Renvyle has been an established hotel for over 100 years, witnessing in that time a procession of luminaries through its doors – Augustus John, Lady Gregory, Yeats and Churchill, drawn no doubt by an atmosphere as warm and convivial then as it is today. Renvyle now welcomes visitors with turf fires glowing in public areas, wood-beamed interiors and comfortable, relaxed furnishings in the easy rooms. The bedrooms are comfortably appointed and all have been refurbished in the past 3 years. In the dining room, meals from a constantly-changing menu are served with emphasis on local fish and Renvyle lamb. In the grounds activities include tennis, croquet, riding, bowls and golf. Beyond the hotel, there are walks in the heather-clad hills, or swimming and sunbathing on empty beaches.

Our inspector loved: *The new rooms and additions to this Connemara hotel.*

PARK HOTEL KENMARE & SÁMAS

KENMARE, CO. KERRY, IRELAND

"Mystical," "magical," "wonderful" and "green" are some of the words one would use in relation to describing Ireland. Due to SÁMAS, a Deluxe Destination Spa at the applauded Park Hotel Kenmare, the word "holistic" can be added. Adjoining the hotel and staffed by a professional team, the Spa offers over 60 Holistic treatments combined with heat experiences and relaxation to rejuvenate body, mind and spirit. There are both male and female spas to meet individual, distinctive requirements. Retaining the character and ambience of a past era, the Park Hotel Kenmare combines elegant accommodation and superb amenities with glorious countryside views and is holder of numerous awards, including Egon Ronay and AA 'Hotel of the Year', AA Three Rosettes, RAC Gold Ribbon and Condé Nast Gold List. Bedrooms and suites are furnished in traditional style with fine antiques and objects d'art and have every modern amenity. The elegant dining room, with silver-laden sideboards and views over the terraced gardens, offers acclaimed seasonal a la carte and set dinner menus with a leaning towards local seafood. The hotel has its own 12-seat cinema, tennis and croquet. Adjacent is Kenmare Golf Club's 18-hole parkland course and within easy reach are numerous championship links courses.

Directions: The hotel is in the centre of Kenmare on the N70 or the N71, just 27 miles away from Kerry International Airport.

Web: www.johansens.com/parkkenmare
E-mail: info@parkkenmare.com
Tel: 00 353 64 41200
Fax: 00 353 64 41402

Price Guide:
double €205–€349

Dingle
Tralee
Killarney

Our inspector loved: *Feeling totally relaxed after a SÀMAS experience.*

CAHERNANE HOUSE HOTEL

MUCKROSS ROAD, KILLARNEY, CO KERRY, IRELAND

Directions: 1 mile from Killarney on the Muckross Road.

Web: www.johansens.com/cahernane
E-mail: info@cahernane.com
Tel: 00 353 64 31895
Fax: 00 353 64 34340

Price Guide:
single €150
double €240
suite €360

A shady tunnel of greenery frames the ¼-mile long drive leading to the welcoming twin entrance doors to this historic house, a place of peace and tranquillity where time moves at a calming slow pace. A delightful, family-run hotel, Cahernane is the former home of the Earls of Pembroke and dates back to the 17th century. Standing in gorgeous parklands on the edge of Killarney's National Park, this is a designated area of outstanding beauty with an untamed landscape of lakes, mountains, woodland walks and gardens where giant rhododendrons and tropical plants grow in abundance. The Browne family pride themselves on their hospitality and attentive service that ensures guests enjoy the hotel's charm and grace. Each of the individually designed bedrooms and suites is elegantly furnished, tastefully decorated and has a lovely bathroom, some boast a Jacuzzi. The award-winning Herbert Room restaurant offers à la carte, table d'hôte and vegetarian menus whilst less formal dining can be enjoyed in the Cellar Bar. The Wine Celler forms the backdrop to the Celler Bar and stocks more than 300 selections. Challenging golf courses are within easy reach as well as a variety of outdoor pursuits and national treasures such as Muckross House and Ross Castle.

Our inspector loved: The deer that visit the garden from the adjoining Killarney National Park.

PARKNASILLA HOTEL

GREAT SOUTHERN HOTEL, PARKNASILLA, CO. KERRY, IRELAND

County Kerry has an equitable climate from the warm Gulf Stream. Parknasilla is a splendid Victorian mansion surrounded by extensive parkland and subtropical gardens leading down to the seashore. New arrivals appreciate the graceful reception rooms which, like the luxurious bedrooms, look out on the mountains, across the verdant countryside or down to Kenmare Bay. Wonderful damask and chintz harmonize with the period furniture and thoughtful 'extras' have been provided. The bathrooms are lavishly appointed. George Bernard Shaw's many visits are reflected in the names of the inviting Doolittle Bar and the elegant Pygmalion Restaurant. The sophisticated menus always include fish fresh from the sea and the international wine list will please the most discerning guests. Corporate activities and private celebrations are hosted in the traditional Shaw Library or handsome Derryquin Suite. Leisure facilities abound: a private 12-hole golf course with challenging championship courses close by, horse riding, water sports, sailing, clay pigeon shooting and archery. Parknasilla has 7 recomended walks through the estate and its own boat for cruises round the coast. Indoors there is a superb pool, sauna, steam room, Jacuzzi, hot tub, hydrotherapy seaweed baths, aromatherapy and massage

Our inspector loved: The sensitive moderisation of this Victorian favourite.

Directions: The hotel is south west of Killarney off N70.

Web: www.johansens.com/parknasilla
E-mail: res@parknasilla-gsh.com
Tel: 00 353 64 45122
Fax: 00 353 64 45323

Price Guide: (room only)
single/double/twin €150–€250
suite €500

329

KILLASHEE HOUSE HOTEL

KILLASHEE, NAAS, CO KILDARE, IRELAND

Directions: 30 minutes from Dublin on N7/M7 to Naas, then 1 mile along R448 Kilcullen Road.

Web: www.johansens.com/killashee
E-mail: reservations@killasheehouse.com
Tel: 00 353 45 879277
Fax: 00 353 45 879266

Price Guide: (per person sharing)
single from €144
double/twin from €99
classic from €125
suites €107.50–€247.50

Originally a Victorian hunting lodge, Killashee House still bears the coats of arms of its founders, the Moore family. Guests are treated to tantalising views of its Jacobean-style facade and eye-catching bell tower as they approach on an elegant curving driveway, although the house actually dates from Victorian times when it was built for the influential Moore Family in the early 1860s. Today it is a glorious hotel situated within 80 acres of gardens and woodland, just 30 minutes from Dublin. There are 142 luxurious and comfortable guest rooms including junior and executive suites, many with four-poster beds and stunning views of the gardens and, sometimes, the Wicklow Mountains. All bedrooms have multi-line telephone, data port and voicemail. Traditional Irish and Mediterranean cuisine can be enjoyed in the award-winning Turners Restaurant. State-of-the-art conference facilities include sophisticated audio-visual equipment as well as broadband, video conferencing and fibre optic data ports. Killashee House Country Club and Health Spa with numerous treatment rooms is the ultimate in luxury and sheer relaxation. The National Stud and the racecourses of Curragh, Punchestown and Naas are all within easy reach, as are several championship golf courses, including the K Club and the Curragh. There is car racing at Mondello Park, and the Japanese and St Fiachra's Gardens provide a tranquil setting for horticultural enthusiasts.

Our inspector loved: The large and luxurious new rooms.

MOUNT JULIET CONRAD

THOMASTOWN, CO KILKENNY, IRELAND

Mount Juliet Conrad is an architectural gem, a magnificent 18th-century Georgian mansion standing proudly on the banks of the River Nore in the heart of a lush 1,500-acre estate. The entrance doorway leads into an impressive hall featuring elaborate stucco work with bas-reliefs on walls and ceilings. A feeling of opulence pervades all reception rooms, the bars recall a glorious equestrian past whilst the homeliness of the library and drawing rooms provide comfortable venues for relaxation. Afternoon tea or a pre-dinner glass of champagne can be enjoyed in the elegant Majors Room. Jewel in the crown, however, is the exquisite Lady Helen Dining Room, famed for its original stucco plasterwork, pastoral views and superb cuisine. The 32 en-suite guest rooms are individually designed and are full of the character and charm that reflects the quiet good taste and refinement of the Georgian period. Centre of activity for guests is Hunters Yard, which is situated on the edge of a championship golf course, host to the American Express World Golf Championships in 2002 and 2004. The Hunters Yard is the epicentre of the estate's sporting and leisure life and offers stylish dining in Kendals Restaurant and 16 "Club" style rooms which offer direct access to the hotels sybaritic spa. For guests who require a greater degree of space and privacy, there are 10 lodges located beside the magnificent Rose Gardens.

Our inspector loved: The Trompe-L'œil in the entrance hall.

Directions: 16 miles from Kilkenny on the N9 via N10.

Web: www.johansens.com/mountjuliet
E-mail: mountjulietinfo@ConradHotels.com
Tel: 00 353 56 777 3000
Fax: 00 353 56 777 3019

Price Guide:
single from €175
double/twin from €230
suite €560

Castlecomer

Kilkenny

Thomastown

GLIN CASTLE

GLIN, CO LIMERICK, IRELAND

Home to the 29th Knight of Glin and Madam FitzGerald, Glin Castle has received accolades from all over the world, and maintains a reputation as one of the most unique places to stay in Ireland. The present castle was built with entertaining in mind in the late 18th century and has been sympathetically restored for modern day guests. Its famous collections of Irish furniture and paintings, built up over the centuries, fill reception rooms, whilst family portraits and photographs adorn the walls and mahogany side tables. Beautiful features are endless; the Corinthian pillars and rare flying staircase of the entrance hall, the Sittingroom's crackling fire, the Drawingroom with its 6 long windows overlooking the croquet lawn, the library with its secret bookcase doorway. Each of the sumptuous bedrooms is furnished with period pieces including rugs, chaise longues, and chintz covered beds. Those at the back look across the garden and those at the front have views of the River Shannon. The castle stands within 500 acres of grounds which comprise formal gardens, a series of follies, a parade of yew trees and a walled garden that supplies the hotel kitchen with fresh fruit and vegetables for its good Irish country house cooking, as well as fresh flowers for the rooms.

Directions: From Ennis and Shannon airport via N68 take the ferry from Kilimer. Alternatively take the N69 from Limerick.

Web: www.johansens.com/glincastle
E-mail: knight@iol.ie
Tel: 00 353 68 34173
Fax: 00 353 68 34364

Price Guide:
standard €280
superior €360
de luxe €440

Our inspector loved: *The aristocratic opulence of this wonderful castle home.*

ASHFORD CASTLE

CONG, CO MAYO

Ashford Castle is set on the northern shores of Lough Corrib amidst acres of beautiful gardens and forests. Once the country estate of Lord Ardilaun and the Guinness family, it was transformed into a luxury hotel in 1939. The castle's Great Hall is lavishly decorated with rich panelling, fine period pieces, objets d'art and masterpiece paintings. Guest rooms are of the highest standards and many feature high ceilings, enormous bathrooms and delightful lake views. The main dining room offers superb continental and traditional menus, while the gourmet restaurant, The Connaught Room, specialises in excellent French cuisine. Before and after dinner in the Dungeon Bar guests are entertained by a harpist or pianist. Ashford Castle offers a full range of country sports, including fishing on Lough Corrib, clay pigeon shooting, riding, an exclusive 9-hole golf course and Ireland's only school of falconry. The hotel has a modern health centre comprising a whirlpool, sauna, steam room, fully equipped gymnasium and conservatory. Ashford is an ideal base for touring the historic West of Ireland, places like Kylemore Abbey, Westport House and the mediaeval town of Galway. A member of Leading Hotels of the World.

Our inspector loved: *The stunning views across Lough Corrib.*

Directions: 30 minutes from Galway on the shore of Lough Corrib, on the left when entering the village of Cong.

Web: www.johansens.com/ashfordcastle
E-mail: ashford@ashford.ie
Tel: 00 353 94 95 46003
Fax: 00 353 94 95 46260

Price Guide:
single/twin/double €215–€515
stateroom/suite €570–€995

KNOCKRANNY HOUSE HOTEL & SPA

KNOCKRANNY, WESTPORT, CO MAYO, IRELAND

Within secluded grounds overlooking the picturesque heritage town of Westport, Knockranny enjoys unrivalled views of Croagh Patrick, Clew Bay and the Atlantic Ocean. This Victorian-style hotel is privately owned and managed by Adrian and Geraldine Noonan, who guarantee the best in Irish hospitality. The 54 charming bedrooms and suites are tastefully furnished and offer luxury, comfort and every up-to-date amenity. The opulent Executive Suites have four poster beds, spa baths, DVD and CD players and a sunken lounge area with panoramic views. Fresh flowers in spring to roaring open log fires in winter create a relaxing ambience in the utmost comfort. La Fougère serves imaginative modern Irish cuisine with international influences, complemented by a selection of fine wines. Golf, fishing, sailing, horse riding and much more can be enjoyed in the dramatic surrounding countryside, whilst a climb to the top of Croagh Patrick makes an exhilarating day's journey. Alternatively, relax in the new destination spa, opening in December 2004. The ideal location to combine business with pleasure, extensive conference facilities for up to 500 are available. The Conference Suites are fully air conditioned with state-of-the-art communication and audio visual equipment.

Directions: Turn left off the N60 before entering Westport town. Complimentary bottle of house wine and chocolates for guests staying for 2 nights or more.

Web: www.johansens.com/knockranny
E-mail: info@khh.ie
Tel: 00 353 98 28600
Fax: 00 353 98 28611

Price Guide:
single €120–€170
double/twin €190–€240
suite €255–€305

Ballina

Knock Airport

Westport

Ballyhaunis

Our inspector loved: The stunning view of the mountain Croagh Patrick and the Atlantic Ocean from the circular dining room windows.

           SPA

NUREMORE HOTEL AND COUNTRY CLUB

CARRICKMACROSS, CO MONAGHAN, IRELAND

Nestling on the outskirts of Carrickmacross, Nuremore Hotel and Country Club is set in 200 acres of rolling countryside with beautifully landscaped gardens. Its wide range of facilities include a swimming pool, tennis courts, treatment rooms and a health club featuring a gymnasium, spa bath, sauna and steam room. The hotel's renowned 18-hole championship golf course makes superb use of the surrounding lakes and landscape and has been described as one of the most picturesque parkland courses in the country. Resident professional, Maurice Cassidy, is on hand to offer advice and tuition. All 72 bedrooms and suites are beautifully appointed to ensure a generous feeling of personal space and guests can sample the classic European cuisine with Irish and French influences, prepared by award-winning chef Raymond McArdle. The restaurant has been listed in Food & Wine magazine and it also features in the Bridgestone Guide to Ireland's best 100 restaurants. Nuremore's impressive conference centre constantly evolves to ensure it remains at the cutting edge for business events. Conference and syndicate rooms boast natural lighting, AV equipment, air conditioning, fax and ISDN lines. A dedicated conference team ensures that all functions run smoothly.

Our inspector loved: The extensive sporting and health facilities, newly refurbished swimming pool and gym.

Directions: From Dublin Airport take the M1 to the Ardee sliproad then take the N33 to Carrickmacross. Nuremore is situated on the main N2 Dublin-Ardee Road, just before Carrickmacross town. There is a toll charge applicable on the M1. 45 minutes from Dublin Airport. 75 minutes from Belfast Airport.

Monaghan

Castleblayney

Carrickmacross

Web: www.johansens.com/nuremore
E-mail: nuremore@eircom.net
Tel: 00 353 42 9661438
Fax: 00 353 42 9661853

Price Guide:
single €155–€210
double/twin €225–€265
suite €255–€310

DUNBRODY COUNTRY HOUSE & COOKERY SCHOOL

ARTHURSTOWN, CO WEXFORD, IRELAND

Once home to the Marquess of Donegal, this beautiful Georgian country house hotel stands in the heart of 20 acres of woodland and gardens on the dramatic hook peninsula of Ireland's sunny south-east coast. The charming interior is adorned with comfortable furniture, furnishings and paintings, fresh flowers, potted plants and crackling log fires in period fireplaces during cooler months. Owners Kevin and Catherine Dundon have perfected the art of relaxed elegance. Public rooms are large and comfortable with views over to distant parkland. Bedrooms and suites are understated opulence: spacious, delightfully decorated, superbly appointed and with a high standard of facilities including luxurious bathrooms. Kevin acquired star status as Master Chef in Canada and creates gastronomic delights for a discerning clientele in an elegant dining room overlooking the lawned garden. The Dunbrody Cookery school also offers residential cookery courses and demonstrations. Also highly acclaimed is the late breakfast which is served daily until noon. Waterford and Wexford are close, as are Tintern Abbey, Dunbody Abbey and a multitude of sandy coves. Croquet and clay pigeon shooting is on site, golf, riding and fishing nearby.

Directions: From Wexford take R733 to Duncannon and Arthurstown. Dunbrody is on the left coming into Arthurstown village.

Web: www.johansens.com/dunbrody
E-mail: dunbrody@indigo.ie
Tel: 00 353 51 389 600
Fax: 00 353 51 389 601

Price Guide:
single €135
double/twin €200–€400
suite €310–€500

Our inspector loved: The international influence in Kevin Dundon's fine cooking.

MARLFIELD HOUSE

GOREY, CO WEXFORD, IRELAND

Staying at Johansens award-winning Marlfield House is a memorable experience. Set in 34 acres of woodland and gardens, this former residence of the Earl of Courtown preserves the Regency lifestyle in all its graciousness. Built in 1820 and situated just 55 miles south of Dublin, it is recognised as one of the finest country houses in Ireland and is supervised by its welcoming hosts and proprietors, Raymond and Mary Bowe and their daughter Margaret. The State Rooms have been built in a very grand style and have period fireplaces where open fires burn even in cooler weather. All of the furniture is antique and the roomy beds are draped with sumptuous fabrics. The bathrooms are made of highly polished marble and some have large freestanding bathtubs. There is an imposing entrance hall, luxurious drawing room and an impressive curved Richard Turner conservatory. The kitchen's gastronomic delights have earned it numerous awards. Located 2 miles from fine beaches and within easy reach of many golf courses, including Seafield, Woodenbridge, Druids Glen, The European Club and Coolattin, the house is central to many touring high points: Glendalough, Waterford Crystal and Powerscourt Gardens and the medieval city of Kilkenny. Closed mid-December to the end of January.

Our inspector loved: The instant calming influence caused by the Bowe family's devotion to quality.

Directions: On the Gorey–Courtown road, just over a mile east of Gorey.

Web: www.johansens.com/marlfieldhouse
E-mail: info@marlfieldhouse.ie
Tel: 00 353 55 21124
Fax: 00 353 55 21572

Price Guide:
single from €130
double/twin €245–€265
state rooms from €425–€730

337

KELLY'S RESORT HOTEL

ROSSLARE, CO WEXFORD, IRELAND

Directions: Follow signs for Wexford/ Rosslare. Situated 20km outside Wexford Town.

Web: www.johansens.com/kellysresort
E-mail: kellyhot@iol.ie
Tel: 00 353 53 32114
Fax: 00 353 53 32222

Price Guide:
single €84–€90
double/twin €148–€187

Situated beside the long, sandy beach at Rosslare, Kelly's is very much a family hotel, now managed by the fourth generation of Kellys. With a firm reputation as one of Ireland's finest hotels, based on a consistently high standard of service, Kelly's extends a warm welcome to its guests, many of whom return year after year. The hotel has won numerous endeavour awards for tourism. The public rooms are tastefully decorated and feature a collection of carefully selected paintings. All bedrooms are en suite and have been refurbished in the last 4 years. The hotel restaurant is highly regarded for its superb cuisine and great attention to detail. An extensive wine list includes individual estate wines imported from France. To complement Chef Aherne's fine cuisine, Kelly's have a French bar/bistro, "La Marine", which is an inspired assemblage of design and offers the ideal venue for pre-dinner drinks. Step inside the new spa, "SeaSpa", where healing sea waters, heat and steam experiences, therapeutic lighting and textured surrounds will help service the body, mind and soul. For excercise, The Aqua Club has 2 swimming pools and a range of water facilities, steam room and Canadian hot tub as well as a gymnasium. Golfers have courses at Rosslare, St Helens' Bay and Wexford, which has an excellent shopping centre. Places of interest nearby include the Irish National Heritage Park at Ferrycarrig.

Our inspector loved: A complete family resort with something for everyone.

Recommendations in Scotland appear on pages 340-384

For further information on Scotland, please contact:

Visit Scotland
23 Ravelston Terrace, Edinburgh EH4 3TP
Tel: +44 (0)131 332 2433
Internet: www.visitscotland.com

or see pages 412-414 for details of
local attractions to visit during your stay.

Images from www.britainonview.com

DARROCH LEARG

BRAEMAR ROAD, BALLATER, ABERDEENSHIRE AB35 5UX

Directions: At the western edge of Ballater on the A93.

Web: www.johansens.com/darrochlearg
E-mail: info@darrochlearg.co.uk
Tel: 0870 381 8477
International: +44 (0)13397 55443
Fax: 013397 55252

Price Guide:
single £87–£102
double/twin £134–£164

Peterhead

Aberdeen City

Aberdeen

● Ballater

4 acres of leafy grounds surround Darroch Learg, situated on the side of the rocky hill which dominates Ballater. The hotel, which was built in 1888 as a fashionable country residence, offers panoramic views over the golf course, River Dee and Balmoral Estate to the fine peaks of the Grampian Mountains. All bedrooms are individually furnished and decorated, providing modern amenities. The reception rooms in Darroch Learg are similarly elegant and welcoming, a comfortable venue in which to enjoy a relaxing drink. Log fires create a particularly cosy atmosphere on chilly nights. The beautifully presented food has been awarded 3 AA Rosettes. A wide choice of wines, a former winner of the AA "Wine List of the Year for Scotland", complements the cuisine, which is best described as modern and Scottish in style. To perfect the setting, there is a wonderful outlook south towards the hills of Glen Muick. The wealth of outdoor activities on offer include walking, riding, mountain-biking, loch and river fishing, gliding and skiing. The surrounding areas are interesting with an old ruined Kirk and ancient Celtic stones. A few miles away stands Balmoral Castle, the Highland residence of the British sovereign.

Our inspector loved: The personal attention of the charming owners and staff, wonderful understated food, wine and décor.

LOCH MELFORT HOTEL & RESTAURANT

ARDUAINE, BY OBAN, ARGYLL PA34 4XG

Spectacularly located on the west coast of Scotland, the Loch Melfort Hotel is a quiet hideaway on Asknish Bay, with the awe-inspiring backdrop of woodlands and the magnificent mountains of Argyll. Friendly staff attend to every need and there is a warm, welcoming atmosphere. Spacious bedrooms are lavishly appointed with bold bright fabrics, comfortable furnishings and have large patio windows overlooking the islands of Jura, Shuna and Scarba. The award-winning restaurant, which has breathtaking views stretching as far as the eye can see, is perfect for a romantic meal. Guests may feast on the sumptuous fresh local fish, shellfish and meat complemented by an extensive selection of fine wines. There is also a mouth-watering array of home-made desserts, delicious ice creams and Scottish cheeses. Skerry Bistro serves informal meals, lunches, suppers and afternoon teas. Outdoor activities include fishing, sailing, riding, windsurfing, walking and mountain biking. Visitors can explore the nearby islands and local places of interest include Mull, Kilchoan Castle, Castle Stalker and the stunning Dunstaffnage Castle (home of Clan Campbell). The Arduaine Gardens, situated adjacent to the hotel, are extremely beautiful and home to a diversity of plants and trees from all over the world. The Marine Sanctuary and Kilmartin Glen are well worth a visit.

Our inspector loved: The super views and great food.

Directions: From Oban take the A816 south for 19 miles. From Loch Lomond area follow A82 then A83, finally A816 north to Arduaine.

Web: www.johansens.com/lochmelfort
E-mail: reception@lochmelfort.co.uk
Tel: 0870 381 8699
International: +44 (0)1852 200233
Fax: 01852 200214

Price Guide: (including dinner)
double/twin £118-£178
superior £138-£218

341

ARDANAISEIG

KILCHRENAN BY TAYNUILT, ARGYLL PA35 1HE

Directions: Reaching Taynuilt on the A85, take the B845 to Kilchrenan.

Web: www.johansens.com/ardanaiseig
E-mail: ardanaiseig@clara.net
Tel: 0870 381 8319
International: +44 (0)1866 833333
Fax: 01866 833222

Price Guide:
single £80–£125
double/twin £108–£276

This romantic small luxury hotel, built in 1834, stands alone in a setting of almost surreal natural beauty at the foot of Ben Cruachan. Directly overlooking Loch Awe and surrounded by wild wooded gardens, Ardanaiseig is evocative of the romance and history of the Highlands. Skilful restoration has ensured that this lovely old mansion has changed little since it was built. The elegant drawing room has log fires, bowls of fresh flowers, superb antiques, handsome paintings and marvellous views of the islands in the Loch and of faraway mountains. The traditional library, sharing this outlook, is ideal for postprandial digestifs. The charming bedrooms are peaceful, appropriate to the era of the house, yet equipped thoughtfully with all comforts. True Scottish hospitality is the philosophy of the Ardanaiseig Restaurant, renowned for its inspired use of fresh produce from the Western Highlands. The wine list is magnificent. Artistic guests enjoy the famous 100-acre Ardanaiseig gardens and nature reserve, filled with exotic shrubs and trees brought back from the Himalayas over the years. Brilliant rhododendrons and azaleas add a riot of colour. The estate also offers fishing, boating, tennis and croquet (snooker in the evenings) and exhilarating hill or lochside walks.

Our inspector loved: *The feeling of complete escape.*

CAMERON HOUSE

LOCH LOMOND G83 8QZ

Set amidst 108 acres of beautiful countryside on the southern shores of Loch Lomond, in the Trossachs, with views of Ben Lomond and beyond, this 5-star resort is the perfect destination for business and leisure travellers. Once the home of the illustrious Smollett family, Cameron House has been sympathetically restored to provide an elegant, timeless ambience. The bedrooms are luxuriously appointed, and the suites have 4-poster beds and panoramic views over the loch. There are various dining options, including the elegant 3 AA Rosette Georgian Room Restaurant and the more informal Smolletts Restaurant, whilst traditional afternoon tea is served in the Drawing Room. Casual dining can be enjoyed in the stylish Marina Restaurant and Bar, a contemporary restaurant centred around an open kitchen. Leisure facilities include a large lagoon-style swimming pool, sauna, steam room, Turkish bath and spa bath as well as gym, tennis, children's club, and a wide range of treatments offered at the Éspa health and beauty salon. There is golf on the "Wee Demon" 9-hole golf course, quad biking, clay pigeon shooting, and numerous water sports on the loch. The hotel's 46-foot luxury motor cruiser, the Celtic Warrior, can be hired for private cruises, weddings and other celebrations as well as small business meetings.

Our inspector loved: *The great location and the food which is just the best around.*

Directions: From Glasgow Airport, follow M8 towards Greenock, leave at jct 30, go over Erskine Toll Bridge. Join A82 towards Loch Lomond and Crianlarich. Approx 14 miles on, at Balloch roundabout, carry straight on. Hotel is 1 mile on the right.

Isle of Mull   Oban

Dunoon

Glasgow

Campbelltown

Web: www.johansens.com/cameronhouse
E-mail: reservations@cameronhouse.co.uk
Tel: 0870 381 8588
International: +44 (0)1389 755565
Fax: 01389 759522

Price Guide:
single £178–£208
double/twin £245–£275
suite £395–£495

STONEFIELD CASTLE

TARBERT, LOCH FYNE, ARGYLL PA29 6YJ

Nestled within 60 acres of its own woodland garden, Stonefield Castle stands high on the Kintyre peninsula overlooking the craggy Argyll coastline and Loch Fyne. Famed for their fisheries and smoke-houses this area has much to be proud of and guests sitting in the restaurant will have a heady combination of exemplary Scottish cuisine and the most spectacular scenery on the West Coast. The Castle was built in 1837 and stands today as a fine example of Scottish Baronial architecture, with long elegant windows, gothic turrets and imposing castellations. Each of its 33 bedrooms has been carefully designed to ensure that this period elegance is retained and indeed some of the original pieces of furniture remain in the hotel. The woodland gardens at Stonefield lure horticulturalists from far and wide to see its rare examples of exotic rhododendrons and shrubs. In fact Stonefield has the United Kingdom's second largest collection of Himalayan rhododendrons. The spectacular scenery of the local countryside makes this a stunning backdrop for summer walks or cosy autumn retreats.

Directions: Take the A82 from Glasgow along Loch Lomond side, then the A83 at Tarbert towards Campbelltown. The hotel is 10 miles past Lochgilphead on left hand side

Web: www.johansens.com/stonefield
E-mail: enquiries@stonefieldcastle.co.uk
Tel: 0870 381 8918
International: +44 (0)1880 820836
Fax: 01880 820929

Our inspector loved: Some of the finest views and gardens in Scotland.

Price Guide:
single £90–£125
double/twin £180–£200
suite £250

BALCARY BAY HOTEL

AUCHENCAIRN, NR CASTLE DOUGLAS, DUMFRIES & GALLOWAY DG7 1QZ

Enjoying a very warm climate due to its proximity to the Gulf Stream, Balcary Bay is one of Scotland's more romantic and secluded hideaways, yet only ½ hour from the bustling market town of Dumfries. As you sit in the lounge overlooking Balcary Bay, the calling of birds and the gently lapping waves compete for your attention. Guests will be greeted by genuine Scottish hospitality, which includes the provision of modern facilities with a traditional atmosphere, imaginatively prepared local delicacies such as lobsters, prawns and salmon, plus the reassuring intimacy of a family-run hotel. This hotel is a true haven for those wishing to get away from their hectic lives and an ideal break for a romantic weekend. This exciting corner of Scotland offers numerous great coastal and woodland walks, whilst nearby are several 9 and 18-hole golf courses at Colvend, Kirkcudbright, Castle Douglas, Southerness and Dumfries. There are also salmon rivers and trout lochs, sailing, shooting, riding and bird-watching facilities. The area abounds with National Trust historic properties and gardens. Seasonal short breaks and reduced inclusive rates are available for 3 and 7 night stays.

Our inspector loved: The views from this hotel, which complete the feeling of total escape.

Directions: Located off the A711 Dumfries–Kirkcudbright road, 2 miles out of Auchencairn on the Shore Road.

Web: www.johansens.com/balcarybay
E-mail: reservations@balcary-bay-hotel.co.uk
Tel: 0870 381 8334
International: +44 (0)1556 640217/640311
Fax: 01556 640272

Price Guide:
single £65
double/twin £115–£135

CALLY PALACE HOTEL

GATEHOUSE OF FLEET, DUMFRIES & GALLOWAY DG7 2DL

Directions: 60 miles west of Carlisle, turn right off the A75 from Gatehouse of Fleet. The hotel entrance is on the left after approximately 1 mile.

Web: www.johansens.com/callypalace
E-mail: info@callypalace.co.uk
Tel: 0870 381 8401
International: +44 (0)1557 814341
Fax: 01557 814522

Price Guide: (including dinner, minimum 2-night stay)
single £91–£135
double/twin £172–£196

Set in over 150 acres of forest and parkland, on the edge of Robert Burns country, this 18th-century country house has been restored to its former glory by the McMillan family, the proprietors since 1981. On entering the hotel, guests will initially be impressed by the grand scale of the interior. 2 huge marble pillars support the original moulded ceiling of the entrance hall. All the public rooms have ornate ceilings, original marble fireplaces and fine reproduction furniture. Combine these with grand, traditional Scottish cooking and you have a hotel par excellence. Awarded 1 Rosette for cuisine, Cally Palace offers a delightful dining experience enhanced by the atmospheric piano playing every evening. The 55 en-suite bedrooms have been individually decorated. Some are suites with a separate sitting room; others are large enough to accommodate a sitting area. An indoor leisure complex, completed in the style of the marble entrance hall, includes heated swimming pool, Jacuzzi and saunas. The hotel has an all-weather tennis court, a putting green, croquet and a lake. Also, for hotel guests' use only, is an 18-hole golf course, par 71, length 6,062 yards set around the lake in the grounds. Special weekend breaks are available out of season. Closed January and mid week in February.

Our inspector loved: *The style and comfort of the hotel in a beautiful part of Scotland with golf on the doorstep.*

KNOCKINAAM LODGE

PORTPATRICK, WIGTOWNSHIRE DG9 9AD

With an unsurpassed tradition of quality and excellence, Knockinaam Lodge has the reputation of being one of Scotland's finest hotels. At the foot of a wooded glen, surrounded by 30 acres of greenery, hills and magnificent unspoilt countryside, this beautiful country house displays traditional elegance and charm. Inside, there is a wonderful, welcoming atmosphere, enhanced by stunning arrangements of fresh flowers and extremely friendly staff. The large secluded grounds, shelterd by cliffs, include immaculate lawns and gardens that stretch all the way down to the hotel's own private sandy beach and majestic cove where spectacular views of the rugged coastline are to be savoured. Guests can relax and enjoy the soothing sound of rolling waves or the tuneful accompaniment of birds creating a sense of harmonious serenity. The 3-Rosetted restaurant uses fresh and local ingredients for its delicious contemporary French menu§ with an eclectic twist. There is an extensive international wine list, which boasts some outstanding top vintages. After dinner, the perfect place for a nightcap is the cosy wood-panelled bar with roaring log fire, where guests will have difficulty in choosing from the impressive collection of 160 whiskies. The bedrooms are sunny, warm and comfortable with an emphasis on stylish décor and luxury.

Our inspector loved: *The great views and feeling of privacy within the*

Directions: From the A77 follow signs to Portpatrick. Turn left at the Knockinaam sign, 2 miles west of Lochans and continue past Smokehouse. The lodge is approximately 3 miles along this road.

Web: www.johansens.com/knockinaam
E-mail: reservations@knockinaamlodge.com
Tel: 0870 381 9166
International: +44 (0)1776 810471
Fax: 01776 810435

Price Guide:
single £135–£155
double/twin £210–£290
master/suite £260–£375

KIRROUGHTREE HOUSE

NEWTON STEWART, WIGTOWNSHIRE DG8 6AN

Directions: The hotel entrance is situated on the A712 Newton Stewart - New Galloway road approx 250 metres on the left from the junction with the A75 Dumfries/Stranrear road.

Web: www.johansens.com/kirroughtreehouse
E-mail: info@kirroughtreehouse.co.uk
Tel: 0870 381 8659
International: +44 (0)1671 402141
Fax: 01671 402425

Price Guide:
single £80–£113
double/twin £140–£180
suite £180

A previous winner of the Johansens Most Excellent Service Award and the Good Hotel Guide's Scottish Hotel of the Year, Kirroughtree House is situated in the foothills of the Cairnsmore of Fleet, on the edge of Galloway Forest Park. Standing in 8 acres of landscaped gardens, guests can relax and linger over the spectacular views. Built by the Heron family in 1719, the oak-panelled lounge, with open fireplace, reflects the style of that period. From the lounge rises the original staircase, where Robert Burns often recited his poems. Each bedroom is well furnished; guests may choose to spend the night in one of the hotel's spacious de luxe bedrooms with spectacular views over the surrounding countryside. Many guests are attracted by Kirroughtree's culinary reputation, awarded 2 AA rosettes – only the finest produce is used to create meals of originality and finesse. An ideal venue for small meetings, family parties and weddings; exclusive use of the hotel can be arranged. Pitch and putt and croquet can be enjoyed in the grounds and the hotel's position makes it an ideal base for great walking expeditions. Residents can play golf on the many local courses and also have use of the exclusive 18-hole course at Cally Palace. Trout and salmon fishing, shooting and deer stalking during the season can all be organised. Short breaks available. Closed 3 January to mid February.

Our inspector loved: *The classic elegance of this beautiful hotel.*

THE BONHAM

35 DRUMSHEUGH GARDENS, EDINBURGH EH3 7RN

This award-winning, boutique-style hotel is situated just a few minutes walk from the West End of Edinburgh and is equally suitable for a restful weekend or a high-intensity business trip. Many of the original Victorian features of the 3 converted town houses have been maintained. The interior has been designed to create a contemporary ambience within the classic timelessness of a Victorian town house. Each room has been elegantly and dramatically created with modern furniture and art, using rich, bold colours to produce tasteful oversized abundance throughout. The Bonham offers a traditional feel with a modern twist, coupled with impeccable standards and individuality. Purely for pleasure, each of the 48 bedrooms offers 55 channel cable TV, a mini-bar and e-TV, which provides a complete PC capability, Internet and E-mail access as well as DVD video and CD player. The Events Room is a perfect setting for a range of select meetings and private dining. Restaurant at The Bonham, the most timeless contemporary restaurant in Edinburgh, serves distinct European inspired cuisine which is complemented by provocative wines. Along with its famous castle and numerous shops, Edinburgh houses Scotland's national galleries and some splendid museums.

Our inspector loved: The design and décor of the hotel make it surely one of the coolest in Edinburgh.

Directions: The Hotel is situated in the city centre's West End.

Web: www.johansens.com/bonham
E-mail: reserve@thebonham.com
Tel: 0870 381 8373
International: +44 (0)131 623 9301
Fax: 0131 226 6080

Price Guide:
single: £105–£165
double/twin £127–£195
suprior double/twin £168–£245
suites £247–£335

BRUNTSFIELD HOTEL

69 BRUNTSFIELD PLACE, EDINBURGH EH10 4HH

This elegant Victorian town house first became a hotel in the 1920s and has maintained a reputation for its special charm and character ever since. Located just a few minutes from the hustle and bustle of the city centre, guests arriving here will relish the peace and tranquillity of its setting overlooking the leafy Bruntsfield Links, one of Edinburgh's oldest golfing areas and now an elegant park. The traditional Victorian architecture is mirrored inside the building with carefully decorated bedrooms and lounges to ensure that a welcoming ambience of warmth and comfort is maintained throughout the hotel. Many of the 73 carefully appointed bedrooms have delightful views, either of the Links or Edinburgh Castle and beyond towards the Old Town; there are also a number of larger rooms with 4-poster beds. The hotel offers 2 dining settings: the Cardoon restaurant with its relaxed-style and atmosphere, which serves an award-winning selection of freshly prepared dishes using local produce, and the less formal Kings Bar, a popular meeting place which is open all day for drinks, light meals, snacks and coffees. Bruntsfield Hotel is the ideal base from which to explore the vibrant and cosmopolitan Scottish capital with its excellent shopping, wonderful historic sites and many festivals.

Directions: Join the A702 city bypass, exit at Lothianburn to Bruntsfield Place. The hotel overlooks Bruntsfield Links Park.

Web: www.johansens.com/bruntsfield
E-mail: sales@thebruntsfield.co.uk
Tel: 0870 381 8388
International: +44 (0)131 229 1393
Fax: 0131 229 5634

Price Guide:
single £79-£120
double/twin £120-£250

Our inspector loved: The different dining options and the great outlook over a grass meadow despite being in the city centre.

CHANNINGS

15 SOUTH LEARMONTH GARDENS, EDINBURGH EH4 1EZ

Channings is located on a quiet cobbled street only 10 minutes' walk from the centre of Edinburgh, with easy access to the shops on Princes Street and the timeless grandeur of Edinburgh Castle. The hotel, formerly 5 Edwardian town houses, retains its original features, which have been restored with flair and consideration, and the atmosphere is like that of an exclusive country club. With an ambience of country-style tranquillity, guests can relax in one of the fully refurbished lounges with coffee or afternoon tea served by the friendliest of staff. For those who like to browse, the hotel has an interesting collection of antique prints, furniture, objets d'art, periodicals and books. The atmosphere is perfect for discreet company meetings, small conferences and private or corporate events, which may be held. These may be held in the oak-panelled Library or Kingsleigh. Fine dining at Channings can be experienced in the exclusive, refurbished Channings Restaurant which boasts distinctive food in a warm and welcoming ambience. Alternatively, Ochre Vita is a delight with its vibrant and flavoursome Mediterranean food and wines.

Our inspector loved: *The location; in the heart of Edinburgh yet overlooking green grass and with the friendliest of staff.*

Directions: Go north-west from Queensferry Street, over Dean Bridge on to Queensferry Road. Take the 3rd turning on the right down South Learmonth Avenue, then turn right at the end into South Learmonth Gardens.

Web: www.johansens.com/channings
E-mail: reserve@channings.co.uk
Tel: 0870 381 8413
International: +44 (0)131 623 9302
Fax: 0131 332 9631

Price Guide:
single £100–£155
double/twin £131–£225
four poster/suite £157–£260

NEW

THE CHESTER RESIDENCE

9 CHESTER STREET, EDINBURGH EH3 7RF

Directions: Situated in Edinburgh city's West End.

Web: www.johansens.com/chesterresidence
E-mail: enquiries@chester-residence.com
Tel: 0870 381 9281
International: +44 (0)131 226 2075
Fax: 0131 226 2191

Price Guide: (per apartment, excluding VAT)
second floor £190-£230
first floor £190
ground floor £180
garden £170
patio £120

This stylish terraced Georgian townhouse features 5 exclusive self-contained apartments situated in Edinburgh's West End, within walking distance of its commercial districts, art galleries and museums. Each of the suites comprises airy, light rooms, superbly decorated with a mixture of antique and contemporary furnishings. Soothing colours such as creams, browns and oranges coupled with open fireplaces and soft lighting create a cosy atmosphere in these spacious rooms with their high ceilings and large windows. The Garden Apartment features a private walled garden perfect for relaxing in during the summer and the Second Floor Apartment, with 2 bedrooms, overlooks the gardens and spires of St Mary's Cathedral. Chic bathrooms are decorated in black and white marble and each of the superbly modern kitchens is conveniently stocked with ingredients for a continental breakfast as well as fresh fruit and hot and cold drinks. A house menu of fine wines and champagne is available and a supper menu for house dining. This is a unique location to hold a business meeting; a relaxed setting with all the facilities on-hand expected from a 5-star hotel. Broadband Internet access, direct dial telephone, widescreen TV and DVD player with a library of 50 films are all standard. Gym facilities can be arranged in a nearby leisure centre.

Our inspector loved: *The exceptional quality and feeling of spaciousness, and the contemporary feel in this beautiful Georgian building.*

CHRISTOPHER NORTH HOUSE

6 GLOUCESTER PLACE, EDINBURGH EH3 6EF

Behind its graceful grey-stone façade highlighted by tall, colourfully draped windows and slender, decorative wrought-iron pavement railings this lovely old house is the epitome of elegance and style. Surrounded by similarly attractive architecture it stands serenely in the splendid residential area of Edinburgh's New Town, a short walk from Princes Street and the business district of Charlotte Square. Originally the home of poet, writer and moral philosopher Christopher North, who lived here from 1823 to 1854, the house has been tastefully refurbished and extended over the years, and today it is an attractive boutique-style residence with a contemporary ambience that blends superbly into the classic timelessness of a Georgian town house. Many original features have been retained in lounges and bedrooms, which have been delightfully decorated and furnished to ensure a welcoming atmosphere of warmth and comfort. Each en-suite guest room is individually designed to appeal to the most discerning leisure and business traveller alike. Home-from-home comforts include colour television, direct dial telephone, tea and coffee making tray and baby listening service. Guests can enjoy pre-dinner drinks in the friendly Mozart Kaffee Haus before sampling the Bacchus restaurant's delicious and varied menu.

Our inspector loved: The warm and personal welcome.

Directions: In the heart of Georgian Edinburgh, Only 5 minutes walk from Princes Street, down Charlotte Square to Moray Place and the hotel.

Web: www.johansens.com/christophernorth
E-mail: reservations@christophernorth.co.uk
Tel: 0870 381 9310
International: +44 (0)131 225 2720
Fax: 0131 220 4706

Price Guide:
single £88–£110
double/twin £98–£120
Executive double £120–£140
Executive suite £160–£220

THE EDINBURGH RESIDENCE

7 ROTHESAY TERRACE, EDINBURGH EH3 7RY, SCOTLAND

Directions: From the West End of Princes Street head towards West Register Street. Princes Street becomes Rutland Place then Shandwich Place. Turn right into Coates Crescent then right again into Walker Street. Walker Street turns into Drumsheugh Gardens. Turn left at Rothesay Terrace.

Web: www.johansens.com/edinburghres
E-mail: reserve@theedinburghresidence.com
Tel: 0870 381 8913
International: +44 (0)131 623 9304
Fax: 0131 226 3381

Price Guide:
suite £112–£265
town house apartment £260–£395

Space, luxury, privacy and convenience can be enjoyed at this stylish, grey-stone venue situated in Edinburgh's West End, just a short stroll from the city's main shopping area and attractions. With its central yet peaceful location, The Edinburgh Residence consists of 29 superbly equipped suites in a row of 3 terraced town houses. These comprise classic suites, 3 with their own private entrance, grand suites and 8 apartments whose average floor area is approximately the size of a tennis court. Each is tastefully and comfortably furnished, beautifully appointed and has every modern facility, including crockery and discreetly stored microwave oven. The spacious bathrooms are particularly delightful; some have a traditional roll-top bath, others offer a Jacuzzi big enough for 2. There is wood panelling and sweeping staircases throughout, a splendid Georgian morning room and an elegant drawing room where visitors can relax with a drink from the honesty bar and take in the stunning views over Edinburgh and beyond. There is no dining room, but 24-hour room service is available, and just a short walk away is the Residence's sister restaurant, The Bonham, whose European-inspired cuisine has earned it a high reputation. Small private or corporate events can be accommodated.

Our inspector loved: *This stylish and relaxed alternative to a traditional hotel; great service with great style.*

THE HOWARD

34 GREAT KING STREET, EDINBURGH EH3 6QH

Situated in the heart of Edinburgh, with good connections by train and easily accessible from Edinburgh Airport, this 5-star hotel, originally built as a private house, ensures that each guest is made to feel special and experiences traditional Georgian pampering as if a guest in a private home. Visitors take a step back in time at The Howard where attention to detail and attentive service is paramount. A dedicated butler will take care of guests' unpacking, serve afternoon tea and will even arrange a social itinerary for exploring nearby Edinburgh, with its chic designer boutiques just a 10-minute walk away in George Street. Some of the 18 individually decorated bedrooms boast free-standing roll-top baths, Jacuzzi and a power or double shower; 3 suites feature exclusive terraced gardens and private entrances. 24-hour room service is available and dinner, selected from the à la carte menu, may be served in the comfort of guests' bedrooms by their personal butler. Alternatively, dining at The Atholl is an unforgettable experience where the talented team of chefs create meticulously prepared cuisine. This is an elegant Georgian setting ideal for personal entertaining and private corporate gatherings.

Our inspector loved: *The most discreet personal service and the incredible consideration to detail.*

Directions: From Queen Street turn north into Dundas Street, then take the third right into Great King Street. The hotel is on the left.

Web: www.johansens.com/howardedinburgh
E-mail: reserve@thehoward.com
Tel: 0870 381 8626
International: +44 (0)131 623 9303
Fax: 0131 557 6515

Price Guide:
single £108–£210
double/twin £180–£275
suite £243–£395
grand suite £356–£475

THE OLD MANOR COUNTRY HOUSE HOTEL

LEVEN ROAD, LUNDIN LINKS, NEAR ST ANDREWS KY8 6AJ

Directions: The hotel lies 12 miles south west of St Andrews on the A915.

Web: www.johansens.com/oldmanorfife
E-mail: enquiries@oldmanorhotel.co.uk
Tel: 0870 381 9322
International: +44 (0)1333 320368
Fax: 01333 320911

Price Guide:
single £95–£110
double £135–£200

This delightful hotel has the most attractive setting, overlooking 2 championship golf courses and Largo Bay, and on clear days the view extends some 30 miles to the coast of East Lothian. Pretty sandy coves and fishing villages are all within easy reach, whilst the cosmopolitan city of Edinburgh is within a 45-minute drive. Each of the 23 en-suite bedrooms is newly decorated with cherry or mahogany furniture and elegant fabrics, and the public rooms are light, spacious and comfortable. Great care has been taken to offer guests a choice of dining options: the Terrace Brasserie serves an imaginative menu of locally caught fish and game, whilst the delightfully informal Coachman's Bistro serves steaks and seafood within a lively atmosphere. The Library Lounge has an impressive selection of over 100 single malts, armagnacs, cognacs and liqueurs and is the ideal spot in which to unwind after a hard day on the Links. The hotel takes great pride in its wide appeal and has something to offer for the business executive, family holidaymaker and romantic weekender.

Our inspector loved: *The bright and airy rooms in this professionally run hotel.*

ONE DEVONSHIRE GARDENS

1 DEVONSHIRE GARDENS, GLASGOW, G12 0UX

One Devonshire Gardens is set in the heart of Glasgow's fashionable West End with its tree-lined terraces and Victorian mansions. Quite simply for those who expect and appreciate the finest of standards, this multi-award-winning hotel is situated in a series of converted period townhouses offering luxurious accommodation and exquisite cuisine. It's all about individuality, and all 35 bedrooms have their own distinctive identity, imaginative and unusual use of classic and contemporary furnishings. Public areas reflect the grandeur of a bygone era with antiques and original Scottish artwork throughout, and guests are entrusted to old-fashioned values of genuine personal service in relaxing comfort and style. The terraced garden is perfect for afternoon teas on a sunny day or pre-dinner drinks on a balmy evening. The hotel has an air-conditioned residents-only gym, equipped with a range of cardio and resistance equipment, together with cardio-theatre; a personal trainer can be organised. Guests can enjoy a range of in-room spa treatments and can request a personalized yoga instructor in the comfort of their own room, both by prior arrangement. 2 dining options are offered including the hotel's award-winning fine dining 2 AA Rosette No 5 Restaurant, and Room Glasgow offering classic cuisine with a contemporary twist.

Our inspector loved: The incredible effort made to add those little touches that make this hotel the very best there is.

Directions: From the M8 take junction 17 and follow signs for the A82 Dumbarton/Kelvinside (Great Western Road).

Web: www.johansens.com/onedevonshire
E-mail: info@onedevonshiregardens.com
Tel: 0870 381 9146
International: +44 (0)141 3392001
Fax: 0141 3371663

Price Guide:
continental breakfast £12
full Scottish breakfast £17
single/double £145-£285
town house suite £355-£485

INVERLOCHY CASTLE

TORLUNDY, FORT WILLIAM PH33 6SN

Directions: 3m north-east of Fort William on the A82.

Web: www.johansens.com/inverlochy
E-mail: info@inverlochy.co.uk
Tel: 0870 381 9278
International: +44 (0)1397 702177
Fax: 01397 702953

Price Guide:
single £205-£290
double £290-£475
suite £400-£550

Set amidst gorgeous scenery in the foothills of Ben Nevis, Inverlochy was built in 1863 by the first Lord Abinger, and as a visitor in 1873 Queen Victoria wrote of it, "I never saw a lovelier or more romantic spot." Today, with new manager, Norbert Lieder, the castle is a splendid hotel. A massive reception room has Venetian crystal chandeliers, a Michaelangelo-style ceiling and a handsome staircase leading through to 3 elaborately decorated dining rooms and the Drawing Room, which has views over the castle's private loch and recently underwent a designer makeover. Spacious bedrooms, all with individual furnishings, offer every comfort. Michelin-starred chef Matt Gray, continues to create menus featuring modern British cuisine using the finest local ingredients including local game, hand picked wild mushrooms and scallops from the Isle of Skye. Various outdoor activities are available to guests, such as golf, clay pigeon shooting, guided walking, fly fishing for brown trout, pony trekking and tennis. Stunning places of landscape and history await exploration nearby: the mountains of Glencoe, the falls at Glen Nevis, the monument at Glenfinnan and many more.

Our inspector loved: The Victorian splendour combining tasteful, contemporary grandeur, great wines and wonderful food.

John O'Groats
Portree
Inverness
Fort William
Glasgow

ROYAL MARINE HOTEL

GOLF ROAD, BRORA, SUTHERLAND KW9 6QS

Overlooking the mouth of River Brora, the Royal Marine, designed by Sir Robert Lorimer in 1913, has undergone great restoration to its original antique furniture, woodwork and panelling. Passing under the wooden arches of the entrance hall and ascending the grand staircase, guests step back in time to refined living of a bygone era. All 22 en suite bedrooms offer modern comfort whilst retaining the ambience of early 20th century elegance. Scottish cuisine is served in the Sir Robert Lorimer Dining Room where fresh seafood, local salmon, meat and game, are all on the menu, complemented by a varied wine list. Less formal meals are taken in the Hunter's Lounge where a fine selection of malt whiskies can be sampled and the Garden Room Café Bar in The Dolphin Leisure Centre also serves lighter snacks all day. The Leisure Centre features an indoor swimming pool, gymnasium, sauna, steam room and Jacuzzi. There are several golf courses nearby, including Royal Dunoch and the Brora Championship course is just a 1 minute walk from the hotel. Sea angling, walking and hawking expeditions can all be arranged. The hotel maintains 2 fishing boats on Loch Brora, which are available for hire. A unique facility to the hotel is its four lane curling rink, which is open from October-March.

Our inspector loved: *This very traditional hotel with excellent facilities and great golf on the doorstep.*

Directions: One hour's drive from Inverness. Travel north on the A9, signposted Wick. In Brora cross bridge turn right and the hotel is 100 yards on the left.

Web: www.johansens.com/royalmarine
E-mail: info@highlandescape.com
Tel: 0870 381 9133
International: +44 (0)1408 621252
Fax: 01408 621181

Price Guide:
single £75–£95
double £120-£138
suite £158

THE ROYAL GOLF HOTEL

THE 1ST TEE, DORNOCH, HIGHLAND IV25 3LG

Directions: Enter the town from the A9 and travel up the hill, across the cross roads and past the police station. The hotel is 200 yards on the right.

Web: www.johansens.com/royalgolf
E-mail: rooms@morton-hotels.com
Tel: 0870 381 9199
International: +44 (0)1667 458800
Fax: 01667 458818

John O'Groats
Portree
Inverness
Fort William
Glasgow

Price Guide:
(dinner £26)
single £55-£120
double £195-£225
suite £200-£275

This handsome sandstone building has recently seen an altogether tasteful renovation, however the focus ultimately remains on golf and its location on the 1st tee of the Royal Dornoch Golf Club lends itself perfectly. Indeed many famous names including Nick Faldo, Tom Watson and Ben Crenshaw have raved about the world's second oldest Links course, established in the 16th century. 20 Highlands courses are within an hour's drive of Dornoch, and include other championship courses such as Nairn, or more hidden gems such as Brora, Golspie or Nairn Dunbar. The hotel is happy to take care of golfing arrangements, from tuition to personalised itineraries. Bedrooms – no two of which are identical – are comfortable, and furnished in a blend of the traditional and contemporary. Dining is available in the informal Conservatory with its views across the golf course and the Dornoch Firth, or the fine main restaurant, which serves the freshest local game, seafood, beef and lamb. The Tom Morris Bar features real log fires and the Malt Whisky Wall with an array of over 100 unusual malts. Nearby activities include birdwatching, fishing and hillwalking. Places of interest include Dunrobin Castle, Skibo Castle, Glenmorangie Distillery and "Harrods" of the north at the falls of Shin.

Our inspector loved: *The majestic location of this stylish, revamped hotel.*

MUCKRACH LODGE HOTEL & RESTAURANT

DULNAIN BRIDGE, BY GRANTOWN-ON-SPEY, INVERNESS-SHIRE PH26 3LY

Set in 10 acres of landscaped grounds and surrounded by the woods and farms of Muckrach estate, this former sporting lodge has a relaxed and informal ambience with an awe-inspiring backdrop of the scenery of the Cairngorms National Park. Quality of service is paramount in this welcoming hotel, where a comfortable atmosphere has been lovingly created with plump sofas, log fires and vases of fresh flowers. The finest quality beef, lamb, game, fish and shellfish are sourced from local farms and ports to be served in the hotel's excellent 2 AA Rosette restaurant, with its distinguished cellar of fine wines and rare malts. There is a large selection of books, magazines and games to enjoy by the fireside or, for the more energetic, the beautiful National Park offers stunning mountains, heather moors, ancient forests and sparkling lochs in the valley of the River Spey. Muckrach Lodge is the ideal base for touring the Highlands, Loch Ness, Royal Deeside and the picturesque Moray coastal villages. The Malt Whisky and Castle Trails are extremely interesting and Strathspey's turbulent history can be discovered by visiting the area's cathedrals, forts and museums. The area is renowned for its rare natural history and offers superb golf with Royal Dornoch, Nairn, Boat of Garten and many others. Alternatively, fishing, riding and watersports are available.

Our inspector loved: The relaxed style and the absence of pretentiousness.

Directions: Muckrach Lodge is 3 miles South West of Grantown-on-Spey on the B9102 and A95, through Dulnain Bridge Village on the A938.

Web: www.johansens.com/muckrachlodge
E-mail: stay@muckrach.co.uk
Tel: 0870 381 8751
International: +44 (0)1479 851257
Fax: 01479 851325

Price Guide:
single £60–£105
double/twin £120–£160
good value short breaks available

361

KINCRAIG HOUSE HOTEL

INVERGORDON, ROSS-SHIRE, SCOTLAND IV18 0LF

Directions: Located on the A9, on the left-hand side 2 miles north of the turn off signposted Alness and Invergordon.

Web: www.johansens.com/kincraighouse
E-mail: info@kincraig-house-hotel.co.uk
Tel: 0870 381 9323
International: +44 (0)1349 852587
Fax: 01349 852193

Price Guide:
single £45
double £90–£140

Built in 1820, this historic country house is full of character and is set within 5 acres of its own elevated gardens with picturesque views over the Cromarty Firth. Inverness Airport is only 35 minutes away, and some of Scotland's finest golf courses, beaches and scenery are situated on the doorstep. The hotel has 15 bedrooms, all with en-suite facilities, each with its own distinct charm. Four-poster beds, moulded ceilings and elegant fireplaces retain a period feel, whilst the lounge has oak panelled walls that add warmth and atmosphere to this fine buiding. The restaurant overlooking the gardens has a relaxed atmosphere and offers guests the chance to enjoy some excellent cuisine. Service is friendly and unobtrusive, with the lounge an exceptional and popular spot amongst regular guests wishing to enjoy a Dalmore malt whisky after dinner from the local distillery. The beautiful Loch Ness, Isle of Skye and Inverness the Highland capital are all within easy access of the hotel.

Our inspector loved: The beautiful period features.

BUNCHREW HOUSE HOTEL

INVERNESS IV3 8TA

This splendid 17th-century Scottish mansion, "Hotel on the Shore", is set amidst 20 acres of landscaped gardens and woodlands on the shores of the Beauly Firth. Guests can enjoy breathtaking views of Ben Wyvis and the Black Isle, while just yards from the house the sea laps at the garden walls. Bunchrew has been carefully restored to preserve its heritage, whilst still giving its guests the highest standards of comfort and convenience. A continual schedule of refurbishment is on-going. The bedrooms are beautifully furnished and decorated to enhance their natural features. The elegant panelled drawing room is the ideal place to relax at any time, and during winter log fires lend it an added appeal which has given the hotel 4-star status. In the candle-lit restaurant the traditional cuisine includes prime Scottish beef, fresh lobster and langoustines, locally caught game and venison and freshly grown vegetables which has been rewarded with 2 AA Rosettes. A carefully chosen wine list complements the menu. Local places of interest include Cawdor Castle, Loch Ness, Castle Urquhart and a number of beautiful glens. For those who enjoy sport there is skiing at nearby Aviemore, sailing, cruising, golf, shooting and fishing.

Our inspector loved: The cosy charm and splendid shore location.

Directions: From Inverness follow signs to Beauly, Dingwall on the A862. 1 mile from the outskirts of Inverness the entrance to the hotel is on the right.

Web: www.johansens.com/bunchrewhouse
E-mail: welcome@bunchrew–inverness.co.uk
Tel: 0870 381 8393
International: +44 (0)1463 234917
Fax: 01463 710620

Price Guide:
single £90–£127.50
double/twin £140–£210

GLEN MHOR HOTEL

9-12 NESS BANK, INVERNESS IV2 4SG

Directions: Opposite Eden Court Theatre, the hotel is best approached from Bank Street, straight across the crossroads on the north side of the bridge.

Web: www.johansens.com/glenmhor
E-mail: glenmhorhotel@btconnect.com
Tel: 0870 381 8407
International: +44 (0)1463 234308
Fax: 01463 713170

Price Guide:
single £59-£85
double £88-£120
junior suite £120-£150
suite £140-£160

This well-established family business is situated in a quiet location on the River Ness. Dapper owner, Nicol Manson, runs the hotel along with his wife and his son-in-law who is the chef. The traditional and modern cuisine of the classic River restaurant is long renowned. It operates for dinner from June to September only, or may be pre-booked for private parties. Specialities include local seafood, salmon, lamb, beef and game in season. The informal Nicos Bistro & Wine Bar, a genuine Victorian Oak Room, serves local and international dishes in a relaxed, tavern style, and offers an extensive wine list. Al fresco dining on the terrace is available, weather permitting. Finally, Nicky Tams, a former baker's stables complete with log fire, provides a wide range of pure malt whiskies along with a cheery lounge bar atmosphere. All of the en-suite bedrooms are tidy and well furnished with individual heating, direct dial telephones and televisions, and some have river views. A number of the guest rooms are housed in the adjacent cottage-annexe, a charming riverside building. The hotel is a short walk from the town centre, and Inverness itself is ideally located for golf and fishing, which the Glen Mhor is happy to arrange on guests' behalf.

Our inspector loved: The traditional comforts of this classic hotel.

THE GLENMORISTON TOWN HOUSE HOTEL & LA RIVIERA RESTAURANT

NESS BANK, INVERNESS IV2 4SF

Superbly located on the banks of the River Ness and just a short walk from the town centre, The Glenmoriston has most recently been chosen as the AA Courtesy and Care Award Winner for Scotland 2003-2004. Its owners have have taken a real interest in progressing the hotel and have refurbished it in a most tasteful way. Now split between 2 magnificent buildings its classic town-house style comprises 30 individually designed bedrooms. New rooms feature marble bathrooms, pocket sprung mattresses and beautiful hand-made furniture. Future developments for the annexed building include a conservatory, and bedrooms in the original building will be refurbished this year. La Terrazza and La Riviera combine the finest local Scottish produce to create classic and contemporary menus; The Glenmoriston holds 2 prestigious AA Rosettes and a listing in the Michelin Red Guide for its outstanding cuisine. Dedicated business facilities and meeting rooms are available, and the hotel provides the perfect base for exploring the Scottish Highlands.

Our inspector loved: The vitality and wonderful rooms added by the new owners.

Directions: On the opposite side of the river to the Eden Court Theatre, the Hotel is best approached from Bank St, straight across the crossroads on the north side of the bridge.

Web: www.johansens.com/glenmoriston
E-mail: glenmoriston@cali.co.uk
Tel: 0870 381 8555
International: +44 (0)1463 223777
Fax: 01463 712378

Price Guide:
single £95-£115
double/twin £120–£150

CULLODEN HOUSE

CULLODEN, INVERNESS, INVERNESS-SHIRE IV2 7BZ

A majestic circular drive leads to the splendour of this handsome Georgian mansion, battle headquarters of Bonnie Prince Charlie 253 years ago. 3 miles from Inverness, this handsome Palladian country house stands in 40 acres of beautiful gardens and peaceful parkland roamed by roe deer. Princes past and present and guests from throughout the world have enjoyed the hotel's ambience and hospitality. Rich furnishings, sparkling chandeliers, impressive Adam fireplaces and ornate plaster reliefs add to the grandness of the hotel's luxurious, high-ceilinged rooms. The bedrooms are appointed to the highest standard, many having four-poster beds and Jacuzzis. 4 non-smoking suites are in the Pavilion Annex, which overlooks a 3-acre walled garden and 2 in the West Pavilion. In the Dining Room guests can savour superb cuisine prepared by chef Michael Simpson, who trained at Gleneagles Hotel and the Hamburg Conference Centre. There is an outdoor tennis court and indoor sauna. Shooting, fishing and pony-trekking can be arranged, while nearby are Cawdor Castle, the Clava Cairns Bronze Age burial ground and Culloden battlefield. AA 4 stars and 2 Rosettes, Scottish Tourist Board 4 stars. From the USA Toll Free fax/phone 0800 980 4561.

Directions: Leave Inverness on the A96 towards Aberdeen and take the right turn off to Culloden. The hotel is signposted on the left ¾ mile after turning.

Web: www.johansens.com/cullodenhouseinverness
E-mail: info@cullodenhouse.co.uk
Tel: 0870 381 9137
International: +44 (0)1463 790461
Fax: 01463 792181

Price Guide:
single £155–£189
double £199–£249
suite £249–£279

Our inspector loved: The elegant exterior and great comfort and service once inside.

CUILLIN HILLS HOTEL

PORTREE, ISLE OF SKYE IV51 9QU

Spectacular views of the majestic Cuillin Mountains and Portree Bay on the beautiful Isle of Skye make this hotel the perfect choice for any discerning visitor. Originally built in the 1870s as a hunting lodge, Cuillin Hills Hotel benefits from 15 acres of private mature grounds, which create a secluded setting and tranquil atmosphere. Quality and comfort is a priority, reflected in the beautiful furniture and décor of the lounge, where guests can relax in front of the log fire and sample the extensive choice of malt whiskys. Spacious bedrooms are elegantly furnished and decorated to the highest standard with all modern conveniences. Imaginative and traditional cuisine combine to create award-winning delights, which are served in the stylish restaurant overlooking the bay. Guests may feast on highland game, lobster, scallops and other deliciously fresh local produce as well as tasty homemade desserts. An interesting selection of informal meals is served in the bar. The island's rich history can be discovered through its castles, museums and visitor centres. There is an abundance of beautiful unspoilt coastal paths and woodland walks nearby. The town of Portree is a mere 10 minutes' walk away.

Our inspector loved: The panoramic position of this well-kept, friendly hotel.

Directions: Skye can be reached by bridge from Kyle of Localsh or by ferry from Mallaig or Glenelg. From Portree take the A855 to Staffin. After ½ mile take the road to Budhmor.

Web: www.johansens.com/cuillinhills
E-mail: info@cuillinhills-hotel-skye.co.uk
Tel: 0870 381 8467
International: +44 (0)1478 612003
Fax: 01478 613092

Price Guide:
single £60–£110
double/twin £120–£210

NEW

SKEABOST COUNTRY HOUSE

SKEABOST BRIDGE, PORTREE IV51 9NP

On the banks of the serene Loch Snizort, surrounded by majestic mountains and fast flowing rivers, the recently refurbished Skeabost Country House is the ultimate in style and opulent good taste. Whilst enjoying the highest quality of personal attention, guests can immerse themselves in the warm atmosphere of the hotel with its open fires and comfortable public rooms or sip a champagne cocktail before sampling the most deliciously fresh Highland fare and fine wines. The bustling public bar features live music every Saturday. Bedrooms and bathrooms are individually designed with luxurious fabrics and colour co-ordinated décor to create an atmosphere of elegance and serenity. In a separate building the hotel has 3 rooms that are perfect for a self-catering holiday. There are plenty of outdoor activities at the hotel: guests can wander along the shoreline of the loch, play golf at the challenging 9-hole course or take advantage of the excellent local salmon and trout fishing. Historic Skeabost is a fascinating place to explore with its long ago battles and places of real antiquity. On colder days simply relax and read a book in front of the fire or play snooker in the old family chapel.

Our inspector loved: *The new stylish bedrooms with splendid drapes and décor.*

Directions: Leave Portree on the A87 for Uig but turn left after 4 miles onto the A850 signposted Dunvegan. The hotel entrance is 1.75 miles on the right.

Web: www.johansens.com/skeabost
E-mail: reception@skeabostcountryhouse.com
Tel: 0870 381 9294
International: +44 (0)1470 532202
Fax: 01470 532454

Price Guide:
single £90
double £110-£350

John O'Groats

Portree

Inverness

Fort William

Glasgow

THE GOLF VIEW HOTEL & LEISURE CLUB

THE SEAFRONT, NAIRN, BY INVERNESS IV12 4HD

This well kept and appointed 4-star hotel has seen much re-investment recently, and its tasteful, individually designed bedrooms offer great comfort and modern facilities such as DVD players and satellite television. Many overlook the Moray Firth, some have romantic four-poster beds and spa baths, and family units come equipped with integral bunk rooms and games consoles. A selection of menus is served in the informal conservatory and the restaurant, both of which take full advantage of the excellent local produce such as lamb, venison and salmon. Guests can swim in the pool, work out in the gymnasium or enjoy a pampering beauty treatment. There are also outdoor tennis courts, and the hotel has mountain bikes available for hire. Excellent nearby beaches offer perfect spots for bathing, relaxing, and leisurely walks along the seafront. Golfers are spoilt for choice, with 2 championship courses in town and 20 courses within easy driving distance. The closest is Nairn Golf Course, established in 1897 and host to the Walker Cup in 1999. Elsewhere, places of interest include the historic Cawdor Castle, Culloden Battlefield and Fort George, Urquhart Castle and the infamous Loch Ness. Many events such as the Nairn Highland Games and Nairn Jazz festival are held throughout the year.

Our inspector loved: This compact, tasteful hotel with its splendid leisure facilities and wonderful views over the Moray Firth.

Directions: Driving through the town on the A96, the hotel is signposted off the main road, down Seabank Road.

John O'Groats

Portree

Inverness

Fort William

Glasgow

Web: www.johansens.com/golfview
E-mail: rooms@morton-hotels.com
Tel: 0870 381 8404
International: +44 (0)1667 458800
Fax: 01667 458818

Price Guide: (dinner £26)
single £92-£113
double £139-£216
suite £209-£266

369

LOCH TORRIDON COUNTRY HOUSE HOTEL

TORRIDON, BY ACHNASHEEN, WESTER-ROSS IV22 2EY

Directions: The hotel is 10 miles from Kinlochewe on the A896. Do not turn off to Torridon village.

Web: www.johansens.com/lochtorridon
E-mail: enquiries@lochtorridonhotel.com
Tel: 0870 381 9136
International: +44 (0)1445 791242
Fax: 01445 791296

Price Guide:
single £64–£107
double/twin £107–£248
master suite £202–£323

Loch Torridon is gloriously situated at the foot of wooded mountains on the shores of the loch from which it derives its name. Built as a shooting lodge for the first Earl of Lovelace in 1887, in a 58-acre estate containing formal gardens, mature trees and resident Highland cattle. Today, Daniel and Rohaise Rose-Bristow welcome guests into their home offering the best in Highland hospitality. Awarded Top 200 status in the AA and 3 Red Stars, the hotel has 18 bedrooms which are luxuriously decorated. The Victorian kitchen garden provides chef, Kevin Broome, with fresh herbs, salad and a variety of fruits and vegetables. Dinner is served from 7pm - 8.45pm where an extensive fine dining table d'hôte menu is offered. Guests may begin with white bean and barley slice, wrapped in home cured wild sea salmon with garden beetroot and Marjoram fondue followed by roast fillet and braised aromatic belly free-range Highland pork, chickpea and olive casserole, shallot mash, jus of pork. Providing a seasonal alternative, dinner is also served in the more informal Ben Damph Bar and Restaurant with rooms where alternative accommodation is available. Outdoor pursuits: archery; mountain biking; clay pigeon shooting; a huge choice of low and high level walks; boating; fishing; and the opportunity to watch otters, seals and whales.

Our inspector loved: The highly appropriate hotel legend, "where spirits soar and eagles fly."

DALHOUSIE CASTLE AND SPA

NR EDINBURGH, BONNYRIGG EH19 3JB

For over 700 years Dalhousie Castle has nestled in beautiful parkland, providing warm Scottish hospitality. There are fascinating reminders of a rich and turbulent history, such as the 2 AA Rosette Vaulted Dungeon Restaurant; a delightful setting in which to enjoy classical French and traditional Scottish "Castle Cuisine". 15 of the 27 Castle bedrooms are historically themed and include the James VI, Mary Queen of Scots, Robert the Bruce and William Wallace. The "de Ramseia" suite houses the 500-year-old "Well". There are also 7 en-suite bedrooms in the 100-year-old Lodge. Five carefully renovated function rooms provide a unique setting for conferences for up to 120 delegates, banquets and weddings for up to 100 guests. Extensive parking and a helipad are on site. Dalhousie Castle is only 7 miles from Edinburgh city centre and just 14 miles from the International Airport. The Castle has a Scottish Tourist Board 4 Star classification. The Aqueous Spa includes a hydro pool, Laconium, Ottoman and treatment rooms. The Orangery Restaurant, overlooking the South Esk River, offers contemporary Scottish/European dining. Activities including Dalhousie Castle Falconry with its own mews where guests can enjoy a private display and learn to fly Eagles, Owls, Hawks and Falcons. Clay pigeon shooting can be arranged given prior notice as well as golf at nearby courses.

Our inspector loved: The contrast between lunch in the bright, modern conservatory and dinner in the dungeon restaurant.

Directions: From Edinburgh on city by pass A7 south, through Newtongrange. Turn right at the junction onto B704, hotel is ³/₄ mile and well signposted.

Web: www.johansens.com/dalhousiecastle
E-mail: info@dalhousiecastle.co.uk
Tel: 0870 381 8472
International: +44 (0)1875 820153
Fax: 01875 821936

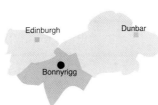

Price Guide:
single from £95
double £120–£325

KNOCKOMIE HOTEL

GRANTOWN ROAD, FORRES, MORAYSHIRE IV36 2SG

Dating back some 150 years, this elegant house owes much of its defining style to the Arts and Crafts movement, which in 1914 transformed the house into what it is today. Paying guests are recorded as early as the 1840s, although its metamorphosis into a stylish hotel is somewhat more recent! With just 15 bedrooms, the hotel has a winning combination of personal service and intimate atmosphere combined with an extremely stylish and elegant interior that ensures guests can relax from the moment they arrive and enjoy the local hospitality. This is Malt Whisky country and Knockomie has a fine collection for guests to savour, although a trip to one of the local distilleries is a must. It is a beautiful region with Loch Ness on the west and Speyside to the east. Country pursuits are plentiful including shooting, fishing and golf which can all be arranged by the hotel, whilst the less sporting can enjoy trips to nearby Brodie and Cawdor castles. At the end of such a day, guests can look forward to a relaxing drink in the comfortable surroundings of the bar, followed by a carefully prepared dinner from a menu that boasts a successful balance of traditional Scottish ingredients and lighter recipes.

Directions: Knockomie Hotel is located 1 mile south of Forres on the A940 to Grantown on Spey.

Web: www.johansens.com/knockomiehotel
E-mail: stay@knockomie.co.uk
Tel: 0870 381 8663
International: +44 (0)1309 673146
Fax: 01309 673290

Price Guide:
single £95–£130
double/twin £138–£180

Our inspector loved: The unexpected pleasure of coming across this stylish hotel nicely positioned outside the town.

GLENEAGLES

AUCHTERARDER, PERTHSHIRE PH3 1NF

Known as the "great palace in the glen" this luxurious hotel nestles in the heart of the Ochil Hills on the edge of the Highlands in the White Muir of Auchterarder. From its Georgian-style windows and lush green grounds guests can marvel at views of Ben Lomond and the Grampians. Gleneagles is enveloped by clean, crisp air and an artistic landscape capped by an ever-changing sky of blue, violet and autumnal gold. It is a haven of comfort and impeccable service. The interior has been redesigned and refurbished with 21st-century amenities, whilst offering the charm and atmosphere of a Scottish country house. The elegant public rooms are enhanced by superb antique furniture. The 257 bedrooms and 13 suites have every home-from-home comfort, in subtle, yet dramatic colours with sensual fabrics and spacious bathrooms. Many have stunning views across Gleneagles' lawns, estate and golf courses. Guests may dine in the sophisticated Strathearn and Michelin-starred Andrew Fairlie restaurants, whilst a cosy bar serves light lunches and afternoon teas. Championship golf facilities and a variety of country sports and pursuits can be enjoyed. Superb leisure facilities. Less than 50 miles from Edinburgh and Glasgow Airports.

Our inspector loved: This ever-improving star of Scottish hotels, great food options, polished service and everything to do, golf especially.

Directions: From the north, leave the A9 at the exit for the A823 and follow the sign for Gleneagles Hotel. From the south, turn off the M9/A9 at junction with the A823 signed Crieff and Gleneagles.

Web: www.johansens.com/gleneagles
E-mail: resort.sales@gleneagles.com
Tel: 0870 381 8553
International: +44 (0)1764 662231
Fax: 01764 662134

Price Guide:
double/twin £265–£465
suite £605–£1,560

THE ROYAL HOTEL

MELVILLE SQUARE, COMRIE, PERTHSHIRE PH6 2DN

Directions: Located in the centre of the village, on the A85.

Web: www.johansens.com/royalcomrie
E-mail: reception@royalhotel.co.uk
Tel: 0870 381 8875
International: +44 (0)1764 679200
Fax: 01764 679219

Price Guide:
single £70
double £110
suite £150

Set in an area of outstanding natural beauty, this former inn was once frequented by personalities such as Rob Roy McGregor and Queen Victoria, whose stay bestowed the name of The Royal Hotel on Comrie's major inn. Its homely yet luxurious and elegant atmosphere is enhanced by open log fires, period furnishings and genuine Highland hospitality provided by the cheerful staff and the Milsom family, who also own the Tufton Arms Hotel, Appleby. Each of the 11 bedrooms has been individually designed and shows exceptional attention to detail. An ideal place to unwind, the comfortable Lounge Bar is popular for pre-dinner drinks which include a choice of over 130 whiskies. Guests may enjoy Scottish cuisine and fine wines in the conservatory-style Brasserie or the more intimate Royal Restaurant, where chef David Milsom and his team, awarded an AA Rosette, create delicious dishes based on fresh local produce. The hotel is located amidst superb walking country; guests can go for gentle walks in the nearby Glens and across the hills and moorlands. The hotel has its own stretch of the river Earn for fishing, and horse riding and fowl or clay pigeon shooting can be arranged. Comrie is surrounded by excellent golf courses, which range from scenic Highland layouts to idyllic parkland settings, such as the famous Gleneagles.

Our inspector loved: *This modern inn 'Par Excellence'.*

KINNAIRD

KINNAIRD ESTATE, BY DUNKELD, PERTHSHIRE PH8 0LB

Offering a panoramic vista across the Tay valley, Kinnaird is surrounded by a beautiful estate of 9,000 acres and is ideally located for those seeking a relaxing break or enthusiasts of outdoor pursuits. Built in 1770, the Edwardian house now features 8 individually decorated bedrooms with exquisite fabrics, gas log fires and opulent bathrooms. There are also 6, 2 to 4 bedroomed guest cottages on the estate. These delightfully decorated cottages offer ultimate seclusion and feature unique touches with amazing views. Throughout the house, rare pieces of antique furniture, china and fine paintings abound. The panelled Cedar Room is the essence of comfort where guests may relax before enjoying gourmet cuisine in the restaurants, enhanced by hand-painted Italian frescoes. The hotel's 2 dining rooms serve imaginative seasonal cuisine whilst magnificent views of the surrounding Perthshire countryside can be enjoyed. The original wine cellars are stocked with an extensive range of wines, liqueurs and malt whiskies. Sporting facilities include salmon and trout fishing, bird-watching, shooting of pheasant, grouse, duck and partridge and deer stalking can be arranged. The estate also features an all-weather tennis court and croquet and bowling lawns.

Our inspector loved: The spacious luxury of the rooms and overall grand elegance with food and wine to match.

Directions: 2 miles north of Dunkeld on the A9, take B898 for 4½ miles.

Web: www.johansens.com/kinnaird
E-mail: enquiry@kinnairdestate.com
Tel: 0870 381 9124
International: +44 (0)1796 482440
Fax: 01796 482289

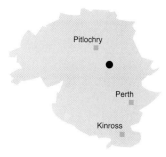

Price Guide:
double/twin £375–£525
Winter rates £325 or £275 for
2 or more nights

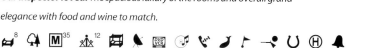

CROMLIX HOUSE

KINBUCK, BY DUNBLANE, NR STIRLING FK15 9JT

Directions: Cromlix House lies 4 miles north of Dunblane, north of Kinbuck on the B8033 and 4 miles south of Braco.

Web: www.johansens.com/cromlixhouse
E-mail: reservations@cromlixhouse.com
Tel: 0870 381 8460
International: +44 (0)1786 822125
Fax: 01786 825450

Price Guide:
single £140–£210
double/twin £220–£290
suite with private sitting room£275–£420

Set in a 2,000-acre estate in the heart of Perthshire, just off the A9, the STB 5 Star Cromlix House is a rare and relaxing retreat. Built as a family home in 1874, much of the house remains unchanged including many fine antiques acquired over the generations. Proprietors, David and Ailsa Assenti, are proud of their tradition of country house hospitality. The individually designed bedrooms and spacious suites have been redecorated with period fabrics to enhance the character and fine furniture whilst retaining the essential feeling of a much loved home. Unpretentious, restful and most welcoming, the large public rooms have open fires. In the restaurant, the finest local produce is used. Cromlix is an ideal venue for small exclusive conferences and business meetings. The private Chapel is a unique feature and perfect for weddings. Cromlix House was one of the AA top 10 hotels in Scotland 2003. Extensive sporting and leisure facilities include trout and salmon fishing and game shooting in season. There are several challenging golf courses within easy reach including Gleneagles, Rosemount, Carnoustie and St Andrews. The location is ideal for touring the Southern Highlands, with Edinburgh and Glasgow only an hour away.

Our inspector loved: *The peaceful atmosphere where it's easy to believe you are in your own luxury house.*

BALLATHIE HOUSE HOTEL

KINCLAVEN, STANLEY, PERTHSHIRE PH1 4QN

Set in an estate overlooking the River Tay near Perth, Ballathie House Hotel offers Scottish hospitality in a house of character and distinction. Dating from 1850, this mansion has a French baronial façade and handsome interiors. Overlooking lawns which slope down to the riverside, the drawing room is an ideal place to relax with coffee and the papers or to enjoy a malt whisky after dinner. The premier bedrooms are large and elegant, whilst the standard rooms are designed in a cosy, cottage style. On the ground floor there are several bedrooms suitable for guests with disabilities. Local ingredients such as Tay salmon, Scottish beef, seafood and piquant soft fruits are used by chef, Kevin MacGillivray, winner of the title Scottish Chef of the Year 1999–2000, to create menus catering for all tastes. The hotel has 2 Rosettes for fine Scottish cuisine. Activities available on the estate include salmon fishing, river walks, croquet and putting. The new Riverside Rooms are ideal for both house guests or sportsmen. The area has many good golf courses. Perth, Blairgowrie and Edinburgh are within an hour's drive. STB 4 star and AA 3 Red Stars (Top 200). Dogs are permitted in certain rooms only. 2 day breaks from £95, including dinner.

Our inspector loved: Something of the grand hotel in rural Perthshire, with polished service and classic comforts.

Directions: From the A93 at Beech Hedges, follow the signs for Kinclaven and Ballathie or take the A9 and turn right 2 miles north of Perth, at the sign for Stanley. The hotel is well signposted from this point and lies 10 miles north of Perth.

Web: www.johansens.com/ballathiehouse
E-mail: email@ballathiehousehotel.com
Tel: 0870 381 8337
International: +44 (0)1250 883268
Fax: 01250 883396

Price Guide:
single £79–£110
double/twin £158–£220
suite £228–£250

EDNAM HOUSE HOTEL

BRIDGE STREET, KELSO, ROXBURGHSHIRE TD5 7HT

Overlooking the River Tweed, in 3 acres of gardens, Ednam House is one of the region's finest examples of Georgian architecture. This undulating, pastoral countryside was immortalised by Sir Walter Scott. Ednam House has been owned and managed by the Brooks family for over 70 years, spanning 4 generations. Although the grandiose splendour may seem formal, the warm, easy-going atmosphere is all-pervasive. The lounges and bars are comfortably furnished and command scenic views of the river and grounds. All 32 bedrooms are en suite, individually decorated and well-equipped. In the elegant dining room which overlooks the river, a blend of traditional and creative Scottish cuisine, using fresh local produce, is served. The wine list is very interesting and reasonably priced. Ednam House is extremely popular with fishermen, the Borders being renowned for its salmon and trout. Other field sports such as stalking, hunting and shooting can be arranged as can riding, golfing and cycling. Local landmarks include the abbeys of Kelso, Melrose, Jedburgh and Dryburgh. The hotel is closed Christmas and New Year.

Directions: From the south, reach Kelso via A698; from the north, via A68. The hotel is just off the market square by the river.

Web: www.johansens.com/ednamhouse
E-mail: contact@ednamhouse.com
Tel: 0870 381 8500
International: +44 (0)1573 224168
Fax: 01573 226319

Price Guide:
single from £67
double/twin £89–£124

Our inspector loved: The beautiful views from the hotel out to the River Tweed on one side and the short walk into the bustling market town.

THE ROXBURGHE HOTEL & GOLF COURSE

KELSO, ROXBURGHSHIRE TD5 8JZ

Converted by its owners, the Duke and Duchess of Roxburghe, into a luxury hotel of character and charm, The Roxburghe is situated in over 200 acres of rolling grounds on the bank of the River Teviot. There are 22 bedrooms, including four-poster rooms and suites, and like the spacious reception rooms, they are furnished with care and elegance. The menu, which is changed daily, reflects the hotel's position at the source of some of Britain's finest fish, meat and game – salmon and trout from the waters of the Tweed, or grouse, pheasant and venison from the Roxburghe estate – complemented with wines from the Duke's own cellar. Fine whiskies are served in the Library Bar, with its log fire and leather-bound tomes. The Beauty Clinic brings to guests the régimes of Decleor, Paris. Surrounding the hotel is the magnificent Roxburghe Golf Course, designed by Dave Thomas. This parkland course, host to Charles Church Scottish seniors Open is the only championship golf course in the Scottish Borders. A full sporting programme can be arranged, including fly and coarse fishing, and falconry. The shooting school offers tuition in game and clay shooting. 7 great country houses are within easy reach including Floors Castle, the home of the Duke and Duchess of Roxburghe, guests receive complimentary access from April to October.

Directions: The hotel is at Heiton, just off the A698 Kelso–Jedburgh road.

Web: www.johansens.com/roxburghekelso
E-mail: hotel@roxburghe.net
Tel: 0870 381 8873
International: +44 (0)1573 450331
Fax: 01573 450611

Price Guide:
single £110-£145
double/twin £145-£185
four-poster £205-£230
suite £235-£280

Our inspector loved: A championship golf course on the doorstep.

CRINGLETIE HOUSE

EDINBURGH ROAD, PEEBLES EH45 8PL

Directions: Take the A703 from Edinburgh to Peebles. The hotel is on the right approximately 2 miles south of Eddleston village

Web: www.johansens.com/cringletiehouse
E-mail: enquiries@cringletie.com
Tel: 0870 381 9279
International: +44 (0)1721 725750
Fax: 01721 725751

Price Guide:
single £95-£120
double/twin £115–£240

A distinguished baronial mansion set within 28 acres of manicured gardens and lush woodland, Cringletie House is the epitome of style and fine country living. Elegant turrets combine with the traditional red Borders' sandstone to capture the quiet dignity of a bygone era. All of the beautifully appointed bedrooms have been individually decorated and boast breathtaking views over the surrounding Peeblesshire countryside. The splendid panelled dining room has an impressive carved oak and marble fireplace, many original artworks and an eye catching hand painted ceiling depicting a heavenly classical scene. Highly acclaimed cuisine is created with flair and imagination with menus designed around the fruits and vegetables available in Scotland's only 17th-century walled kitchen garden. Specialities include deliciously prepared fresh game and fish. Guests can play tennis, attempt the 9-hole putting green, play lawn croquet or simply stroll around the manicured lawns and lush woodlands surrounding the hotel. Fishing is available on the River Tweed and for golf lovers there is an excellent golf course in Peebles. Other activities such as archery, shooting, quad biking and hot air ballooning can be arranged. Cringletie is a good base from which to explore the rich historical and cultural heritage of the Borders and is only 30 minutes from Edinburgh.

Our inspector loved: The attention to detail shown by the new owners.

CASTLE VENLAW

EDINBURGH ROAD, PEEBLES EH45 8QG

Just 40 minutes from the city of Edinburgh, yet within the peaceful Borders countryside, the Castle sits majestically on the slopes of Venlaw Hill overlooking the royal and ancient town of Peebles. Originally built as a private house in 1782, it was bought by John and Shirley Sloggie in 1997. Now recognised as one of the leading 4-star hotels in the area, Castle Venlaw keeps the country house tradition alive and offers an air of elegance and relaxed informality. From the welcoming Library with its oak panelling and log fire to the 12 bedrooms – all named after Scotland's finest malt whiskies – great care has been taken to preserve the castle's charm and character. Guests can choose from a range of suites and, at the top of the tower, a family suite comes complete with children's den. The spacious and airy 2 AA Rosette restaurant provides the perfect ambience in which to enjoy menus where delicious local produce such as Borders salmon, lamb and game are given an international flavour. Outside, acres of beautiful woodland grounds can be explored, golf or fishing enjoyed and the history in the ruined Abbeys and historic houses can be appreciated. Edinburgh, Glasgow and Stirling are within easy reach. Short breaks, including dinner, are available throughout the year starting from £70.

Our inspector loved: The exceptionally large rooms, the peace and quiet and the proximity to Edinburgh.

Directions: From Edinburgh, follow the A703 to Peebles. After 30mph sign, the hotel drive is signposted on the left. From Peebles follow the A703 to Edinburgh the Hotel is on the right after .75 mile.

Web: www.johansens.com/venlaw
E-mail: enquiries@venlaw.co.uk
Tel: 0870 381 8410
International: +44 (0)1721 720384
Fax: 01721 724066

Price Guide:
single £70–£95
double/twin £140–£200

NEW

DRYBURGH ABBEY HOTEL

ST BOSWELLS, MELROSE, SCOTTISH BORDERS TD6 0RQ

Directions: Take the A68 from Edinburgh to St Boswells then turn onto the B6404. Continue on this road for two miles then turn left onto the B6356 signposted Scott's view and Earlston. The hotel entrance is approximately 2 miles further on this road.

Web: www.johansens.com/dryburghabbey
E-mail: enquiries@dryburgh.co.uk
Tel: 0870 381 9311
International: +44 (0)1835 822261
Fax: 01835 823945

Price Guide:
single £63.50–£103.50
double/twin £60–£80

This is quintessential Scotland with its russet and yellow moorlands, cool green pastures, rivers running with princely salmon, darting trout and hillsides speckled with sheep whose wool is used to produce the world famous Borderlands tweed. Dryburgh Abbey Hotel stands in the heart of this glorious, Sir Walter Scott countryside just 5 miles south east of the small historic town of Melrose, which nestles in the shelter of the 3 peaks of lovely Eildon Hills. Beautifully restored, this delightful old country house is superbly located on the banks of the River Tweed next to the ruins of the 12th-century abbey from which it takes its name, home to the tombs of the novelist Sir Walter Scott and Field Marshal Earl Haig, the British Army's Commander-in-Chief during World War I. Solid and traditional on the outside, the interior of the hotel is grand and opulent with all the luxuries and modern comforts expected from a leading leisure and business residence. Bedrooms are elegantly furnished and decorated, well equipped and proffer superb views. 2 lounges offer peaceful relaxation and guests can choose to dine in style in the tranquil setting of the Tweed Restaurant overlooking the river, alternatively there is the bistro-style ambience of the Courtyard Bar. Indoor swimming pool, shooting and fishing by arrangement.

Our inspector loved: *The great backdrop of the abbey ruins and River Tweed.*

ENTERKINE COUNTRY HOUSE

ANNBANK, BY AYR, AYRSHIRE KA6 5AL

A winding tree-lined avenue leads to this elegant 1930s country house, which is an ideal base for leisure and sporting holidaymakers, and has won numerous awards including a Scottish Tourist Board 5 Star Rating, 3 RAC Dining Awards and 2 AA Rosettes. Built originally as a private residence, Enterkine is situated near the village of Annbank, 5 miles east of Ayr, and surrounded by 310 acres of woodland and meadows that are a mecca for those who like walking and countryside peace and quiet. Delightful soft furnishings and tasteful colour coordination grace the hotel's interior and create a warm and welcoming ambience. Privacy is a priority and the staff place emphasis on individual service and comfort. The 6 bedroom suites have luxurious bathrooms, are spacious, light and stunningly decorated. An oval-shaped library with open fire offers the perfect venue for relaxation whilst the restaurant provides first-class cuisine incorporating the best Scottish ingredients. There are 7 championship golf courses within a 30-minute drive, ranging from the famous links of Turnberry and Royal Troon to Western Gailes and Prestwick, and arrangements can be made for guests to play them. Also within easy reach is some of the finest fishing and game shooting in Scotland, which visitors can enjoy on inclusive outings.

Our inspector loved: The lovely setting and absolute attention to detail.

Directions: From the A77 take A70 to Edinburgh, turn left onto B744 through Annbank turn right after Annbank towards Coylton. The Hotel is on the left.

Web: www.johansens.com/enterkine
E-mail: mail@enterkine.com
Tel: 0870 381 8505
International: +44 (0)1292 520580
Fax: 01292 521582

Price Guide: (including dinner)
single £110
double/twin £220

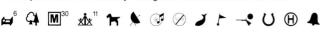

BUCHANAN ARMS HOTEL & LEISURE CLUB

DRYMEN, STIRLINGSHIRE G63 0BQ

Directions: From Glasgow (17 miles) follow signs to Aberfoyle on the A81. At Bearsden Cross roundabout take the A809 to Drymen.

Web: www.johansens.com/buchananarms
E-mail: enquiries@buchananarms.co.uk
Tel: 0870 381 9301
International: +44 (0)1360 660588
Fax: 01360 660943

Price Guide:
single £100
double £160

With its warm welcome, attractive décor, comfortable furnishings and superb setting this is a haven of relaxation that attracts guests time and time again. Built and opened in 1752 as a droving inn this sparkling white-fronted hotel, highlighted by attractive roof peaks and a large half-moon shaped roadside window, stands in the heart of a picturesque conservation village between the vibrant city of Glasgow and historic town of Stirling, just about 3 miles from the scenic beauty of the eastern edge of Loch Lomond. It is the perfect location for touring city, town and countryside and within easy reach are Balloch Castle, Glengoyne Distillery and the magnificent Trossachs. The Buchanan Arms Hotel has been sympathetically and skillfully restored to provide a comfortable, timeless grace that exudes a blend of character and charm combined with 21st-century facilities. Each of the 52 guest rooms are individually designed, delightfully decorated and offer the highest standard of amenities and thoughtful little comforts. True Scottish hospitality is the philosophy of the hotel's attentive staff, particularly in the Tapestries Restaurant where courteous service presents creatively prepared dishes featuring the freshest of local produce. Leisure facilities include a swimming pool, sauna, spa, gymnasium, squash courts and health and beauty suite.

Our inspector loved: *The great location for Loch Lomond and Trossachs.*

Tanqueray ®

The International Mark of Excellence

For further information, current news,
e-club membership, hotel search, Preferred Partners,
online bookshop and special offers visit:

www.johansens.com

For further information on Wales, please contact:

Wales Tourist Board
Brunel House, 2 Fitzalan Road, Cardiff CF24 0UY
Tel: +44 (0)29 2049 9909
Web: www.visitwales.com

North Wales Tourism
Tel: +44 (0)1492 531731
Web: www.nwt.co.uk

Mid Wales Tourism
Tel: (Freephone) 0800 273747
Web: www.visitmidwales.co.uk

South West Wales Tourism Partnership
Tel: +44 (0)1558 669091
Web: www.swwtp.co.uk

or see pages 412-414 for details of
local attractions to visit during your stay.

Images from www.britainonview.com

LLECHWEN HALL

LLANFABON, NR ABERCYNON, CARDIFF, MID GLAMORGAN CF37 4HP

Visitors step back in time when they enter this lovely 17th-century Welsh Long-House with its Victorian frontage standing in 6 acres of mature gardens on the hillside overlooking the Aberdare and Merthyr valleys. There are 4-foot thick walls with narrow embrasures, low ceilings, stout-blackened oak beams, huge fireplaces and stone-roofed outbuildings. Careful restoration and sympathetic refurbishment over the years, since being purchased as a near derelict building in 1988, has created a 3-star country house hotel with an award-winning restaurant. The 20 superbly appointed bedrooms are individually decorated and furnished to provide a truly comfortable environment. Guests have a choice of restaurants for memorable dining. Outstanding, freshly prepared cusine, with seasonal changes to the menu, is served either in the intimate atmosphere of the oak-beamed restaurant in part of the original Welsh Long-House or in the light and airy Victorian dining room with its stunning views across the valleys. Pre and after-dinner drinks can be enjoyed in an elegant cocktail lounge. The hotel is just a 20 minute drive from Cardiff and 15 minutes from the foothills of the Brecon Beacons.

Directions: Exit the M4 at junction 32 and follow the A470 towards Merthyr Tydfil for approximately 11 miles. Join the A472 towards Nelson and then the A4054 towards Cilfynydd. The hotel is on the left after ½ mile.

Web: www.johansens.com/Llechwenhall
E-mail: llechwen@aol.com
Tel: 0870 381 8698
International: +44 (0)1443 742050
Fax: 01443 742189

Price Guide:
single £54.50–£65.50
double/twin £75–£106

Our inspector loved: The spacious and well appointed bedrooms and spectacular setting in 6 acres of wooded gardens.

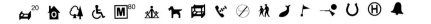

388

BODYSGALLEN HALL & SPA

LLANDUDNO, NORTH WALES LL30 1RS

Nestling in 200 acres of magnificent parkland to the south of Llandudno and west of Pydew Mountain, Grade I listed Bodysgallen Hall & Spa exudes a mixture of history, great comfort and sophistication. With spectacular views of Snowdonia and Conwy Castle it provides all that is best in country house hospitality and expectations. Bodysgallen has grown and developed from a 13th-century fortified tower into one of the grandest family houses in Wales and is now a superb, charismatic hotel. Large, beautiful gardens include a 17th-century parterre of box hedges filled with scented herbs, a rockery with cascade, a superbly restored formal walled rose garden and several follies. Within these beautiful grounds is a cluster of 16 self-contained cottages, for guests requiring total privacy. The 19 comfortable bedrooms inside the house, are individually and stylishly furnished and are non-smoking. All guest accommodation has the latest facilities, with selected Sky TV channels in most of the rooms and some have air conditioning. The antique furnished entrance hall and first-floor drawing rooms, with large fireplaces and splendid oak panelling, are particularly appealing, as are the 2 dining rooms where award-winning head chef John Williams serves imaginative cuisine. A short walk through the garden takes guest to the fully equipped spa and indoor swimming pool.

Our inspector loved: This wonderful historic gem; such charm.

Directions: On the A470, 1 mile from the intersection with the A55. Llandudno is a mile further on the A470.

Web: www.johansens.com/bodysgallenhall
E-mail: info@bodysgallen.com
Tel: 0870 381 8372
International: +44 (0)1492 584466
Fax: 01492 582519

Price Guide:
single £120–£185
double/twin £165–£300
suite £195–£320

389

St Tudno Hotel & Restaurant

NORTH PROMENADE, LLANDUDNO LL30 2LP

Directions: On the promenade opposite the pier entrance and gardens. Car parking and garaging is available for up to 12 cars.

Web: www.johansens.com/sttudno
E-mail: sttudnohotel@btinternet.com
Tel: 0870 381 8907
International: +44 (0)1492 874411
Fax: 01492 860407

Llandudno

Chester

Betws-y-Coed

Price Guide:
single from £70
double/twin £90–£200
suite from £260

Without doubt one of the most delightful small hotels to be found on the coast of Britain, St. Tudno Hotel, a former winner of the Johansens Hotel of the Year Award for Excellence, certainly offers a very special experience. The hotel has been elegantly and lovingly furnished with meticulous attention to detail, and offers a particularly warm welcome from owners, Janette and Martin Bland now in their 33rd year. Each beautifully co-ordinated bedroom has been individually designed with many thoughtful extras, half are equipped with spa baths. The bar lounge and sitting room, which overlook the sea, have an air of Victorian charm. Regarded as one of Wales' leading restaurants, the air-conditioned Terrace Restaurant has won 3 AA Rosettes for its excellent cuisine for the 11th consecutive year. This AA Red Star Hotel has won a host of other prestigious awards: Best Seaside Resort Hotel in Great Britain (Good Hotel guide); Welsh Hotel of the Year; Runner up for Johansens Tattinger Wine List Award 2004; the AA's Wine Award for Wales 2004 and even an accolade for having the Best Hotel Loos in Britain! St Tudno is ideally situated for visits to Snowdonia, Conwy and Caernarfon Castles, delightful walks on the Great Orme, Bodnant Gardens and Anglesey. Golf, riding, swimming, dry-slope skiing and tobogganing can all be enjoyed locally.

Our inspector loved: The recently decorated restaurant- delicious dining and superb wines.

WILD PHEASANT HOTEL

BERWYN ROAD, LLANGOLLEN, DENBIGHSHIRE LL20 8AD

Set within beautiful countryside overlooking the Vale of Llangollen, the Berwyn Mountains and Castell Dinas Bran, this new hotel is a haven of tranquillity, yet easily accessible from the A5. The original building, dating back to the 19th century, has been sympathetically renovated and extended to provide a luxurious hotel, which retains its former country house charm whilst offering all modern amenities and an eclectic blend of contemporary and traditional design. The bedrooms and suites in the extension are spacious and tastefully furnished, and the more traditional bedrooms in the old part have been updated and are small but extremely comfortable. The Penthouse Suite is simply superb and boasts a hot tub on the balcony. Excellent dining options include the Cinnamon Restaurant, which has been awarded 1 Rosette for its daily changing menus based on fresh local produce. The more informal Bistro Bar is ideal for light meals and drinks. Guests can completely unwind and relax in the hotel's Spa of Tranquillity, which offers a wide range of pampering health and beauty treatments. The Wild Pheasant is the ideal location for weddings, with the Glanafon Suite accommodating 120 guests in comfort and style. Comprehensive meeting and conference facilities, awarded Gold standard by the Welsh Tourist Board, are also available.

Our inspector loved: The tremendous range of bedrooms, and the spa- a very relaxing facility.

Directions: From the north: M6, then take M56 to Chester, then follow A483 past Wrexham and take A5 to Langollen. From south: M6, then take M54 past Shrewsbury, onto A5 to Langollen.

Rhyl

Denbigh

Llangollen

Web: www.johansens.com/wildpheasant
E-mail: wild.pheasant@talk21.com
Tel: 0870 381 8633
International: +44 (0)1978 860629
Fax: 01978 861837

Price Guide:
single £70–£85
double/twin £104–£130
suite £190–£230

 SPA

PALÉ HALL

PALÉ ESTATE, LLANDDERFEL, BALA, GWYNEDD LL23 7PS

Directions: Situated off the B4401 Corwen to Bala Road, Palé Hall is 4 miles from Llandrillo.

Web: www.johansens.com/palehall
E-mail: enquiries@palehall.co.uk
Tel: 0870 381 8799
International: +44 (0)1678 530285
Fax: 01678 530220

Price Guide:
single £80–£140
double/twin £105–£200

Set in acres of peaceful, tranquil woodland on the edge of Snowdonia National Park, Palé Hall is a magnificent building, beautifully preserved by its current owners, and gives guests the opportunity to sample true country house lifestyle. Shooting parties are a regular occurrence on the surrounding estates, whilst clay shooting can be arranged, fishing on the Dee is available on site. A venture with Land Rover Experience also enables guests to experience off road driving in their preferred choice of 4-wheel drive, whilst the less adventurous can walk for miles on the beautiful Palé estate. The staff at Palé Hall carefully maintain the beautiful period interior of the building including the galleried staircase and painted ceilings, which have survived largely due to the house's unusual electricity system. Supplied by a turbine powered by water, the Palé's 18 electric fires were left burning during 22 years of unoccupancy! Queen Victoria and Winston Churchill have stayed at the Hall. The 17 individually designed suites with luxurious bathrooms have breathtaking views of the surrounding scenery. The restaurant has 2 AA Rosettes and serves seasonal table d'hôte menus complemented by a fine wine selection. Exclusive use is available for conferences, product launches and weddings.

Our inspector loved: *The wonderful new bathrooms, in this delightful rural estate. So relaxing.*

PENMAENUCHAF HALL

PENMAENPOOL, DOLGELLAU, GWYNEDD LL40 1YB

Climbing the long tree lined driveway you arrive at Penmaenuchaf Hall to behold its idyllic setting. With stunning panoramic views across the spectacular Mawddach Estuary and wooded mountain slopes in the distance, this handsome Victorian mansion is truly an exceptional retreat. Set within the Snowdonia National Park, the 21-acre grounds encompass lawns, a formal sunken rose garden, a water garden and woodland. The beautiful interiors feature oak and mahogany panelling, stained-glass windows, log fires in winter, polished Welsh slate floors and freshly cut flowers. There are 12 luxurious bedrooms, some with four-poster and half-tester beds and all with interesting views. In the restaurant guests can choose from an imaginative menu prepared with the best seasonal produce and complemented by an extensive list of wines. An elegant panelled dining room can be used for private dinners or meetings. Penmaenuchaf Hall is perfect for a totally relaxed holiday. For recreation, guests can fish for trout and salmon along 10miles of the Mawddach River or take part in a range of water sports. They can also enjoy scenic walks, visit sandy beaches and historic castles and take trips on narrow-gauge railways. Special offers for early booking are available.

Our inspector loved: *The tranquillity and loving care given to this delightful hotel.*

Directions: The hotel is off the A493 Dolgellau–Tywyn road, about 2 miles from Dolgellau.

Web: www.johansens.com/penmaenuchafhall
E-mail: relax@penhall.co.uk
Tel: 0870 381 8813
International: +44 (0)1341 422129
Fax: 01341 422787

Price Guide:
single £75–£135
double/twin £120–£180

393

HOTEL MAES-Y-NEUADD

TALSARNAU, NEAR HARLECH, GWYNEDD LL47 6YA

Directions: Hotel is 3½ miles north of Harlech, off the B4573, signposted at the end of the lane.

Web: www.johansens.com/maesyneuadd
E-mail: maes@neuadd.com
Tel: 0870 381 9332
International: +44 (0)1766 780200
Fax: 01766 780211

Price Guide: (including dinner)
single £80
double/twin £159–£230

Bangor

Pwllheli

Dolgellau

Set amidst spectacular scenery, with views across Snowdonia National Park, this 14th-century Welsh manor house has won many awards including AA Red Stars and an RAC Gold Ribbon in 1999 and 2000. Owned and managed by the Jackson and Payne families, this welcoming country house has been sympathetically restored to provide comfort and luxury. Furnished and equipped to a very high standard, the 16 individually designed bedrooms reflect the various periods during which the house was built. Features include dormer windows, high-ceilinged Georgian rooms, 16th-century beams and even two 14th-century rooms. The sunlit conservatory is perfect for enjoying morning coffee or afternoon tea, whilst the terrace offers the magnificent spectacle of the sun setting over the Lleyn Peninsula. Delicious regional dishes, awarded 2 Rosettes, are served in the elegant restaurant, where chef patron Peter Jackson uses the succulent fresh produce for which Wales is renowned. The hotel's 2 walled kitchen gardens are currently being restored and provide the kitchens with salads, vegetables, herbs and fruit. The perfect venue for small meetings and exclusive use, the grounds provide a wonderful backdrop for weddings. Explore numerous tourist attractions nearby such as the North Wales coast, Portmeirion and the Ffestiniog Railway.

Our inspector loved: *The most wonderful kitchen garden.*

THE TREARDDUR BAY HOTEL

LON ISALLT, TREARDDUR BAY, ANGLESEY LL65 2UN

For both business traveller and holidaymaker, here is one of the most delightful retreats to be found on the Anglesey coast. The comfortable and welcoming Trearddur Bay Hotel, the 1st independent hotel in Wales to be awarded Hospitality Assured, is situated opposite a "Blue Flag Beach" and enjoys panoramic views across the sandy bay. This prime location is conveniently just 1¾ miles from the fully completed A55 North Wales Expressway, which makes the hotel a comfortable drive from the Midlands, Yorkshire and the North West. Guests have the choice of a variety of sporting and leisure facilities from kayaking, diving and sailing to bird watching, walking and golf. Close by are places of historical interest such as a medieval chapel, Beaumaris Castle and a Celtic burial mound. For a day out with a difference, take the 99-minute fast ferry service to Ireland from the nearby port of Holyhead. Inside the hotel's sparkling white exterior are spacious en-suite bedrooms, with first-class furnishings and facilities. All of the 16 charming studio suites have sea views and many boast their own private balconies. Morning coffee and afternoon tea are served in a relaxing lounge, whilst aperitifs can be enjoyed in an elegant cocktail bar as a prelude to sampling culinary delights from the restaurant's extensive table d'hôte menu. A heated indoor swimming pool is a popular alternative to the Irish Sea.

Our inspector loved: The 6 new rooms in Tower House.

Directions: From Bangor, when the A55 Expressway terminates at Holyhead, at the 1st roundabout turn left onto the B4545, signposted Trearddur. Continue for 1.7 miles. Turn right at the Power Garage onto Lon Isallt. The hotel is 350 yards on the right.

Web: www.johansens.com/trearddurbay
E-mail: enquiries@trearddurbayhotel.co.uk
Tel: 0870 381 8949
International: +44 (0)1407 860301
Fax: 01407 861181

Price Guide:
single £85–£105
double/twin £124–£150

LLANSANTFFRAED COURT HOTEL

LLANVIHANGEL GOBION, ABERGAVENNY, MONMOUTHSHIRE NP7 9BA

Directions: From M4 J24 (Via A449) off B4598 (formerly A40 old road) Leave A40 D/C at Abergavenny or Raglan. Follow signs to Clytha and the hotel is approx 4½ miles away.

Web: www.johansens.com/llansantffraedcourt
E-mail: reception@llch.co.uk
Tel: 0870 381 8697
International: +44 (0)1873 840678
Fax: 01873 840674

Price Guide:
single from £86
double/twin from £106
suites £140

Llansantffraed Court is a perfect retreat from the fast pace of modern life. This elegant Georgian-style country house hotel, part of which dates back to the 14th century, is set in spacious grounds on the edge of the Brecon Beacons and the Wye Valley. Guests are provided with the highest level of personal, yet unobtrusive service. Most of the tastefully decorated and luxuriously furnished bedrooms offer views over the hotel's gardens and ornamental trout lake. While one has a four-poster bed, others feature oak beams and dormer windows. An excellent reputation is enjoyed by the 2 AA Rosette restaurant; the menus reflect the changing seasons and the availability of fresh local produce. Exquisite cuisine is complemented by fine wines. Afternoon tea can be taken in the lounge, where guests enjoy a blazing log fire during the cooler months and savour the views of the South Wales countryside. A range of excellent facilities is available for functions, celebrations and meetings. Llansantffraed Court is an ideal base for exploring the diverse history and beauty of this area and there are plenty of opportunities to take advantage of energetic or relaxing pursuits, including golf, trekking, walking, and salmon and trout fishing.

Our inspector loved: *This elegant Georgian hotel surrounded by rolling parkland as far as the eye can see.*

ALLT-YR-YNYS HOTEL

WALTERSTONE, NR ABERGAVENNY, HR2 0DU

Nestling in the foothills of the Black Mountains, on the fringes of the Brecon Beacons National park, Allt-yr-Ynys is an impressive Grade II 16th-century manor house hotel. The Manor was the home of the Cecil family whose ancestry dates back to Rhodri Mawr, King of Wales in the 8th century. A more recent Cecil was Lord Burleigh, Chief Minister to Queen Elizabeth I, portrayed by Sir Richard Attenborough in the recent film, "Elizabeth". Features of this interesting past still remain and include moulded ceilings, oak panelling and beams and a 16th-century four-poster bed in the Jacobean suite. However, whilst the charm and the character of the period remains, the house has been sympathetically adapted to provide all the comforts expected of a modern hotel. The former outbuildings have been transformed into spacious and well-appointed guest bedrooms. Fine dining is offered in the award-winning restaurant and the conference/function suite accommodates up to 200 guests. Facilities include a heated pool, Jacuzzi, clay pigeon shooting range and private river fishing. Pastimes include exploring the scenery, historic properties and plethora of tourist attractions.

Our inspector loved: *The spacious individually decorated bedrooms, all with glorious secluded views of the countryside.*

Directions: 5 miles north of Abergavenny on A465 Abergavenny/ Hereford trunk road, turn west at Old Pandy Inn in Pandy. After 400 metres turn right down lane at grey/green barn. The hotel is on the right after 400 metres.

Web: www.johansens.com/alltyrynys
E-mail: reception@allthotel.co.uk
Tel: 0870 381 8309
International: +44 (0)1873 890307
Fax: 01873 890539

Price Guide: (per room)
single from £75
double/twin from £110
suite from £150

WARPOOL COURT HOTEL

ST DAVID'S, PEMBROKESHIRE SA62 6BN

Directions: The hotel is signposted from St David's town centre.

Web: www.johansens.com/warpoolcourt
E-mail: warpool@enterprise.net
Tel: 0870 381 8968
International: +44 (0)1437 720300
Fax: 01437 720676

Price Guide:
single £80–£110
double/twin £135–£200

Originally built as St David's Cathedral Choir School in the 1860s, Warpool Court enjoys spectacular scenery at the heart of the Pembrokeshire National Park, with views over the coast and St Bride's Bay to the islands beyond. First converted to a hotel over 40 years ago, continuous refurbishment has ensured all its up-to-date comforts are fit for the new century. All 25 bedrooms have immaculate en-suite facilities of which 14 enjoy sea views. The 2 AA Rosette restaurant enjoys a splendid reputation. Imaginative menus, including vegetarian, offer a wide selection of modern and traditional dishes. Local produce, including Welsh lamb and beef, is used whenever possible, with crab, lobster, sewin and sea bass caught just off the coast. Salmon and mackerel are smoked on the premises. The hotel gardens are ideal for a peaceful stroll or an after-dinner drink in the summer. There is a covered heated swimming pool (open April to the end of October) and an all-weather tennis court in the grounds. A path from the hotel leads straight on to the Pembrokeshire Coastal Path, with its rich variety of wildlife and spectacular scenery. Boating and water sports are available locally. St David's Peninsula offers a wealth of history and natural beauty and has inspired many famous artists. Closed in January.

Our inspector loved: *The spectacular views of the coast from the dining room complementing the superb 2 Rosette cuisine.*

PENALLY ABBEY

PENALLY, TENBY, PEMBROKESHIRE SA70 7PY

Penally Abbey, a beautiful listed Pembrokeshire country house, offers comfort and hospitality in a secluded setting by the sea. Standing in 5 acres of gardens and woodland on the edge of Pembrokeshire National Park, the hotel overlooks Carmarthen Bay and Caldey Island. The bedrooms in the main building and in the adjoining coach house are well furnished, many with four-poster beds. The emphasis is on relaxation – enjoy a late breakfast and dine at leisure. Fresh seasonal delicacies are offered in the candlelit restaurant, with its chandeliers and colonnades. Guests can enjoy a game in the snooker room or relax in the elegant sunlit lounge, overlooking the terrace and gardens. In the grounds there is a wishing well and a ruined chapel – the last surviving link with the hotel's monastic past. Water skiing, surfing, sailing, riding and parascending are available nearby. Sandy bays and rugged cliffs are features of the Pembrokeshire coastal park.

Our inspector loved: *The romantic location and ambience of the hotel full of personal touches.*

Directions: Penally Abbey is situated adjacent to the church on Penally village green.

Web: www.johansens.com/penallyabbey
E-mail: penally.abbey@btinternet.com
Tel: 0870 381 8810
International: +44 (0)1834 843033
Fax: 01834 844714

Price Guide:
single £134
double/twin £126–£150
suite £150

LAMPHEY COURT HOTEL

LAMPHEY, NR TENBY, PEMBROKESHIRE SA71 5NT

Directions: From M4, exit at Junction 49 onto the A40 to Carmarthen. Then follow the A477 and turn left at Milton Village for Lamphey.

Web: www.johansens.com/courtpembroke
E-mail: info@lampheycourt.co.uk
Tel: 0870 381 8675
International: +44 (0)1646 672273
Fax: 01646 672480

Price Guide:
single £78–£90
double/twin £110–£150

Idyllically located for enjoying spectacular coastal walks and the pretty resorts of Tenby and Saundersfoot, Lamphey Court Hotel is a welcoming country house with excellent facilities. The well-proportioned, richly decorated public rooms are in-keeping with the era when the house was built. The attractive bedrooms offer an extremely high standard of comfort; family suites are located in a former coach house with generously sized rooms and extra space for families. The formal, candlelit Georgian restaurant offers a dinner menu featuring locally caught fish such as Teifi salmon and freshwater Bay lobster. The light and airy Conservatory Restaurant provides a more informal alternative for lunch and lighter meals. Guests may take advantage of the hotel's modern leisure spa, with its large indoor swimming pool overlooking the gardens and floodlit tennis courts, spa pool, saunas and a gymnasium. Skilled therapists provide a range of treatments. The Pembrokeshire National Park offers an unprecedented choice of activities closeby including golf, sailing, fishing and cycling. Alternatively, visit the medieval Bishop's Palace located within the hotel grounds.

Our inspector loved: *The extensive leisure centre offering an indoor swimming pool, well equipped gymnasium, hairdresser, sauna and solarium.*

POWYS - BRECON (LLYSWEN)

LLANGOED HALL

LLYSWEN, BRECON, POWYS, WALES LD3 0YP

Llangoed Hall dates back to 560 AD when it is thought to have been the site of the first Welsh Parliament. Inspired by this legend, the architect, Sir Clough Williams-Ellis transformed the Jacobean mansion he found here in 1914 into an Edwardian country house. Situated deep in the Wye valley, surrounded by a walled garden, the hotel commands magnificent views of the Black Mountains and Brecon Beacons. Its welcoming rooms are furnished with antiques, Oriental rugs on the walls and an outstanding collection of paintings acquired by the owner, Sir Bernard Ashley, whilst the bedrooms are spacious and luxurious. The restaurant, with new chef, Sean Ballington, using only the finest local produce to create imaginative dishes, matched by a wine list of over 100 Old and New World wines. Two delightful rooms can accommodate up to 200 guests for weddings or conferences. Outdoor pursuits include golf, riding, shooting, mountain walking and gliding, and for expeditions, there is Hay-on-Wye and the castles of Hereford and Leominster. Based in the grounds are the Elanbach Shop, Studio and Print-works of Sir Bernard Ashley's fabric company, founded in 2000. The team at Elanbach has a broad experience in the textile industry and offer their own designs, as well as a bespoke service for their customers to create, colour and print their own designs.

Our inspector loved: One really does imagine being back in time - faded elegance and quite delightful.

Directions: 9 miles west of Hay, 11 miles north of Brecon on A470. Bristol and Cardiff Airports just under an hour away.

Welshpool
Llandrindod Wells
Brecon
Abergavenny

Web: www.johansens.com/llangoedhall
E-mail: enquiries@llangoedhall.com
Tel: 0870 381 8696
International: +44 (0)1874 754525
Fax: 01874 754545

Price Guide:
single from £140
double/twin from £180
suite from £340

GLIFFAES COUNTRY HOUSE HOTEL

CRICKHOWELL, POWYS NP8 1RH

Directions: Gliffaes is signposted from the A40, 21/2 miles west of Crickhowell.

Web: www.johansens.com/gliffaescountryhouse
E-mail: calls@gliffaeshotel.com
Tel: 0870 381 8557
International: +44 (0)1874 730371
Fax: 01874 730463

Price Guide:
single from £57–£77.50
double/twin £119–£170

Welshpool

Llandrindod Wells

Brecon

Abergavenny

This elegant Italianate building is set in an idyllic location 150ft above the River Usk, and is home to some of the most prolific salmon and trout fishing. The fisheries at the hotel can offer both slow flowing and fast, rapid water and is a fisherman's dream. The hotel itself is a stunning piece of architecture and commands glorious views over the surrounding countryside. There are 4 clock faces on each side of the Gliffaes tower, which symbolise the timeless nature of the hotel, and there is a real atmosphere of gentle tranquillity. The elegant panelled sitting room is an excellent place to unwind in the winter months, whilst in summer the terrace is a wonderful spot from which to enjoy a first-class afternoon tea. The dining room serves an imaginative menu that cleverly combines some traditional Welsh favourites with contemporary Mediterranean specialities, accompanied by an extensive wine list. The hotel grounds comprise 33 acres with some rare trees and shrubs as well as well-tended croquet lawn. There are 2 golf courses within easy reach and riding can be arranged at a nearby riding school.

Our inspector loved: *Its total timelessness - a country hotel at its best.*

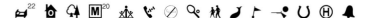

LAKE VYRNWY HOTEL

LAKE VYRNWY, LLANWDDYN, MONTGOMERYSHIRE SY10 0LY

A stunning location and relaxing environment are the hallmark of this impressive Victorian country house hotel, which has been maintained since 1890 as a peaceful retreat for lovers of nature and fine dining. Standing majestically on the hillside of the Berwyn Mountain range, Lake Vyrnwy Hotel offers breathtaking views over gardens, lake waters, a 24,000-acre estate teaming with wildlife and a background landscape of mountains, moor land and forest. As well as being an RSPB sanctuary the estate also provides 56 miles of forest tracks, excellent driven and rough shooting for pheasant and duck and some of the best fly-fishing in Wales. Other pursuits include sailing, quad trekking, clay shooting, archery, cycling and tennis. Horses can be accommodated in the livery. All 35 spacious bedrooms are individually decorated and furnished, some have four-posters beds, Jacuzzis, suites and balconies and most afford panoramic views. Dining is a delight in the 2 Rosettes awarded candle-lit restaurant where courteous staff provide the most attentive service. Mouth-watering menus change seasonally with even the breakfast marmalade and afternoon tea jams made by the talented kitchen team. Awarded "Best use of local produce in Wales". Dedicated meeting and private dining facilities are available.

Our inspector loved: *The ambience and warmth of welcome with wonderful views, truly relaxing. So was the bath!*

Directions: From Shrewsbury take the A458 to Welshpool, then turn right onto the B4393 just after Ford (signposted to Lake Vyrnwy 28 miles).

Welshpool

Llandrindod Wells

Brecon

Abergavenny

Web: www.johansens.com/lakevyrnwy
E-mail: res@lakevyrnwy.com
Tel: 0870 381 8671
International: +44 (0)1691 870 692
Fax: 01691 870 259

Price Guide:
single £90–£155
double/twin £120–£190
suite £190–£220

THE LAKE COUNTRY HOUSE

LLANGAMMARCH WELLS, POWYS LD4 4BS

Directions: From the A483, follow signs to Llangammarch Wells and then to the hotel.

Web: www.johansens.com/lakecountryhouse
E-mail: info@lakecountryhouse.co.uk
Tel: 0870 381 8668
International: +44 (0)1591 620202
Fax: 01591 620457

Price Guide:
single £120
double/twin £160–£200
suite £200–£250

A welcoming Welsh Country house set in its own 50 acres with rhododendron lined pathways, riverside walks and a large well-stocked trout lake. Within the hotel, airy rooms filled with fine antiques, paintings and fresh flowers make this the perfect place to relax. Delicious homemade teas are served everyday beside log fires. From the windows, ducks and geese can be glimpsed wandering in the gardens which cascade down to the river. In the award-winning restaurant, fresh produce and herbs from the gardens are used for seasonal country house menus, complemented by one of the finest wine lists in Wales. Each of the supremely comfortable bedrooms or suites with beautifully appointed sitting rooms are furnished with the thoughtful attention to detail seen throughout the hotel. Guests can fish for trout or salmon on the four miles of river which runs through the grounds and the 3-acre lake regularly yields trout of 5 pounds and over. The grounds are a haven for wildlife: herons, dippers and kingfishers skim over the river, there are badgers in the woods and swans and waterfowl abound. There is a large billiard room in the hotel and a 9-hole par 3 golf course, tennis court, croquet lawn and putting green. Awarded an AA 3 Red star and RAC Gold Ribbon.

Our inspector loved: This wonderful retreat, the delicious dining and a perfect day wandering by the lake listening to the rush of the river.

MORGANS

SOMERSET PLACE, SWANSEA SA1 1RR

When it opened to great acclaim in 2002, Morgans not only made a dream come true for local entrepreneur Martin Morgan and his wife Louisa, it also brought a touch of 21st-century style to Wales's "City by the Sea". Swansea's Grade II listed Victorian Port Authority building has been transformed, yet behind the red brick exterior it retains many of its classic features, from mouldings to staircases, wooden floors and intricate windows. Each of the 20 individually named bedrooms is bursting with personality, the coolly elegant Zeta, the vibrant Digby Grande and the plush Henry Belle representing just a small selection. Sumptuous furnishings of suede, satin and fine Egyptian cotton combine with more fun interior design elements that include double showers, plasma screens and DVD players. Sophistication and attention to detail abound throughout the non-smoking hotel's public spaces, and no more so than in the chocolate and cream Morgans Bar with its one red chair, or the gently neon-lit Champagne Bar. Visitors can enjoy dinner in Morgans restaurant or the buzzing Plimsoll Line bar, relax on the decked courtyard, or gaze at the exquisite stained glass of the cuppola.

Our inspector loved: The contemporary elegance and attention to detail throughout; simply stunning.

Directions: From the M4 take junction 42 and follow signs to the city centre. After the 6th set of traffic lights take a left turn to Dylan Thomas Centre and the hotel and car park are on the right.

Web: www.johansens.com/morgans
E-mail: fdesk@morganshotel.co.uk
Tel: 0870 381 9158
International: +44 (0)1792 484856
Fax: 01792 484849

Price Guide:
double £100-£250

405

MITRE
INTERNATIONAL CONTRACT TEXTILES & FURNISHINGS

Bathrobes
Bedspreads:
• Quilted
• Throwover
Blankets
Chefs Wear
Cleaning Cloths
Divan Beds & Mattresses
Duvet Covers:
• Easy Care
• Egyptian Cotton
• Flame Retardant
• Patterned Poly/cotton
Duvets & Pillows
Furniture
Lighting
Made To Measure:
• Curtains
• Tie Backs
Mattress Protectors
Sheets:
• Easy Care
• Egyptian Cotton
• Flame Retardant
Shower Curtains & Mats
Table Linen & Napkins
Table Skirtings
Tea Towels
Towels & Bath Mats

**CALL FOR A COPY OF
OUR CATALOGUE TO
SEE OUR FULL RANGE
OF HIGH QUALITY
PRODUCTS
AND GREAT PRICES.**

Mitre Furnishing Group have been working within the hotel industry for over sixty years, specialising in bedroom, bathroom, restaurant and kitchen textiles and providing a complete furnishings service to our wide range of clients from the smallest guesthouse to the largest corporate hotel chain.

Mitre Furnishing Group Ltd, 1 Goat Mill Road, Dowlais, Merthyr Tydfil CF48 3TD
Telephone: 01685 353456   Fax: 01685 353444
Email: sales@MitreFurnGrp.co.uk   Web: www.MitreFurnGrp.co.uk

MINI LISTINGS COUNTRY HOUSES

Condé Nast Johansens are delighted to recommend over 240 country houses, small hotels and inns across Great Britain & Ireland.
Call 0800 269 397 or see the order forms on page 459 to order Guides.

England

Bath & North East Somerset

The County Hotel - 18/19 Pulteney Road, Bath, Somerset BA2 4EZ. Tel: 0870 381 8455

Dorian House - One Upper Oldfield Park, Bath BA2 3JX. Tel: 0870 381 8650

Oldfields - 102 Wells Road, Bath, Somerset BA2 3AL. Tel: 0870 381 8792

The Ring O' Roses - Stratton Road, Holcombe, Near Bath BA3 5EB. Tel: 0870 381 9181

Tasburgh House Hotel - Warminster Road, Bath BA2 6SH. Tel: 0870 381 8941

Bedfordshire

Mill House Hotel & Restaurant - Mill House, Mill Road, Sharnbrook, Bedfordshire MK44 1NP. Tel: 0870 381 9189

Berkshire

Cantley House - Milton Road, Wokingham, Berkshire RG40 5QG. Tel: 0870 381 9233

The Cottage Inn - Maidens Green, Winkfield, Berkshire SL4 4SW. Tel: 0870 381 9234

Crown & Garter - Great Common, Inkpen, Berkshire RG17 9QR. Tel: 0870 381 9354

The Inn on the Green - The Old Cricket Common, Cookham Dean, Berkshire SL6 9NZ. Tel: 0870 381 8639

The Leatherne Bottel Riverside Restaurant - The Bridleway, Goring-on-Thames, Berkshire RG8 0HS. Tel: 0870 381 8685

The Royal Oak Restaurant & Hotel - Yattendon, Newbury RG16 0UF. Tel: 0870 381 9346

Buckinghamshire

The Dinton Hermit - Water Lane, Ford, Aylesbury, Buckinghamshire HP17 8XH. Tel: 0870 381 9295

The Greyhound - High Street, Chalfont-St-Peter, Buckinghamshire SL9 9RA. Tel: 0870 381 9216

The Ivy House - London Road, Chalfont-St-Giles, Buckinghamshire HP8 4RS. Tel: 0870 381 9236

The Nags Head - London Road, Great Missenden, Buckinghamshire HP16 0DG. Tel: 0870 381 9237

Cambridgeshire

The Meadowcroft Hotel - Trumpington Road, Cambridge CB2 2EX. Tel: 0870 381 8651

Cheshire

Broxton Hall - Whitchurch Road, Broxton, Chester, Cheshire CH3 9JS. Tel: 0870 381 8387

Frogg Manor Hotel & Restaurant - Fullers Moor, Nantwich Road, Broxton, Chester CH3 9JH. Tel: 0870 381 8534

Willington Hall Hotel - Willington, Nr Tarporley, Cheshire CW6 0NB. Tel: 0870 381 8999

Cornwall

▼
Cormorant On The River, Hotel & Riverside Restaurant - Golant By Fowey, Cornwall PL23 1LL. **Tel: 0870 381 8446**

Highland Court Lodge - Biscovey Road, Biscovey, Near St Austell, Cornwall PL24 2HW. Tel: 0870 381 9290

The Old Quay House Hotel - 28 Fore Street, Fowey, Cornwall PL23 1AQ. Tel: 0870 381 8783

Tredethy House - Helland Bridge, Bodmin, Cornwall PL30 4QS. Tel: 0870 381 9142

Trehaven Manor Hotel - Station Road, Looe, Cornwall PL13 1HN. Tel: 0870 381 8952

Trehellas House Hotel & Restaurant - Washaway, Bodmin, Cornwall PL30 3AD. Tel: 0870 381 8953

Trelawne Hotel - The Hutches Restaurant - Mawnan Smith, Nr Falmouth, Cornwall TR11 5HT. Tel: 0870 381 8954

Trevalsa Court Country House Hotel - School Hill, Mevagissey, St Austell, Cornwall PL26 6TH. Tel: 0870 381 8955

Wisteria Lodge & Country Spa - Boscundle, Tregrehan, St Austell, Cornwall PL25 3RJ. Tel: 0870 381 9183

Cumbria

Broadoaks Country House - Bridge Lane, Troutbeck, Windermere, Cumbria LA23 1LA. Tel: 0870 381 8380

Crosby Lodge Country House Hotel - High Crosby, Crosby-on-Eden, Carlisle, Cumbria CA6 4QZ. Tel: 0870 381 8461

Dale Head Hall Lakeside Hotel - Thirlmere, Keswick, Cumbria CA12 4TN. Tel: 0870 381 8470

Fayrer Garden House Hotel - Lyth Valley Road, Bowness-on-Windermere, Cumbria LA23 3JP. Tel: 0870 381 8517

Gilpin Lodge - Crook Road, Windermere, Cumbria LA23 3NE. Tel: 0870 381 8546

Grizedale Lodge - Grizedale Forest, Hawkshead, Ambleside, Cumbria LA22 0QL. Tel: 0870 381 9342

The Leathes Head - Borrowdale, Keswick, Cumbria CA12 5UY. Tel: 0870 381 8686

Linthwaite House Hotel - Crook Road, Bowness-on-Windermere, Cumbria LA23 3JA. Tel: 0870 381 8694

The Pheasant - Bassenthwaite Lake, Nr Cockermouth, Cumbria CA13 9YE. Tel: 0870 381 9227

The Queen's Head Hotel - Main Street, Hawkshead, Cumbria LA22 0NS. Tel: 0870 381 8844

Sawrey House Country Hotel & Restaurant - Near Sawrey, Hawkshead, Ambleside, Cumbria LA22 0LF. Tel: 0870 381 8886

Temple Sowerby House Hotel - Temple Sowerby, Penrith, Cumbria CA10 1RZ. Tel: 0870 381 8942

Underwood - The Hill, Millom, Cumbria LA18 5EZ. Tel: 0870 381 8959

Derbyshire

Boar's Head Hotel - Lichfield Road, Sudbury, Derbyshire DE6 5GX. Tel: 0870 381 8371

The Chequers Inn - Froggatt Edge, Hope Valley, Derbyshire S32 3ZJ. Tel: 0870 381 8422

Dannah Farm Country House - Bowman's Lane, Shottle, Nr Belper, Derbyshire DE56 2DR. Tel: 0870 381 8476

Kegworth House - 42 High Street, Kegworth, Derbyshire DE74 2DA. Tel: 0870 381 9102

Littleover Lodge Hotel - 222 Rykneld Road, Littleover, Derby, Derbyshire DE23 7AN. Tel: 0870 381 8695

The Peacock At Rowsley - Rowsley, Near Matlock, Derbyshire DE4 2EB. Tel: 0870 381 8805

The Plough Inn - Leadmill Bridge, Hathersage, Derbyshire S30 1BA. Tel: 0870 381 8827

The Wind In The Willows - Derbyshire Level, Glossop, Derbyshire SK13 7PT. Tel: 0870 381 9001

Devon

Bickleigh Castle - Bickleigh, Devon EX16 8RP. Tel: 0870 381 9316

Browns Hotel, Wine Bar & Brasserie - 80 West Street, Tavistock, Plymouth, Devon PL19 8AQ. Tel: 0870 381 8386

Combe House Hotel & Restaurant - Gittisham, Honiton, Nr Exeter, Devon EX14 3AD. Tel: 0870 381 8440

The Edgemoor - Haytor Road, Bovey Tracey, South Devon TQ13 9LE. Tel: 0870 381 8499

The Galley Restaurant & Rooms - 41 Fore Street, Topsham, Exeter EX3 0HU. Tel: 0870 381 9307

▼
Gidleigh Park - Chagford, Devon TQ13 8HH. **Tel: 0870 381 8545**

MINI LISTINGS COUNTRY HOUSES

Condé Nast Johansens are delighted to recommend over 240 country houses, small hotels and inns across Great Britain & Ireland.
Call 0800 269 397 or see the order forms on page 459 to order Guides.

Hewitt's - Villa Spaldi - North Walk, Lynton,
Devon EX35 6HJ. Tel: 0870 381 8593

Home Farm Hotel - Wilmington, Nr Honiton,
Devon EX14 9JR. Tel: 0870 381 8604

Ilsington Country House Hotel - Ilsington Village, Near
Newton Abbot, Devon TQ13 9RR. Tel: 0870 381 8635

Kingston House - Staverton, Totnes, Devon TQ9 6AR.
Tel: 0870 381 8655

The New Inn - Coleford, Crediton, Devon EX17 5BZ.
Tel: 0870 381 8757

Percy's Country Hotel & Restaurant - Coombeshead Estate,
Virginstow, Devon EX21 5EA. Tel: 0870 381 8817

Yeoldon House Hotel - Durrant Lane, Northam,
Nr Bideford EX39 2RL. Tel: 0870 381 9019

Dorset

The Grange At Oborne - Oborne, Nr Sherborne,
Dorset DT9 4LA. Tel: 0870 381 9240

Kemps Country Hotel & Restaurant - East Stoke, Wareham,
Dorset BH20 6AL. Tel: 0870 381 8647

The Lord Bute - 181/185 Lymington Road, Highcliffe On
Sea, Christchurch, Dorset BH23 4JS. Tel: 0870 381 9341

Summer Lodge - Summer Lane, Evershot,
Dorset DT2 0JR. Tel: 0870 381 8926

Yalbury Cottage Hotel - Lower Bockhampton, Dorchester,
Dorset DT2 8PZ. Tel: 0870 381 9015

Essex

The Cricketers' Arms - The Inn on the Green, Rickling
Green, Saffron Walden, Essex CB11 3YG.
Tel: 0870 381 9351

The Crown House - Great Chesterford, Saffron Walden,
Essex CB10 1NY. Tel: 0870 381 8465

The Mistley Thorn - High Street, Mistley,
Colchester CO11 1HE. Tel: 0870 381 9347

The Pump House Apartment - 132 Church Street,
Great Burstead, Essex CM11 2TR. Tel: 0870 381 8842

Gloucestershire

Bibury Court - Bibury Court, Bibury,
Gloucestershire GL7 5NT. Tel: 0870 381 8360

Charlton Kings Hotel - Charlton Kings, Cheltenham,
Gloucestershire GL52 6UU. Tel: 0870 381 8416

Lower Brook House - Blockley, Nr Moreton-in-marsh,
Gloucestershire GL56 9DS. Tel: 0870 381 9297

The Malt House - Broad Campden,
Gloucestershire GL55 6UU. Tel: 0870 381 8714

New Inn At Coln - Coln St-Aldwyns, Nr Cirencester,
Gloucestershire GL7 5AN. Tel: 0870 381 8758

The Snooty Fox - Market Place, Tetbury,
Gloucestershire GL8 8DD. Tel: 0870 381 9306

Three Choirs Vineyards Estate - Newent,
Gloucestershire GL18 1LS. Tel: 0870 381 8946

The Wild Duck Inn - Drakes Island, Ewen, Cirencester,
Gloucestershire GL7 6BY. Tel: 0870 381 8997

Hampshire

Langrish House - Langrish, Nr Petersfield,
Hampshire GU32 1RN. Tel: 0870 381 8679

The Mill At Gordleton - Silver Street, Hordle, Nr Lymington,
New Forest, Hampshire SO41 6DJ. Tel: 0870 381 8558

The Nurse's Cottage - Station Road, Sway, Lymington,
New Forest, Hampshire SO41 6BA. Tel: 0870 381 8774

▼

**Thatched Cottage Hotel & Restaurant - 16 Brookley Road,
Brockenhurst, New Forest, Hampshire SO42 7RR.
Tel: 0870 381 8943**

Whitley Ridge Country House Hotel - Beaulieu Road,
Brockenhurst, New Forest, Hampshire SO42 7QL.
Tel: 0870 381 8994

Herefordshire

Ford Abbey - Pudleston, Nr Leominster,
Herefordshire HR6 0RZ. Tel: 0870 381 9144

Glewstone Court - Nr Ross-on-Wye,
Herefordshire HR9 6AW. Tel: 0870 381 8556

The Pilgrim Hotel - Much Birch, Hereford HR2 8HJ.
Tel: 0870 381 9335

Rhydspence Inn - Whitney-on-Wye, Near Hay-on-Wye,
Herefordshire HR3 6EU. Tel: 0870 381 9156

The Verzon - Hereford Road, Trumpet, Nr Ledbury,
Herefordshire HR8 2PZ. Tel: 0870 381 9348

Wilton Court Hotel - Wilton, Ross-on-Wye,
Herefordshire HR9 6AQ. Tel: 0870 381 9000

Hertfordshire

Redcoats Farmhouse Hotel And Restaurant - Redcoats
Green, Near Hitchin, Hertfordshire SG4 7JR.
Tel: 0870 381 8851

The White House and Lion & Lamb Bar & Restaurant -
Smiths Green, Dunmow Road, Takeley, Bishops
Stortford, Hertfordshire CM22 6NR. Tel: 0870 381 9334

Isle of Wight

Rylstone Manor - Rylstone Gardens, Shanklin,
Isle of Wight PO37 6RE. Tel: 0870 381 8882

The Wellington Hotel - Belgrave Road, Ventnor,
Isle of Wight PO38 1JH. Tel: 0870 381 9320

Kent

The George Hotel - Stone Street, Cranbrook,
Kent TN17 3HE. Tel: 0870 381 8540

Hempstead House - London Road, Bapchild, Sittingbourne,
Kent ME9 9PP. Tel: 0870 381 8649

Ringlestone Inn and Farmhouse Hotel - 'Twixt Harrietsham
And Wormshill, Nr Maidstone, Kent ME17 1NX.
Tel: 0870 381 8856

Romney Bay House Hotel - Coast Road, Littlestone, New
Romney, Kent TN28 8QY. Tel: 0870 381 8863

Wallett's Court Hotel & Spa - West Cliffe, St Margaret's-at-
Cliffe, Dover, Kent CT15 6EW. Tel: 0870 381 8966

Lancashire

The Inn At Whitewell - Forest Of Bowland, Clitheroe,
Lancashire BB7 3AT. Tel: 0870 381 8638

Tree Tops Country House Restaurant & Hotel - Southport
Old Road, Formby, Nr Southport, Lancashire L37 0AB.
Tel: 0870 381 8950

Leicestershire

Abbots Oak Country House - Abbots Oak, Warren Hills
Road, Near Coalville, Leicestershire LE67 4UY.
Tel: 0870 381 8303

Horse & Trumpet - Old Green, Medbourne, Near Market
Harborough, Leicestershire LE16 8DX.
Tel: 0870 381 9340

The Red House - 23 Main Street, Nether Broughton,
Leicestershire LE14 3HB. Tel: 0870 381 9350

Rothley Court Hotel - Westfield lane, Rothley,
Leicestershire LE7 7LG. Tel: 0870 381 9339

Sysonby Knoll Hotel - Ashfordby Road, Melton Mowbray,
Leicestershire LE13 0HP. Tel: 0870 381 9352

Lincolnshire

The Crown Hotel - All Saints Place, Stamford,
Lincolnshire PE9 2AG. Tel: 0870 381 8464

The Lea Gate Inn - Leagate Road, Coningsby,
Lincolnshire LN4 4RS. Tel: 0870 381 8684

Washingborough Hall - Church Hill, Washingborough,
Lincoln LN4 1BE. Tel: 0870 381 8971

Merseyside

Racquet Club - Hargreaves Building, 5 Chapel Street,
Liverpool L3 9AA. Tel: 0870 381 9287

Norfolk

Beechwood Hotel - Cromer Road, North Walsham,
Norfolk NR28 0HD. Tel: 0870 381 8353

Condé Nast Johansens are delighted to recommend over 240 country houses, small hotels and inns across Great Britain & Ireland.
Call 0800 269 397 or see the order forms on page 459 to order Guides.

Broom Hall Country Hotel - Richmond Road, Saham Toney, Thetford, Norfolk IP25 7EX. Tel: 0870 381 8384

Brovey Lair - Carbrooke Road, Ovington, Thetford, Norfolk IP25 6SD. Tel: 0870 381 8385

Catton Old Hall - Lodge Lane, Catton, Norwich, Norfolk NR6 7HG. Tel: 0870 381 9353

Elderton Lodge Hotel & Langtry Restaurant - Gunton Park, Thorpe Market, Nr North Walsham, Norfolk NR11 8TZ. Tel: 0870 381 8502

Felbrigg Lodge - Aylmerton, North Norfolk NR11 8RA. Tel: 0870 381 8520

The Great Escape Holiday Company - Docking, Kings Lynn, Norfolk PE31 8LY. Tel: 0870 381 8568

Idyllic Cottages At Vere Lodge - South Raynham, Fakenham, Norfolk NR21 7HE. Tel: 0870 381 8961

The Manor House - Barsham Road, Great Snoring, Norfolk NR21 OHP. Tel: 0870 381 8716

The Moat House - Rectory Lane, Hethel, Norwich NR14 8HD. Tel: 0870 381 9317

▼
The Norfolk Mead Hotel - Coltishall, Norwich, Norfolk NR12 7DN. Tel: 0870 381 8764

The Old Rectory - 103 Yarmouth Road, Norwich, Norfolk NR7 OHF. Tel: 0870 381 8784

The Stower Grange - School Road, Drayton, Norwich, Norfolk NR8 6EF. Tel: 0870 381 8921

The White Horse - Brancaster Staithe, Norfolk PE31 8BY. Tel: 0870 381 8986

Northamptonshire

The Falcon Hotel - Castle Ashby, Northamptonshire NN7 1LF. Tel: 0870 381 8512

The Windmill At Badby - Main Street, Badby, Daventry, Northamptonshire NN11 3AN. Tel: 0870 381 9002

Northumberland

The Otterburn Tower - Otterburn, Northumberland NE19 1NS. Tel: 0870 381 8796

Waren House Hotel - Waren Mill, Bamburgh, Northumberland NE70 7EE. Tel: 0870 381 8967

Nottinghamshire

Cockliffe Country House Hotel - Burnt Stump Country Park, Burnt Stump Hill, Nottinghamshire NG5 8PQ. Tel: 0870 381 8435

The Saracens Head Hotel - Market Place, Southwell, Nottinghamshire NG25 OHE. Tel: 0870 381 9337

Oxfordshire

Duke Of Marlborough Country Inn - Woodleys, Woodstock, Oxford OX20 1HT. Tel: 0870 381 9219

The George Hotel - High Street, Dorchester-on-Thames, Oxford OX10 7HH. Tel: 0870 381 8539

The Kings Head Inn & Restaurant - The Green, Bledington, Nr Kingham, Oxfordshire OX7 6XQ. Tel: 0870 381 8654

The Lamb Inn - Sheep Street, Burford, Oxfordshire OX18 4LR. Tel: 0870 381 8674

The Plough At Clanfield - Bourton Road, Clanfield, Oxfordshire OX18 2RB. Tel: 0870 381 8826

The White Hart Hotel - Nettlebed, Henley-on-Thames, Oxfordshire RG9 5DD. Tel: 0870 381 9292

Rutland

Barnsdale Lodge - The Avenue, Rutland Water, Nr Oakham, Rutland, Leicestershire LE15 8AH. Tel: 0870 381 8342

Shropshire

The Hundred House Hotel, Norton - Bridgnorth Road, Norton, Nr Shifnal, Telford, Shropshire TF11 9EE. Tel: 0870 381 8629

The Old Vicarage Hotel - Worfield, Bridgnorth, Shropshire WV15 5JZ. Tel: 0870 381 8790

Overton Grange Hotel - Overton, Nr Ludlow, Shropshire SY8 4AD. Tel: 0870 381 9135

Pen-Y-Dyffryn Hall Hotel - Rhydycroesau, Nr Oswestry, Shropshire SY10 7JD. Tel: 0870 381 8809

Soulton Hall - Nr Wem, Shropshire SY4 5RS. Tel: 0870 381 8899

Somerset

Ashwick Country House Hotel - Dulverton, Somerset TA22 9QD. Tel: 0870 381 8327

Beryl - Wells, Somerset BA5 3JP. Tel: 0870 381 8358

Compton House - Townsend, Axbridge, Somerset BS26 2AJ. Tel: 0870 381 8441

Farthings Hotel & Restaurant - Hatch Beauchamp, Somerset TA3 6SG. Tel: 0870 381 8515

Glencot House - Glencot Lane, Wookey Hole, Nr Wells, Somerset BA5 1BH. Tel: 0870 381 8552

Karslake House Hotel & Restaurant - Halse Lane, Winsford, Exmoor National Park, Somerset TA24 7JE. Tel: 0870 381 9134

The Old Rectory - Cricket Malherbie, Ilminster, Somerset TA19 OPW. Tel: 0870 381 8785

Porlock Vale House - Porlock Weir, Somerset TA24 8NY. Tel: 0870 381 8830

Three Acres Country House - Three Acres, Brushford, Dulverton, Somerset TA22 9AR. Tel: 0870 381 9229

Staffordshire

▼
Somerford Hall - Brewood, Staffordshire ST19 9DQ. Tel: 0870 381 9120

Suffolk

The Brome Grange Hotel - Brome, Eye, Suffolk IP23 8AP. Tel: 0870 381 9299

Clarice House - Horringer Court, Horringer Road, Bury St Edmunds Suffolk IP29 5PH. Tel: 0870 381 8431

Worlington Hall Country House Hotel - Worlington, Suffolk IP28 8RX. Tel: 0870 381 9161

Surrey

Chase Lodge - 10 Park Road, Hampton Wick, Kingston-upon-Thames, Surrey KT1 4AS. Tel: 0870 381 8419

Stanhill Court Hotel - Stan Hill Road, Charlwood, Nr Horley, Surrey RH6 0EP. Tel: 0870 381 8908

East Sussex

The Hope Anchor Hotel - Watchbell Street, Rye, East Sussex TN31 7HA. Tel: 0870 381 8607

West Sussex

Crouchers Country Hotel & Restaurant - Birdham Road, Apuldram, Near Chichester, West Sussex PO20 7EH. Tel: 0870 381 8462

The Mill House Hotel - Mill Lane, Ashington, West Sussex RH20 3BX. Tel: 0870 381 8735

The Old Tollgate Restaurant And Hotel - The Street, Bramber, Steyning, West Sussex BN44 3WE. Tel: 0870 381 8789

MINI LISTINGS COUNTRY HOUSES

Condé Nast Johansens are delighted to recommend over 240 country houses, small hotels and inns across Great Britain & Ireland. Call 0800 269 397 or see the order forms on page 459 to order Guides.

The Royal Oak Inn - Pook Lane, East Lavant, Nr Goodwood, Chichester, West Sussex PO18 0AX. Tel: 0870 381 9218

Wiltshire

The George Inn - Longbridge Deverill, Warminster, Wiltshire BA12 7DG. Tel: 0870 381 8542

Hinton Grange - Nr Hinton, Dryham, Wiltshire SN14 8HG. Tel: 0870 381 8596

Lucknam Park, Bath - Colerne, Chippenham, Wiltshire SN14 8AZ. Tel: 0870 381 8707

The Old Manor Hotel - Trowle, Nr Bradford-on-Avon, Wiltshire BA14 9BL. Tel: 0870 381 8782

Stanton Manor - Stanton Saint Quintin, Nr Chippenham, Wiltshire SN14 6DQ. Tel: 0870 381 8910

Whatley Manor - Easton Grey, Malmesbury, Wiltshire SN16 0RB. Tel: 0870 381 9197

Widbrook Grange - Widbrook, Bradford-on-Avon, Nr Bath, Wiltshire BA15 1UH. Tel: 0870 381 8996

Worcestershire

The Boot Inn - Radford Road, Flyford Flavell, Worcestershire WR7 4BS. Tel: 0870 381 9319

Buckland Manor - Near Broadway, Worcestershire WR12 7LY. Tel: 0870 381 9175

Colwall Park - Colwall, Near Malvern, Worcestershire WR13 6QG. Tel: 0870 381 8437

The Old Rectory - Ipsley Lane, Ipsley, Near Redditch, Worcestershire B98 0AP. Tel: 0870 381 9169

The Old Windmill - Withybed Lane, Inkberrow, Worcester WR7 4JL. Tel: 0870 381 9167

Riverside Restaurant And Hotel - The Parks, Offenham Road, Near Evesham, Worcestershire WR11 8JP. Tel: 0870 381 9298

The White Lion Hotel - High Street, Upton-upon-Severn, Nr Malvern, Worcestershire WR8 0HJ. Tel: 0870 381 8989

North Yorkshire

The Austwick Traddock - Austwick, Via Lancaster, North Yorkshire LA2 8BY. Tel: 0870 381 8331

The Boar's Head Hotel - The Ripley Castle Estate, Harrogate, North Yorkshire HG3 3AY. Tel: 0870 381 8370

Dunsley Hall - Dunsley, Whitby, North Yorkshire YO21 3TL. Tel: 0870 381 8494

Hob Green Hotel And Restaurant - Markington, Harrogate, North Yorkshire HG3 3PJ. Tel: 0870 381 8600

The Kings Head Hotel - Market Place, Richmond, North Yorkshire DL10 4HS. Tel: 0870 381 9224

Middleham Grange - Market Place, Middleham, North Yorkshire DL8 4NR. Tel: 0870 381 9336

The Red Lion - By The Bridge At Burnsall, Near Skipton, North Yorkshire BD23 6BU. Tel: 0870 381 8850

Rookhurst Country House Hotel - West End, Gayle, Hawes, North Yorkshire DL8 3RT. Tel: 0870 381 8865

Stow House Hotel - Aysgarth, Leyburn, North Yorkshire DL8 3SR. Tel: 0870 381 8920

West Yorkshire

Hey Green Country House Hotel - Waters Road, Marsden, West Yorkshire HD7 6NG. Tel: 0870 381 8652

Channel Islands

Jersey

Eulah Country House - Mont Cochon, St Helier, Jersey, Channel Islands JE2 3JA. Tel: 0870 381 8509

Herm Island

The White House - Herm Island, Guernsey, Channel Islands GY1 3HR. Tel: 0870 381 8988

Sark

Aval du Creux Hotel - Harbour Hill, Sark, Guernsey, Channel Islands GY9 0SB. Tel: 0870 381 9173

La Sablonnerie - Little Sark, Sark, Channel Islands GY9 0SD. Tel: 0870 381 8666

Ireland

Clare

▼
Gregans Castle - Ballyvaughan, Co Clare, Ireland. **Tel: 00 353 65 7077005**

Cork

Ballylickey Manor House - Ballylickey, Bantry, Co Cork. Tel: 00 353 27 50071

Dublin

Merrion Hall Hotel - 54-56 Merrion Road, Ballsbridge, Dublin 4, Ireland. Tel: 00 353 1 668 1426

Galway

Ross Lake House Hotel - Rosscahill, Oughterard, Co Galway, Ireland. Tel: 00 353 91 550109

Zetland Country House Hotel - Cashel Bay, Connemara, Co Galway, Ireland. Tel: 00 353 95 31111

Kerry

Caragh Lodge - Caragh Lake, Co Kerry, Ireland. Tel: 00 353 66 9769115

Emlagh House - Dingle, Co Kerry, Ireland. Tel: 00 353 66 915 2345

Gorman's Clifftop House & Restaurant - Glaise Bheag, Ballydavid, Dingle Peninsula - Tralee, Co Kerry, Ireland. Tel: 00 353 66 9155162

Sligo

Coopershill House - Riverstown, Co Sligo, Ireland. Tel: 00 353 71 9165108

Scotland

Aberdeenshire

Balgonie Country House - Braemar Place, Ballater, Royal Deeside, Aberdeenshire AB35 5NQ. Tel: 0870 381 8335

Angus

Castleton House Hotel - Glamis, By Forfar, Angus DD8 1SJ. Tel: 0870 381 8411

Argyll & Bute

Ballachulish House - Ballachulish, Argyll PH49 4JX. Tel: 0870 381 8336

The Frog At Port Dunstaffnage - Dunstaffnage Marina, Connel, By Oban, Argyll PA37 1PX. Tel: 0870 381 8533

Highland Cottage - Breadalbane Street, Tobermory, Isle of Mull PA75 6PD. Tel: 0870 381 9184

Ptarmigan House - The Fairways, Tobermory PA75 6PS. Tel: 0870 381 9343

Condé Nast Johansens are delighted to recommend over 240 country houses, small hotels and inns across Great Britain & Ireland.
Call 0800 269 397 or see the order forms on page 459 to order Guides.

Clackmannanshire

Castle Campbell Hotel - 11 Bridge Street, Dollar, Clackmannanshire FK14 7DE. Tel: 0870 381 9232

Dumfries & Galloway

Fernhill Hotel - Heugh Road, Portpatrick DG9 8TD. Tel: 0870 381 8521

Gill Bank - 8 East Morton Street, Thornhill, Dumfriesshire DG3 5LZ. Tel: 0870 381 9355

Trigony House Hotel - Closeburn, Thornhill, Dumfriesshire DG3 5EZ. Tel: 0870 381 9121

Highland

▼
Corriegour Lodge Hotel - Loch Lochy, By Spean Bridge, Inverness-shire PH34 4EB. Tel: 0870 381 8447

The Cross at Kingussie - Tweed Mill Brae, Kingussie, Inverness-shire PH21 1TC. Tel: 0870 381 9349

Hotel Eilean Iarmain - Sleat, Isle of Skye IV43 8QR. Tel: 0870 381 8619

The Steadings Hotel - Flichity, Farr, South Loch Ness, Inverness IV2 6XD. Tel: 0870 381 9138

Toravaig House Hotel - Knock Bay, Sleat, Isle of Skye IV44 8RE. Tel: 0870 381 9344

Perth & Kinross

Cairn Lodge Hotel - Orchil Road, Auchterarder, Perthshire PH3 1LX. Tel: 0870 381 9284

The Four Seasons Hotel - St Fillans, Perthshire PH6 2NF. Tel: 0870 381 8528

Knockendarroch House - Higher Oakfield, Pitlochry, Perthshire PH16 5HT. Tel: 0870 381 8662

The Lake Hotel - Port of Menteith, Perthshire FK8 3RA. Tel: 0870 381 8669

Monachyle Mhor - Balquhidder, By Lochearnhead, Perthshire FK19 8PQ. Tel: 0870 381 9231

Scottish Borders

Traquair House - Innerleithen, Peebleshire EH44 6PW. Tel: 0870 381 9104

South Ayrshire

Culzean Castle - The Eisenhower Apartment - Maybole, Ayrshire KA19 8LE. Tel: 0870 381 8469

Wales

Bridgend

The Great House - High Street, Laleston, Bridgend, Wales CF32 0HP. Tel: 0870 381 8570

Cardiff

The Inn At The Elm Tree - St Brides, Wentlooge, Nr Newport NP10 8SQ. Tel: 0870 381 8637

Carmarthenshire

Ty Mawr Country Hotel - Brechfa, Carmarthenshire SA32 7RA. Tel: 0870 381 9318

Ceredigion

Conrah Country House Hotel - Rhydgaled, Chancery, Aberystwyth, Ceredigion SY23 4DF. Tel: 0870 381 8444

Ynyshir Hall - Eglwysfach, Machynlleth, Ceredigion SY20 8TA. Tel: 0870 381 9020

Conwy

The Old Rectory Country House - Llanrwst Road, Llansanffraid Glan Conwy, Conwy LL28 5LF. Tel: 0870 381 8787

Tan-Y-Foel - Capel Garmon, Nr Betws-y-coed, Conwy LL26 0RE. Tel: 0870 381 8938

Gwynedd

Bae Abermaw - Panorama Hill, Barmouth, Gwynedd LL42 1DQ. Tel: 0870 381 8332

Llwyndu Farmhouse - Llanaber, Nr Barmouth, Gwynedd LL42 1RR. Tel: 0870 381 9143

Plas Dolmelynllyn - Ganllwyd, Dolgellau, Gwynedd LL40 2HP. Tel: 0870 381 8825

Porth Tocyn Country House Hotel - Abersoch, Pwllheli, Gwynedd LL53 7BU. Tel: 0870 381 8832

Isle of Anglesey

Ye Olde Bull's Head - Castle Street, Beaumaris, Isle of Anglesey LL58 8AP. Tel: 0870 381 9017

Monmouthshire

▼
The Bell At Skenfrith - Skenfrith, Monmouthshire NP7 8UH. Tel: 0870 381 8354

Parva Farmhouse And Restaurant - Tintern, Chepstow, Monmouthshire NP16 6SQ. Tel: 0870 381 8803

Pembrokeshire

The Gower Hotel & Orangery Restaurant - Milford Terrace, Saundersfoot, Pembrokeshire SA69 9EL. Tel: 0870 381 9149

Wolfscastle Country Hotel & Restaurant - Wolf's Castle, Haverfordwest, Pembrokeshire SA62 5LZ. Tel: 0870 381 9162

Powys

Felin Fach Griffin - Felin Fach, Brecon, Powys LD3 0UB. Tel: 0870 381 9345

Swansea

Fairyhill - Reynoldston, Gower, Near Swansea SA3 1BS. Tel: 0870 381 9321

Vale Of Glamorgan

Egerton Grey - Porthkerry, Nr Cardiff, Vale Of Glamorgan CF62 3BZ. Tel: 0870 381 8501

HISTORIC HOUSES, CASTLES & GARDENS

Incorporating Museums & Galleries

We are pleased to feature over 150 places to visit during your stay at a Condé Nast Johansens recommended hotel.

England

Bedfordshire

Woburn Abbey - Woburn, Bedfordshire MK17 9WA. Tel: 01525 290666

Berkshire

Anderton House - The Landmark Trust, Shottesbrooke, Maidenhead, Berkshire SL6 3SW. Tel: 01628 825920

Dolbelydr - The Landmark Trust, Shottesbrooke, Maidenhead, Berkshire SL6 3SW. Tel: 01628 825920

Old Campden House - The Landmark Trust, Shottesbrooke, Maidenhead, Berkshire SL6 3SW. Tel: 01628 825920

Savill Garden - Windsor Great Park, Berkshire. Tel: 01753 847518

Taplow Court - Berry Hill, Taplow, Nr Maidenhead, Berkshire SL6 0ER. Tel: 01628 591209

Buckinghamshire

Hughenden Manor - High Wycombe, Buckinghamshire HP14 4LA. Tel: 01494 755573

Stowe Landscape Gardens - Stowe, Buckingham, Buckinghamshire MK18 5EH. Tel: 01280 818809

Waddesdon Manor - Waddesdon, Nr Aylesbury, Buckinghamshire HP18 0JH. Tel: 01296 653211

Cambridgeshire

Ely Cathedral - The Chapter House, The College, Ely, Cambridgeshire CB7 4DL. Tel: 01353 667735

The Manor of Green Knowe - Hemingford Grey, Cambridgeshire PE28 9BN. Tel: 01480 463134

Cheshire

Dorfold Hall - Nantwich, Cheshire CW5 8LD. Tel: 01270 625245

Gawsworth Hall - Gawsworth, Macclesfield, Cheshire SK11 9RN. Tel: 01260 223456

Norton Priory Museum & Gardens - Tudor Road, Manor Park, Cheshire WA7 1SX. Tel: 01928 569895

Tabley House Stately Home - Tabley House, Knutsford, Cheshire WA16 0HB. Tel: 01565 750151

Co Durham

Raby Castle - Staindrop, Darlington, Co Durham DL2 3AH. Tel: 01833 660207 / 660202

Cornwall

Mount Edgcumbe House & Park - Cremyll, Nr. Plymouth, Cornwall PL10 1HZ. Tel: 01752 822236

Royal Cornwall Museum - River Street, Truro, Cornwall TR1 2SJ. Tel: 01872 272205

Cumbria

Dove Cottage & The Wordsworth Museum - Grasmere, Cumbria LA22 9SH. Tel: 015394 35544

Isel Hall - Cockermouth, Cumbria CA13 0QG.

Levens Hall & Gardens - Kendal, Cumbria LA8 0PD. Tel: 01539 560321

Mirehouse & Keswick - Mirehouse, Keswick, Cumbria CA12 4QE. Tel: 01768 772287

Windermere Steamboat Centre - Rayrigg Road, Windermere, Cumbria LA23 1BN. Tel: 01539 445565

Derbyshire

Haddon Hall - Bakewell, Derbyshire DE45 1LA. Tel: 01629 812855

Melbourne Hall & Gardens - Melbourne, Derbyshire DE73 1EN. Tel: 01332 862502

Devon

▼
Bickleigh Castle - Bickleigh, Tiverton, Devon EX16 8RP. Tel: 01884 855363

Downes Estate at Crediton - Crediton, Devon EX17 3PL. Tel: 01392 439046

Ugbrooke Park - Ugbrooke, Chudleigh, Devon TQ13 0AD. Tel: 01626 852179

Dorset

Chiffchaffs - Chaffeymoor, Bourton, Gillingham, Dorset SP8 5BY. Tel: 01747 840841

Cranborne Manor Garden - Cranborne, Wimborne, Dorset BH21 5PP. Tel: 01725 517248

Deans Court Garden - Deans Court, Wimborne, Dorset BH21 1EE. Tel: 01202 886116

Lulworth Castle - The Lulworth Estate, East Lulworth, Wareham, Dorset BH20 5QS. Tel: 01929 400352

Mapperton - Mapperton, Beaminster, Dorset DT8 3NR. Tel: 01308 862645

Russell-Cotes Art Gallery & Museum - East Cliff, Bournemouth, Dorset BH1 3AA. Tel: 01202 451800

Essex

Ingatestone Hall - Hall Lane, Ingatestone, Essex CM4 9NR. Tel: 01277 353010

The Gardens of Easton Lodge - Warwick House, Easton Lodge, Essex CM6 2BB. Tel: 01371 876979

Gloucestershire

Cheltenham Art Gallery & Museum - Clarence Street, Cheltenham, Gloucestershire GL50 3JT. Tel: 01242 237431

Hardwicke Court - Gloucester, Gloucestershire GL2 4RS. Tel: 01452 720212

Hampshire

Beaulieu - John Montagu Building, Beaulieu, Hampshire SO42 7ZN. Tel: 01590 612345

Beaulieu Vineyard and Gardens - Beaulieu Estate, John Montagu Building, Beaulieu, Hampshire SO42 7ZN. Tel: 01590 612345

Broadlands - Romsey, Hampshire SO51 9ZD. Tel: 01794 505010

Gilbert White's House and The Oates Museum - Selborne, Hampshire GU34 3JH. Tel: 01420 511275

Greywell Hill House - Greywell, Hook, Hampshire RG29 1DG.

Pylewell House - South Baddesley, Lymington, Hampshire SO41 5SJ. Tel: 01329 833130

Herefordshire

Eastnor Castle - Eastnor, Ledbury, Herefordshire HR8 1RL. Tel: 01531 633160

Kentchurch Court - Kentchurch, Nr Pontrilas, Hereford, HR2 0DB. Tel: 01981 240228

Hertfordshire

Ashridge - Ringshall, Berkhamsted, Hertfordshire HP4 1NS. Tel: 01442 843491

Hatfield House, Park & Gardens - Hatfield, Hertfordshire AL9 5NQ. Tel: 01707 287010

Isle of Wight

Deacons Nursery - Moor View, Godshill, Isle of Wight PO38 3HW. Tel: 01983 840750

Kent

Cobham Hall - Cobham, Kent DA12 3BL. Tel: 01474 823371

Graham Clarke Up the Garden Studio - Green Lane, Boughton Monchelsea, Maidstone, Kent ME17 4LF. Tel: 01622 743938

Groombridge Place Gardens & Enchanted Forest - Groombridge, Tunbridge Wells, Kent TN3 9QG. Tel: 01892 861444

Hever Castle & Gardens - Edenbridge, Kent TN8 7NG. Tel: 01732 865224

Leeds Castle - Maidstone, Kent ME17 1PL. Tel: 01622 765400

Marle Place Gardens - Marle Place Road, Brenchley, Kent TN12 7HS. Tel: 01892 722304

Mount Ephraim Gardens - Hernhill, Nr Faversham, Kent ME13 9TX. Tel: 01227 751496

Penshurst Place & Gardens - Penshurst, Nr Tonbridge, Kent TN11 8DG. Tel: 01892 870307

HISTORIC HOUSES, CASTLES & GARDENS

Incorporating Museums & Galleries

www.historichouses.co.uk

Scotney Castle, Garden & Estate - Lamberhurst, Tunbridge Wells, Kent TN3 8JN. Tel: 01892 891081

The New College of Cobham - Cobhambury Road, Graves End, Kent DA12 3BG. Tel: 01474 814280

Lancashire

Townhead House - Slaidburn, Via Clitheroe, Lancashire BBY 3AG.

London

Pitzhanger Manor House - Walpole Park, Mattock Lane, Ealing, London W5 5EQ. Tel: 020 8567 1227

Sir John Soane's Museum - 13 Lincoln's Inn Fields, London WC2A 3BP. Tel: 020 7405 2107

Spencer House - 27 St. James's Place, London SW1A 1NR. Tel: 0207-514 1964

Merseyside

Knowsley Hall - Prescot, Merseyside L32 4AF. Tel: 0151 489 4437 / 0468 698640

Middlesex

Syon Park - London Road, Brentford, Middlesex TW8 8JF. Tel: 020 8560 0882

Norfolk

Walsingham Abbey Grounds - c/o The Estate Office, Little Walsingham, Norfolk NR22 6BP. Tel: 01328 820259 / 820510

Wolterton and Mannington Estate - Mannington Hall, Norwich, Norfolk NR11 7BB. Tel: 01263 584175

Northamptonshire

Althorp - Northampton, Northamptonshire NN7 4HQ. Tel: 01604 770107

Boughton House - Kettering, Northamptonshire NN14 1BJ. Tel: 01536 515731

Coton Manor Garden - Coton, Nr Guilsborough, Northamptonshire NN6 8RQ. Tel: 01604 740219

Cottesbrooke Hall and Gardens - Cottesbrooke, Northampton, Northamptonshire NN6 8PF. Tel: 01604 505808

Haddonstone Show Garden - The Forge House, Church Lane, East Haddon, Northamptonshire NN6 8DB. Tel: 01604 770711

Northumberland

Alnwick Castle - Alnwick, Northumberland NE66 1NQ. Tel: 01665 510777/ 511100

Chipchase Castle - Chipchase, Wark on Tyne, Hexham, Northumberland NE48 3NT. Tel: 01434 230203

Paxton House & Country Park - Berwick-upon-Tweed, Northumberland TD15 1SZ. Tel: 01289 386291

Seaton Delaval Hall - Seaton Sluice, Whitley Bay, Northumberland NE26 4QR. Tel: 0191 237 1493 / 0786

Oxfordshire

Kingston Bagpuize House - Kingston Bagpuize, Abingdon, Oxfordshire OX13 5AX. Tel: 01865 820259

Mapledurham House - Mapledurham, Nr Reading, Oxfordshire RG4 7TR. Tel: 01189 723350

River & Rowing Museum - Mill Meadows, Henley-on-Thames, Oxfordshire RG9 1BF. Tel: 01491 415600

Wallingford Castle Gardens - Castle Street, Wallingford, Oxfordshire. Tel: 01491 835373

Shropshire

Hawkstone Park & Follies - Weston-under-Redcastle, Shrewsbury, Shropshire SY4 5UY. Tel: 01939 200 611

Hodnet Hall Gardens - Hodnet, Market Drayton, Shropshire TF9 3NN. Tel: 01630 685786

The Dorothy Clive Garden - Willoughbridge, Market Drayton, Shropshire TF9 4EU. Tel: 01630 647237

Weston Park - Weston-under-Lizard, Nr Shifnal, Shropshire TF11 8LE. Tel: 01952 852100

Somerset

▼

Cothay Manor & Gardens - Cothay Manor, Greenham, Nr Wellington, Somerset TA21 OJR. Tel: 01823 672283

Great House Farm - Wells Road, Theale, Wedmore, Somerset BS28 4SJ. Tel: 01934 713133

Museum of Costume & Assembly Rooms - Bennett Street, Bath, Somerset BA1 2QH. Tel: 01225 477789 / 477785

Robin Hood's Hut - Halswell, Goathurst, Somerset. Tel: 01628 825920

Roman Baths & Pump Room - Abbey Church Yard, Bath, Somerset BA1 1LZ. Tel: 01225 477785

Staffordshire

Ancient High House - Greengate Street, Stafford, Staffordshire ST16 2JA. Tel: 01785 223181

Izaak Walton's Cottage - Shallowford, Nr Stafford, Staffordshire ST15 OPA. Tel: 01785 760 278

Stafford Castle - Newport Road, Stafford, Staffordshire ST16 1DJ. Tel: 01785 257 698

Whitmore Hall - Whitmore, Newcastle-under-Lyme, Staffordshire ST5 5HW. Tel: 01782 680478

Suffolk

Ancient House - Clare, Suffolk CO10 8NY. Tel: 01628 825920

Freston Tower - Nr Ipswich, Suffolk. Tel: 01628 825920

Newbourne Hall - Newbourne, Nr Woodbridge, Suffolk IP12 4NP. Tel: 01473 736764

Shrubland Park Gardens - Shrubland Estate, Coddenham, Ipswich, Suffolk IP6 9QQ. Tel: 01473 830221

Surrey

Claremont House - Claremont Drive, Esher, Surrey KT10 9LY. Tel: 01372 467841

Goddards - Abinger Common, Dorking, Surrey RH5 6TH. Tel: 01628 825920

Painshill Landscape Garden - Portsmouth Road, Cobham, Surrey KT11 1JE. Tel: 01932 868113

East Sussex

Merriments Gardens - Hurst Green, E Sussex TN19 7RA. Tel: 01580 860666

Firle Place - The Estate Office, Lewes, East Sussex BN8 6NS. Tel: 01273 858043

Garden and Grounds of Herstmonceux Castle - Herstmonceux Castle, Hailsham, East Sussex BN27 1RN. Tel: 01323 833816

Wilmington Priory - Wilmington, Nr Eastbourne, East Sussex BN26 5SW. Tel: 01628 825920

West Sussex

Borde Hill Garden - Balcombe Road, West Sussex RH16 1XP. Tel: 01444 450326

Denmans Garden - Clock House, Denmans, Fontwell, West Sussex BN18 0SU. Tel: 01243 542808

Goodwood House - Goodwood, Chichester, West Sussex PO18 0PX. Tel: 01243 755000

High Beeches Gardens - High Beeches, Handcross, West Sussex RH17 6HQ. Tel: 01444 400589

Weald and Downland Open Air Museum - Singleton, Chichester, West Sussex PO21 4JU. Tel: 01243 811363

West Dean Gardens - West Dean, Chichester, West Sussex PO18 0QZ. Tel: 01243 818210

Warwickshire

Arbury Hall - Nuneaton, Warwickshire CV10 7PT. Tel: 024 7638 2804

Shakespeare Houses - The Shakespeare Centre, Henley Street, Stratford-upon-Avon, Warwickshire CV37 6QW. Tel: 01789 204016

Barber Institute of Fine Arts - The University of Birmingham, Edgbaston, Birmingham, West Midlands B15 2TS. Tel: 0121 414 7333

Castle Bromwich Hall Gardens - Chester Road, Castle Bromwich, Birmingham, West Midlands B36 9BT. Tel: 0121 749 4100

Coventry Cathedral - 7 Priory Row, Coventry, West Midlands CV1 5ES. Tel: 0203 227597

The Birmingham Botanical Gardens and Glasshouses - Westbourne Road, Edgbaston, Birmingham, West Midlands B15 3TR. Tel: 0121 454 1860

HISTORIC HOUSES, CASTLES & GARDENS

Incorporating Museums & Galleries

www.historichouses.co.uk

North Yorkshire

Allerton Park - Knaresborough, North Yorkshire HG5 OSE. Tel: 01423 330927

Duncombe Park - Helmsley, York, North Yorkshire YO62 5EB. Tel: 01439 770213

Kiplin Hall - Nr Scorton, Richmond, North Yorkshire. Tel: 01748 818178

Newby Hall & Gardens - Ripon, North Yorkshire HG4 5AE. Tel: 01423 322583

Ripley Castle - Ripley Castle Estate, Harrogate, North Yorkshire HG3 3AY. Tel: 01423 770152

Skipton Castle - Skipton, North Yorkshire BD23 1AQ. Tel: 01756 792442

The Forbidden Corner - The Tupgill Park Estate, Coverham, Middleham, North Yorkshire DL8 4TJ. Tel: 01969 640638

Thorp Perrow Arboretum & The Falcons of Thorp Perrow - Bedale, North Yorkshire DL8 2PR. Tel: 01677 425323

West Yorkshire

Bramham Park - Estate Office, Bramham Park, Wetherby, West Yorkshire LS23 6ND. Tel: 01937 846000

Harewood House - The Harewood House Trust, Moorhouse, Harewood, Leeds, West Yorkshire LS17 9LQ. Tel: 0113 218 1010

Ledston Hall - Hall Lane, Ledstone, West Yorkshire WF10 3BB. Tel: 01423 523 423

Lotherton Estate & Garden - Aberford, Leeds, West Yorkshire LS25 3EB. Tel: 0113 281 3259

Temple Newsam House & Estate - Leeds, West Yorkshire LS15 0AE. Tel: 0113 264 7321

Wiltshire

Charlton Park House - Charlton, Malmesbury, Wiltshire SN16 9DG. Tel: 01666 824389

Hamptworth Lodge - Landford, Salisbury, Wiltshire SP5 2EA. Tel: 01794 390215

▼
Longleat - Warminster, Wiltshire BA12 7NW. Tel: 01985 844400

Salisbury Cathedral - Visitor Services, 33 The Close, Salisbury, Wiltshire SP1 2EJ. Tel: 01722 555120

Worcester

Harvington Hall - Harvington, Kidderminster, Worcestershire DY10 4LR. Tel: 01562 777846

Spetchley Park Gardens - Spetchley Park, Worcester Worcestershire WR5 1RS. Tel: 01453 810303

Little Malvern Court - Nr Malvern, Worcestershire WR14 4JN. Tel: 01684 892988

N. Ireland

Co Down

Seaforde Gardens - Seaforde, Downpatrick, Co Down BT30 8PG. Tel: 028 4481 1225

Ireland

Co Cork

Bantry House & Gardens - Bantry, Co Cork. Tel: + 353 2 750 047

Co Offaly

Birr Castle Demesne & Ireland's Historic Science Centre - Birr, Co Offaly. Tel: + 353 509 20336

Scotland

Aberdeenshire

Craigston Castle - Turriff, Aberdeenshire AB53 5PX. Tel: 01888 551228

Ayrshire

Auchinleck House - Ochiltree, Ayrshire. Tel: 01628 825920

Blairquhan Castle and Gardens - Straiton, Maybole, Ayrshire KA19 7LZ. Tel: 01655 770239

Maybole Castle - Maybole, Ayrshire KA19 7BX. Tel: 01655 883765

Isle of Skye

Armadale Castle, Gardens & Museum of the Isles - Armadale, Sleat, Isle of Skye IV45 8RS. Tel: 01471 844305

Kincardineshire

Arbuthnott House and Garden - Arbuthnott, Laurencekirk, Kincardineshire AB30 1PA. Tel: 0561 361226

Orkney Islands

Balfour Castle - Shapinsay, Orkney Islands KW17 2DL. Tel: 01856 711282

Peebles

▼
Traquair House - Innerleithen, Peebles EH44 6PW. Tel: 01896 830323

Scottish Borders

Bowhill House & Country Park - Bowhill, Selkirk, Scottish Borders TD7 5ET. Tel: 01750 22204

West Lothian

Newliston - Kirkliston, West Lothian EH29 9EB. Tel: 0131 333 3231

Wales

Flintshire

Golden Grove - Llanasa, Nr Holywell, Flintshire CH8 9NA. Tel: 01745 854452

Gwynedd

Plas Brondanw Gardens - Menna Angharad, Plas Brondanw, Llanfrothen, Gwynedd LL48 6SW. Tel: 01766 770484

Pembrokeshire

St Davids Cathedral - The Deanery, The Close, St. David's, Pembrokeshire SA62 6RH. Tel: 01437 720199

Powys

The Judge's Lodging - Broad Street, Presteigne, Powys LD8 2AD. Tel: 01544 260650

Continental Europe

France

Château Royal D'Amboise - Chateau Royal, B.P. 271, 37403 Amboise, France. Tel: +33 2 47 57 00 98

The Netherlands

Palace Het Loo National Museum - Koninklijk Park 1, 7315 JA Apeldoorn, The Netherlands. Tel: +31 55 577 2400

Now all your guests can have a room with the best view. Philips offers a dedicated range of LCD and Plasma screen technology for the Hotel environment. With a wide choice of FlatTV's from 15" to 42" we have the right size screen for any room, and all models are designed to operate with interactive systems for in-room movies, games and internet connection. For the most discerning hotelier, Philips' unique Mirror TV creates a high quality video picture through a polarized mirror. You choose the frame to complement the decor of your establishment. Whether in a hallway, reception area, or as a guest-room centrepiece, Philips Mirror TV delivers high visual impact.

If you're not quite ready for FlatTV, there is a comprehensive range of conventional Philips Hotel TV's to choose from. All models incorporate a Welcome Message and give you the ability to lock the settings as you want them. The ProPlus range features a Digital Clock Alarm and FM Radio and the Smartcard range is designed to operate with interactive systems. Isn't it time you upgraded to Philips Hotel TV?

For more information please contact your local Philips head office, or visit our website www.philips.com/itv

MINI LISTINGS EUROPE

Condé Nast Johansens are delighted to recommend over 360 properties across Europe and The Mediterranean.
Call 0800 269 397 or see the order forms on page 459 to order guides.

Austria

KÄRNTEN (VELDEN)
Seeschlössl Velden, Klagenfurter Strasse 34, 9220
Velden, Austria. Tel: +43 4274 2824

VORARLBERG (LECH AM ARLBERG)
Sporthotel Kristiania, Omesberg 331, 6764 Lech am
Arlberg, Austria. Tel: +43 5583 25 610

VORARLBERG (ZÜRS)
Thurnhers Alpenhof, 6763 Zürs - Arlberg, Austria.
Tel: +43 5583 2191

Belgium

ANTWERP
Firean Hotel, Karel Oomsstraat 6, 2018 Antwerp,
Belgium. Tel: +32 3 237 02 60

BRUGES
Hotel de Tuilerieën, Dyver 7, 8000 Bruges, Belgium.
Tel: +32 50 34 36 91

BRUGES
Hotel Die Swaene, 1 Steenhouwersdijk (Groene Rei),
8000 Bruges, Belgium. Tel: +32 50 34 27 98

BRUGES
Hotel Prinsenhof, Ontvangersstraat 9, 8000 Bruges,
Belgium. Tel: +32 50 34 26 90

KORTRIJK
Hotel Damier, Grote Markt 41, 8500 Kortrijk, Belgium.
Tel: +32 56 22 15 47

MALMÉDY
Hostellerie Trôs Marets, Route des Trôs Marets, 4960
Malmédy, Belgium. Tel: +32 80 33 79 17

POPERINGE
Hotel Recour, Guido Gezellestraat 7, 8970 Poperinge,
Belgium . Tel: +32 57 33 57 25

POPERINGE
Manoir Ogygia, Veurnestraat 108, 8970 Poperinge,
Belgium. Tel: +32 57 33 88 38

TURNHOUT
Hostellerie Ter Driezen, Herentalsstraat 18, 2300
Turnhout, Belgium. Tel: +32 14 41 87 57

Croatia

DUBROVNIK
Grand Hotel Villa Argentina, Frana Supila 14, 20000
Dubrovnik, Croatia. Tel: +385 20 440 555

Cyprus

LIMASSOL
Four Seasons Hotel, Po Box 57222, 3313 Limassol,
Cyprus. Tel: +357 258 58000

PAPHOS
Almyra, Poseidonos Avenue, 8042 Paphos, Cyprus.
Tel: +357 26 93 30 91

PAPHOS
The Annabelle Hotel, Poseidonos Avenue, 8042 Paphos,
Cyprus. Tel: +357 26 938 333

PAPHOS
Elysium, Queen Verenikis Street, PO Box 60701, 8107
Paphos, Cyprus. Tel: +357 26 844 444

POLIS
Anassa, PO Box 66006, Latsi, 8830 Polis, Cyprus.
Tel: +357 688 80 00

Czech Republic

PRAGUE
Art Hotel Prague, Nad Královskou Oborou 53, 170 00
Prague 7, Czech Republic. Tel: +420 233 101 331

PRAGUE
Bellagio Hotel Prague, U Milosrdnych 2, 110 00 Prague 1,
Czech Republic. Tel: +420 221 778 999

PRAGUE
Hotel Hoffmeister, Pod Bruskou 7, Klárov,
11800 Prague 1, Czech Republic. Tel: +420 251 017 111

PRAGUE
Romantik Hotel U Raka, Cernínská 10/93,
11800 Prague 1, Czech Republic. Tel: +420 2205 111 00

Denmark

MIDDELFART
Hindsgavl Slot, Hindsgavl Allé 7, 5500 Middelfart,
Denmark. Tel: +45 64 41 88 00

NYBORG
Hotel Hesselet, Christianslundsvej 119, 5800 Nyborg,
Denmark. Tel: +45 65 31 30 29

Estonia

PÄRNU
Ammende Villa , Mere Pst 7, 80010 Pärnu, Estonia.
Tel: +372 44 73888

TALLINN
Domina City Hotel, Vana-Posti 11/13, 10146 Tallinn,
Estonia. Tel: +372 681 3900

TALLINN
The Three Sisters Hotel, Pikk 71/Tolli 2, 10133 Tallinn,
Estonia. Tel: +372 630 6300

France

ALSACE~LORRAINE (COLMAR)
Hostellerie Le Maréchal, 4 Place Six Montagnes Noires,
Petite Venise, 68000 Colmar, France.
Tel: +33 3 89 41 60 32

ALSACE~LORRAINE (COLMAR)
Hôtel Les Têtes, 19 Rue des Têtes, 68000 Colmar, France.
Tel: +33 3 89 24 43 43

ALSACE~LORRAINE (COLMAR - ROUFFACH)
Château d'Isenbourg, 68250 Rouffach, France.
Tel: +33 3 89 78 58 50

ALSACE~LORRAINE (GÉRARDMER - VOSGES)
Hostellerie Les Bas Rupts, 88400 Gérardmer, Vosges,
France. Tel: +33 3 29 63 09 25

ALSACE~LORRAINE (MURBACH - BUHL)
Hostellerie St Barnabé, 68530 Murbach - Buhl, France.
Tel: +33 3 89 62 14 14

ALSACE~LORRAINE (OBERNAI)
Hotel à la Cour d'Alsace, 3 Rue de Gail, 67210 Obernai,
France. Tel: +33 3 88 95 07 00

ALSACE~LORRAINE (STRASBOURG)
Romantik Hotel Beaucour Baumann, 5 Rue des Bouchers,
67000 Strasbourg, France. Tel: +33 3 88 76 72 00

ALSACE~LORRAINE (STRASBOURG - OSTWALD)
Château de L'Ile, 4 Quai Heydt, 67540 Ostwald, France.
Tel: +33 3 88 66 85 00

ALSACE~LORRAINE (THIONVILLE)
Romantik Hotel L'Horizon, 50 Route du Crève~Cœur,
57100 Thionville, France. Tel: +33 3 82 88 53 65

ALSACE~LORRANIE (JUNGHOLTZ)
Les Violettes, Thierenbach, 68500 Jungholtz, France.
Tel: +33 3 89 76 91 19

BRITTANY (BILLIERS)
Domaine de Rochevilaine, Pointe de Pen Lan, 56190
Billiers, France. Tel: +33 2 97 41 61 61

BRITTANY (BRÉLIDY)
Château Hotel de Brélidy, Noblance, 22140 Brélidy,
France. Tel: +33 1 96 95 69 38

BRITTANY (LA GOUESNIÈRE - SAINT~MALO)
Château de Bonaban, 35350 La Gouesnière, France.
Tel: +33 2 99 58 24 50

BRITTANY (LA ROCHE~BERNARD)
Domaine de Bodeuc, Route Saint Dolay, La
Roche~Bernard, 56130 Nivillac, France. Tel: +33 2 99 90
89 63

▼
BRITTANY (MOËLAN~SUR~MER)
Manoir de Kertalg, Route de Riec~Sur~Belon, 29350
Moëlan~sur~Mer, France. Tel: +33 2 98 39 77 77

BRITTANY (SAINT MALO - PLEVEN)
Manoir du Vaumadeuc, 22130 Pleven, France.
Tel: +33 2 96 84 46 17

BRITTANY (TREBEURDEN)
Ti Al Lannec, 14 Allée de Mézo~Guen, BP 3, 22560
Trebeurden, France. Tel: +33 296 15 01 01

BURGUNDY - FRANCHE~COMTÉ (AVALLON)
Château de Vault de Lugny, 11 Rue du Château, 89200
Avallon, France. Tel: +33 3 86 34 07 86

BURGUNDY - FRANCHE~COMTÉ (BEAUNE)
Ermitage de Corton, R.N. 74, 21200 Chorey~les~Beaune,
France. Tel: +33 3 80 22 05 28

BURGUNDY - FRANCHE~COMTÉ (POLIGNY - JURA)
Hostellerie des Monts de Vaux, Les Monts de Vaux,
39800 Poligny, France. Tel: +33 3 84 37 12 50

BURGUNDY - FRANCHE~COMTÉ (VOUGEOT)
Château de Gilly, Gilly~les~Cîteaux, 21640 Vougeot,
France. Tel: +33 3 80 62 89 98

CHAMPAGNE~ARDENNES (ETOGES)
Château d'Etoges, 51270 Etoges~en~Champagne,
France. Tel: +33 3 26 59 30 08

CHAMPAGNE~ARDENNES (FÈRE~EN~TARDENOIS)
Château de Fère, 02130 Fère~en~Tardenois, France.
Tel: +33 3 23 82 21 13

MINI LISTINGS EUROPE

Condé Nast Johansens are delighted to recommend over 360 properties across Europe and The Mediterranean.
Call 0800 269 397 or see the order forms on page 459 to order guides.

CHAMPAGNE~ARDENNES (SAINTE PREUVE)
Domaine du Château de Barive, 02350 Sainte-Preuve, France. Tel: +33 3 23 22 15 15

CHAMPAGNE~ARDENNES (TINQUEUX - REIMS)
L'Assiette Champenoise, 40 Avenue Paul Vaillant Couturier, 51430 Tinqueux, France.
Tel: +33 3 26 84 64 64

CÔTE D'AZUR (AUPS)
Bastide du Calalou, Village de Moissac-Bellevue, 83630 Aups, France. Tel: +33 4 94 70 17 91

CÔTE D'AZUR (ÈZE VILLAGE)
Château Eza, Rue de la Pise, 06360 Èze Village, France.
Tel: +33 4 93 41 12 24

CÔTE D'AZUR (GRASSE)
Bastide Saint Mathieu, 35 Chemin de Blumenthal, 06130 Saint Mathieu, Grasse, France. Tel: +33 4 97 01 10 00

CÔTE D'AZUR (JUAN~LES~PINS)
Hôtel Juana, La Pinède, Avenue G. Gallice, 06160 Antibes Juan~les~Pins, France. Tel: +33 4 93 61 08 70

CÔTE D'AZUR (LE RAYOL - CANADEL~SUR~MER)
Le Bailli de Suffren, Avenue des Américains, Golfe de Saint~Tropez, 83820 Le Rayol - Canadel, France.
Tel: +33 4 98 04 47 00

CÔTE D'AZUR (MOUGINS)
Les Muscadins, 18 Boulevard Courteline, 06250 Mougins, France. Tel: +33 4 92 28 28 28

CÔTE D'AZUR (NICE)
Hôtel La Pérouse, 11, Quai Rauba~Capeu, 06300 Nice, France. Tel: +33 4 93 62 34 63

CÔTE D'AZUR (SAINT~PAUL~DE~VENCE)
Le Mas d'Artigny, Route de la Colle, 06570 Saint~Paul~de~Vence, France. Tel: +33 4 93 32 84 54

CÔTE D'AZUR (SAINT~TROPEZ - RAMATUELLE)
La Ferme d'Augustin, Plage de Tahiti, 83350 Ramatuelle, Near Saint-Tropez, France. Tel: +33 4 94 55 97 00

CÔTE D'AZUR (VENCE)
Hôtel Cantemerle, 258 Chemin Cantemerle, 06140 Vence, France. Tel: +33 4 93 58 08 18

LOIRE VALLEY (AMBOISE)
Château de Pray, Route de Chargé, 37400 Amboise, France. Tel: +33 2 47 57 23 67

LOIRE VALLEY (AMBOISE)
Le Choiseul, 36 Quai Charles Guinot, 37400 Amboise, France. Tel: +33 2 47 30 45 45

LOIRE VALLEY (AMBOISE)
Le Manoir Les Minimes, 34 Quai Charles Guinot, 37400 Amboise, France. Tel: +33 2 47 30 40 40

LOIRE VALLEY (LANGEAIS)
Château de Rochecotte, 37130 Saint~Patrice, (Near Langeais) France. Tel: +33 2 47 96 16 16

LOIRE VALLEY (SAINT~AMOND MONTROND)
Château de la Commanderie, Farges Allichamps, 18200 Saint~Amand de Montrond, France.
Tel: +33 2 48 61 04 19

LOIRE VALLEY (SAINTE~MAURE~DE~TOURAINE)
Hostellerie des Hauts de Sainte Maure, 2-4 avenue du Général-de-Gaulle, 37800 Sainte~Maure~de~Touraine, France. Tel: +33 2 47 65 51 18

LOIRE VALLEY (SAUMUR-CHÊNEHUTTE~LES~TUFFEAUX)
Le Prieuré, 49350 Chênehutte~Les~Tuffeaux, France.
Tel: +33 2 41 67 90 14

LOIRE VALLEY (TOURS - LUYNES)
Domaine de Beauvois, Le Pont Clouet, Route de Cléré~les~Pins, 37230 Luynes, France.
Tel: +33 2 47 55 50 11

LOIRE VALLEY (TOURS - MONTBAZON)
Château d'Artigny, 37250 Montbazon, France.
Tel: +33 2 47 34 30 30

▼
LOIRE VALLEY (TOURS - MONTBAZON)
Domaine de La Tortinière, Route de Ballan~Miré, 37250 Montbazon, France. Tel: +33 2 47 34 35 00

MIDI~PYRÉNÉES (CORDES~SUR~CIEL)
Le Grand Ecuyer, Haut de la Cité, 81170 Cordes~sur~Ciel, France. Tel: +33 5 63 53 79 50

MIDI~PYRÉNÉES (FLOURE~CARCASSONNE)
Château de Floure, 1, Allée Gaston Bonheur, 11800 Floure, France. Tel: +33 4 68 79 11 29

NORMANDY (ETRETAT)
Domaine Saint Clair, Le Donjon, Chemin de Saint Clair, 76790 Etretat, France. Tel: +33 2 35 27 08 23

NORMANDY (FECAMP - SASSETOT)
Château de Sassetot, 76540 Sassetot~Le~Mauconduit, France. Tel: +33 2 35 28 00 11

NORMANDY (HONFLEUR - CRICQUEBOEUF)
Manoir de la Poterie, Chemin Paul Ruel, 14113 Cricqueboeuf, France. Tel: +33 2 31 88 10 40

NORTH - PICARDY (ALBERT)
Hôtel Royal Picardie, Avenue du Général Leclerc, 80300 Albert, France. Tel: +33 3 22 75 37 00

NORTH - PICARDY (BETHUNE - GOSNAY)
La Chartreuse du Val Saint Esprit, 62199 Gosnay, France.
Tel: +33 3 21 62 80 00

NORTH - PICARDY (CALAIS - RECQUES~SUR~HEM)
Château de Cocove, 62890 Recques~sur~Hem, France.
Tel: +33 3 21 82 68 29

NORTH - PICARDY (LILLE)
Carlton Hotel, Rue de Paris, 59000 Lille, France.
Tel: +33 3 20 13 33 13

NORTH - PICARDY (VERVINS)
La Tour du Roy, 02140 Vervins, France.
Tel: +33 3 23 98 00 11

PARIS (CHAMPS~ELYSÉES)
Hôtel Plaza Athénée, 25 Avenue Montaigne, 75008 Paris, France. Tel: +33 1 53 67 66 65

PARIS (CHAMPS~ELYSÉES)
Hôtel San Régis, 12 Rue Jean Goujon, 75008 Paris, France. Tel: +33 1 44 95 16 16

PARIS (CHAMPS~ELYSÉES)
La Trémoille, 14 Rue de La Trémoille, 75008 Paris, France.
Tel: +33 1 56 52 14 00

PARIS (ÉTOILE - PORTE MAILLOT)
L'Hôtel Pergolèse, 3 Rue Pergolèse, 75116 Paris, France.
Tel: +33 1 53 64 04 04

PARIS (ÉTOILE - PORTE MAILLOT)
La Villa Maillot, 143 Avenue de Malakoff, 75116 Paris, France. Tel: +33 1 53 64 52 52

PARIS (INVALIDES)
Hôtel Le Tourville, 16 Avenue de Tourville, 75007 Paris, France. Tel: +33 1 47 05 62 62

PARIS (JARDIN DU LUXEMBOURG)
Le Sainte~Beuve, 9 Rue Sainte~Beuve, 75006 Paris, France. Tel: +33 1 45 48 20 07

PARIS (JARDIN DU LUXEMBOURG)
Relais Médicis, 23 Rue Racine, 75006 Paris, France.
Tel: +33 1 43 26 00 60

PARIS (MADELEINE)
Hôtel de L'Arcade, 9 Rue de L'Arcade, 75008 Paris, France. Tel: +33 1 53 30 60 00

PARIS (MADELEINE)
Hôtel Le Lavoisier, 21 rue Lavoisier, 75008 Paris, France.
Tel: +33 1 53 30 06 06

PARIS (MADELEINE)
Hôtel Opéra Richepanse, 14 Rue du Chevalier de Saint-George, 75001 Paris, France. Tel: +33 1 42 60 36 00

PARIS (MONTPARNASSE)
Hôtel Mayet, 3 Rue Mayet, 75006 Paris, France.
Tel: +33 1 47 83 21 35

PARIS (MONTPARNASSE)
Victoria Palace Hôtel, 6, Rue Blaise Desgoffe, 75006 Paris, France. Tel: +33 1 45 49 70 00

PARIS (OPÉRA)
Pavillon de Paris, 7 Rue de Parme, 75009 Paris, France.
Tel: +33 1 55 31 60 00

PARIS (SAINT~GERMAIN)
Hôtel Le Saint~Grégoire, 43 Rue de L'Abbé Grégoire, 75006 Paris, France. Tel: 33 1 45 48 23 23

PARIS (SAINT~GERMAIN)
L' Hôtel, 13, Rue des Beaux Arts, 75006 Paris, France.
Tel: +33 1 44 41 99 00

PARIS REGION (GRESSY~EN~FRANCE - CHANTILLY)
Le Manoir de Gressy, 77410 Gressy~en~France, Roissy Cdg, Nr Paris, France. Tel: +33 1 60 26 68 00

PARIS REGION (SAINT SYMPHORIEN~LE~CHÂTEAU)
Château d'Esclimont, 28700 Saint Symphorien~Le~Château, France. Tel: +33 2 37 31 15 15

POITOU~CHARENTES (COGNAC - CHÂTEAUBERNARD)
Château de L'Yeuse, 65 Rue de Bellevue, Quartier de Echassier, 16100 Châteaubernard, France.
Tel: +33 5 45 36 82 60

POITOU~CHARENTES (CRAZANNES - SAINTES)
Château de Crazannes, 17350 Crazannes, France.
Tel: +33 6 80 65 40 96

POITOU~CHARENTES (MASSIGNAC)
Domaine des Etangs, 16310 Massignac, France.
Tel: +33 5 45 61 85 00

POITOU~CHARENTES (MOSNAC)
Moulin du Val de Seugne, Marcouze, 17240 Mosnac, France. Tel: +33 5 46 70 46 16

POITOU~CHARENTES (POITIERS - SAINT~MAIXENT~L'ECOLE)
Le Logis Saint Martin, Chemin de Pissot, 79400 Saint~Maixent~L'Ecole, France. Tel: +33 549 0558 68

PROVENCE (AIX~EN~PROVENCE)
Le Pigonnet, 5 Avenue du Pigonnet, 13090 Aix~en~Provence, France. Tel: +33 4 42 59 02 90

PROVENCE (ARLES)
L'Hôtel Particulier, 4 rue de la Monnaie, 13200 Arles, France. Tel: +33 4 90 52 51 40

Mini Listings Europe

Condé Nast Johansens are delighted to recommend over 360 properties across Europe and The Mediterranean. Call 0800 269 397 or see the order forms on page 459 to order guides.

PROVENCE (BONNIEUX~EN~PROVENCE)
La Bastide de Capelongue, 84480 Bonnieux~en~Provence, France. Tel: +33 4 90 75 89 78

PROVENCE (GRIGNAN)
Le Clair de la Plume, Place du Mail, 26230 Grignan, France. Tel: +33 4 75 91 81 30

PROVENCE (GRIGNAN)
Manoir de la Roseraie, Route de Valréas, 26230 Grignan, France. Tel: +33 4 75 46 58 15

PROVENCE (LES~BAUX~DE~PROVENCE)
Mas de l'Oulivié, 13520 Les~Baux~de~Provence, France. Tel: +33 4 90 54 35 78

PROVENCE (LOURMARIN)
Le Moulin de Lourmarin, 84160 Lourmarin, Provence, France. Tel: +33 4 90 68 06 69

PROVENCE (MAZAN)
Château de Mazan, Place Napoléon, 84380 Mazan, France. Tel: +33 4 90 69 62 61

PROVENCE (PORT CAMARGUE)
Le Spinaker, Pointe de la Presqu'île, Port Camargue, 30240 Le Grau~du~Roi, France. Tel: +33 4 66 53 36 37

PROVENCE (SAINT~RÉMY~DE~PROVENCE)
Château des Alpilles, Route Départementale 31, Ancienne Route du Grès, 13210 Saint~Rémy~de~Provence, France. Tel: +33 4 90 92 03 33

PROVENCE (TORNAC-ANDUZE)
Les Demeures du Ranquet, Tornac, 30140 Anduze, France. Tel: +33 4 66 77 51 63

RHÔNE~ALPES (CONDRIEU)
Le Beau Rivage, 2 rue du Beau-Rivage, 69420 Condrieu, France. Tel: +33 4 74 56 82 82

RHÔNE~ALPES (COURCHEVEL 1850)
La Sivolière, 73120 Courchevel 1850, France. Tel: +33 4 79 08 08 33

RHÔNE~ALPES (DIVONNE~LES~BAINS)
Château de Divonne, 01220 Divonne~les~Bains, France. Tel: +33 4 50 20 00 32

RHÔNE~ALPES (DIVONNE~LES~BAINS)
Le Domaine de Divonne Casino, Golf & Spa Resort, Avenue des Thermes, 01220 Divonne-les-Bains, France. Tel: +33 4 50 40 34 34

RHÔNE~ALPES (LES GÊTS)
Chalet Hôtel La Marmotte, 61 Rue du Chêne, 74260 Les Gêts, France. Tel: + 33 4 50 75 80 33

RHÔNE~ALPES (LYON)
La Tour Rose, 22 Rue du Boeuf, 69005 Lyon, France. Tel: +33 4 78 92 69 10

RHÔNE~ALPES (MEGÈVE)
Le Fer à Cheval, 36 route du Crêt d'Arbois, 74120 Megève, France. Tel: +33 4 50 21 30 39

RHÔNE~ALPES (SAVIGNEUX)
Domaine de Fontanelle, Chemin de la rose, 01480 Savigneux, France. Tel: +33 4 74 08 12 15

RHÔNE~ALPES (SCIEZ~SUR~LÉMAN)
Château de Coudrée, Domaine de Coudrée, Bonnatrait, 74140 Sciez~sur~Léman, France. Tel: +33 4 50 72 62 33

RHÔNE~ALPES (SERRE~CHEVALIER)
L'Auberge du Choucas, 05220 Monetier~les~Bains, Serre~Chevalier, Hautes~Alpes, France. Tel: +33 4 92 24 42 73

SOUTH WEST (BIARRITZ)
Hôtel du Palais, 1 Avenue de L'Impératrice, 64200 Biarritz, France. Tel: +33 5 59 41 64 00

SOUTH WEST (SAINTE~RADEGONDE - SAINT~EMILION)
Château de Sanse, 33350 Sainte~Radegonde, France. Tel: +33 5 57 56 41 10

WESTERN LOIRE (CHAMPIGNÉ)
Château des Briottières, 49330 Champigné, France. Tel: +33 2 41 42 00 02

Great Britain & Ireland

ENGLAND (AMBERLEY)
Amberley Castle, Amberley, Near Arundel, West Sussex BN18 9LT, England. Tel: +44 1798 831 992

ENGLAND (DEVON - DARTMOOR NATIONAL PARK)
Bovey Castle, North Bovey, Dartmoor National Park, Devon TQ13 8RE, England. Tel: +44 1647 445 016

ENGLAND (FAWSLEY)
Fawsley Hall, Fawsley, Near Daventry, Northamptonshire NN11 3BA, England. Tel: +44 1327 892000

ENGLAND (LONDON)
The Carlton Tower, One Cadogan Place, London SW1X 9PY, England. Tel: +44 20 7235 1234

ENGLAND (LONDON)
The Cranley, 10 Bina Gardens, South Kensington, London SW5 0LA, England. Tel: +44 20 7373 0123

ENGLAND (LONDON)
The Dorchester, Park Lane, Mayfair, London W1A 2HJ, England. Tel: +44 (0)20 7629 8888

ENGLAND (LONDON)
Draycott House Apartments, 10 Draycott Avenue, Chelsea, London SW3 3AA, England. Tel: +44 20 7584 4659

ENGLAND (LONDON)
The Lowndes Hotel, 21 Lowndes Street, Knightsbridge, London SW1X 9ES, England. Tel: +44 20 7823 1234

ENGLAND (LONDON)
Mayflower Hotel, 26-28 Trebovir Road, London SW5 9NJ, England. Tel: +44 20 7370 0991

ENGLAND (LONDON)
Pembridge Court Hotel, 34 Pembridge Gardens, London W2 4DX, England. Tel: +44 20 7229 9977

ENGLAND (LONDON)
The Royal Park, 3 Westbourne Terrace, Lancaster Gate, Hyde Park, London W2 3UL, England. Tel: +44 20 7479 6600

ENGLAND (LONDON)
Twenty Nevern Square, 20 Nevern Square, London SW5 9PD, England. Tel: +44 20 7565 9555

ENGLAND (ROWSLEY - DERBYSHIRE)
The Peacock at Rowsley, Rowsley, Near Matlock, Derbyshire DE4 2EB, England. Tel: +44 1629 733518

ENGLAND (SONNING ON THAMES)
The French Horn, Sonning on Thames, Berkshire RG4 6TN, England. Tel: +44 1189 692204

IRELAND (DUBLIN)
Aberdeen Lodge, 53-55 Park Avenue, Ballsbridge, Dublin 4, Ireland. Tel: +353 1 283 8155

SCOTLAND (BRORA)
Royal Marine Hotel, Golf Road, Brora, Sutherland KW9 6QS, Scotland. Tel: +44 1408 621252

SCOTLAND (GRANTOWN~ON~SPEY)
Muckrach Lodge Hotel & Restaurant, Dulnain Bridge, By Grantown~on~Spey, Inverness-shire PH26 3LY, Scotland. Tel: +44 1479 851257

SCOTLAND (HIGHLAND)
Skeabost Country House, Skeabost Bridge, Portree IV51 9NP, Scotland. Tel: +44 470 532202

SCOTLAND (SCOTTISH BORDERS)
Castle Venlaw Hotel, Edinburgh Road, Peebles, Scotland EH45 8QG. Tel: +44 1721 720384

Greece

ATHENS
Astir Palace Vouliagmeni, 40 Apollonos Street, 166 71 Vouliagmeni, Athens, Greece. Tel: +30 210 890 2000

ATHENS
Hotel Pentelikon, 66 Diligianni Street, 14562 Athens, Greece. Tel: +30 2 10 62 30 650

CRETE
Athina Suites, Ksamoudochori, Platanias, 73014 Chania, Crete, Greece. Tel: +30 28210 20960

CRETE
The Peninsula at Porto Elounda De Luxe Resort, 72053 Elounda, Crete, Greece. Tel: +30 28410 68000

CRETE
Pleiades Luxurious Villas, Plakes, 72100 Aghios Nikolaos, Crete, Greece. Tel: +30 28410 90450

▼
CRETE
St Nicolas Bay Hotel, PO Box 47, 72100 Aghios Nikolaos, Crete, Greece. **Tel: +30 2841 025041**

MYKONOS
Apanema, Tagoo, Mykonos, Greece. Tel: +30 22890 28590

MYKONOS
Tharroe of Mykonos, Angelika, 84600 Mykonos, Greece. Tel: +30 22890 27370

PAROS
Acquamarina Resort, New Golden Beach, 84400 Paros, Greece. Tel: +30 228404 3281

Italy

CALABRIA (VILLA SAN GIOVANNI)
Altafiumara Hotel, Santa Trada di Cannitello, 89010 Villa San Giovanni (Reggio Calabria), Italy. Tel: +39 096 575 9804

CAMPANIA (RAVELLO)
Hotel Villa Maria, Via S. Chiara 2, 84010 Ravello (SA), Italy. Tel: +39 089 857255

Condé Nast Johansens are delighted to recommend over 360 properties across Europe and The Mediterranean.
Call 0800 269 397 or see the order forms on page 459 to order guides.

CAMPANIA (SORRENTO)
Grand Hotel Cocumella, Via Cocumella 7, 80065
Sant'Agnello, Sorrento, Italy. Tel: +39 081 878 2933

EMILIA ROMAGNA (BOLOGNA)
Monte del Re, 40050 Dozza (Bologna), Italy.
Tel: +39 0542 678400

EMILIA ROMAGNA (FERRARA)
Ripagrande Hotel, Via Ripagrande 21, 44100 Ferrara,
Italy. Tel: +39 0532 765250

EMILIA ROMAGNA (REGGIO EMILIA)
Hotel Posta (Historical Residence), Piazza del Monte, 2,
42100 Reggio Emilia, Italy. Tel: +39 05 22 43 29 44

EMILIA ROMAGNA (RICCIONE)
Hotel des Nations, Lungomare Costituzione 2, 47838
Riccione (RN), Italy. Tel: +39 0541 647878

FRIULI VENEZIA GIULIA (BUDOIA)
Ciasa de Gahja, Via Anzolet 13, 33070 Budoia (PN), Italy.
Tel: +39 0434 654 897

LAZIO (PALO LAZIALE - ROME)
La Posta Vecchia Hotel Spa, Palo Laziale, 00055 Ladispoli,
Rome, Italy. Tel: +39 0699 49501

LAZIO (ROME)
The Duke Hotel, Via Archimede 69, 00197 Rome, Italy.
Tel: +39 06 367221

LAZIO (ROME)
Hotel Aventino, Via San Domenico 10, 00153 Rome, Italy.
Tel: +39 06 5745 231

LAZIO (ROME)
Hotel dei Borgognoni, Via del Bufalo 126 (Piazza di
Spagna), 00187 Rome, Italy. Tel: +39 06 6994 1505

LAZIO (ROME)
Hotel dei Consoli, Via Varrone 2/d, 00193 Roma, Italy.
Tel: +39 0668 892972

LAZIO (ROME)
Hotel Fenix, Viale Gorizia 5/7, 00198 Rome, Italy.
Tel: +39 06 8540 741

LAZIO (ROME)
Hotel Giulio Cesare, Via degli Scipioni 287, 00192 Rome,
Italy. Tel: +39 06 321 0751

LAZIO (ROME)
Hotel Piranesi, Via del Babuino 196, 00187 Rome, Italy.
Tel: +39 06328041

LIGURIA (DIANO MARINA)
Grand Hotel Diana Majestic, Via Oleandri 15, 18013
Diano Marina (IM), Italy. Tel: +39 0183 402 727

LIGURIA (FINALE LIGURE)
Hotel Punta Est, Via Aurelia 1, 17024 Finale Ligure (SV)
Italy. Tel: +39 019 600611

LIGURIA (GENOA NERVI)
Romantik Hotel Villa Pagoda, Via Capolungo 15, 16167
Genoa Nervi, Italy. Tel: +39 010 372 6161

LIGURIA (SANTA MARGHERITA LIGURE)
Grand Hotel Miramare, Via Milite Ignoto, 30, 16038 Santa
Margherita Ligure, Liguria, Italy. Tel: +39 0185 287013

LIGURIA (SESTRI LEVANTE)
Hotel Vis à Vis & Ristorante Olimpo, Via della Chiusa 28,
16039 Sestri Levante (GE), Italy. Tel: +39 0185 42661

LOMBARDY (BELLAGIO - LAKE COMO)
Grand Hotel Villa Serbelloni, Via Roma 1, 22021 Bellagio,
Lake Como, Italy. Tel: +39 031 950 216

LOMBARDY (BRESCIA-LAKE GARDA)
Grand Hotel Gardone Riviera, Via Zanardelli 84, 25083
Gardone Riviera (BS), Lago di Garda, Italy.
Tel: +39 0365 20261

LOMBARDY (DESENZANO DEL GARDA)
Park Hotel, Via Lungolago Cesare Battisti 19, 25015
Desenzano del Garda, Brescia, Italy.
Tel: +39 030 914 3494

LOMBARDY (MONZA - MILANO)
Hotel de la Ville, Viale Regina Margherita 15, 20052
Monza (MI), Italy. Tel: +39 039 382 581

LOMBARDY (SALÒ - LAKE GARDA)
Hotel Bellerive, Via Pietro da Salò 11, 25087 Salò (BS),
Italy. Tel: +39 0365 520 410

PIEMONTE (BELGIRATE - LAKE MAGGIORE)
Villa Dal Pozzo d'Annone, Strada Statale del Sempione 5,
28832 Belgirate (VB), Lake Maggiore, Italy.
Tel: +39 0322 7255

PIEMONTE (STRESA - LAKE MAGGIORE)
Hotel Villa Aminta, Via Sempione Nord 123, 28838 Stresa
(VB), Italy. Tel: +39 0323 933 818

PIEMONTE (VERBANIA - LAKE MAGGIORE)
Grand Hotel Majestic, Via Vittorio Veneto 32, Pallanza,
28922 Verbania (Lake Maggiore), Italy.
Tel: +39 0323 504305

PUGLIA (FASANO)
Masseria Marzalossa, C.da Pezze Vicine 65, 72015 Fasano
(BR), Italy. Tel: +39 080 4413 780

PUGLIA (MARTINA FRANCA)
Villa San Martino, Via Taranto, Zona G - 59, 74015
Martina Franca (TA), Italy. Tel: +39 080 485 7719

▼
PUGLIA (SAVELLETRI DI FASANO)
Masseria San Domenico, Litoranea 379, 72010 Savelletri
di Fasano (Brindisi) Italy. Tel: +39 080 482 7769

SARDINIA (GOLFO DI MARINELLA - PORTO ROTONDO)
Domina Palumbalza, 07026 Olbia (SS) Golfo della
Marinella, Porto Rotondo, Italy. Tel: +39 0789 32005

SICILY (SIRACUSA)
Hotel des Etrangers et Miramare, Passeggio Adorno
10/12, 96100 Siracusa, Italy. Tel: +39 0931 62671

SICILY (TAORMINA MARE)
Grand Hotel Atlantis Bay, Via Nazionale 161, Taormina
Mare, Italy. Tel: +39 0942 612111

SICILY (TAORMINA MARE)
Grand Hotel Mazzarò Sea Palace, Via Nazionale 147,
98030 Taormina (ME), Italy. Tel: +39 0942 612111

SICILY (TAORMINA RIVIERA - MARINA D'AGRO)
Hotel Baia Taormina, Statale dello Ionio 39, 98030
Marina d'Agro (ME), Italy. Tel: +39 0942 756292

TRENTINO - ALTO ADIGE / DOLOMITES (BRESSANONE)
Hotel Dominik am Park, Unterdrittelgasse 13, Via Terzo
di Sotto, I-39042 Brixen/Bressanone, Italy.
Tel: +39 0472 830 144

TRENTINO - ALTO ADIGE / DOLOMITES (COLFOSCO - CORVARA)
Art Hotel Cappella, Str. Pecei 17, Alta Badia - Dolomites,
39030 Colfosco/Corvara (BZ), Italy. Tel: +39 0471 836183

TRENTINO - ALTO ADIGE / DOLOMITES
(MADONNA DI CAMPIGLIO)
Hotel Lorenzetti, Via Dolomiti di Brenta 119, 38084
Madonna Di Campiglio (Tn) Italy. Tel: +39 0465 44 14 04

TRENTINO - ALTO ADIGE / DOLOMITES (MARLING - MERAN)
Romantik Hotel Oberwirt, St Felixweg 2, 39020 Marling -
Meran, Italy. Tel: +39 0473 22 20 20

TRENTINO - ALTO ADIGE / DOLOMITES (MERAN)
Park Hotel Mignon, Via Grabmayr 5, 39012 Meran (BZ),
Italy. Tel: +39 0473 230353

TRENTINO - ALTO ADIGE / DOLOMITES (NOVA LEVANTE)
Posthotel Cavallino Bianco, Via Carezza 30, 39056 Nova
Levante (Bz), Dolomites, Italy. Tel: +39 0471 613113

TRENTINO - ALTO ADIGE / DOLOMITES (VÖLS AM SCHLERN)
Romantik Hotel Turm, Piazza della Chiesa 9, 39050 Völs
Am Schlern, Süd Tirol (Bz), Italy. Tel: +39 0471 725014

TUSCANY (ASCIANO - SIENA)
Castello di Leonina Relais, Strada di Leonina 5, 53041
Asciano (Siena), Italy. Tel: +39 0577 716088

TUSCANY (CAMPIGLIA MARITTIMA)
Castello di Magona, Via di Venturina 27, 57021
Campiglia Marittima (Livorno), Italy.
Tel: +39 0565 851235

TUSCANY (COLLE VAL D'ELSA - SIENA)
Relais della Rovere, Via Piemonte 10, Loc Badia, 53034
Colle Val d'Elsa (SI), Italy. Tel: +39 0577 924696

TUSCANY (CORTONA)
Relais Villa Baldelli, San Pietro a Cegliolo 420, 52044
Cortona (AR), Italy. Tel: +39 0575 612406

TUSCANY (FLORENCE)
Hotel Lorenzo Il Magnifico, Via Lorenzo Il Magnifico 25,
50129 Florence, Italy. Tel: +39 055 4630878

TUSCANY (FLORENCE)
J and J Historic House Hotel, Via di Mezzo 20, 50121
Florence, Italy. Tel: +39 055 26312

TUSCANY (FLORENCE)
Marignolle Relais & Charme, Via di S Quirichino a
Marignolle 16, 50124 Florence, Italy.
Tel: +39 055 228 6910

TUSCANY (FLORENCE)
Villa Montartino, Via Gherardo Silvani 151, 50125
Florence, Italy. Tel: +39 055 223520

TUSCANY (FORTE DEI MARMI - LUCCA)
Hotel Byron, Viale A Morin 46, 55042 Forte dei Marmi
(Lucca), Italy. Tel: +39 0584 787 052

TUSCANY (MONTEBENICHI)
Country House Casa Cornacchi, Loc. Montebenichi,
52021 Arezzo, Tuscany, Italy. Tel: +39 055 998229

TUSCANY (MONTEPULCIANO - SIENA)
Dionora, Via Vicinale di Poggiano, 53040 Montepulciano
(Siena), Italy. Tel: +39 0578 717 496

TUSCANY (MONTERIGGIONI - SIENA)
Hotel Monteriggioni, Via 1 Maggio 4, 53035
Monteriggioni (SI), Italy. Tel: +39 0577 305009

TUSCANY (MONTERIGGIONI - STROVE)
Castel Pietraio, Strada di Strove 33, 53035 Monteriggioni,
Italy. Tel: +39 0577 300020

TUSCANY (MONTEVARCHI - VALDARNO)
Villa Sassolini, Largo Moncioni 85-88, 52020 Moncioni
Montevarchi (Arezzo), Italy. Tel: +39 055 9702246

Mini Listings Europe

Condé Nast Johansens are delighted to recommend over 360 properties across Europe and The Mediterranean.
Call 0800 269 397 or see the order forms on page 459 to order guides.

TUSCANY (PIETRASANTA)
Albergo Pietrasanta - Palazzo Barsanti Bonetti, Via Garibaldi 35, 55045 Pietrasanta (Lucca), Italy.
Tel: +39 0584 793 727

TUSCANY (PIEVESCOLA)
Relais La Suvera, 53030 Pievescola - Siena, Italy.
Tel: +39 0577 960300

TUSCANY (PISA)
Hotel Relais Dell'Orologio, Via della Faggiola 12/14, 56126 Pisa, Italy. Tel: +39 050 830 361

TUSCANY (PORTO ERCOLE)
Il Pellicano Hotel & Spa, Loc. Sbarcatello, 58018 Porto Ercole (Gr), Tuscany, Italy. Tel: +39 0564 858111

TUSCANY (RADDA IN CHIANTI - SIENA)
Relais Fattoria Vignale, Via Panigiani 9, 53017 Radda in Chianti (Siena), Italy. Tel: +39 0577 738300

TUSCANY (ROCCATEDERIGHI - GROSSETO)
Pieve di Caminino (Historical Residence), Via Prov. di Peruzzo, 58028 Roccatederighi (Grosseto), Italy.
Tel: +39 0564 569 737

TUSCANY (VIAREGGIO - LUCCA)
Hotel Plaza e de Russie, Piazza d'Azeglio 1, 55049 Viareggio, Luca, Italy. Tel: +39 0584 44449

UMBRIA (ASSISI)
Romantik Hotel Le Silve di Armenzano, 06081 Loc Armenzano, Assisi (PG), Italy. Tel: +39 075 801 9000

UMBRIA (COLLE SAN PAOLO - PERUGIA)
Romantik Hotel Villa di Monte Solare, Via Montali 7, 06070 Colle San Paolo - Panicale (PG), Italy.
Tel: +39 075 832376

UMBRIA (GUBBIO)
Castello di Petroia, Località Petroia, 06020 Gubbio (Pg), Italy. Tel: +39 075 92 02 87

UMBRIA (MORRA - CITTÀ DI CASTELLO)
Palazzo Terranova, Loc. Ronti Morra, 06010 Morra (PG), Italy. Tel: +39 075 857 0083

UMBRIA (ORVIETO)
Villa Ciconia, Via dei Tigli 69, Loc Ciconia, 05018 Orvieto (TR), Italy. Tel: +39 0763 305582/3

UMBRIA (PETRIGNANO - CORTONA)
Alla Corte del Sole Relais, Loc. I Giorgi, 06061 Petrignano del Lago (PG), Italy. Tel: +39 075 9689008

UMBRIA (PIEVE SAN QUIRICO)
Le Torri di Bagnara, Strada della Bruna 8, 06080 Perugia, Italy. Tel: +39 075 604 136

UMBRIA (SPOLETO)
Convento di Agghielli, Frazione Pompagnano, Località Agghielli, 06049 Spoleto (PG), Italy.
Tel: +39 0743 225 010

UMBRIA (SPOLETO)
Hotel San Luca, Via Interna delle Mura 21, 06049 Spoleto, Italy. Tel: +39 0743 223 399

VALLE D'AOSTA (COURMAYEUR - MONT BLANC)
Romantik Hotel Villa Novecento, Viale Monte Bianco 64, 11013 Courmayeur, Aosta, Italy. Tel: +39 0165 843 000

VENETIA (ASOLO - TREVISO)
Albergo Al Sole, Via Collegio 33, 31011 Asolo, Treviso, Italy. Tel: +39 0423 951 332

VENETIA (BARDOLINO - LAKE GARDA)
Color Hotel, Via Santa Cristina 5, 37011 Bardolino (VR), Italy. Tel: +39 045 621 0857

VENETIA (BASSANO DEL GRAPPA)
Hotel Ca' Sette, Via Cunizza da Romano 4, 36061 Bassano del Grappa, Italy. Tel: +39 0424 383350

VENETIA (CISON-TREVISO)
Castelbrando, Via Brandolini 29, 31030 Cison di Valmarino (TV), Italy. Tel: +39 0438 9761

VENETIA (GARDA - LAKE GARDA)
Villa Madrina, Via Paolo Veronese, 37016 Garda (VR), Italy. Tel: +39 045 6270 144

VENETIA (LAKE GARDA)
Hotel Madrigale, Via Ghiandare 1, 37010 Marciaga, Lake Garda (VR), Italy. Tel: +39 045 627 9001

VENETIA (LIDO DI JESOLO)
Park Hotel Brasilia, Via Levantina, 30017 Lido di Jesolo, Italy. Tel: +39 0421 380851

VENETIA (VALPOLICELLA - VERONA)
Relais La Magioca, Via Moron 3, 37024 Valpolicella (Verona), Italy. Tel: +39 045 600 0167

VENETIA (VENICE)
Domina Prestige Giudecca, Corte Ferrando, Giudecca, 30100 Venice, Italy. Tel: +39 041 2960 168

VENETIA (VENICE)
Hotel Giorgione, SS Apostoli 4587, 30131 Venice, Italy. Tel: +39 041 522 5810

VENETIA (VENICE)
Hotel Londra Palace, Riva degli Schiavoni, 4171, 30122 Venice, Italy. Tel: +39 041 5200533

VENETIA (VENICE - LIDO)
Albergo Quattro Fontane - Residenza d'Epoca, 30126 Lido di Venezia, Venice, Italy. Tel: +39 041 526 0227

VENETIA (VERONA)
Hotel Gabbia d'Oro (Historical Residence), Corso Porta Borsari 4A, 37121 Verona, Italy. Tel: +39 045 8003060

VENETIA (VERONA)
Palazzo San Fermo, Strada San Fermo 8, 37121 Verona, Italy. Tel: +39 045 800 3060

Luxembourg

REMICH
Hotel Saint~Nicolas, 31 Esplanade, 5533 Remich, Luxembourg. Tel: +352 2666 3

Monaco

MONTE~CARLO
Monte~Carlo Beach Hotel, Avenue Princesse Grace, 06190 Roquebrune - Cap~Martin, France.
Tel: +377 92 16 25 25

Norway

VOSS
Fleischers Hotel, 5700 Voss, Norway. Tel: +47 56 52 05 00

Portugal

ALENTEJO (REDONDO)
Convento de São Paulo, Aldeia da Serra, 7170 -120 Redondo, Portugal. Tel: +351 266 989 160

ALGARVE (ALBUFEIRA)
Grande Real Santa Eulália Resort & Hotel Spa, Praia de Santa Eulália, PO Box 2445, 8200-916 Albufeira, Portugal.
Tel: +351 289 598 000

ALGARVE (ALBUFEIRA)
Vila Joya, Praia da Galé, PO Box 120, P-8200 Albufeira, Algarve, Portugal. Tel: +351 289 59 1795

ALGARVE (LAGOS)
Romantik Hotel Vivenda Miranda, Porto de Mós, 8600 Lagos, Portugal. Tel: +351 282 763222

ALGARVE (LAGOS)
Villa Esmeralda, Porto de Mós, 8600 Lagos, Portugal.
Tel: +351 282 760 430

LISBON & TAGUS VALLEY (LISBON)
As Janelas Verdes, Rua das Janelas Verdes 47, 1200-690 Lisbon, Portugal. Tel: +351 21 39 68 143

LISBON & TAGUS VALLEY (LISBON)
Hotel Britania, Rua Rodrigues Sampaio 17, 1150-278 Lisbon, Portugal. Tel: +351 21 31 55 016

LISBON & TAGUS VALLEY (LISBON)
Lisboa Plaza Hotel, TV Salitre / Av Liberdade, 1269-066 Lisbon, Portugal. Tel: +351 213 218 218

LISBON & TAGUS VALLEY (LISBON)
Solar do Castelo, Rua das Cozinhas 2, 1100-181 Lisbon, Portugal. Tel: +351 218 870 909

LISBON & TAGUS VALLEY (LISBON - CASCAIS)
Albatroz Palace, Luxury Suites, Rua Frederico Arouca 100, 2750-353 Cascais, Lisbon, Portugal.
Tel: +351 21 484 73 80

LISBON & TAGUS VALLEY (SANTARÉM)
Casa da Alcáçova, Largo da Alcáçova 3, Portas do Sol, 2000 Santarém, Portugal. Tel: +351 343 304 030

▼
LISBON & TAGUS VALLEY (SINTRA)
Convento De São Saturnino, 2705-001 Azoia - Sintra, Portugal. Tel: +351 21 928 3192

MADEIRA (FUNCHAL)
Quinta da Bela Vista, Caminho do Avista Navios 4, 9000 Funchal, Madeira, Portugal. Tel: +351 291 706400

MADEIRA (PONTA DO SOL)
Estalagem da Ponta do Sol, Quinta da Rochinha, 9360 Ponta do Sol, Madeira, Portugal. Tel: +351 291 970 200

OPORTO & NORTHERN PORTUGAL (PINHÃO)
Vintage House, Lugar da Ponte, 5085-034 Pinhão, Portugal. Tel: +351 254 730 230

OPORTO & NORTHERN PORTUGAL (VIDAGO)
Vidago Palace Hotel, Parque de Vidago, 5425-307 Vidago, Portugal. Tel: +351 276 990 900

Slovak Republik

BRATISLAVA
Hotel Marrol's, Tobrucká ul 4, 81102 Bratislava, Slovak Republik. Tel: +421 25 77 84 600

MINI LISTINGS EUROPE

Condé Nast Johansens are delighted to recommend over 360 properties across Europe and The Mediterranean.
Call 0800 269 397 or see the order forms on page 459 to order guides.

Spain

ANDALUCÍA (ARCOS DE LA FRONTERA)
Hacienda El Santiscal, Avda. El Santiscal 129 (Lago de Arcos), 11630 Arcos de La Frontera, Spain.
Tel: +34 956 70 83 13

ANDALUCÍA (BAEZA)
Hotel Puerta de la Luna, C/ Canónigo Melgares Raya s/n, 23440 Baeza, Jaén, Spain. Tel: +34 953 747 019

▼
ANDALUCÍA (BENHAVIS - MARBELLA)
Hotel Villa Padierna & Flamingos Golf Club, Ctra. de Cádiz Km 166, 29679 Marbella, Spain.
Tel: +34 952 88 91 50

ANDALUCÍA (CASARABONELA)
Hotel La Era, Partido Martina, Los Cerrillos, p.85, 29566 Casarabonela, Málaga, Spain. Tel: +34 952 1125 25

ANDALUCÍA (ÉCIJA)
Hotel Palacio de Los Granados, Emilio Castelar 42, 41400 Écija (Sevilla), Spain. Tel: +34 955 905 344

ANDALUCÍA (ESTEPONA)
Gran Hotel Elba Estepona & Thalasso Spa, Urb Arena Beach, Ctra Estepona-Cadiz 151, 29680 Estepona, Spain.
Tel: +34 952 794 308

ANDALUCÍA (GRANADA)
Hotel Casa Morisca, Cuesta de la Victoria 9, 18010 Granada, Spain. Tel: +34 958 221 100

ANDALUCÍA (GRANADA)
Hotel La Bobadilla, Finca La Bobadilla, Apto 144, 18300 Loja, Granada, Spain. Tel: +34 958 32 18 61

ANDALUCÍA (GRANADA)
Hotel Palacio de Santa Inés, Cuesta de Santa Inés 9, 18010 Granada, Spain. Tel: +34 958 22 23 62

ANDALUCÍA (MÁLAGA)
El Molino de Santillán, Ctra de Macharaviaya, Km 3, 29730 Rincón de la Victoria, Málaga, Spain.
Tel: +34 952 40 09 49

ANDALUCÍA (MÁLAGA)
La Posada del Torcal, 29230 Villanueva de la Concepción, Málaga, Spain. Tel: +34 952 03 11 77

ANDALUCÍA (MARBELLA)
Gran Hotel Guadalpin, Blvd Príncipe Alfonso de Hohenlohe, CN 340, Km 179, 29600 Marbella (Málaga), Spain . Tel: +34 952 899 400

ANDALUCÍA (MARBELLA)
Hotel Los Monteros, Ctra Cadiz, Km 187, 29600 Marbella, Spain. Tel: +34 952 771 700

ANDALUCÍA (MARBELLA)
Vasari Vacation Resort, Urb La Alzambra, Edif Vasari Center, 29660 Marbella, Málaga, Spain.
Tel: +34 952 907 806

ANDALUCÍA (MIJAS~COSTA)
Hotel Byblos Andaluz, Mijas Golf, 29650 Mijas~Costa, Málaga, Spain. Tel: +34 952 47 30 50

ANDALUCÍA (OSUNA - SEVILLE)
Palacio Marqués de la Gomera, C/ San Pedro 20, 41640 Osuna, Seville, Spain. Tel: +34 95 4 81 22 23

ANDALUCÍA (SAN JOSÉ)
Hotel Cortijo el Sotillo, Carretera entrada a San José s/n, 04118 San José-Níjar, Spain. Tel: +34 950 61 11 00

ANDALUCÍA (SEVILLA)
Hotel Las Casas Del Rey de Baeza, C/Santiago, Plaza Jesús de la Redención 2, 41003 Sevilla, Spain.
Tel: +34 954 561 496

ANDALUCÍA (SEVILLE)
Hotel Cortijo Águila Real, Ctra. Guillena-Burguillos Km 4, 41210 Guillena, Seville, Spain. Tel: +34 955 78 50 06

ANDALUCÍA (SEVILLE)
Hotel Hacienda La Boticaria, Ctra Alcalá - Utrera Km 12, 41500 Alcalá de Guadaira (Seville), Spain.
Tel: +34 955 69 88 20

ANDALUCÍA (SOTOGRANDE)
NH Almenara Golf Hotel & Spa, A-7 (National Road), 11310 Sotogrande, Spain. Tel: + 34 956 58 20 00

ANDALUCÍA (TARIFA)
Cortijo el Aguilon, Cn 340, km 68.3, Facinas, 11391 Tarifa (Cádiz), Spain. Tel: +34 637 424 251

ANDALUCÍA (TOLOX)
Cerro de Hijar Hotel, s/n - 29109 Tolox, Málaga, Spain.
Tel: +34 952 11 21 11

ANDALUCÍA (ÚBEDA)
Palacio de la Rambla, Plaza del Marqués 1, 23400 Úbeda, Jaén, Spain. Tel: +34 953 75 01 96

ARAGON (VALDERROBRES)
La Torre del Visco, 44587 Fuentespalda, Teruel, Spain.
Tel: +34 978 76 90 15

ASTURIAS (VILLAMAYOR)
Palacio de Cutre, La Goleta S/N Villamayor, 33583 Infiesto, Asturias, Spain. Tel: +34 985 70 80 72

BALEARIC ISLANDS (IBIZA)
Atzaró Agroturismo, Ctra San Juan, Km 15, 07840 Santa Eulalia, Ibiza, Balearic Islands . Tel: +34 971 33 88 38

BALEARIC ISLANDS (IBIZA)
Can Curreu, Ctra. Sant Carles, km 12, Apdo. Correos 240, 07840 Santa Eulària, Ibiza, Balearic Islands.
Tel: +34 971 335 280

BALEARIC ISLANDS (IBIZA)
Can Lluc, Crta. Santa Inés, km 2, 07816 San Rafael, Ibiza, Balearic Islands. Tel: +34 971 198 673

BALEARIC ISLANDS (IBIZA)
Cas Gasi, Apdo. Correos 117, 07814 Santa Gertrudis, Ibiza, Balearic Islands. Tel: +34 971 197 700

BALEARIC ISLANDS (MALLORCA)
Agroturismo Es Puig Moltó, Ctra. Pina-Montuiri, 07230 Montuiri, Mallorca, Balearic Islands. Tel: +34 971 18 17 58

BALEARIC ISLANDS (MALLORCA)
Ca's Xorc, Carretera de Deía, Km 56.1, 07100 Sóller, Mallorca, Balearic Islands. Tel: +34 971 63 82 80

BALEARIC ISLANDS (MALLORCA)
Can Furiós, Camí Vell Binibona 11, Binibona, 07314 Caimari, Mallorca, Balearic Islands. Tel: +34 971 51 57 51

BALEARIC ISLANDS (MALLORCA)
Gran Hotel Son Net, 07194 Puigpunyent, Mallorca, Balearic Islands. Tel: +34 971 14 70 00

BALEARIC ISLANDS (MALLORCA)
Hotel Dalt Murada, C/ Almudaina 6-A, 07001 Palma de Mallorca, Mallorca, Balearic Islands. Tel: +34 971 425 300

BALEARIC ISLANDS (MALLORCA)
Hotel Maricel, Carretera d'Andratx 11, Cas Català, Palma de Mallorca, 07184 Calvià, Balearic Islands.
Tel: +34 971 707 744

BALEARIC ISLANDS (MALLORCA)
La Moraleja Hotel, Urbanización Los Encinares s/n, 07469 Cala San Vicente, Mallorca, Balearic islands.
Tel: +34 971 534 010

BALEARIC ISLANDS (MALLORCA)
Palacio Ca Sa Galesa, Carrer de Miramar 8, 07001 Palma de Mallorca, Balearic Islands. Tel: +34 971 715 400

BALEARIC ISLANDS (MALLORCA)
Read's, Ca'n Moragues, 07320 Santa María, Mallorca, Balearic Islands. Tel: +34 971 14 02 62

BALEARIC ISLANDS (MALLORCA)
Sa Posada d'Aumallia, Camino Son Prohens 1027, 07200 Felanitx, Mallorca, Balearic Islands. Tel: +34 971 58 26 57

BALEARIC ISLANDS (MALLORCA)
Valldemossa Hotel, Ctra. Vieja de Valldemossa s/n, 07170 Valldemossa, Mallorca, Balearic Islands.
Tel: +34 971 61 26 26

CANARY ISLANDS (FUERTEVENTURA)
Elba Palace Golf Hotel, Urb. Fuerteventura Golf Club, Cta de Jandia, km11, 35610 Antigua, Fuerteventura, Canary Islands. Tel: +34 928 16 39 22

CANARY ISLANDS (FUERTEVENTURA)
Gran Hotel Atlantis Bahía Real, Avenida Grandes Playas s/n, 35660 Corralejo, Fuerteventura, Canary Islands.
Tel: +34 928 53 64 44

CANARY ISLANDS (GRAN CANARIA)
Gran Hotel Costa Meloneras, C/Mar Mediterráneo 1, 35100 Maspalomas, Gran Canaria, Canary Islands.
Tel: +34 928 12 81 00

CANARY ISLANDS (LANZAROTE)
Hesperia Lanzarote Hotel, Urb. Cortijo Viejo, Puerto Calero, 35570 Yaiza, Lanzarote, Canary Islands.
Tel: +34 828 0808 00

CANARY ISLANDS (LANZAROTE)
Princesa Yaiza Suite Hotel***,** Avenida Papagayo s/n, 35570 Playa Blanca, Yaiza, Lanzarote, Canary Islands.
Tel: +34 928 519 222

▼
CANARY ISLANDS (TENERIFE)
Gran Hotel Bahía del Duque Resort, C/Alcalde Walter Paetzmann, s/n 38660 Costa Adeje, Tenerife South, Canary Islands. Tel: +34 922 74 69 00

MINI LISTINGS EUROPE

Condé Nast Johansens are delighted to recommend over 360 properties across Europe and The Mediterranean.
Call 0800 269 397 or see the order forms on page 459 to order guides.

CANARY ISLANDS (TENERIFE)
Hotel Jardín Tropical, Calle Gran Bretaña, 38670 Costa Adeje, Tenerife, Canary Islands. Tel: +34 922 74 60 11/2/3

CANARY ISLANDS (TENERIFE)
Hotel La Quinta Roja, Glorieta de San Francisco, 38450 Garachico, Tenerife, Canary Islands.
Tel: +34 922 13 33 77

CASTILLA Y LEÓN (AMPUDIA)
Posada de la Casa del Abad de Ampudia, Plaza Francisco Martín Gromaz 12, 34160 Ampudia (Palencia), Spain.
Tel: +34 979 768 008

CASTILLA Y LEÓN (ÁVILA)
El Milano Real, C/Toleo s/n, Hoyos del Espino, 05634 Ávila, Spain. Tel: +34 920 349 108

CASTILLA Y LEÓN (SALAMANCA)
Hotel Rector, Rector Esperabé 10-Apartado 399, 37008 Salamanca, Spain. Tel: +34 923 21 84 82

CASTILLA Y LEÓN (TOPAS - SALAMANCA)
Castillo de Buen Amor, Carretera National 630 Km 317, 6, 37799 Topas , Salamanca, Spain. Tel: +34 923 355 002

CATALUÑA (ALCANAR)
Tancat de Codorniu, Ctra N340, Km 1059, Alcanar, 43 43530 Tarragona, Spain. Tel: +34 977 737 194

CATALUÑA (BARCELONA)
Claris Hotel , Pau Claris 150, 08009 Barcelona, Spain.
Tel: +34 934 87 62 62

CATALUÑA (BARCELONA)
Gallery Hotel, Rosselló 249, 08008 Barcelona, Spain.
Tel: +34 934 15 99 11

CATALUÑA (BARCELONA)
Gran Hotel La Florida, Carreta Vallvidrera al Tibidabo 83-93, 08035 Barcelona, Spain. Tel: +34 93 259 30 00

CATALUÑA (BARCELONA)
Hotel Casa Fuster, Passeig de Gràcia 132, 08008 Barcelona, Spain. Tel: +34 93 255 30 00

CATALUÑA (BARCELONA)
Hotel Colón, Avenida de la Catédral 7, 08002 Barcelona, Spain. Tel: +34 933 01 14 04

CATALUÑA (BARCELONA)
Hotel Omm, Rosselló 265, 08008 Barcelona, Spain.
Tel: +34 93 445 40 00

CATALUÑA (CALDERS)
Hotel Urbisol, Ctra Manresa to Moià (N-141c), Km 20, 08279 Calders, Barcelona, Spain. Tel: +34 93 830 9153

CATALUÑA (COSTA BRAVA)
Hotel Santa Marta, Playa de Santa Cristina, 17310 Lloret de Mar, Spain. Tel: +34 972 364 904

CATALUÑA (COSTA BRAVA)
Rigat Park & Spa Hotel, Av. America 1, Playa de Fenals, 17310 Lloret de Mar, Costa Brava, Gerona, Spain.
Tel: +34 972 36 52 00

CATALUÑA (GERONA)
Mas Falgarona, Avinyonet de Puigventos, 17742 Gerona, Spain. Tel: +34 972 54 66 28

CATALUÑA (LA SELVA DEL CAMP)
Hotel Mas Passamaner, Camí de la Serra 52, 43470 La Selva del Camp (Tarragona), Spain. Tel: +34 977 766 333

CATALUÑA (REGENCÓS)
Hotel del Teatre, Plaça Major s/n, 17214 Regencós, Costa Brava, Girona, Spain. Tel: +34 972 30 62 70

CATALUÑA (ROSES)
Romantic Villa - Hotel Vistabella , Cala Canyelles Petites, PO Box 3, 17480 Roses (Gerona), Spain.
Tel: +34 972 25 62 00

CATALUÑA (SITGES)
San Sebastian Playa Hotel, Calle Port Alegre 53, 08870 Sitges (Barcelona), Spain. Tel: +34 93 894 86 76

CATALUÑA (ST JULIÀ DE VILATORTA)
Hotel Torre Martí, C/ Ramon Llull 11, 08504 St Julià de Vilatorta, Spain. Tel: +34 938 88 83 72

GALICIA (ISLA DE LA TOJA)
Gran Hotel Hesperia La Toja, Isla de La Toja s/n, 36991 Pontevedra, Spain. Tel: +34 986 73 00 25

GALICIA (ISLA DE LA TOJA)
Hesperia Isla de la Toja, Isla de La Toja s/n, 36991 Pontevedra, Spain. Tel: +34 986 73 00 50

MADRID (MADRID)
Antiguo Convento, C/ de Las Monjas, s/n Boadilla del Monte, 28660 Madrid, Spain. Tel: + 34 91 632 22 20

MADRID (MADRID)
Gran Meliá Fénix, Hermosilla 2, 28001 Madrid, Spain.
Tel: +34 91 431 67 00

MADRID (MADRID)
Hotel Orfila, C/Orfila, No 6, 28010 Madrid, Spain.
Tel: +34 91 702 77 70

MADRID (MADRID)
Hotel Quinta de los Cedros, C/Allendesalazar 4, 28043 Madrid, Spain. Tel: +34 91 515 2200

MADRID (MADRID)
Hotel Villa Real, Plaza de las Cortes 10, 28014 Madrid, Spain. Tel: +34 914 20 37 67

MADRID (MADRID)
Mirasierra Suites Hotel, C/ Alfredo Marquerié 43, 28034 Madrid, Spain. Tel: +34 91 727 79 00

VALENCIA (ALICANTE)
Amérigo, C/ Rafael Altamira 7, 03002 Alicante, Spain.
Tel: +34 965 14 65 70

VALENCIA (ALICANTE)
Hesperia Alicante Golf, Spa, Hotel, Avenida de las Naciones, s/n Playa de San Juan, 03540 Alicante, Spain.
Tel: +34 965 23 50 00

VALENCIA (ALICANTE)
Hotel Sidi San Juan & Spa, Playa de San Juan, 03540 Alicante, Spain. Tel: +34 96 516 13 00

VALENCIA (ONTINYENT)
Santa Elena, Santa Elena SL, Avda Daniel Gil, No 23, (PO Box 292) 46870 Ontinyent, Valencia, Spain.
Tel: +34 96 291 16 56

VALENCIA (VALENCIA)
Hotel Sidi Saler & Spa, Playa el Saler, 46012 Valencia, Spain. Tel: +34 961 61 04 11

VALENCIA (VALENCIA)
Palau de la Mar, Navrro Reverter 14, 46004 Valencia, Spain. Tel: +34 96 316 2884

Sweden

HESTRA - SMÅLAND
Hestravikens Wärdshus, Vik, 33027, Hestra, Småland, Sweden. Tel: +46 370 33 68 00

Switzerland

WEGGIS - LAKE LUCERNE
Park Hotel Weggis, Hertensteinstrasse 34, CH - 6353 Weggis, Switzerland. Tel: +41 41 392 05 05

The Netherlands

AMSTERDAM
Ambassade Hotel, Herengracht 341, 1016 Az Amsterdam, The Netherlands. Tel: +31 20 5550222

Turkey

ANTALYA
Gloria Select Villas, Aciscu Mevkii, Belek, Antalya, Turkey.
Tel: +90 242 715 2410

ANTALYA
Olympos Lodge, P O Box 38, Çirali - Kemer, Antalya, Turkey. Tel: +90 242 825 7171

ANTALYA
Renaissance Antalya Beach Resort & Spa, PO Box 654, 07004 Beldibi - Kemer, Antalya, Turkey.
Tel: +90 242 824 84 31

ANTALYA
Tekeli Konaklari, Dizdar Hasan Sokak, Kaleici, Antalya, Turkey. Tel: +90 242 244 54 65

ANTALYA
Tuvana Residence, Tuzcular Mahallesi, Karanlik Sokak 7, 07100 Kaleiçi - Antalya, Turkey. Tel: +90 242 247 60 15

▼
BODRUM
Ada Hotel, Bagarasi Mahallesi, Tepecik Caddesi, No 128, PO Box 350, GölTürkbükü, 48400 Bodrum, Turkey.
Tel: +90 252 377 5915

BODRUM
Divan Bodrum Palmira, Kelesharim Caddesi 6, 48483 Göltürkbükü, 48483 Bodrum, Turkey.
Tel: +90 252 377 5601

CAPPADOCIA - ÜRGÜP
Sacred House, Karahandere Mahallesi, Barbaros Hayrettin, Sokak, No 25, 50400 Ürgüp, Turkey.
Tel: +90 384 341 7102

CAPPADOCIA - ÜRGÜP
Ürgüp Evi, Esbelli Mahallesi 54, 50400 Ürgüp-Nevsehir, Turkey. Tel: +90 384 341 3173

GÖCEK - FETHIYE-MUGLA
Swissôtel Göcek Marina & Spa Resort, Cumhuriyet Mahallesi, PO Box 15, Göcek-Fethiye/Mugla, 48310 Göcek, Turkey. Tel: +90 252 645 2760

İZMİR
Sisus, Dalyanköy Yat Limani Mevkii, Çesme - İzmír, Turkey. Tel: +90 232 724 0330

İZMİR
Tas Otel, Kemalpasa Caddesi No 132, Alaçati/Çesme - İzmír, Turkey. Tel: +90 232 716 7772

KALKAN
Hotel Villa Mahal, P.O. Box 4 Kalkan, 07960 Antalya, Turkey. Tel: +90 242 844 32 68

Condé Nast Johansens are delighted to recommend over 240 properties across North America, Mexico, Bermuda, The Caribbean, The Pacific. Call 0800 269 397 or see the order forms on page 459 to order guides.

ARIZONA - SEDONA

Canyon Villa Bed & Breakfast Inn
125 Canyon Circle Drive, Sedona, Arizona 86351
Tel: 1 928 284 1226
Fax: 1 928 284 2114

ARIZONA - SEDONA

L'Auberge De Sedona
301 L'Auberge Lane, Sedona, Arizona 86336
Tel: 1 928 282 1661
Fax: 1 928 282 1064

ARIZONA - SEDONA

The Lodge at Sedona - A Luxury Bed & Breakfast Inn
125 Kallof Place, Sedona, Arizona 86336
Tel: 1 928 204 1942
Fax: 1 928 204 2128

ARIZONA - TUCSON

Arizona Inn
2200 East Elm Street, Tucson, Arizona 85719
Tel: 1 520 325 1541
Fax: 1 520 881 5830

ARIZONA - TUCSON

Tanque Verde Ranch
14301 East Speedway, Tucson, Arizona 85748
Tel: 1 520 296 6275
Fax: 1 520 721 9426

ARIZONA - TUCSON

White Stallion Ranch
9251 West Twin Peaks Road, Tucson, Arizona 85743
Tel: 1 520 297 0252
Fax: 1 520 744 2786

ARKANSAS - EUREKA SPRINGS

The 1886 Crescent Hotel & Spa
75 Prospect Avenue, Eureka Springs, Arkansas 72632
Tel: 1 479 253 9766
Fax: 1 479 253 5296

ARKANSAS - LITTLE ROCK

The Empress of Little Rock
2120 South Louisiana, Little Rock, Arkansas 72206
Tel: 1 501 374 7966
Fax: 1 501 375 4537

ARKANSAS - LITTLE ROCK

The Peabody Little Rock
3 Statehouse Plaza, 72201 Arkansas
Tel: 1 501 375 5000
Fax: 1 501 375 4721

CALIFORNIA - BEL AIR

The Hotel Bel Air
701 Stone Canyon Road, Bel Air, California 90077
Tel: 1 310 472 1211
Fax: 1 310 909 1601

CALIFORNIA - BORREGO SPRINGS

La Casa del Zorro Desert Resort
3845 Yaqui Pass Road, Borrego Springs, California 92004
Tel: 1 760 767 5323
Fax: 1 760 767 5963

CALIFORNIA - CARMEL

Quail Lodge
8000 Valley Greens Drive, Carmel, California 93923
Tel: 1 831 624 2888
Fax: 1 831 624 3726

CALIFORNIA - CARMEL VALLEY

Bernardus Lodge
415 Carmel Valley Road, Carmel Valley California 93924
Tel: 1 831 658 3400
Fax: 1 831 659 3529

CALIFORNIA - CARMEL-BY-THE-SEA

Tradewinds Inn
Mission Street at Third, Carmel-by-the-Sea, California 93921
Tel: 1 831 624 2776
Fax: 1 831 624 0634

CALIFORNIA - EUREKA

Carter House
301 L Street, Eureka, California 95501
Tel: 1 707 444 8062
Fax: 1 707 444 8067

CALIFORNIA - FERNDALE

Gingerbread Mansion Inn
400 Berding Street, Ferndale, California 95536
Tel: 1 707 786 4000
Fax: 1 707 786 4381

CALIFORNIA - FORESTVILLE

Farmhouse Inn and Restaurant
7871 River Road, Forestville, California 95436
Tel: 1 707 887 3300
Fax: 1 707 887 3311

CALIFORNIA - GLEN ELLEN

The Gaige House
13540 Arnold Drive, Glen Ellen, California 95442
Tel: 1 707 935 0237
Fax: 1 707 935 6411

CALIFORNIA - HEALDSBURG

The Grape Leaf Inn
539 Johnson Street, Healdsburg, California 95448
Tel: 1 707 433 8140
Fax: 1 707 433 3140

CALIFORNIA - KENWOOD

The Kenwood Inn and Spa
10400 Sonoma Highway, Kenwood, California 95452
Tel: 1 707 833 1293
Fax: 1 707 833 1247

Condé Nast Johansens are delighted to recommend over 240 properties across North America, Mexico, Bermuda, The Caribbean, The Pacific. Call 0800 269 397 or see the order forms on page 459 to order guides.

CALIFORNIA - LA JOLLA

The Bed & Breakfast Inn At La Jolla
7753 Draper Avenue, La Jolla, California 92037
Tel: 1 858 456 2066
Fax: 1 858 456 1510

CALIFORNIA - LOS GATOS

Hotel Los Gatos & Spa
210 Main Street, Los Gatos, California 95030
Tel: 1 408 335 1700
Fax: 1 408 335 1750

CALIFORNIA - MENDOCINO

The Joshua Grindle Inn
44800 Little Lake Road, Mendocino, California 95460
Tel: 1 707 937 4143
Fax: 1 801 751 4998

CALIFORNIA - MENDOCINO

The Stanford Inn By The Sea
Coast Highway One & Comptche-Ukiah Road, Mendocino, California 95460
Tel: 1 707 937 5615
Fax: 1 707 937 0305

CALIFORNIA - MILL VALLEY

Mill Valley Inn
165 Throckmorton Avenue, Mill Valley, California 94941
Tel: 1 415 389 6608
Fax: 1 415 389 5051

CALIFORNIA - MONTEREY

Old Monterey Inn
500 Martin Street, California 93940
Tel: 1 831 375 8284
Fax: 1 831 375 6730

CALIFORNIA - NAPA

The Carneros Inn
4048 Sonoma Highway, California 94559
Tel: 1 707 299 4900
Fax: 1 707 299 4950

CALIFORNIA - NAPA

Milliken Creek
1815 Silverado Trail, Napa, California 94558
Tel: 1 707 255 1197
Fax: 1 707 255 3112

CALIFORNIA - NAPA VALLEY

1801 First Inn
1801 First Street, Napa, California 94559
Tel: 1 707 224 3739
Fax: 1 707 224 3932

CALIFORNIA - OLEMA

Olema Druids Hall
9870 Shoreline Highway One, Olema, California 94950
Tel: 1 415 663 8727
Fax: 1 415 663 1830

CALIFORNIA - PALM SPRINGS

Caliente tropics Resort
411 East Palm Canyon Drive, Palm Springs, California 92264
Tel: 1 760 327 1391
Fax: 1 760 318 1883

CALIFORNIA - PLAYA DEL REY

Inn At Playa Del Rey
435 Culver Boulevard Playa del Rey, Comer, California 90293
Tel: 1 310 574 1920
Fax: 1 310 574 9920

CALIFORNIA - RANCHO SANTA FE

The Inn at Rancho Santa Fe
5951 Linea del Cielo, Rancho Santa Fe, California 92067
Tel: 1 858 756 1131
Fax: 1 858 759 1604

CALIFORNIA - SAN FRANCISCO

Nob Hill Lambourne
725 Pine Street, San Francisco, California 94108
Tel: 1 415 433 2287
Fax: 1 415 433 0975

CALIFORNIA - SAN FRANCISCO

Union Street Inn
2229 Union Street, San Francisco, California 94123
Tel: 1 415 346 0424
Fax: 1 415 922 8046

CALIFORNIA - SAN FRANCISCO BAY AREA

Gerstle Park Inn
34 Grove Street, San Rafael, California 94901
Tel: 1 415 721 7611
Fax: 1 415 721 7600

CALIFORNIA - SAN JOSE

Hotel Valencia Santana Row
355 Santana Row, San Jose, California 95128
Tel: 1 408 551 0010
Fax: 1 408 551 05550

CALIFORNIA - SANTA BARBARA

Inn of the Spanish Garden
915 Garden Street, Santa Barbara, California 93101
Tel: 1 805 564 4700
Fax: 1 805 564 4701

CALIFORNIA - SANTA YNEZ

The Santa Ynez Inn
3627 Sagunto Street, Santa Ynez, California 93460-0628
Tel: 1 805 688 5588
Fax: 1 805 686 4294

CALIFORNIA - TIBURON

Waters Edge Hotel
25 Main Street, Tiburon, California 94920
Tel: 1 415 789 5999
Fax: 1 415 789 5888

Condé Nast Johansens are delighted to recommend over 240 properties across North America, Mexico, Bermuda, The Caribbean, The Pacific.
Call 0800 269 397 or see the order forms on page 459 to order guides.

CALIFORNIA - BIG SUR

Ventana Inn and Spa
Highway 1, Big Sur, California 93920
Tel: 1 831 667 2331
Fax: 1 831 667 2419

COLORADO - BEAVER CREEK

The Inn at Beaver Creek
10 Elk Track Lane, Beaver Creek Resort, Colorado, 81620
Tel: 1 970 845 5990
Fax: 1 970 845 5911

COLORADO - DENVER

The Brown Palace Hotel
321 17th Street, Denver, Colorado 80202
Tel: 1 303 297 3111
Fax: 1 303 297 2954

COLORADO - DENVER

Castle Marne
1572 Race Street, Denver, Colorado 80206
Tel: 1 303 331 0621
Fax: 1 303 331 0623

COLORADO - EAGLE

Inn & Suites at Riverwalk
27 Main Street, Edwards, Colorado 81632
Tel: 1 970 926 0606
Fax: 1 970 926 0616

COLORADO - ESTES PARK

Taharaa Mountain Lodge
3110 So. St. Vrain, Estes Park, Colorado 80517
Tel: 1 970 577 0098
Fax: 1 970 577 0819

COLORADO - MANITOU SPRINGS

The Cliff House at Pikes Peak
306 Cañon Avenue, Manitou Springs, Colorado 80829
Tel: 1 719 685 3000
Fax: 1 719 685 3913

COLORADO - STEAMBOAT SPRINGS

Vista Verde Guest Ranch
PO Box 770465, Steamboat Springs, Colorado 80477
Tel: 1 970 879 3858
Fax: 1 970 879 1413

DELAWARE - WILMINGTON

The Inn at Montchanin
Route 100 & Kirk Road, Montchanin, Delaware 19710
Tel: 1 302 888 2133
Fax: 1 302 888 0389

DELAWARE - REHOBOTH BEACH

Boardwalk Plaza Hotel
Olive Avenue & The Boardwalk, Rehoboth Beach, Delaware 19971
Tel: 1 302 227 7169
Fax: 1 302 227 0561

DISTRICT OF COLUMBIA - WASHINGTON D.C.

The Hay Adams
Sixteenth & H Streets N.W., Washington D.C. 20006
Tel: 1 202 638 6600
Fax: 1 202 638 2716

DISTRICT OF COLUMBIA - WASHINGTON D.C.

The Madison
15th and M Streets, N.W., Washington D.C. 20005
Tel: 1 202 862 1600
Fax: 1 202 587 2696

FLORIDA - KEY WEST

Simonton Court Historic Inn & Cottages
320 Simonton Street, Key West, Florida 33040
Tel: 1 305 294 6386
Fax: 1 305 293 8446

FLORIDA - LITTLE TORCH KEY

Little Palm Island Resort & Spa
28500 Overseas Highway, Little Torch Key, Florida 33042
Tel: 1 305 872 2524
Fax: 1 305 872 4843

FLORIDA - MIAMI BEACH

Fisher Island Hotel & Resort
One Fisher Island Drive, Fisher Island, Florida 33109
Tel: 1 305 535 6080
Fax: 1 305 535 6003

FLORIDA - MIAMI BEACH

The Tides
1220 Ocean Drive, Miami Beach, Florida 33139
Tel: 1 305 604 5070
Fax: 1 305 604 5180

FLORIDA - NAPLES

LaPlaya Beach & Golf Resort
9891 Gulf Shore Drive, Naples, Florida 34108
Tel: 1 239 597 3123
Fax: 1 239 597 8283

FLORIDA - ORLANDO

Celebration Hotel
700 Bloom Street, Celebration, Florida 34747
Tel: 1 407 566 6000
Fax: 1 407 566 6001

FLORIDA - ORLANDO

Portofino Bay Hotel
5601 Universal Boulevard, Orlando, Florida 32819
Tel: 1 407 503 1000
Fax: 1 407 503 1010

FLORIDA - ORLANDO

Villas of Grand Cypress
One North Jacaranda, Orlando, Florida 32836
Tel: 1 407 239 4700
Fax: 1 407 239 7219

Condé Nast Johansens are delighted to recommend over 240 properties across North America, Mexico, Bermuda, The Caribbean, The Pacific. Call 0800 269 397 or see the order forms on page 459 to order guides.

FLORIDA - PALM COAST

The Lodge at Ocean Hammock

105 16th Road, Palm Coast, Florida 32137
Tel: 1 386 447 4600
Fax: 1 386 447 4601

FLORIDA - SEAGROVE BEACH

WaterColor Inn & Resort

34 Goldenrod Circle, Seagrove Beach, Florida 32459
Tel: 1 850 534 5030
Fax: 1 850 534 5001

FLORIDA - ST. AUGUSTINE

Casablanca Inn

24 Avenida Menendez, St. Augustine, Florida 32084
Tel: 1 904 829 0928
Fax: 1 904 826 1892

FLORIDA - ST. PETE BEACH

Don CeSar Beach Resort

3400 Gulf Boulevard, St. Pete Beach, Florida 33706
Tel: 1 727 360 1881
Fax: 1 727 367 3609

GEORGIA - LITTLE ST. SIMONS ISLAND

The Lodge on Little St. Simons Island

PO Box 21078, Little St. Simons Island, Georgia 31522–0578
Tel: 1 912 638 7472
Fax: 1 912 634 1811

GEORGIA - PERRY

Henderson Village

125 South Langston Circle, Perry, Georgia 31069
Tel: 1 478 988 8696
Fax: 1 478 988 9009

GEORGIA - SAVANNAH

The Eliza Thompson House

5 West Jones Street, Savannah, Georgia 31401
Tel: 1 912 236 3620
Fax: 1 912 238 1920

HAWAII - HILO

Shipman House

131 Ka'iulani Street, Hilo, Hawaii 96720
Tel: 1 808 934 8002
Fax: 1 808 934 8002

HAWAII - HONOMU

The Palms Cliff House

28-3514 Mamalahoa Highway 19, PO Box 189, Honomu, Hawaii 96728-0189
Tel: 1 808 963 6076
Fax: 1 808 963 6316

HAWAII - LAHAINA

Lahaina Inn

127 Lahainaluna Road, Lahaina, Maui, Hawaii 96761
Tel: 1 808 661 0577
Fax: 1 808 667 9480

HAWAII - LAHAINA

The Plantation Inn

174 Lahainaluna Road, Lahaina, Maui, Hawaii 96761
Tel: 1 808 667 9225
Fax: 1 808 667 9293

IDAHO - MCCALL

The Whitetail Club

501 West Lake Street, McCall, Idaho 83638
Tel: 1 208 634 2244
Fax: 1 208 634 7504

LOUISIANA - NAPOLEONVILLE

Madewood Plantation House

4250 Highway 308, Napoleonville, Louisiana 70390
Tel: 1 985 369 7151
Fax: 1 985 369 9848

LOUISIANA - NEW ORLEANS

Hotel Maison De Ville

727 Rue Toulouse, New Orleans, Louisiana 70130
Tel: 1 504 561 5858
Fax: 1 504 528 9939

LOUISIANA - NEW ORLEANS

The LaFayette Hotel

600 St. Charles Avenue, New Orleans, Louisiana 70130
Tel: 1 504 524 4441
Fax: 1 504 962 5537

LOUISIANA - ST. FRANCISVILLE

The Lodge at the Bluffs

Highland 965 at Freeland Road, 70748 Louisiana
Tel: 1 225 634 3410
Fax: 1 225 634 3528

MARYLAND - FROSTBURG

Savage River Lodge

1600 Mt. Aetna Road, Frostburg, Maryland 21536
Tel: 1 301 689 3200
Fax: 1 301 689 2746

MARYLAND - TANEYTOWN

Antrim 1844

30 Trevanion Road, Taneytown, Maryland 21787
Tel: 1 410 756 6812
Fax: 1 410 756 2744

MISSISSIPPI - JACKSON

Fairview Inn

734 Fairview Street, Jackson, Mississippi 39202
Tel: 1 601 948 3429
Fax: 1 601 948 1203

MISSISSIPPI - NATCHEZ

Dunleith

84 Homochitto Street, Natchez, Mississippi 39120
Tel: 1 601 446 8500
Fax: 1 601 446 8554

MINI LISTINGS NORTH AMERICA

Condé Nast Johansens are delighted to recommend over 240 properties across North America, Mexico, Bermuda, The Caribbean, The Pacific.
Call 0800 269 397 or see the order forms on page 459 to order guides.

MISSISSIPPI - NATCHEZ

Monmouth Plantation

36 Melrose Avenue At John A. Quitman Parkway, Natchez, Mississippi 39120
Tel: 1 601 442 5852
Fax: 1 601 446 7762

MISSISSIPPI - VICKSBURG

Anchuca Historic Mansion & Inn

1010 First East Street, Vicksburg, Mississippi 39183
Tel: 1 601 661 0111
Fax: 1 601 661 0111

MISSOURI - ST. LOUIS

The Chase Park Plaza

212-232 North Kingshighway Boulevard, St. Louis, Missouri 63108
Tel: 1 314 633 3000
Fax: 1 314 633 1144

MISSOURI - KANSAS CITY

The Raphael Hotel

325 Ward Parkway, Kansas City, Missouri 64112
Tel: 1 816 756 3800
Fax: 1 816 802 2131

MONTANA - BIG SKY

The Big EZ Lodge

7000 Beaver Creek Road, Big Sky, Montana 59716
Tel: 1 406 995 7000
Fax: 1 406 995 7007

NEW ENGLAND / CONNECTICUT - ESSEX

Copper Beech Inn

46 Main Street, Ivoryton, Connecticut 06442
Tel: 1 860 767 0330
Fax: 1 860 767 7840

NEW ENGLAND / CONNECTICUT - GREENWICH

Delamar Greenwich Harbor Hotel

500 Steamboat Road, Greenwich, Connecticut 06830
Tel: 1 203 661 9800
Fax: 1 203 661 2513

NEW ENGLAND / CONNECTICUT - WESTPORT

The Inn at National Hall

2 Post Road West, Westport, Connecticut 06880
Tel: 1 203 221 1351
Fax: 1 203 221 0276

NEW ENGLAND / MAINE - GREENVILLE

The Lodge At Moosehead Lake

Upon Lily Bay Road, Box 1167, Greenville, Maine 04441
Tel: 1 207 695 4400
Fax: 1 207 695 2281

NEW ENGLAND / MAINE - KENNEBUNKPORT

The Captain Lord Mansion

6 Pleasant Street, Kennebunkport, Maine 04046-0800
Tel: 1 207 967 3141

NEW ENGLAND / MAINE - NEWCASTLE

The Newcastle Inn

60 River Road, Newcastle, Maine 04553
Tel: 1 207 563 5685
Fax: 1 207 563 6877

NEW ENGLAND / MASSACHUSETTS - BOSTON

The Charles Street Inn

94 Charles Street, Boston, Massachusetts 02114–4643
Tel: 1 617 314 8900
Fax: 1 617 371 0009

NEW ENGLAND / MASSACHUSETTS - BOSTON

The Lenox

61 Exeter Street at Boylston, Boston, Massachusetts 02116
Tel: 1 617 536 5300
Fax: 1 617 267 1237

NEW ENGLAND / MASSACHUSETTS - CAPE COD

Wequassett Inn Resort and Golf Club

On Pleasant Bay, Chatham, Cape Cod, Massachusetts 02633
Tel: 1 508 432 5400
Fax: 1 508 430 3131

NEW ENGLAND / MASSACHUSETTS - LENOX

Cranwell Resort, Spa & Golf Club

55 Lee Road, Route 20, Lenox, Massachusetts 01240
Tel: 1 413 637 1364
Fax: 1 413 637 4364

NEW ENGLAND / MASSACHUSETTS - MARTHA'S VINEYARD

Hob Knob Inn

128 Main Street, Edgartown, Massachusetts 02539
Tel: 1 508 627 9510
Fax: 1 508 627 4560

NEW ENGLAND / MASSACHUSETTS - MARTHA'S VINEYARD

The Victorian Inn

24 South Water Street, Edgartown, Massachusetts 02539
Tel: 1 508 627 4784

NEW ENGLAND / MASSACHUSETTS - MARTHA'S VINEYARD

The Winnetu Inn & Resort at South Beach

31 Dunes Road, Edgartown, Massachusetts 02539
Tel: 1 978 443 1733
Fax: 1 978 443 0479

NEW ENGLAND / MASSACHUSETTS - ROCKPORT

Seacrest Manor

99 Marmion Way, Rockport, Massachusetts 01966
Tel: 1 978 546 2211

NEW ENGLAND / NEW HAMPSHIRE - ASHLAND

The Glynn House Inn

59 Highland Street, Ashland, New Hampshire 03217
Tel: 1 603 968 3775
Fax: 1 603 968 9415

Mini Listings North America

Condé Nast Johansens are delighted to recommend over 240 properties across North America, Mexico, Bermuda, The Caribbean, The Pacific.
Call 0800 269 397 or see the order forms on page 459 to order guides.

NEW ENGLAND / NEW HAMPSHIRE - JACKSON

The Wentworth

Jackson Village, New Hampshire 03846
Tel: 1 603 383 9700
Fax: 1 603 383 4265

NEW ENGLAND / RHODE ISLAND - BLOCK ISLAND

The Atlantic Inn

Po Box 1788, Block Island, Rhode Island 02807
Tel: 1 401 466 5883
Fax: 1 401 466 5678

NEW ENGLAND / RHODE ISLAND - NEWPORT

The Agincourt Inn

120 Miantonomi Avenue, Newport, Rhode Island 02842
Tel: 1 401 847 0902
Fax: 1 401 848 6529

RHODE ISLAND - NEWPORT

The Chanler at Cliff Walk

117 Memorail Boulevard, Newport, Rhode Island 02840
Tel: 1 401 847 1300
Fax: 1 401 847 3620

NEW ENGLAND / VERMONT - KILLINGTON

Fox Creek Inn

49 Dam Road, Chittenden, Vermont 05737
Tel: 1 802 483 6213
Fax: 1 802 483 2623

NEW ENGLAND / VERMONT - KILLINGTON

Mountain Top Inn & Resort

195 Mountain Top Road, Chittenden, Vermont 05737
Tel: 1 802 483 2311
Fax: 1 802 483 6373

NEW ENGLAND / VERMONT - KILLINGTON

Red Clover Inn

Woodward Road, Mendon, Vermont 05701
Tel: 1 802 775 2290
Fax: 1 802 773 0594

NEW ENGLAND / VERMONT - MANCHESTER CENTER

Inn at Ormsby Hill

Route 7A, 1842 Main Street, Manchester Center, Vermont
05255
Tel: 1 802 362 1163
Fax: 1 802 362 5176

NEW ENGLAND / VERMONT - STOWE

The Green Mountain Inn

18 Main Street, Stowe, Vermont 05672
Tel: 1 802 253 7301
Fax: 1 802 253 5096

NEW ENGLAND / VERMONT - STOWE

The Mountain Road Resort At Stowe

PO Box 8, 1007 Mountain Road, Stowe, Vermont 05672
Tel: 1 802 253 4566
Fax: 1 802 253 7397

NEW ENGLAND / VERMONT - WOODSTOCK

Woodstock Inn & Resort

Fourteen The Green, Woodstock, Vermont 05091-1298
Tel: 1 802 457 1100
Fax: 1 802 457 6699

NEW MEXICO - SANTA FE

The Bishop's Lodge Resort & Spa

PO Box 2367, Santa Fe, New Mexico 87504
Tel: 1 505 983 6377
Fax: 1 505 989 8739

NEW MEXICO - SANTA FE

Hotel St. Francis

210 Don Gaspar Avenue, Santa Fe, New Mexico 87501
Tel: 1 505 983 5700
Fax: 1 505 989 7690

NEW MEXICO - SANTA FE

Inn of the Anasazi

113 Washington Avenue, Santa Fe, New Mexico 87501
Tel: 1 505 988 3030
Fax: 1 505 988 3277

NEW MEXICO - SANTA FE

The Inn of The Five Graces

150 E Devargas Street, Santa Fe, New Mexico 87501
Tel: 1 505 992 0957
Fax: 1 505 955 0549

NEW MEXICO - SANTA FE

Inn of the Turquoise Bear

342 E. Buena Vista Street, Santa Fe, New Mexico 87505-
2623
Tel: 1 505 983 0798
Fax: 1 505 988 4225

NEW YORK - AURORA

The Aurora Inn

391 Main Street, Aurora, new York 13026
Tel: 1 315 364 8888
Fax: 1 315 364 8887

NEW YORK - CAZENOVIA

The Brewster Inn

6 Ledyard Avenue, Cazenovia, New York 13035
Tel: 1 315 655 9232
Fax: 1 315 655 2130

NEW YORK - DOVER PLAINS

Old Drovers Inn

196 East Duncan Hill Road, Dover Plains, New York 12522
Tel: 1 845 832 9311
Fax: 1 845 832 6356

NEW YORK - EAST AURORA

Roycroft Inn

40 South Grove Street, East Aurora, New York 14052
Tel: 1 716 652 5552
Fax: 1 716 655 5345

Mini Listings North America

NEW YORK - GENEVA

Geneva On The Lake
1001 Lochland Road (Route 14), Geneva, New York 14456
Tel: 1 315 789 7190
Fax: 1 315 789 0322

NEW YORK - LAKE GEORGE

The Sagamore
110 Sagamore Road, Bolton Landing, New York 12814
Tel: 1 518 644 9400
Fax: 1 518 644 2851

NEW YORK - LAKE PLACID

Lake Placid Lodge
Whiteface Inn Road, New York 12946
Tel: 1 518 523 2700
Fax: 1 518 523 1124

NEW YORK - LONG ISLAND

Inn at Great Neck
30 Cutter Mill Road, Great Neck, New York 11021
Tel: 1 516 773 2000
Fax: 1 516 773 2020

NEW YORK - LONG ISLAND

The Mill House Inn
31 North Main Street, East Hampton New York 11937
Tel: 1 631 324 9766
Fax: 1 631 324 9793

NEW YORK - MOUNT TREMPER

The Emerson Inn & Spa
146 Mount Pleasant Road, Mount Tremper, New York 12457
Tel: 1 845 688 7900
Fax: 1 845 688 2789

NEW YORK - NEW YORK CITY

The Benjamin
125 East 50th Street, New York, New York 10022
Tel: 1 212 320 8002
Fax: 1 212 465 3697

NEW YORK - NEW YORK CITY

Hotel Plaza Athenee
37 East 64th Street, New York 10021
Tel: 1 212 734 9100
Fax: 1 212 772 0958

NEW YORK - NEW YORK CITY

The Inn at Irving Place
56 Irving Place, New York, New York 10003
Tel: 1 212 533 4600
Fax: 1 212 533 4611

NEW YORK - SARANAC LAKE

The Point
Saranac Lake, New York 12983
Tel: 1 518 891 5674
Fax: 1 518 891 1152

NORTH CAROLINA - BEAUFORT

The Cedars Inn
305 Front Street, Beaufort, North Carolina 28516
Tel: 1 252 728 7036
Fax: 1 252 728 1685

NORTH CAROLINA - BLOWING ROCK

Gideon Ridge Inn
202 Gideon Ridge Road, Blowing Rock, North Carolina 28605
Tel: 1 828 295 3644
Fax: 1 828 295 4586

NORTH CAROLINA - CASHIERS

Millstone Inn
119 Lodge Lane, Highway 64 West, Cashiers, North Carolina 28717
Tel: 1 828 743 2737
Fax: 1 828 743 0208

NORTH CAROLINA - CHARLOTTE

Ballantyne Resort
10000 Ballantyne Commons Parkway, Charlotte, North Carolina 28277
Tel: 1 704 248 4000
Fax: 1 704 248 4099

NORTH CAROLINA - CHARLOTTE

The Park
2200 Rexford Road, Charlotte, North Carolina 28211
Tel: 1 704 364 8220
Fax: 1 704 365 4712

NORTH CAROLINA - HENDERSONVILLE

Claddagh Inn
755 North Main Street, Hendersonville, North Carolina 28792
Tel: 1 828 697 7778
Fax: 1 828 697 8664

NORTH CAROLINA - HIGHLANDS

Old Edwards Inn and Spa
445 Main Street, Highlands, North Carolina 28741
Tel: 1 828 526 8008
Fax: 1 828 526 8301

NORTH CAROLINA - NEW BERN

Aerie Inn
509 Pollock Street, New Bern, North Carolina 28562
Tel: 1 252 636 5553
Fax: 1 252 514 2157

NORTH CAROLINA - RALEIGH - DURHAM

The Siena Hotel
1505 E Franklin Street, Chapel Hill, North Carolina 27514
Tel: 1 919 929 4000
Fax: 1 919 968 8527

NORTH CAROLINA - ROBBINSVILLE

Snowbird Mountain Lodge
275 Santeetlah Road, Robbinsville, North Carolina 28771
Tel: 1 828 479 3433
Fax: 1 828 479 3473

MINI LISTINGS NORTH AMERICA

Condé Nast Johansens are delighted to recommend over 240 properties across North America, Mexico, Bermuda, The Caribbean, The Pacific.
Call 0800 269 397 or see the order forms on page 459 to order guides.

NORTH CAROLINA - TRYON

Pine Crest Inn

85 Pine Crest Lane, Tryon, North Carolina 28782
Tel: 1 828 859 9135
Fax: 1 828 859 9136

NORTH CAROLINA - WILMINGTON

Graystone Inn

100 South Third Street, Wilmington, North Carolina 28401
Tel: 1 910 763 2000
Fax: 1 910 763 5555

OHIO - CINCINNATI

The Cincinnatian Hotel

601 Vine Street, Cincinnati, Ohio 45202-2433
Tel: 1 513 381 3000
Fax: 1 513 651 0256

OKLAHOMA - BARTLESVILLE

Inn at Price Tower

510 Dewey Avenue, Bartlesville, Oklahoma 74003
Tel: 1 918 336 1000
Fax: 1 918 336 7117

OREGON - ASHLAND

The Winchester Inn & Restaurant

35 South Second Street, Ashland, Oregon 97520
Tel: 1 541 488 1113
Fax: 1 541 488 4604

OREGON - EUGENE

The Campbell House

252 Pearl Street, Eugene, Oregon 97401
Tel: 1 541 343 1119
Fax: 1 541 343 2258

OREGON - GOLD BEACH

Tu Tu' Tun Lodge

96550 North Bank Rogue, Gold Beach, Oregon 97444
Tel: 1 541 247 6664
Fax: 1 541 247 0672

OREGON - PORTLAND

The Benson Hotel

309 Southwest Broadway, Portland, Oregon 97205
Tel: 1 503 228 2000
Fax: 1 503 471 3920

OREGON - PORTLAND

Portland's White House

1914 North East 22nd Avenue, Portland, Oregon 97212
Tel: 1 503 287 7131
Fax: 1 503 249 1641

PENNSYLVANIA - HANOVER

Sheppard Mansion

117 Frederick Street, Hanover, Pennsylvania 17331
Tel: 1 717 633 8075
Fax: 1 717 633 8074

PENNSYLVANIA - LEOLA

Leola Village Inn & Suites

38 Deborah Drive, Route 23, Leola, Pennsylvania 17540
Tel: 1 717 656 7002
Fax: 1 717 656 7648

PENNSYLVANIA - NEW BERLIN

The Inn at New Berlin

321 Market Street, New Berlin, Pennsylvania 17855-0390
Tel: 1 570 966 0321
Fax: 1 570 966 9557

PENNSYLVANIA - PHILADELPHIA

Rittenhouse Square European Boutique Hotel

1715 Rittenhouse Square, Philadelphia, Pennsylvania 19103
Tel: 1 215 546 6500
Fax: 1 215 546 8787

PENNSYLVANIA - SKYTOP

Skytop Lodge

One Skytop, Skytop, Pennyslvania 18357
Tel: 1 800 345 7759
Fax: 1 570 595 8917

SOUTH CAROLINA - CHARLESTON

The Boardwalk Inn at Wild Dunes Resort

5757 Palm Boulevard, Isle of Palms, South Carolina 29451
Tel: 1 843 886 6000
Fax: 1 843 886 2916

SOUTH CAROLINA - CHARLESTON

Vendue Inn

19 Vendue Range, Charleston, South Carolina 29401
Tel: 1 843 577 7970
Fax: 1 843 577 2913

SOUTH CAROLINA - KIAWAH ISLAND

The Sanctuary at Kiawah Island

1 Sanctuary Beach Drive, Kiawah Island, South Carolina 29455
Tel: 1 843 768 6000
Fax: 1 843 768 5150

SOUTH CAROLINA - PAWLEYS ISLAND

Litchfield Plantation

Kings River Road, Box 290, Pawleys Island, South Carolina 29585
Tel: 1 843 237 9121
Fax: 1 843 237 1041

SOUTH CAROLINA - TRAVELERS REST

La Bastide

10 Road Of Vines, Travelers Rest, South Carolina 29690
Tel: 1 864 836 8463
Fax: 1 864 836 4820

TEXAS - AUSTIN

The Mansion at Judges' Hill

1900 Rio Grande, Austin, Texas 78705
Tel: 1 512 495 1800
Fax: 1 512 691 4461

Condé Nast Johansens are delighted to recommend over 240 properties across North America, Mexico, Bermuda, The Caribbean, The Pacific.

Call 0800 269 397 or see the order forms on page 459 to order guides.

TEXAS - GLEN ROSE

Rough Creek Lodge

PO Box 2400, Glen Rose, Texas 76043
Tel: 1 254 965 3700
Fax: 1 254 918 2570

TEXAS - SAN ANTONIO

Hotel Valencia Riverwalk

150 East Houston Street, San Antonio, Texas 78205
Tel: 1 210 227 9700
Fax: 1 210 227 9701

TEXAS - SAN ANTONIO SAN ANTONIO

Beauregard House

215 Beauregard Street, San Antonio, Texas 78204
Tel: 1 210 222 1198
Fax: 1 210 222 9338

VIRGINIA - CHARLOTTESVILLE

200 South Street Inn

200 South Street, Charlottesville, Virginia 22902
Tel: 1 434 979 0200
Fax: 1 434 979 4403

VIRGINIA - CHARLOTTESVILLE

The Clifton Inn

1296 Clifton Inn Drive, Charlottesville, Virginia 22911
Tel: 1 434 971 1800
Fax: 1 434 971 7098

WASHINGTON - BELLINGHAM

The Chrysalis Inn & Spa

804 10th Street, Bellingham, Washington 98225
Tel: 1 360 756 1005
Fax: 1 360 647 0342

WASHINGTON - FRIDAY HARBOR

Friday Harbor House

130 West Street, Washington 98250
Tel: 1 360 378 8455
Fax: 1 360 378 8453

WASHINGTON - SEATTLE

Sorrento Hotel

900 Madison Street, Seattle, Washington 98104-1297
Tel: 1 206 622 6400
Fax: 1 206 343 6155

WASHINGTON - SEATTLE

Woodmark Hotel on Lake Washington

1200 Carillon Point, Kirkland, Washington 98033
Tel: 1 425 822 3700
Fax: 1 425 822 3699

WASHINGTON - SPOKANE

The Davenport Hotel

10 South Post Street, Spokane, Washington 99201
Tel: 1 509 455 8888
Fax: 1 509 624 4455

WASHINGTON - UNION

Alderbrook Resort & Spa

10 East Alderbrook Drive, Union, Washington 98592
Tel: 1 360 898 2200
Fax: 1 360 898 4610

WASHINGTON - WOODINVILLE

The Herbfarm

14590 North East 145th Street, Woodinville, Washington 98072
Tel: 1 425 485 5300
Fax: 1 425 424 2925

WASHINGTON - WOODINVILLE

Willows Lodge

14580 N.E. 145th Street, Woodinville, Washington 98072
Tel: 1 425 424 3900
Fax: 1 425 424 2585

WYOMING - CHEYENNE

Nagle Warren Mansion

222 East 17Th Street, Cheyenne, Wyoming 82001
Tel: 1 307 637 3333
Fax: 1 307 638 6879

WYOMING - JACKSON

The Rusty Parrot Lodge

175 North Jackson Street, Jackson, Wyoming 83001
Tel: 1 307 733 2000
Fax: 1 307 733 5566

WYOMING - JACKSON HOLE

Spring Creek Ranch

1800 Spirit Dance Road, Wyoming 83001
Tel: 1 307 733 8833
Fax: 1 307 733 1524

WYOMING - MORAN

Jenny Lake Lodge

Inner Park Loop Road, Grand Teton National Park, Wyoming 83013
Tel: 1 307 543 3300
Fax: 1 307 543 3358

MEXICO - ACAPULCO

Quinta Real Acapulco

Paseo de la Quinta 6, Desarrollo Turistico Real Diamante, Acapulco, Guerrero 39907
Tel: 52 744 469 1500
Fax: 52 744 469 1516

MEXICO - AGUASCALIENTES

Quinta Real Aguascalientes

Av. Aguascalientes Sur 601, Jardines de la Asuncion, Aguascalientes, Aguascalientes 20070
Tel: 52 449 978 5818
Fax: 52 449 978 5616

MEXICO - BAJA CALIFORNIA

Casa Natalia

Blvd Mijares 4, San Jose Del Cabo, Baja California Sur 23400
Tel: 52 624 14 251 00
Fax: 52 624 14251 10

MINI LISTINGS NORTH AMERICA

Condé Nast Johansens are delighted to recommend over 240 properties across North America, Mexico, Bermuda, The Caribbean, The Pacific. Call 0800 269 397 or see the order forms on page 459 to order guides.

MEXICO - CANCUN

Villas Tacul Boutique Hotel
Boulevard Kukulkan, KM 5.5, Cancun, Quintana Roo 77500
Tel: 52 998 883 00 00
Fax: 52 998 849 70 70

MEXICO - GUADALAJARA

Quinta Real Guadalajara
Av. Mexico 2727 Fraccionamiento Monraz, Guadalajara, Jalisco 44680
Tel: 52 33 3669 0600
Fax: 52 33 3669 0601

MEXICO - GUANAJUATO

Quinta Las Acacias
Paseo de la Presa 168, Guanajuato, Guanajuato 36000
Tel: 52 473 731 1517
Fax: 52 473 731 1862

MEXICO - GUANAJUATO

Quinta Real Casa de Sierra Nevada
Hospicio 35, San Miguel de Allende, Guanajuato 37700
Tel: 52 415 152 7040
Fax: 52 415 152 1436

MEXICO - HUATULCO

Quinta Real Huatulco
Paseo Benito Juarez Lote 2, Bahia de Tangolunda, Huatulco, Oaxaca 70989
Tel: 52 958 58 10428
Fax: 52 958 58 10429

MEXICO - ISLA MUJERES

Secreto
Sección Rocas, Lote 11, Punta Norte, Isla Mujeres, Quintana Roo 77400
Tel: 52 998 877 1039
Fax: 52 998 877 1048

MEXICO - MÉRIDA

Hacienda Xcanatun & Casa de Piedra
Carretera Mérida-Progreso, Km 12, Mérida, Yucatán 97300
Tel: 52 999 941 0273
Fax: 52 999 941 0319

MEXICO - MONTERREY

Quinta Real Monterrey
Diego Rivera 500, Fracc. Valle Oriente, Monterrey, Nuevo León 66260
Tel: 52 81 83 68 1000
Fax: 52 81 83 68 1070

MEXICO - MORELIA

Hotel Los Juaninos
Morelos Sur 39, Centro, Morelia, Michoacán 58000
Tel: 52 443 312 00 36
Fax: 52 443 312 00 36

MEXICO - MORELIA

Villa Montaña Hotel & Spa
201 Patzimba Vista Bella, Morelia, Michoacán 58090
Tel: 52 443 314 02 31
Fax: 52 443 315 14 23

MEXICO - NUEVO VALLARTA

Grand Velas All Suites & Spa Resort
Av. Cocoteros 98 Sur, Nuevo Vallarta, Nayarit 63735
Tel: 52 322 226 8000
Fax: 52 322 297 2005

MEXICO - OAXACA

Casa Cid de Leon
Av. Morelos 602, Centro, Oaxaca, Oaxaca 68000
Tel: 52 951 514 1893
Fax: 52 951 514 7013

MEXICO - OAXACA

Casa Oaxaca
Calle García Vigil 407, Centro, Oaxaca, Oaxaca 68000
Tel: 52 951 514 4173
Fax: 52 951516 4412

MEXICO - OAXACA

Hacienda Los Laureles - Spa
Hildago 21, San Felipe del Agua, Oaxaca 68020
Tel: 52 951 501 5300
Fax: 52 951 501 5301

MEXICO - PUERTO VALLARTA

Las Alamandas Resort
Carretera Barra de Navidad - Puerto Vallarta km 83.5, Col. Quemaro, Jalisco 48980
Tel: 52 322 285 5500
Fax: 52 322 285 5027

MEXICO - PUERTO VALLARTA

Quinta Real Puerto Vallarta
Pelicanos 311, Fracc. Marina Vallarta, Puerto Vallarta, Jalisco 48354
Tel: 52 322 226 6688
Fax: 52 322 226 6699

MEXICO - SALTILLO

Quinta Real Saltillo
Colosio 1385, Saltillo, Coahuila, 25205
Tel: 52 844 485 0471
Fax: 52 844 485 0470

MEXICO - SONORA

Hacienda de los Santos Resort & Spa
Calle Molina 8, Alamos, Sonora 85760
Tel: 52 647 428 0222
Fax: 52 647 428 0367

MEXICO - ZACATECAS

Quinta Real Zacatecas
Av. Ignacio Rayon 434, Centro, Zacatecas, Zacatecas 98000
Tel: 52 492 92 29104
Fax: 52 492 922 8440

MEXICO - ZIHUATANEJO

Hotel Villa Del Sol
Playa La Ropa S/N, Zihuatanejo, Guerrero 40880
Tel: 52 755 555 5500
Fax: 52 755 554 2758

Condé Nast Johansens are delighted to recommend over 240 properties across North America, Mexico, Bermuda, The Caribbean, The Pacific.

Call 0800 269 397 or see the order forms on page 459 to order guides.

BAHAMAS - HARBOUR ISLAND

Pink Sands

Chapel Street, Harbour Island, Bahamas
Tel: 1 242 333 2030
Fax: 1 242 333 2060

BERMUDA - DEVONSHIRE

Ariel Sands

34 South Shore Road, Devonshire, Bermuda
Tel: 1 441 236 1010
Fax: 1 441 236 0087

BERMUDA - HAMILTON

Rosedon Hotel

P.O. Box Hm 290, Hamilton Hmax, Bermuda
Tel: 1 441 295 1640
Fax: 1 441 295 5904

BERMUDA - PAGET

Fourways Inn

PO Box Pg 294, Paget Pg Bx, Bermuda
Tel: 1 441 236 6517
Fax: 1 441 236 5528

BERMUDA - SOMERSET

Cambridge Beaches

Kings Point, Somerset, MA02 Bermuda
Tel: 1 441 234 0331
Fax: 1 441 234 3352

BERMUDA - SOUTHAMPTON

The Reefs

56 South Shore Road, Southampton, SN02 Bermuda
Tel: 1 441 238 0222
Fax: 1 441 238 8372

BERMUDA - WARWICK

Surf Side Beach Club

90 South Shore Road, Warwick, Bermuda
Tel: 1 441 236 7100
Fax: 1 441 236 9765

CARIBBEAN - ANGUILLA

Cap Juluca

Maundays Bay, Anguilla, Leeward Islands, British West Indies
Tel: 1 264 497 6666
Fax: 1 264 497 6617

CARIBBEAN - ANTIGUA

Blue Waters

PO BOX 256, ST. JOHN'S, ANTIGUA, WEST INDIES
Tel: 1 870 360 1245
Fax: 1 870 360 1246

CARIBBEAN - ANTIGUA

Curtain Bluff

P.O. Box 288, Antigua, West Indies
Tel: 1 268 462 8400
Fax: 1 268 462 8409

CARIBBEAN - ANTIGUA

Galley Bay

Five Islands, PO Box 305, St. John's, Antigua, West Indies
Tel: 1 268 462 0302
Fax: 1 268 462 4551

CARIBBEAN - ANTIGUA

The Inn at English Harbour

Po Box 187, St. John's, Antigua, West Indies
Tel: 1 268 460 1014
Fax: 1 268 460 1603

CARIBBEAN - BARBADOS

Coral Reef Club

St. James, Barbados, West Indies
Tel: 1 246 422 2372
Fax: 1 246 422 1776

CARIBBEAN - BARBADOS

The House at Tamarind Cove

Paynes Bay, St. James, Barbados, West Indies
Tel: 1 246 432 5525
Fax: 1 246 432 5255

CARIBBEAN - BARBADOS

Little Arches

Enterprise Beach Road, Christ Church, Barbados, West Indies
Tel: 1 246 420 4689
Fax: 1 246 418 0207

CARIBBEAN - BARBADOS

Lone Star Hotel

Mount Standfast, St. James, Barbados, West Indies
Tel: 1 246 419 0599
Fax: 1 246 419 0597

CARIBBEAN - BARBADOS

The Sandpiper

Holetown, St. James, Barbados, West Indies
Tel: 1 246 422 2251
Fax: 1 246 422 0900

CARIBBEAN - BRITISH VIRGIN ISLANDS (TORTOLA)

Long Bay Beach Resort & Villas

Long Bay, Tortola, British Virgin Islands
Tel: 1 954 481 8787
Fax: 1 954 481 1661

CARIBBEAN - CURAÇAO

Avila Beach Hotel

Penstraat 130, Willemstad, Curaçao, Netherlands Antilles, West Indies
Tel: 599 9 461 4377
Fax: 599 9 461 1493

CARIBBEAN - GRENADA

Spice Island Beach Resort

Grand Anse Beach, Box 6, St. George's, Grenada, West Indies
Tel: 1 473 444 4423/4258
Fax: 1 473 444 4807

Condé Nast Johansens are delighted to recommend over 240 properties across North America, Mexico, Bermuda, The Caribbean, The Pacific. Call 0800 269 397 or see the order forms on page 459 to order guides.

CARIBBEAN - JAMAICA

Half Moon
Montego Bay, Jamaica, West Indies
Tel: 1 876 953 2211
Fax: 1 876 953 2731

CARIBBEAN - JAMAICA

Round Hill Hotel and Villas
P.O. Box 64, Montego Bay, Jamaica, West Indies
Tel: 1 876 956 7050
Fax: 1 876 956 7505

CARIBBEAN - JAMAICA

The Tryall Club
PO Box 1206, Montego Bay, Jamaica, West Indies
Tel: 1 800 238 5290
Fax: 1 876 956 5673

CARIBBEAN - JAMAICA

Sans Souci Resort & Spa
PO Box 103, Ocho Rios, St. Ann, Jamaica, West Indies
Tel: 1 876 994 1206
Fax: 1 876 994 1544

CARIBBEAN - NEVIS

The Hermitage
Figtree Parish, PO Box 497, Charlestown, Nevis, West Indies
Tel: 1 869 469 3477
Fax: 1 869 469 2481

CARIBBEAN - NEVIS

Montpelier Plantation Inn
Montpelier Estate, PO Box 474, Nevis, West Indies
Tel: 1 869 469 3462
Fax: 1 869 469 2932

CARIBBEAN - NEVIS

Nisbet Plantation Beach Club
St. James Parish, Nevis, West Indies
Tel: 1 869 469 9325
Fax: 1 869 469 9864

CARIBBEAN - ST. KITTS

Ottley's Plantation Inn
P.O. Box 345, Basseterre, St. Kitts, West Indies
Tel: 1 869 465 7234
Fax: 1 869 465 4760

CARIBBEAN - SAINT-BARTHÉLEMY

Carl Gustaf Hotel
BP 700, Rue des Normands, Gustavia, 97099 Saint-Barthélemy, French West Indies
Tel: 1 590 590 297 900
Fax: 1 590 590 278 237

CARIBBEAN - ST. LUCIA

Anse Chastanet
SoufriÈre, St. Lucia, West Indies
Tel: 1 758 459 7000
Fax: 1 758 459 7700

CARIBBEAN - ST. LUCIA

The Body Holiday at LeSport
Cariblue Beach, Castries, St. Lucia, West Indies
Tel: 1 758 457 7800
Fax: 1 758 450 0368

CARIBBEAN - ST. LUCIA

Windjammer Landing Villa Beach Resort & Spa
Labrelotte Bay, Castries, St. Lucia, West Indies
Tel: 1 954 481 8787
Fax: 1 954 481 1661

CARIBBEAN - THE GRENADINES (MUSTIQUE)

Firefly
Mustique Island, St. Vincent & The Grenadines
Tel: 1 784 488 8414
Fax: 1 784 488 8514

CARIBBEAN - THE GRENADINES (PALM ISLAND)

Palm Island
St. Vincent & The Grenadines, West Indies
Tel: 1 954 481 8787
Fax: 1 954 481 1661

CARIBBEAN - TURKS & CAICOS

Point Grace
P.O. Box 700, Providenciales, Turks & Caicos Islands, British west indies
Tel: 1 649 946 5096
Fax: 1 649 946 5097

CARIBBEAN - TURKS & CAICOS

Turks & Caicos Club
PO Box 687, Providenciales, Turks & Caicos, British West Indies
Tel: 1 649 946 5800
Fax: 1 649 946 5858

PACIFIC - FIJI ISLANDS (LABASA)

Nukubati Island
P.O. Box 1928, Labasa, Fiji Islands
Tel: 61 2 93888 196
Fax: 61 2 93888 204

PACIFIC - FIJI ISLANDS (LAUTOKA)

Blue Lagoon Cruises
183 Vitogo Parade, Lautoka, Fiji Islands
Tel: 1 679 6661 622
Fax: 1 679 6664 098

PACIFIC - FIJI ISLANDS (QAMEA ISLAND)

Qamea Resort & Spa
P.A. Matei, Tajeuni, Fiji Islands
Tel: 679 888 0220
Fax: 679 888 0092

PACIFIC - FIJI ISLANDS (SAVU SAVU)

Jean-Michel Cousteau Fiji Islands Resort
Lesiaceva Point, Savu Savu, Fiji Islands
Tel: 415 788 5794
Fax: 415 788 0150

MINI LISTINGS NORTH AMERICA

Condé Nast Johansens are delighted to recommend over 240 properties across North America, Mexico, Bermuda, The Caribbean, The Pacific. Call 0800 269 397 or see the order forms on page 459 to order guides.

PACIFIC - FIJI ISLANDS (TOBERUA ISLAND)

Toberua Island Resort
PO Box 3332, Nausori, Fiji Islands
Tel: 679 347 2777
Fax: 679 347 2888

PACIFIC - SAMOA (APIA)

Aggie Grey's Hotel
PO Box 67, Apia, Samoa
Tel: 685 228 80
Fax: 685 236 26 or 685 23203

PACIFIC - FIJI ISLANDS (YASAWA ISLAND)

Yasawa Island Resort
PO Box 10128, Nadi Airport, Nadi, Fiji Islands
Tel: 679 672 2266
Fax: 679 672 4456

The International Mark of Excellence

For further information, current news,
e-club membership, hotel search, Preferred Partners,
online bookshop and special offers visit:

www.johansens.com

Annually Inspected for the Independent Traveller

Index by Property

INDEX BY PROPERTY

INDEX BY LOCATION

Scotland

Wales

≋ Hotels with heated indoor swimming pool

▼

≋ Outdoor pool

Golf course on-site

England

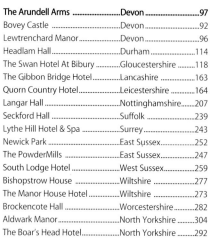

Ireland

Scotland

Wales

Shooting on-site

England

Ireland

Scotland

Fishing on-site

England

Ireland

Scotland

Wales

SPA Dedicated Spa facilities

England

Ⓜ²⁰⁰ Conference facilities for 200 delegates or more

England

INDEX BY CONSORTIUM

LONDON

Hotel location shown in red (hotel) or purple (spa hotel) with page number

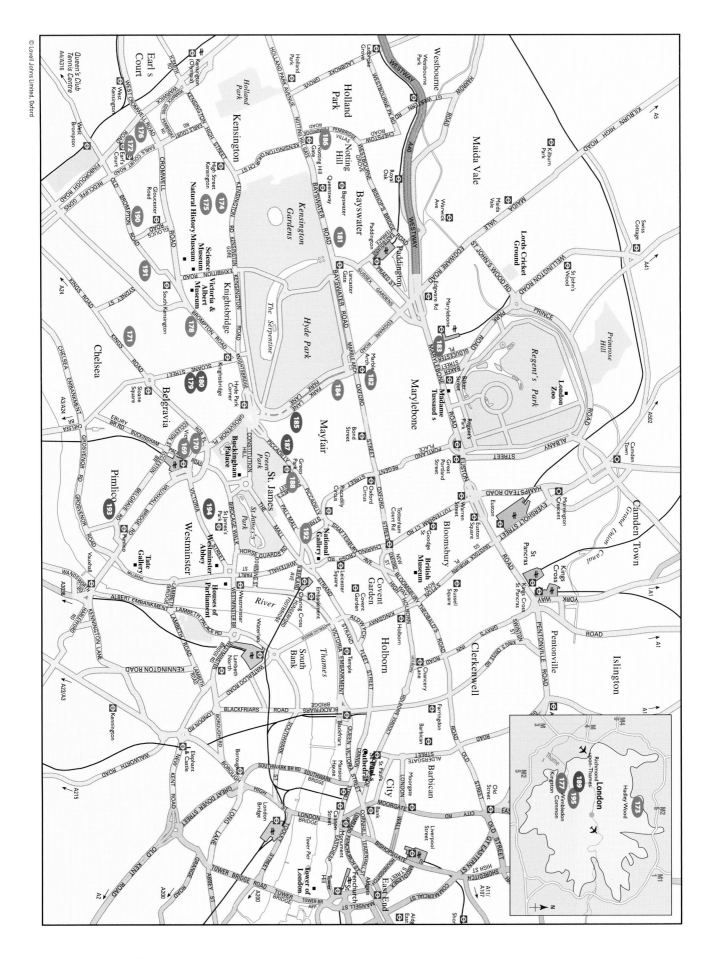

NORTH WEST ENGLAND

Hotel location shown in red (hotel) or purple (spa hotel) with page number

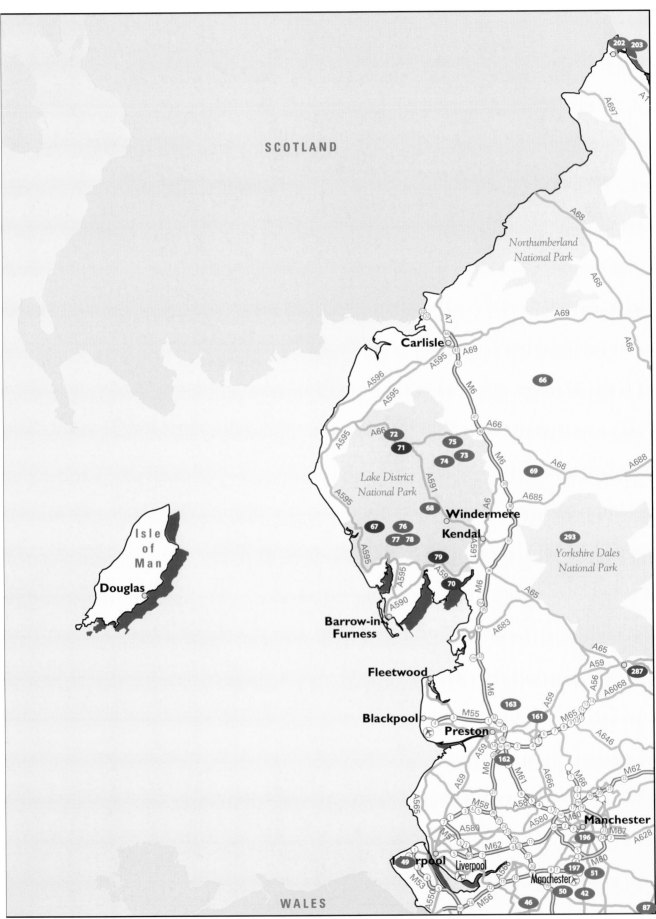

SCOTLAND

Northumberland
National Park

Carlisle

66

A66 72
71   75
        74 73
                69
Lake District
National Park
            68
        Windermere
67 76
77 78 Kendal
        293
    79   Yorkshire Dales
70   National Park

Isle
of
Man

Douglas

Barrow-in-
Furness

Fleetwood

287

163
Blackpool   161
Preston

162

WALES

Liverpool
49   Manchester
                196

            197
            51
        50   42
    46
                87

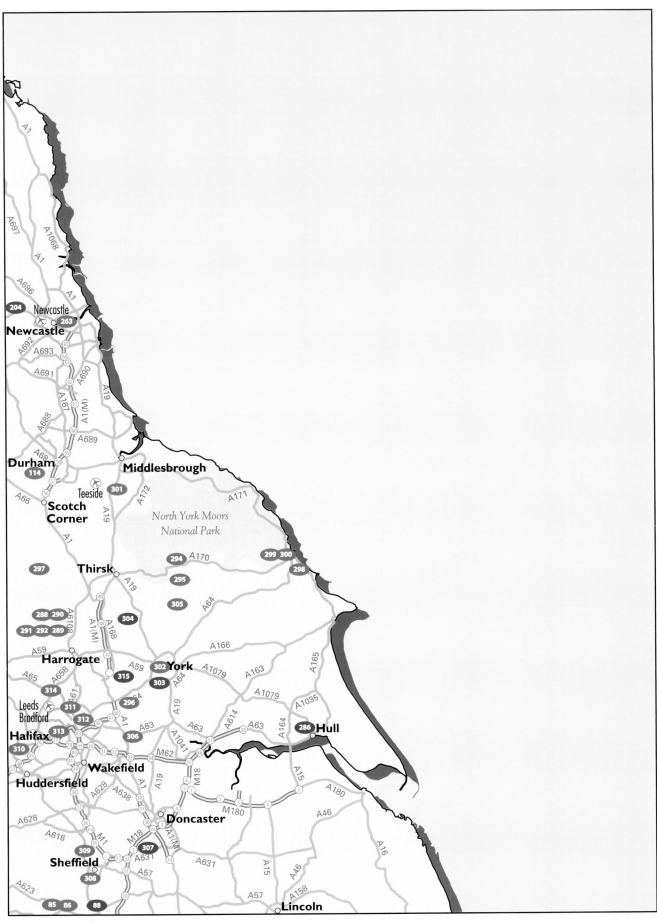

© Lovell Johns Limited, Oxford

CENTRAL ENGLAND

Hotel location shown in red (hotel) or purple (spa hotel) with page number

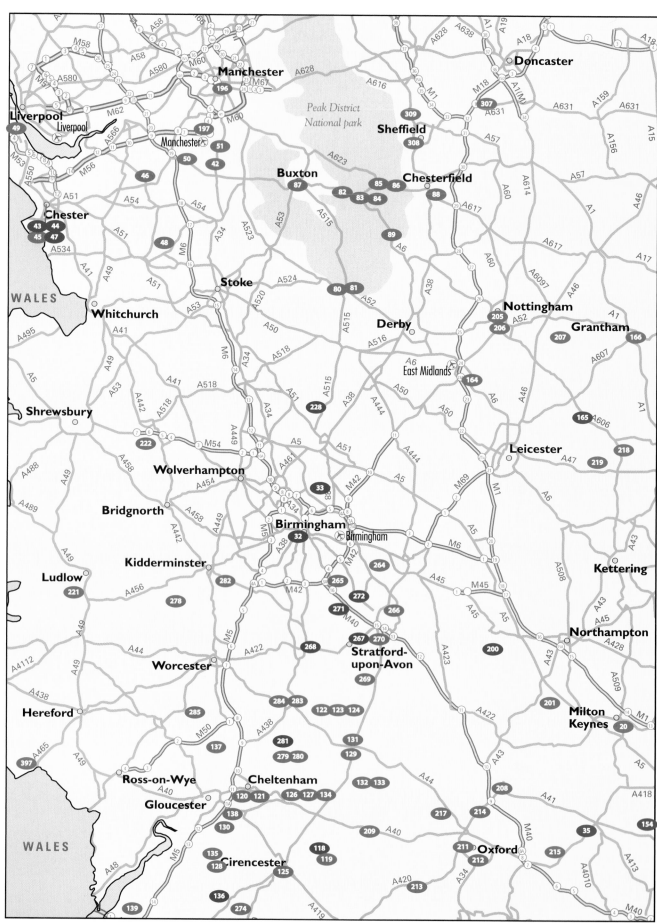

Hotel location shown in red (hotel) or purple (spa hotel) with page number

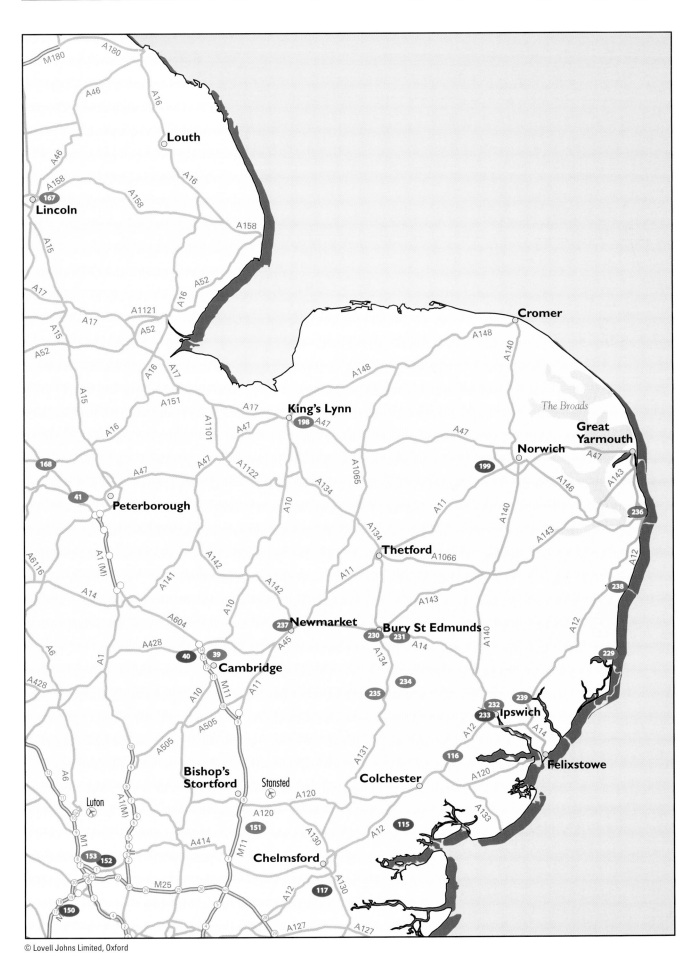

© Lovell Johns Limited, Oxford

CHANNEL ISLANDS & SOUTH WEST ENGLAND

Hotel location shown in red (hotel) or purple (spa hotel) with page number

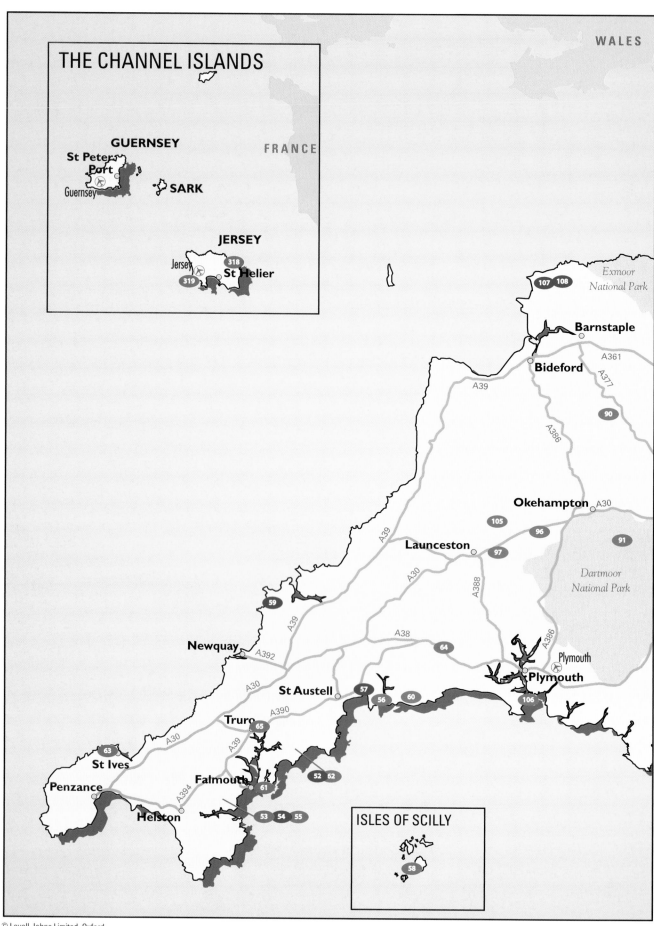

THE CHANNEL ISLANDS

WALES

GUERNSEY
St Peter Port
Guernsey

FRANCE

SARK

JERSEY
Jersey
St Helier
318
319

Exmoor National Park
107 108

Barnstaple
A361
A39
Bideford
A377
A386
90

Okehampton A30
105
96
A39
91
Launceston
97
Dartmoor National Park
A30
A388
A386

59
A39
A38
64
Plymouth
Newquay
A392
St Austell
A30
57
106
A390
56
60
Truro
65
A39
63
A30
St Ives
Falmouth
52 62
61
Penzance
A394
Helston
53 54 55

ISLES OF SCILLY
58

© Lovell Johns Limited, Oxford

452

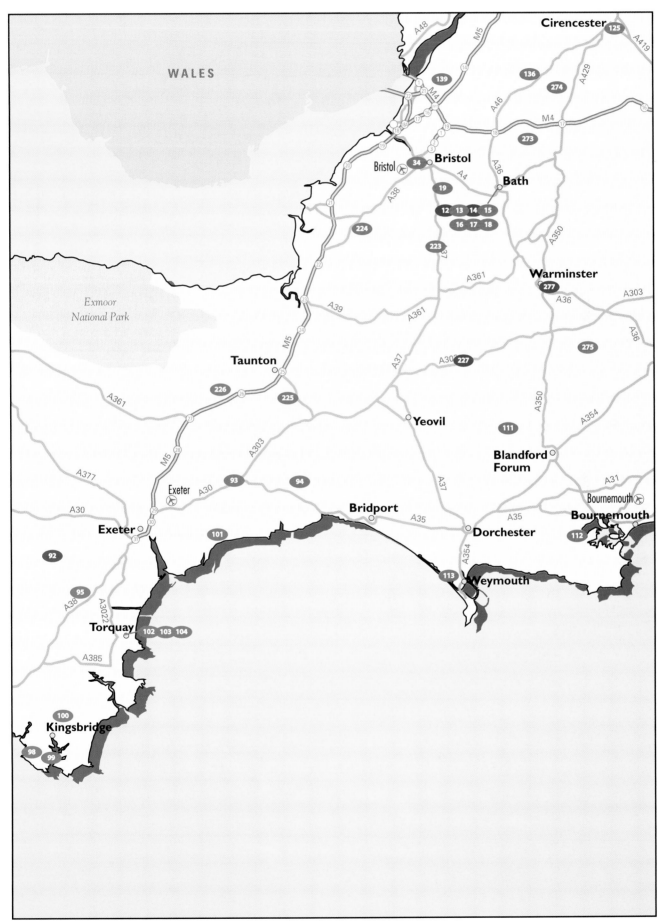

SOUTH WEST ENGLAND

Hotel location shown in red (hotel) or purple (spa hotel) with page number

WALES

Cirencester 125

139

136

274

273

Bristol 34 Bristol

19 Bath

12 13 14 15

16 17 18

224

223

Warminster 277

Exmoor National Park

A361

275

Taunton

226 225

227

Yeovil

111

Blandford Forum

93 94

Exeter

Bridport

Dorchester

Bournemouth

Bournemouth 112

101

92

113 Weymouth

95

Torquay

102 103 104

100
Kingsbridge

98 99

© Lovell Johns Limited, Oxford

453

SOUTHERN ENGLAND

Hotel location shown in red (hotel) or purple (spa hotel) with page number

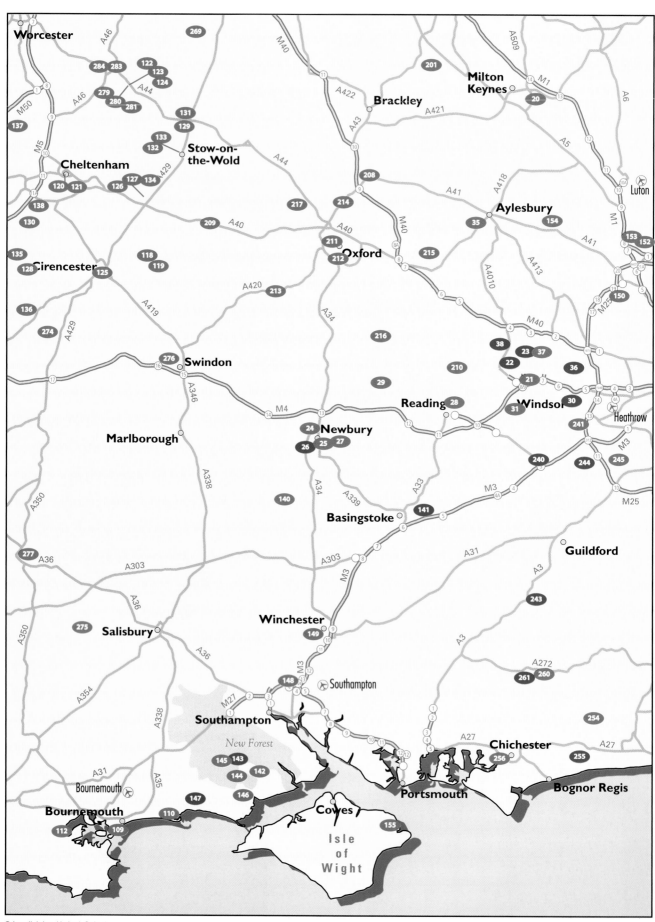

© Lovell Johns Limited, Oxford

SOUTH EAST ENGLAND

Hotel location shown in red (hotel) or purple (spa hotel) with page number

IRELAND

Hotel location shown in red (hotel) or purple (spa hotel) with page number

SCOTLAND

WALES

© Lovell Johns Limited,

WALES

Hotel location shown in red (hotel) or purple (spa hotel) with page number

ORDER FORM

Choose from our wide range of titles below

Up to £20 off when you order more than one guide...

Order 4 guides get £20 off, 3 guides get £10 off, 2 guides £5 off

Hotels & Spas Great Britain & Ireland £19.95	Country Houses Great Britain & Ireland £16.95	Hotels & Spas Europe & Mediterranean £16.95	Hotels, Inns & Resorts N. America, Caribbean £14.95	Business Venues (published Feb 2005) £25.00
QUANTITY £	QUANTITY £	QUANTITY £	QUANTITY £	QUANTITY £

Save over £40 when you order the **The International Collection...**

The International Collection
£70.00

QUANTITY £

a boxed presentation set of the four leisure guides,

PLUS the Business Venues Guide,

PLUS our exclusive silver plated luggage tag.

A great offer for only £70 (RRP £113.80)

(Silver plated luggage tag RRP £15, presentaion box RRP£5)

DISCOUNT - Discount does not apply to the International Collection   2 Guides = £5 off ☐   3 Guides = £10 off ☐   4 Guides = £20 off ☐

PACKING & DELIVERY - All UK Orders add £4.90. (Outside UK add £6 (per Guide) or £25 for The International Collection)   £

GRAND TOTAL - Don't forget to deduct your discount   £

☐ Please charge my Visa/Mastercard/Amex/Switch   ☐ I enclose a cheque payable to Condé Nast Johansens

Card No.:   Exp. Date: Issue No. (Switch only):   Start Date:

Name: Signature:

Address:

Postcode: Tel: E-mail:

Please tick if you would like to receive information or offers from The Condé Nast Publications Ltd by telephone☐ or SMS☐ or E-mail☐
Please tick if you would like to receive information or offers from other selected companies by telephone☐ or SMS☐ or E-mail☐
Please tick this box if you prefer not to receive direct mail from The Condé Nast Publications Ltd ☐ and other reputable companies ☐

Mail to Condé Nast Johansens, FREEPOST (CB264), Eastbourne, BN23 6ZW (no stamp required)
or fax your order on 01323 649 350 or register online at www.cnjguides.co.uk quoting reference below

OR CALL OUR HOTLINE NOW ON FREEPHONE 0800 269 397, quote ref: G006

GUEST SURVEY REPORT

Evaluate your stay in a Condé Nast Johansens Recommendation

Dear Guest,

Following your stay in a Condé Nast Johansens recommendation, please spare a moment to complete this Guest Survey Report. This is an important source of information for Johansens, to maintain the highest standards for our recommendations and to support the work of our team of inspectors.

It is also the prime source of nominations for Condé Nast Johansens Awards for Excellence, which are made annually to those properties worldwide that represent the finest standards and best value for money in luxury, independent travel.

Thank you for your time and I hope that when choosing future accommodation Condé Nast Johansens will be your guide.

Yours faithfully,

Andrew Warren
Managing Director

p.s. Guest Survey Reports may also be completed online at www.johansens.com

1. Your details

Your name: ....

Your address: ....

....

....

Postcode: ....

Telephone: ....

E-mail: ....

2. Hotel details

Name of hotel: ....

Location: ....

Date of visit: ....

3. Your rating of the hotel

Please tick one box in each category below (as applicable)

	Excellent	Good	Disappointing	Poor
Bedrooms	◯	◯	◯	◯
Public Rooms	◯	◯	◯	◯
Food/Restaurant	◯	◯	◯	◯
Service	◯	◯	◯	◯
Welcome/Friendliness	◯	◯	◯	◯
Value For Money	◯	◯	◯	◯

4. Any other comments

If you wish to make additional comments, please write separately to the Publisher, Condé Nast Johansens Ltd, 6-8 Old Bond Street, London W1S 4PH

....

....

....

....

Please return to Condé Nast Johansens, FREEPOST (CB264), EASTBOURNE BN23 6ZW (no stamp required)
or alternatively send by fax on 01323 649350

ORDER FORM
Choose from our wide range of titles below

CONDÉ NAST JOHANSENS

Up to £20 off when you order more than one guide...
Order 4 guides get £20 off, 3 guides get £10 off, 2 guides £5 off

Hotels & Spas
Great Britain & Ireland
£19.95

| QUANTITY | £ |

Country Houses
Great Britain & Ireland
£16.95

| QUANTITY | £ |

Hotels & Spas
Europe & Mediterranean
£16.95

| QUANTITY | £ |

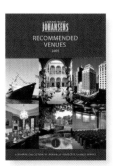

Hotels, Inns & Resorts
N. America, Caribbean
£14.95

| QUANTITY | £ |

Business Venues
(published Feb 2005)
£25.00

| QUANTITY | £ |

Save over £40 when you order the **The International Collection...**

The International Collection
£70.00

| QUANTITY | £ |

a boxed presentation set of the four leisure guides,

PLUS the Business Venues Guide,

PLUS our exclusive silver plated luggage tag.

A great offer for only £70 *(RRP £113.80)*

(Silver plated luggage tag RRP £15, presentaion box RRP£5)

DISCOUNT - Discount does not apply to the International Collection   2 Guides = £5 off ☐   3 Guides = £10 off ☐   4 Guides = £20 off ☐

PACKING & DELIVERY - All UK Orders add £4.90. (Outside UK add £6 (per Guide) or £25 for The International Collection) | £ |

GRAND TOTAL - Don't forget to deduct your discount | £ |

☐ Please charge my Visa/Mastercard/Amex/Switch   ☐ I enclose a cheque payable to Condé Nast Johansens

Card No.:   Exp. Date: Issue No. (Switch only):   Start Date:

Name: Signature:

Address:

Postcode: Tel: E-mail:

Please tick if you would like to receive information or offers from The Condé Nast Publications Ltd by telephone☐ or SMS☐ or E-mail☐
Please tick if you would like to receive information or offers from other selected companies by telephone☐ or SMS☐ or E-mail☐
Please tick this box if you prefer not to receive direct mail from The Condé Nast Publications Ltd ☐ and other reputable companies ☐

Mail to Condé Nast Johansens, FREEPOST (CB264), Eastbourne, BN23 6ZW (no stamp required)
or fax your order on 01323 649 350 or register online at www.cnjguides.co.uk quoting reference below

OR CALL OUR HOTLINE NOW ON FREEPHONE 0800 269 397, quote ref: G006

GUEST SURVEY REPORT

Evaluate your stay in a Condé Nast Johansens Recommendation

CONDÉ NAST
JOHANSENS

Dear Guest,

Following your stay in a Condé Nast Johansens recommendation, please spare a moment to complete this Guest Survey Report. This is an important source of information for Johansens, to maintain the highest standards for our recommendations and to support the work of our team of inspectors.

It is also the prime source of nominations for Condé Nast Johansens Awards for Excellence, which are made annually to those properties worldwide that represent the finest standards and best value for money in luxury, independent travel.

Thank you for your time and I hope that when choosing future accommodation Condé Nast Johansens will be your guide.

Yours faithfully,

Andrew Warren

Andrew Warren
Managing Director

p.s. Guest Survey Reports may also be completed online at www.johansens.com

---

1. Your details

Your name: ....

Your address: ....

....

....

Postcode: ....

Telephone: ....

E-mail: ....

2. Hotel details

Name of hotel: ....

....

Location: ....

Date of visit: ....

3. Your rating of the hotel

Please tick one box in each category below (as applicable)

	Excellent	Good	Disappointing	Poor
Bedrooms	○	○	○	○
Public Rooms	○	○	○	○
Food/Restaurant	○	○	○	○
Service	○	○	○	○
Welcome/Friendliness	○	○	○	○
Value For Money	○	○	○	○

4. Any other comments

If you wish to make additional comments, please write separately to the Publisher, Condé Nast Johansens Ltd, 6-8 Old Bond Street, London W1S 4PH

....

....

....

....

....

Please return to Condé Nast Johansens, FREEPOST (CB264), EASTBOURNE BN23 6ZW (no stamp required)
or alternatively send by fax on 01323 649350

Please tick if you would like to receive information or offers from The Condé Nast Publications Ltd by telephone ☐ or SMS ☐ or E-mail ☐
Please tick if you would like to receive information or offers from other selected companies by telephone ☐ or SMS ☐ or E-mail ☐
Please tick this box if you prefer not to receive direct mail from The Condé Nast Publications Ltd ☐ and other reputable companies ☐

ORDER FORM

Choose from our wide range of titles below

CONDÉ NAST JOHANSENS

Up to £20 off when you order more than one guide...

Order 4 guides get £20 off, 3 guides get £10 off, 2 guides £5 off

Hotels & Spas
Great Britain & Ireland
£19.95

QUANTITY	£

Country Houses
Great Britain & Ireland
£16.95

QUANTITY	£

Hotels & Spas
Europe & Mediterranean
£16.95

QUANTITY	£

Hotels, Inns & Resorts
N. America, Caribbean
£14.95

QUANTITY	£

Business Venues
(published Feb 2005)
£25.00

QUANTITY	£

Save over £40 when you order the **The International Collection...**

The International Collection
£70.00

QUANTITY	£

a boxed presentation set of the four leisure guides,

PLUS the Business Venues Guide,

PLUS our exclusive silver plated luggage tag.

A great offer for only £70 (RRP £113.80)

(Silver plated luggage tag RRP £15, presentaion box RRP£5)

DISCOUNT - Discount does not apply to the International Collection   2 Guides = £5 off ☐   3 Guides = £10 off ☐   4 Guides = £20 off ☐

PACKING & DELIVERY - All UK Orders add £4.90. (Outside UK add £6 (per Guide) or £25 for The International Collection)   £ _____

GRAND TOTAL - Don't forget to deduct your discount   £ _____

☐ Please charge my Visa/Mastercard/Amex/Switch   ☐ I enclose a cheque payable to Condé Nast Johansens

Card No.:   Exp. Date: Issue No. (Switch only):   Start Date:

Name: Signature:

Address:

Postcode: Tel: E-mail:

Please tick if you would like to receive information or offers from The Condé Nast Publications Ltd by telephone☐ or SMS☐ or E-mail☐
Please tick if you would like to receive information or offers from other selected companies by telephone☐ or SMS☐ or E-mail☐
Please tick this box if you prefer not to receive direct mail from The Condé Nast Publications Ltd ☐ and other reputable companies ☐

Mail to Condé Nast Johansens, FREEPOST (CB264), Eastbourne, BN23 6ZW (no stamp required)
or fax your order on 01323 649 350 or register online at www.cnjguides.co.uk quoting reference below

OR CALL OUR HOTLINE NOW ON FREEPHONE 0800 269 397, quote ref: G006

SPECIAL OFFER UPDATES
Receive free monthly E-mail updates of hotels' special offers

In order to keep travellers up to date with the latest developments, we have created an Online Membership scheme. FREE to join, Online Membership gives the user a number of complimentary benefits, including monthly E-mail notification of the latest hotel Special Offers. If you would like us to sign you up, please complete the form below.

Alternatively visit **www.johansens.com** today and take a look for yourself.

Title .... Your name: ....

E-mail ....

Password .... Password Reminder ....

Your Address ....

Postcode .... Telephone ....

Example areas of interest (please tick as applicable)

⭕ Great Britain & Ireland   ⭕ Europe   ⭕ North America   ⭕ Golf   ⭕ Gourmet

⭕ Honeymoon   ⭕ Skiing   ⭕ Weekend   ⭕ Midweek   ⭕ Business use

The details provided may be used to keep you informed of future products and special offers provided by Condé Nast Johansens and other carefully selected third parties. If you do not wish to receive such information please tick this box ☐.

Please return to **Condé Nast Johansens, FREEPOST (CB264), Eastbourne BN23 6ZW** (no stamp required). Alternatively send by fax to 0207 152 3566

SPECIAL OFFER UPDATES
Receive free monthly E-mail updates of hotels' special offers

CONDÉ NAST
JOHANSENS

In order to keep travellers up to date with the latest developments, we have created an Online Membership scheme. FREE to join, Online Membership gives the user a number of complimentary benefits, including monthly E-mail notification of the latest hotel Special Offers. If you would like us to sign you up, please complete the form below.

Alternatively visit **www.johansens.com** today and take a look for yourself.

Title .... Your name: ....

E-mail ....

Password .... Password Reminder ....

Your Address ....

Postcode .... Telephone ....

Example areas of interest (please tick as applicable)

⭕ Great Britain & Ireland   ⭕ Europe   ⭕ North America   ⭕ Golf   ⭕ Gourmet

⭕ Honeymoon   ⭕ Skiing   ⭕ Weekend   ⭕ Midweek   ⭕ Business use

The details provided may be used to keep you informed of future products and special offers provided by Condé Nast Johansens and other carefully selected third parties. If you do not wish to receive such information please tick this box ☐.

Please return to **Condé Nast Johansens, FREEPOST (CB264), Eastbourne BN23 6ZW** (no stamp required). Alternatively send by fax to 0207 152 3566